$1

To order additional copies of *Fusion,* by Melissa and Greg Howell, call
1-800-765-6955.

Visit us at **www.reviewandherald.com** for information on other
Review and Herald® products.

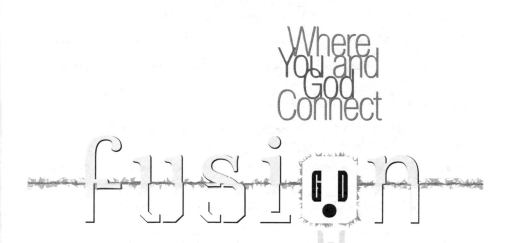

Where
You and
God
Connect

fusion

Melissa
& Greg
Howell
With Contributions
From Seth
Pierce

DAILY DEVOTIONS for TEENS

Review and Herald® titles may be purchased in bulk for educational, business, fund-raising, or sales promotional use. For information, e-mail SpecialMarkets@reviewandherald.com.

The Review and Herald® Publishing Association publishes biblically based materials for spiritual, physical, and mental growth and Christian discipleship.

The author assumes full responsibility for the accuracy of all facts and quotations as cited in this book.

Unless otherwise noted, texts are from the *Holy Bible, New International Version.* Copyright © 1973, 1978, 1984, International Bible Society. Used by permission of Zondervan Bible Publishers.

Scripture quotations credited to ESV are from *The Holy Bible,* English Standard Version, copyright © 2001 by Crossway Bibles, a division of Good News Publishers. Used by permission. All rights reserved.
Texts credited to HCSB are taken from the *Holman Christian Standard Bible,* copyright © 1999, 2000, 2002, 2003 by Holman Bible Publishers. Used by permission.
Bible texts credited to KJV are from the King James Version of the Bible.
Scripture quotations marked NASB are from the *New American Standard Bible,* © 1960, 1962, 1963, 1968, 1971, 1972, 1973, 1975, 1977, 1995 by The Lockman Foundation. Used by permission.
Scripture quotations marked NLT are taken from the *Holy Bible,* New Living Translation, copyright © 1996, 2004. Used by permission of Tyndale House Publishers, Inc., Carol Stream, Illinois 60188. All rights reserved.
Bible texts credited to NRSV are from the New Revised Standard Version of the Bible, copyright © 1989 by the Division of Christian Education of the National Council of the Churches of Christ in the U.S.A. Used by permission.

This book was edited by Penny Estes Wheeler
Copyedited by James Hoffer
Designed by Ron J. Pride
Cover art by Ron J. Pride
Interior design by Tina M. Ivany
Typeset: Adobe Garamond 13.5/11

PRINTED IN U.S.A.

14 13 12 11 10   5 4 3 2 1

Library of Congress Cataloging-in-Publication Data
Howell, Melissa, 1980-
    Fusion : where you and God connect / Melissa and Greg Howell.
       p. cm.
    ISBN 978-0-8280-2547-8
    1. Devotional calendars. 2. Christian teenagers--Religious life. I. Howell, Greg, 1978- II. Title.
    BV4810.H69 2010
    242'.63--dc22

                          2010016910

ISBN 978-0-8280-2547-8

TO THE BIGGEST HEROES OF ALL . . .

Our greatest thanks of all goes out to little **Caleb** and **Toby Jacob,** our precious boys. Caleb, you were only 2 when we started this project, but you were a trooper. Thanks for letting Mommy and Daddy write when you wanted us to take you to the park or play games instead, and for learning to entertain yourself when we were exhausted after writing all night. You are becoming such a sweet, loving child, and we are so proud of you.

Toby Jacob, you were only 3 weeks old when we took on this project, and you, more than anyone else, made it possible. I will always remember the late nights you slept curled up in my lap as I wrote story after story. If you hadn't been such a happy, contented, easygoing baby, we never could have undertaken this task. With hearts full of love, it is to you boys that we dedicate this book. Our greatest hope for you is that you will grow up to love and serve Jesus.

And to Our God . . .

You pulled us through. You gave us energy when we were empty, ideas when our minds were blank, long-forgotten stories from the past, and the determination to write through many a long night. Thanks for Your companionship through this entire project. We wrote for a lot of people, but when it came right down to it, we wrote for You. We fell in love with You long ago, and we hope others will do the same. Thanks for walking with us so closely that writing about You felt like writing about a good friend.

ACKNOWLEDGMENTS

Our names happen to be on the cover of this book, but they would never have made it there if a whole lot of people hadn't stood behind us and held us up, encouraging us along the way. We want you to know about them, because you wouldn't be reading this book without all these great folks: our relatives, friends, ex-boyfriends and ex-girlfriends, students, and dorm kids whose stories appear on countless dozens of these pages. Thanks for giving us something to write about and for being the point of our stories (or sometimes the butt of our jokes). You all have filled our lives with so much color and so much joy. (By the way, we didn't change any of your names, but that's because none of you are innocent. Ha!)

TO OUR FAMILIES . . .

Melissa:

Heather, Russell, and **Josh**: Thanks for beating me up, leaving me on a roof, believing my lies, and pestering and scheming with me. I created my first and favorite stories with you.

Mom and **Dad,** you were my very first storytellers, and sometimes when I read my own writing I think I can still hear your voices. Thank you for telling me stories, making childhood memories, reading to me, praying with me, and teaching me to fall in love with the God that I have written about in these pages. My walk with Jesus began at home with you.

The Palmers and **McGills** (my grandparents): Thank you for always being such pillars of faith in my life, and for praying for me every single day.

Greg, you are not only my loving husband, faithful companion, and the wonderful father of my children—you are also my very best friend. Your love has turned my dreams into realities. Thank you for taking on this project—and its insane deadline—with me, for sometimes writing until the sun rose, sleeping beside me as I wrote, holding our home together, and getting up with the kids the next morning while I slept. There is no end to your strength. I am the luckiest woman alive, and my decision to marry you was the best choice I ever made. I love our life! Thanks for a marriage that is already full of enough great stories to fill a hundred books.

Greg:

Doug, I'm sure you had no idea how all of the persecution you suffered during our childhood at the hands of me, your older brother, would someday be immortalized forever in print. But I'm pretty sure that I wouldn't have even half of my best stories in this book without you. So for all the torture you endured back then, and for being the perfect recipient of my treacherous ways, I want to thank you.

To my parents: Thank you for teaching me about the Bible and instilling in me my first feelings of respect and reverence for what it has to offer in my life. Your patient understanding and encouragement have driven me to rely on it more and more throughout my life.

To Melissa, for knowing the stories of my life almost better than I do, and for remembering them all, even after I've forgotten. You inspire me always to try a little bit harder, and to look a little longer. Thank you so much for what we have. I love you.

TO OUR MENTORS, CHEERLEADERS, AND LIFESAVERS . . .

Melissa:

Pastor Case, thank you for the many years of mentoring and friendship. Your theology has impacted us more profoundly than any other. Your life is an example of living faith. Thanks also for matchmaking in Greek class; you saw the team we could be long before we ever did. Thanks also to our other theology and seminary professors whose theology we used, borrowed, or stole on these pages: **Tom Shepherd, Jon Paulien, Roy Gane, John Baldwin, Rich Carlson,** and **Chris Blake.**

Ladan Quiring, my fifth-grade teacher. You were the *very first person* who told me I could write. Thank you for seeing the possibility in me.

Grandma Gwen, Alicia Johnston, Ashley Blasy, and **Kay Sanborn:** Thanks for being consistent fans of my writing and for repeatedly encouraging me to publish a book.

Sethy, we appreciate the opportunity you gave us to write this devotional and all of the witty and humorous additions you donated as well. *Be saved.*

To the good people at Review and Herald: **Jeannette Johnson,** thank you for taking a chance on "impossible" with new writers and an unbelievable deadline. **Penny Wheeler,** who is terribly interesting—what a joy it was to work with you! Not only were you an amazing editor, but you became a friend as well. Your encouragement and praise kept us going.

Rose and **Dennis Howell:** Thank you for coming to help us meet the first deadline and for all the cooking, cleaning, and child watching while we wrote.

Other deadlines were met thanks to Play-Doh, naptime, bedtime, *Tom and Jerry, The Jungle Book, Finding Nemo,* and the electric swing.

Greg:

Rose Fuller, my freshman English teacher, thank you for encouraging a melodramatic young teen to continue with his feeble attempts at writing. You inspired in me the belief not that I was the next Edgar Allan Poe, but that I could become good enough for publication. I always told you I would send you the first book I wrote, and I trust that you're holding a copy of it right now.

To John Abbot, my youth pastor in high school, who took the risk of being genuine and honest with me in a Denny's restaurant all those years ago. Thank you for answering my questions about the ministry and being humble enough to share both its joys and sorrows. I probably wouldn't have gone much further without that conversation.

To the strange little adventurous man/woman in some far-off land who discovered that jasmine flowers could be shriveled up into black little nubs and boiled in water, my sincerest gratitude. I don't think I could've survived the sleepless nights without you.

To my Swiss Army knife, for always staying faithful and coming back to me every time I lost you, 26 times and counting.

AND FINALLY, TO YOU . . .

Our readers: Thanks for allowing us to journey with you through this new year of your life. We don't know what sorts of trials and surprises the year ahead holds for you, but we want to tell you that we have prayed for you long before this year began and long before you even saw or heard of this book. We hope that somewhere within its pages you will encounter a faith that is practical and relevant, and a God that is worth living for. When we first started reading the Bible as teenagers, we were hooked. It filled our lives with a hope, meaning, and purpose that nothing else compared to. Now we pray that you will have the same experience.

BEFORE YOU BEGIN...

The entrance to the cave is small—you could almost miss it. This is where they died. I've been there, and every time I think about it, it still haunts me. I imagine them there, crouching in the darkness, the cave filling with smoke. Through the chinks between logs, trees, and branches, I imagine that the soldiers in their shiny armor with their steel swords could be seen laughing and throwing more wood on the flames. How had it all actually come to this?

The crowd of more than 100 men, women, and children huddling terrified in the back of the cave had been nicknamed Waldensians, or Vaudois, after the name of a wealthy merchant named Peter Waldo. Waldo had decided to give away everything he had and began to preach the Bible on the streets of Lyon in 1177. As he preached his message of freedom from riches people responded, and soon he had a small following who wanted to be give away all their possessions as well. The problem was that they refused to get permission to preach and teach from the local bishop, and soon the church labeled Waldo and his followers as heretics. They ordered the local cities and regions to hunt down and kill any Waldensians that were found within their borders.

This didn't stop them, though, and only drove the Waldensian believers and their preachers underground. They had to travel secretly from town to town, with small tracts or slips of the translated New Testament sewn into the hem of their clothes. At the right moment during a conversation, if they felt the person was safe, they would pull out the hand-copied texts from their hiding place and share the special truths of the Bible in a plain and simple way. But sometimes they were wrong, and the person they were sharing with wasn't safe. Sometimes they had to run.

In these situations the best places to run to were the mountains of the Alps in northern Italy. They hid themselves in any cave or rocky covering they could find, hounded by bands of soldiers and even neighbors from the local villages. This is how a small group of Waldensian families found themselves crouched against the wet rock walls of an Alpine cave, with soldiers piling more and more wood against the opening until no air could enter. The acrid smoke filled the little chamber, and in less than an hour these families lay dead on the cave's rocky floor.

They died for a book—a book that now freely sits on the shelves of your home. When I look at my own Bible, sitting on that table by my bed, I have to ask myself if I would do the same today. Does it mean that much to me?

Would I die to keep it, though some days I don't even open it?

Many people today simply don't feel any sort of passion at all for the Bible—it seems boring, mysterious, tedious, or just plain out of date. But still, we can't help wondering if maybe there *is* something to it when we observe life after life being changed by its contents. What is it about this book? How does it do that? What's in there that changes lives and inspires millions to be better people?

Join us on a journey, a one-year journey that goes through the entire Bible, book by book. A teacher of mine used to say that trying to read all the way through the Bible makes everyone an expert on Genesis—we don't get any further before we give up! That's why we wanted to write this book, to give you a chance to make your way through the Bible from beginning to end without becoming lost, overwhelmed, or bored out of your mind. There are stories in here that you've probably never heard before, points you've never thought of, and characters who might be a lot more like you than you may have ever realized. So come find out exactly why the Bible has been so powerful to so many.

A Different Beginning

In the beginning God created the heavens and the earth. Genesis 1:1.

The new year began with my sleeping on the street under an old stinky blanket, next to a fresh garbage heap, shivering in the night air, and starving. I wasn't, as you might be suspecting, a homeless bum—though at the time I did feel like one. Rather, I was a southern Californian—a southern Californian who lived within driving distance of the city of Pasadena, where the annual Tournament of Roses Parade is held each and every year on January 1 (except when that happens to fall on Sunday). The night before, thousands of people gather on the streets with lawn chairs and old blankets to stake their claim on a piece of the sidewalk, so the next morning they might see the floats pass by within mere feet of them.

I was typically one of these people. But the experience wasn't the party you might expect. One year I wandered the streets alone till 4:00 a.m. looking for a hot chocolate vendor that everyone kept telling me was "just one more block" over. Another year I woke up covered in someone's spilled Coke, next to a fresh dirty diaper. Still another year I spent 45 minutes waiting in line for a plugged toilet. Several years in a row I walked for miles down the line of floats to witness people frantically pasting on the last few flowers, and ended up shivering and lost with gum and beer glued to the bottom of my shoes.

Why did I keep going year after year? I guess because I wanted to be part of the festivities, I wanted to have a memorable start of the new year, but it always went wrong—I just ended up grouchy, stinky, sleep-deprived, and with a cold. Not a great beginning to the year at all. But then one year I decided to stay home, safe and comfy in my warm bed. It was the best New Year's Day of my life. I've never been back since.

I don't know how you are beginning this year today—whether you are lost, alone, and cold in your life, or feeling warm and at peace. But I have a suggestion for you—make this year different from the others. Put God "in the beginning," as part of every day. Spend time in His Word and with this book, and watch what He is creating anew within you. When you finally experience how warm and comfortable it is to have a daily friendship with Him, I assure you, you will never go back.

—MH

The Arranged Marriage

Then the Lord God made a woman from the rib he had taken out of the man, and he brought her to the man. Genesis 2:22.

We have already arranged a marriage for my 2-year-old son, Caleb. He is betrothed to Madeline Pierce. Some of our best friends just so happened to have a little girl right at the time we had him, and instantly we parents knew it was destined by heaven—a marriage that was meant to be! So this summer when Madeline came to stay with us for two weeks, we all anticipated that there would be excessive toddler romance in the air.

But they spit at each other. He stole her stroller, and she stole his stuffed animals to put in the stroller that she stole back. He hit her, and she screamed. She stuck her fingers in his mouth, and he bit her. They tore food out of each other's hands and cried about bathing in the same tub. This was not the love at first sight that we had anticipated.

In the Garden of Eden we imagine that in the moment Eve and Adam first saw each other it was love at first sight. A perfect romance, a match literally made in heaven! But there is one important key you may not know about this first perfect marriage—they didn't meet each other first. Even though they were the only two human beings on earth, they met Someone else before they met each other. That Someone was God. In both cases the first eyes they gazed into were the eyes of their Creator. God formed Adam, who must have awakened looking into the face of God. Then we see that God formed Eve, and He brought her to the man. That means that God and Eve walked together before Eve met Adam.

If you want to find a match made in heaven for yourself, I suggest you follow the order that God set up: walk with God first, before you find your perfect soul mate. Some of the best romances on earth are made of two people who knew God before they ever knew each other. You may not have yet met the one you are going to marry, but you can prepare for your future marriage even now—by walking with God every day. Get to know Him and learn to love Him first. This is the most important thing you can do for your marriage, and you can do it now.

—MH

The Closet Pooper

The man said, "The woman you put here with me—she gave me some fruit." Genesis 3:12.

There it was, coiled in plain sight in my closet—a brown, steaming, stinking pile of fresh poop. Imagine opening your closet to select some crisp, clean outfit for the day, and finding instead finding such a sight! You've probably never had that experience, so let me tell you that it's quite a shock. My first thought was *Gross!* My second thought was *Who? How?*

An investigation began in our household that day. At first the dog got the blame, but something seemed amiss. He was a good dog, fully grown, who hadn't made any messes in the house in years and years. Besides, how would he have opened the closet door? Something definitely was not fitting into place. In addition to that, my doll's hair had been cut. Was the dog to blame for that as well? My mom made many excuses to console me, even promising that the hair would grow back, but all in all it was a devastating experience.

It was a while later that we discovered my little sister was the one to blame. Thanks to a fight we'd had that afternoon and a fiery passive-aggressive streak in her personality, she decided that pooping in my closet was the best way to express her anger and get even with me! And it was she who had first blamed the dog for the incident. She also admitted to cutting the doll's hair, and my mom now admits that doll hair does not, in fact, grow back. What a chain of blame and excuses all of us were stuck in that day! And poor Jake, the dog—the innocent accused!

But sin always leads to blaming, doesn't it? The very first reaction after Adam and Eve sinned was to blame, blame, blame—each other, the snake, even God. They pointed fingers. They made excuses. Just as my sister blamed the dog and my mom made excuses about the doll's hair, they tried to weasel their way out of the predicament. But sin is permanent—just as permanent as a doll's haircut. What's severed cannot be put back. What's done cannot be undone—without Jesus.

So this year if you find yourself desperately blaming other people, wise up and realize that chances are, you're the one at fault. Decide to face up to the mistakes you make instead of getting stuck in the blame game!

—MH

The Gloved Attacker

If you do what is right, will you not be accepted? But if you do not do what is right, sin is crouching at your door; it desires to have you, but you must master it. Genesis 4:7.

The sucker punch came at the very moment I least expected it. I simply rounded the corner of my own house, entered the living room, and *BAM!* A gloved hand came out of nowhere and hit me with full force square in the stomach. I gasped for air, but none came—the wind had been knocked out of me. I fell to the floor, writhing in pain, waiting for my breath to come back. In those split seconds while I could not breathe, I caught a glimpse of the perpetrator: my little brother, dressed in full karate uniform with every piece of sparring equipment he owned, including the boxing gloves.

Apparently the story he told my parents later (after receiving a good spanking, I hope) was that he was just dying to try out his new sparring equipment before karate lessons the next day. So he put it all on and waited, telling himself that whoever came around the corner of the hallway next would get his first punch. Well, that person just happened to be me. To this day I still remember how much that punch hurt. And to this day my brother falls on the floor laughing when he recounts the tale.

When Cain tried to cheat God by not bringing the right offering to Him, God had a very immediate lesson to give Cain, and it is written in the verse above: If you don't decide to do the right thing, sin is crouching at your door. When I think of sin crouching at the door, I think of my brother, crouching in full sparring gear, at the end of the hallway. The Lord says that sin desires to have us, as though it can't wait to sink its gloved hand into our bellies and make a full frontal impact in our lives. What is God's advice for us? "You must master it." So don't think you can just mess around with sin and not get hurt. It's tougher than you think. It's not some innocent thing floating around out there—it's actually more like a predator, lying in wait, wanting to own you forever. You can't just play with sin and expect to jump out anytime. You have to steer clear. You have to stay away. You have to master it. Today when your favorite temptation comes along, remember that it's not worth playing with, and that you will ultimately lose the game. Purpose in your heart to master it, and God will give you the strength to do so.

—MH

Ape Versus Adam

For forty days the flood kept coming on the earth, and as the waters increased they
lifted the ark high above the earth. The waters rose and increased greatly on the earth,
and the ark floated on the surface of the water. Genesis 7:17, 18.

Unless you're a hermit who prefers to read old newspapers by candlelight in some middle-of-nowhere mountain range, you've probably sat through your share of radio, TV, and Internet commercials. As we all know, the goal of advertising is to entice you to buy the product being sold. Any savvy consumer will tell you that you shouldn't just take what people say without looking deeper, and this applies not only to shopping around for the latest version of the iPod, but also to the world of ideas and beliefs.

When it comes to the biblical story of the Flood, there are lots of things flying around. On the one hand we have the theory of evolution, which says that the Bible's creation story is a myth, and the geologic column proves there was no worldwide flood. On the flip side of the arguments we find creationists, many of whom believe that scientific evidence points toward a worldwide flood, and attempt to gather and study this data.

Some of the more interesting things they've found have to do with basic math. If you look at the present rate of erosion on the continents, all of them should be under water by now—if the earth is really millions of years old. On the other hand, when geologists started figuring out how much sediment and dirt settles to the bottom of the ocean every year, they realized that in the amount of time science tells us the earth has been here, we shouldn't have any ocean left. They all should've filled up with dirt by now! Or take us humans. The current population of earth could have been reached in about 3,200 years, give or take a few famines and wars along the way. But if science says we humans have been around almost 100 times that long, why aren't there more of us? But even with all of these great discoveries and new evidence, does our faith depend on being able to *prove* that the Flood really happened? Not at all. In fact, God always leaves room for a little bit of doubt so that we have to trust Him. Faith still has to exist, even in a world full of mathematical equations and particle accelerators. The point of the Bible isn't to answer every last question. It's to start a relationship with the One who can.

—GH

17

All in the Family?

Say you are my sister, so that I will be treated well for your sake and my life will be spared because of you. Genesis 12:13.

I've tried to pass my husband off as a whole lot of things. One time for a college play, I dressed him up as a big-breasted woman with long flowing hair, dark lashes, and bright-red lipstick. When I was an academy teacher and hadn't made lesson plans for the day, I would send him in as my substitute. Once I even had him pretend he was me when on the telephone. He did a pretty good high girly voice.

However, Greg is not totally innocent either. I remember the afternoon he was late for his first job and we were speeding to get there. I ended up taking the ticket for him, because he already had two on his record that year. Then there was the time in Paris when he made me act like a stranger and flirt madly with a security guard so he could try to sneak into the tunnels of the opera house. I've actually written sermons for him that he preached and took credit for!

In spite of all the things Greg and I have tried to pass each other off as, there is one limit we have not crossed—we have never ever, not even once, tried to pass each other off as brother and sister. Because, um, that would just be wrong.

That's why it is so surprising to me that Abraham, the father of nations, the man of faith and devotion, lied and said that his wife was his sister! But Sarah was quite beautiful, and he was truly afraid that people would kill him to get her. The first time was during their move to Egypt because of a famine. The pharaoh actually took Abraham's "sister" into his palace to be part of his harem. The second time, Abraham told King Abimelech that Sarah was his sister, and he took her too! Both times God had to step in to rescue her. He inflicted Pharaoh and his household with serious diseases, and He came to Abimelech in a dream to say he was as good as dead.

Don't waste a lot of time this year trying to pass yourself off as something you're not. It's unoriginal, and it's lame. It's OK to be honest about who you'd like to be, but have the courage to admit who you really are. Chances are, people will appreciate you a whole lot more, and you won't have to be begging God to get you out of another mess.

—MH

Alone in the World

She gave this name to the Lord who spoke to her: "You are the God who sees me."
Genesis 16:13.

He spent three entire days stranded in the extreme summer heat of Death Valley, unable to hike out, and lived to tell the tale. Mr. McMullen was hiking in Death Valley National Park in September 2001 when he sprained his ankle and could not go on. So he sat down under the shelter of a solitary fig tree and waited for a rescue helicopter to find him. He expected it. Why? Because before he had left home McMullen had given a detailed hike itinerary to his wife, telling her where he'd be and when. This document not only saved his life, but during the long wait it gave McMullen hope that someone was out there looking for him.

When Sarah's servant Hagar fled into the desert to get away from Sarah, she didn't have the same assurance McMullen did. Because Sarah could not get pregnant, she had forced Hagar to sleep with her husband, Abraham. But when Hagar did get pregnant, she became high-handed with Sarah. Sarah, who was jealous and angry anyway, started mistreating her. So Hagar fled, probably thinking that nobody would come looking for her. But God did.

The angel of the Lord found her near a desert spring and assured her that her misery had been noticed. He told her to return to Sarah, promising that both Hagar and her unborn child would survive. Even more, someday he would become a great nation. After all this encouragement, the Bible says that Hagar gave a special name to the Lord: "You are the God who sees me." She thought she was completely alone in the world, but God came to assure her that He not only saw her misery, but would see her through it. This is especially interesting, as Hagar was a pagan from Egypt, not a Jew. Yet the Bible records the name she gave God.

Maybe you've felt like Hagar—stranded in the desert of life, completely alone in the world, with nobody to look for you and no one who cares. But that's not true! God is still looking for you. He is the God who sees you. He sees and knows your pain, your predicaments, and your life. And what's more, He's on His way to find you. Keep your eyes open today for where He might show up, and be assured that you are not alone, and you are not invisible. You belong to "the God who sees."

— MH

Slipping and Sliding

On the third day Abraham looked up and saw the place in the distance. He said to his servants, "Stay here with the donkey while I and the boy go over there. We will worship and then we will come back to you." Genesis 22:4, 5.

Dangling over a high precipice with little more than some webbing strapped to your waist is usually enough to make you feel anywhere from slightly nervous to babbling incoherently with fear. My brother was somewhere in between the two when he finally made it through the ritual of squeezing himself into a climbing harness. I had decided that some good brother bonding time would be to get out and try rappelling, and even though Doug wasn't super excited about heights, he went along with the plan.

I looked closely at his configuration of metal carabiners, self-belay device, and safety knots. Satisfied that everything looked fine, I finally told him to start slowly backing himself up to the edge of the cliff. Just as he was sucking up the courage to step off the cliff, I suddenly noticed that his main locking carabiner wasn't locked! "Doug, your carabiner!" I yelled. He looked down and kind of panicked, and suddenly the ground fell away and he went slipping and sliding over the edge. Luckily the belay device caught him, and he smacked into the side of the wall with a loud yell. After I hauled him up over the edge, I looked closer and realized that he had been locked in all the time, and I had made a mistake. As he stomped off mad, I heard him mutter, "Don't know why I trusted you in the first place!" Trust *is* the bottom line, isn't it?

The story of Abraham sacrificing Isaac sounds crazy. I couldn't imagine having to sacrifice my own son. But when I read the story, one word jumped out at me. "*We* will come back to you." This is trust! Despite the command to sacrifice his son, Abraham believed that something would still work out, because God had promised to make him into a great nation.

Trusting in God's promises means believing in things that sometimes don't make sense to our limited viewpoints. But God always has a way of making things work out. So when you read the Bible promises that say the Lord will take care of you, or that He won't allow you to experience temptations you can't handle, you know He means what He says. All we have to do is trust, and wait for Him to show us how it all works out in the end.

—GH

The Seven-Year Engagement

So Jacob served seven years to get Rachel, but they seemed like only a few days to him because of his love for her. Genesis 29:20.

The first time I had my heart broken I was in seventh grade. His name was Vincent, and he was, in my opinion, the most beautiful boy on earth. We "dated," which in seventh grade pretty much means simply that we called each other boyfriend and girlfriend and held hands once or twice but didn't even talk on the playground some days. On Valentine's Day he gave me a box of mint truffles. At the roller rink he skated with me all night. On my birthday a timid peck on the lips counted for both of us as our first kiss. But then after about six months of "dating" he decided it wasn't working out for him, so he ended it. I was crushed; I was devastated. I thought I would never find another boy I could love so much as I had loved Vincent. I gave up hope of ever getting married.

But, as you can imagine, more boys did in fact come along. And more heartbreaks seemed to come along with them, but over the years I began to realize that the promise of marriage didn't end with each relationship—it was still out there somewhere, and I was still waiting for it. When I finally did meet my husband, it was quite a while until I realized that he was the person I wanted to marry (that's another story). But once I did figure it out, all the heartbreaks of the past seemed like a mere blur, a trifle, compared to the joy of having him.

It was the same with Jacob and Rachel. He had to work a total of 14 years to get her; the last seven were extra after being tricked into first marrying her older sister, Leah. You would think that seven years would seem like a pretty long time to wait for the person you love, but the Bible says that they seemed like only a few days to him because he loved her so much.

At your age, it can feel next to impossible to wait for the one you will marry. You might feel as if you'll never find him or her at all. Or you might feel as if some things are not worth saving for them because the wait is so dreadfully long—how could you possibly control yourself for years and years? But take a lesson from Jacob. When you do find that person, the wait will suddenly seem as if it were only a few days, because your love for them is so great. Assure yourself today that waiting will be worth it.

—MH

Hanging On for Dear Life

Then the man said, "Let me go, for it is daybreak." But Jacob replied, "I will not let you go unless you bless me." Genesis 32:26.

My husband faithfully runs out of gas and gets stranded on the side of the road about twice a month. Every few weeks I can count on getting a call to come rescue him, or his stumbling in the door about an hour late explaining that he had to hike to another gas station. It's not that his gas gauge is broken— it's that he just "doesn't feel like taking the time" to stop for gas. Of all his run-ning-out-of-gas stories (more to come later), my favorite was the night he ended up dangling from the back of a pickup truck at midnight.

Greg and his friend Tim were driving home from college when—true to form—Greg ran out of gas. And it was the middle of the night, in the middle of nowhere. They began walking down the dark highway when an old woman pulled up beside them in a pickup truck that was packed to the gills. She yelled that she had no room for them in the car, but they could hang on to the tailgate if they wanted, and she'd drive really slow into the next town. Well, they hopped on, and she proceeded to zoom off at 50 miles an hour. Greg told me later that he was afraid for his life, but he just kept focusing all of his energy on the single most important task: never letting go of that tailgate.

Jacob could have made that midnight ride with Greg. When God came to Jacob in the night and wrestled with him until daybreak, Jacob refused to let go. All night long he pitted his strength against the Stranger's, determined to get a blessing. And he got one. "You have struggled with God and with men and have overcome," God said (Genesis 32:28).

At one time or another, most of us in this life will have a significant struggle with God. We will doubt, we will question, we will rage and blame—we will wrestle. And as far as I can understand, that's OK. It's OK to wrestle with God, as so many have before us. What's not OK is to let go. I don't know what you're wrestling with today, but I want to challenge you to commit in your heart to be a man or a woman like Jacob—though he wrestled with God all night long, he absolutely refused to let go. You may struggle for a time, but refuse to let go of God. Wait till morning, and your blessing will come.

—MH

Making a Jerk of Yourself

But Esau ran to meet Jacob and embraced him; he threw his arms around his neck and kissed him. And they wept. Genesis 33:4.

'll never forget the shameful fit I threw when I got suspended from school my senior year in college for staying out all night. My curfew was 3:00 a.m., but I'd fallen asleep on a friend's couch and hadn't come in at all. When I got suspended for this accident, I decided to respond with a wave of angry letters and defiant diatribes. These would have made my situation worse if one of the deans—Mrs. Merth—hadn't publicly stood up for me and said, "She is just upset. She's a good girl—she doesn't mean to be like this." I don't know if I deserved that vote of confidence, but I certainly never forgot it. For years after that, I felt ashamed each time I remembered the way I'd acted.

Recently I returned to Union College on a visit, and I ran into good old Mrs. Merth. Immediately all the shame and regret about my suspension behavior came flooding back over me, and as we visited I knew I finally had to get it off my chest. "I'm so sorry about my behavior all those years ago," I apologized.

There was silence. I raised my eyes to see a totally blank look on her face. "Thank you," she said, "but I honestly don't remember what you are talking about." All those years of being ashamed had been for nothing—she had forgiven me long ago. Finally I had peace!

When Jacob met his brother, Esau, whom he had deceived and stolen from 20 years before, he came in shame—bowing low to the ground seven times, sending ahead exorbitant gifts, and begging profusely for forgiveness. But instead of remembering the injustice, Esau ran to meet him and engulfed him in a giant hug. All had been forgiven long ago, but Jacob never knew. He had spent the past 20 years living in shame.

The point is that when you wrong someone and it feels good at the time, you aren't actually hurting them in the long run. You are hurting yourself. Most people will move on and let it go, but you are the one who will have to carry around the shame of your behavior for many years to come. The wrongs you inflict on other lives actually last longest in your life. Remember this today and treat the people you struggle with kindly.

—MH

He So Had It Coming to Him!

Now Israel loved Joseph more than any of his other sons, because he had been born to him in his old age; and he made a richly ornamented robe for him. When his brothers saw that their father loved him more than any of them, they hated him. Genesis 37:3, 4.

You could tell this kid was a brat just by looking at him. There was just something in his pudgy little face, something that said, "I'm going to drive you crazy and then run crying to Mama when you try to stop me." And so in those first few minutes at my very first Pathfinder Camporee I realized that I was about to have the worst tentmate of my entire life. He rolled around squealing when we were trying to sleep, he stole the best candy our parents had sent us, and if we finally caught him he'd yell for his uncle, who just happened to be the head cook. We didn't want to upset him, or we'd lose out in the end.

So we slowly developed a plan for getting this kid back. We'd learned that after a mega helping of dessert he'd go crazy for about an hour, but then the sugar would catch up with him and he'd crash in a tired heap, finally sleeping like a baby. If we could capture him in such a state of exhaustion, there'd be little chance of his raising a ruckus to stop us. So one night we loaded him up with all of our desserts, and watched with self-satisfied grins as he spun himself into a tizzy. After the inevitable crash we surrounded his sleeping bag, pillows and suitcases in hand. Suddenly we let fly with everything all at once, mercilessly jumping on and pounding his sleeping form. His cries of distress were muffled because of the pillows and his state of exhaustion, and by the time we'd finished he had promised not to bother any of us ever again.

I always think of that incident when I read the story of Joseph, because, really, you can't blame his brothers for not liking him. Not only was he obviously his father's favorite, but he went around telling them that in his dreams they all bowed down and worshipped him. Not exactly a short list of endearing qualities when you're the second-youngest of 12 brothers.

Today, think about the kind of person you are. Are you giving the people around you reason to treat you the way they are? And even beyond that, are you taking the label of "Christian" but acting in such a way that makes people think, *If that's a Christian, I want nothing to do with them*? We have to remember that we aren't here just to represent ourselves.

—GH

When You Have the Right to Be Angry

So then, it was not you who sent me here, but God. Genesis 45:8.

My back was turned to her when she took away the ladder. I was completely unaware that I'd just been trapped on top of a roof. We had climbed up onto the garage and were picking plums from the neighbor's tree that grew down over our roof. My sister and I had collected almost two buckets of plums and were getting ready to head down the ladder when I turned to tell her something and saw that the ladder was gone. And so was she. She had crawled down silently and purposely removed the ladder. Now she was nowhere in sight.

I called for her. I yelled and screamed for her. I yelled and screamed for Mom, or Dad, or the neighbors, or anyone who would save me from an entire afternoon trapped alone on a rooftop. But nobody came. I don't know exactly how long I sat up on that burning hot roof on that summer day—an hour? Maybe more? She sat inside, watching and laughing.

My siblings and I have done a lot of mean things to each other, but nothing compared to what Joseph's brothers did to him. They actually sold him into slavery. Imagine how angry you would feel, how hateful and resentful you'd be, if your own brothers or sisters sold you to be a slave! Would you spend the rest of your days hating them? Joseph didn't. He worked hard and earned respect, gaining success in Potiphar's household. But then he was thrown into prison after being falsely accused by Potiphar's wife of attempted rape. He spent two years in a dungeon, forgotten. You would guess that his anger for his brothers would return, that he would plot revenge or wish them harm. But Joseph didn't. When he finally got the chance to face them again, he was prime minister of Egypt, and they all bowed before him, asking to buy food to stave off starvation. They didn't recognize him, of course, and when he finally told them who he was, they begged his forgiveness. Joseph's response was surprising: "It was not you who sent me here, but God." You see, all along Joseph hadn't been angry—he'd believed that God had had a plan for him.

What about you? What are the struggles going on in your life right now that you could get very angry about? Are you wasting time on hatred and resentment? Instead, choose to believe that God has a plan to bring good out of your struggles. Trust Him, and let that anger go.

—MH

Suspended for Bare Feet

Moses said to God, "Suppose I go to the Israelites and say to them, 'The God of your fathers has set me to you,' and they ask me, 'What is his name?' Then what shall I tell them?" God said to Moses, "I am who I am." Exodus 3:13, 14.

I used to think that I could control my teachers. It was one of the many misconceptions I held during my high school years. This erroneous belief really came to the forefront during my junior year. We lived in Phoenix, which for about 363 days out of the year is blazing hot outside. On a campus covered in soft cool grass, I saw no reason of any sort to be wearing hot sticky shoes or sweaty rubber sandals, so I went barefoot. Everywhere—classrooms, cafeteria, chapel, and dorm—my bare feet led the way.

Most people ignored my bare feet, but Mrs. Ault did not. For some reason she made it her mission to get some shoes back on my naked feet. It was technically in the rulebook—for insurance reasons, I'd imagine—that students had to wear shoes while on campus. She would remind me whenever she saw me, but I ignored her. Like a defiant child screaming, "You are not the boss of me!" I stomped all over campus without footwear. I even dared to prop my dirty feet up on my desk in her classroom, and when she asked me to put my shoes on I proudly announced, "I left them at home!" I was pretty sure that I ran the show . . . until one fine day she landed me in discipline committee. All of a sudden, it became very clear to me that I was not in control.

The ancient Egyptians believed that if you could discover the name of a god, then you could control that god or evoke him to act whenever you wanted. That's probably why we see Moses, a man highly trained in Egyptian ways, begging God to share His name. But God doesn't do it. He says only, "I am who I am" (a more exact translation is "I shall be what I shall be"). It's as though God is making a very clear statement: You humans cannot control Me. You cannot force Me to do anything. I am in control. I am the one in charge.

And you know—that really comforts me. I don't want a God that I can control or boss around, because then He wouldn't really be God, would He? Today, take comfort in the fact that God is in control—of this world, of your life, of your future.

—MH

Nobody Will Know You Are Lousy

Moses said to the Lord, "O Lord, I have never been eloquent, neither in the past nor since you have spoken to your servant. I am slow of speech and tongue." The Lord said to him, "Who gave man his mouth? . . . Now go; I will help you speak and will teach you what to say." Exodus 4:10-12.

Even after playing for 23 long years, I have still managed to turn out to be a really lousy harpist. I'm a slow sight reader. I don't have a musician's ear. I can't memorize my music. I have played for dozens upon dozens of weddings, some funerals, quite a few banquets and galas, and churches all over the country, but to be honest with you, all that time I've played the same songs I learned when I was about 8. And I still make mistakes when I play those songs!

I've become so timid about my playing that I've begun to beg off when someone asks me to play. Even the other day at church, when the music coordinator asked me to play for the Christmas program, I just wanted to tell him, "I'm lousy; I stink! Ask someone else!"

But then I realized something: the man has no idea how lousy I am. For that matter, nobody does. You see, the harp just so happens to be one of those instruments that would sound good even if you played it with your toes, so I'm the only person who really knows about my shortcomings. But because I know them, I am afraid. I say no.

For the same reason Moses was afraid to lead the nation of Israel out of Egypt. When God met him at the burning bush and asked him to go to the pharaoh, Moses thought of his shortcomings. He listed his failures and pleaded with God to send someone else. God basically responded by saying, "Is anything too hard for Me? If I could design your mouth, don't you think I can also help you figure out how to use it?"

We get afraid to do things for God because we are busy looking at our own shortcomings. We forget that God is more than able to compensate for them. The next time you have a chance to do something or say something for God, remember that He will be there helping you speak. As He did with Moses, He will teach you what to say. Your part is to stop focusing on your shortcomings and just be willing to let Him use you any way He can.

—MH

If You Have Trouble Worshipping God . . .

Then the Lord said to Moses, "Go to Pharaoh and say to him, 'This is what the Lord says: Let my people go, so that they may worship me.'" Exodus 8:1.

I think there is such as thing as too much freedom. When I was 17, I didn't have a curfew, but I had my own car and a gas card to fill it up with. I was on the school's Student Association, so sometimes I stayed late at the school working on programs or setting up events. My parents got tired of remembering which night I had which meeting, etc., so they got into the habit of letting me roll into the driveway whenever I jolly well pleased, which gave me a whole lot of freedom —too much freedom. I remember one night I stayed out with friends so long that the sun was rising as I turned into our neighborhood. I had just enough time to shower and change before heading back out to the car again!

The later I stayed out, the more exhausted I became. I started to fall asleep in classes. Then I started to skip classes completely to sleep in the dorm. As the months went by and my attendance grade dropped, I began to realize that I wasn't doing the right thing with my freedom. Instead of feeling free, all I ever felt was downright exhausted. Instead of enjoying my freedom, I was trapped in a cycle of sleep deprivation.

When God sent Moses to Pharaoh to demand that His people be set free, God repeatedly gave a purpose for the freedom: so they could worship Him. There is something about slavery that takes away from the full experience of worship. God knew that until the people were living in freedom, they would not be completely available to worship Him with their whole minds, hearts, and bodies.

The point of freedom is to worship God. We cannot worship Him fully when we are not free. And while none of us today really find ourselves in literal slavery, we all struggle with being slaves to one particular sin or another, don't we? If you are finding it difficult right now in your life to truly worship God, could it be that you are not free? Could it be that you are in some serious bondage to a certain sin in your life? Ask the Lord today to set you free from that sin, and see what a difference its absence makes in your ability to worship Him.

—MH

Why Did God Create Idiots and Mean People?

But I have raised you up for this very purpose, that I might show you my power and that my name might be proclaimed in all the earth. Exodus 9:16.

The kicking on the back of my chair never stopped, and neither did the taunting. "Check out the guy who can't get a girl here. Hey, you and your idiot friend gonna go to some nerdfest this weekend?" I hated fifth-period geometry for this one single reason: Chad. Sure, I suppose my best friend, Darin, and I cutting up over our own inside jokes was probably annoying to people, but having the "cool" guy in class constantly harassing you is enough to make anyone crazy. In fact, it's not too much to say I truly hated Chad. From all accounts, he pretty much hated me too, and was fond of letting me know in very public ways. If there was any one person on the face of the earth I could have erased, it would have been him. In my book he was a completely worthless human being. "Why did You even create this guy?" I would ask God.

However, by the end of my junior year something had happened. In completely separate ways, both of us had had a real conversion experience with God, and all of a sudden we found ourselves preaching together and working small group Bible studies together. I realized that there was actually a lot about Chad that I liked. So he wasn't totally worthless after all! And what's more, I began to realize that God had a real purpose for Chad's life. Today, believe it or not, Chad is a successful pastor. I never would have guessed it. (I still hope he has really annoying kids in his youth group, though.)

If I had been an Israelite slave, I know I would have been asking God every single day why He even allowed Pharaoh to live. But God says something so surprising—He says He Himself actually raised Pharaoh up and allowed him to rule, so that God's power might be shown! God had a plan that the Israelites could never have guessed.

Don't forget that the Lord has purposes for other people's lives that you know nothing about. You may be dealing with someone you think is useless, worthless, or just a general waste of space, but God doesn't see them the way you do. Even someone who is causing visible harm, such as Pharaoh, God had a purpose for. Remember that you don't know the end of the story. Decide to see even the troublemakers in your life as people for whom God has a purpose too.

—GH and MH

Takin' the Long Way Around

When Pharaoh let the people go, God did not lead them on the road through the Philistine country, though that was shorter. For God said, "If they face war, they might change their minds and return to Egypt." Exodus 13:17.

After driving wildly around town for more than an hour, I was shocked to arrive right back at my own house. My sister and best friend Alicia had blindfolded me with the promise of a surprise mystery date, and so I wouldn't figure out where we were headed, apparently they drove in circles around dozens of neighborhoods. When they finally led me out of the car, up a driveway, and through a door, the warm scent of my own home caught my nose, and I was completely confused—until the blindfold was ripped off and I was standing in my own living room, surrounded by a huge group of family and friends yelling, "Surprise!" It was my surprise going-away party before I left for college—not at some place an hour away, but right there in my own home! Everyone laughed and joked the rest of the evening about how I really took the long way getting home that day. All that wandering around had been for a good reason, though. Had they only driven around the block once or twice, I would have known where I was all along, and the surprise wouldn't have worked out.

When Pharaoh finally let the Israelite people leave Egypt, God did not lead them the shortest way, because it would have gone through enemy country and they might have gotten into a war. God knew their weak, tired hearts might not have been able to handle that, and they would have wanted to return to Egypt. So instead He led them the long way around, and they wound up on the desert road toward the Red Sea—a seemingly dead end. But God had plans that they didn't know about—to open the sea and let them walk right through!

Maybe you've been feeling as if God is taking you the long way. Maybe you aren't sure why He hasn't worked some things out quicker, or better, or differently. But trust Him. He knows your weak heart better than you do. Though the shortcuts seem better, perhaps He knows reasons they aren't. Remember— His whole goal is to get you home, to the real Promised Land: heaven. So trust the route He's taking you.

—MH

Fight or Flight

The Lord will fight for you; you need only to be still. Exodus 14:14.

My first fistfight took place when I was 12 years old, and it was not with another girl—it was with Jeremy, a boy who wore glasses. He was hitting me on the head with the spine of his book, so I slapped him, and he kicked me. My friends standing nearby retold the rest of the story by saying that I screamed out in anger, "I hate you!" as I tore the glasses off his face with my right hand, then punched him directly in the eye with my left. He had a black eye for the rest of that week, and I remember that every time I looked at it, I wondered, *What made me do that?* I don't remember making a decision to hit him—I only remember reacting in anger. Every cell in my 12-year-old body said, "You need to fight back!"

I've heard that all animals, including humans, come with a built-in fight or flight response. When they're threatened, their response will be in one of two directions—to fight back or to flee. What about you? Are you a fighter? Or would you rather flee the scene?

You'll remember that after they fled Egypt the Israelites stood trapped against the Red Sea with Pharaoh's best military forces advancing toward them. Pharoah had ordered his 600 best chariots for the battle, plus all his officers, horsemen, and troops. Impossible odds for escape, and the Israelites were terrified—and angry. "Was it because there were no graves in Egypt that you brought us to the desert to die?" they demanded of Moses. Their memories were so short! "Didn't we say to you, 'Leave us alone; let us serve the Egyptians'?" (Exodus 14:11, 12). We would expect Moses to suggest one of these two options—fight the Egyptians or try to flee. But strangely, he comes up with a third option—an entirely different approach: "The Lord will fight for you; you need only to be still." Be still? At a time like that? It sounded crazy, but it was exactly what they needed to do so that the Lord could work His miracle to open the sea and save them.

Are you trapped in a position in which you feel you must either fight or flee? Don't forget that when you're in trouble you have a third option—to be still and let the Lord fight for you. It might sound crazy, but it's exactly what we need to do if we want to give Him the chance to work a miracle. Today, if you're backed up against impossible odds, choose to be still and let God work it out for you.

—MH

Hands Over the Valley

When Moses' hands grew tired, they took a stone and put it under him and he sat on it. Aaron and Hur held his hands up—one on one side, one on the other—so that his hands remained steady till sunset. Exodus 17:12.

Our dusty little jeep rattled on through the desert sands, headed for the mountainous region of Egypt's Sinai Peninsula. Suddenly we stopped and found ourselves in a cramped little valley, rock walls not more than 500 feet apart towering above us on each side. Randall Younker, our archaeologist guide, motioned for us to get out of our jeeps and join him on the side of the road. "This is the valley in the ancient region of Rephidim," he said. When our puzzled expressions showed that he might as well have spoken to us in the local Arabic language, he explained, "You know, the place where the Israelites fought the Amalekites, and Moses held his staff up to help them win." Suddenly the old story came back . . .

Exodus records that the Israelites were attacked by the Amalekites and fought them for an entire day. Moses climbed a nearby hill and held up his arms with his staff outstretched. As long as he kept his arms up, the Israelites kept winning. But when he got tired and his arms began to sag, they began to lose heart—*and* the battle.

But this valley where we were standing didn't fit all the pictures that I'd seen in my Sabbath school classes growing up. Those pictures showed the battle on a large open plain, with a small hill and a tiny little guy way up on top. After sharing the obvious mistake with our professor, he simply smiled and shook his head. "Nope; it wasn't on a plain, and there wasn't a hill like that. It was right here in this valley, and Moses would've been standing at the top of the valley wall, looking down over the army." As that sank in, the whole story took on new light in my mind. Instead of being distant and tiny, Moses stood less than 100 feet above his men, catching their gaze as they looked up to see if he was still there supporting them. They would've seen the fatigue and known his struggles, just as he could see theirs.

And really, that's the same way God is with us in our lives. He doesn't wait off in the distance. He's right there nearby, looking down and offering His encouragement and help if we will look up and see Him. Are you looking up to Him these days, or are your own worries and fears taking all of your attention away from Him? All we have to do is look up.

—GH

BFF

The people all responded together, "We will do everything the Lord has said." So Moses brought their answer back to the Lord. Exodus 19:8.

It was petty and it was childish, but every girl in the class liked this one guy, and I was seriously tired of being ignored. The new guy in school always gets extra attention from the girls, but if you add to that a very strong physique, blue eyes, and a deep, manly voice that made the rest of our sixth-grade falsetto-cracking voices sound like chipmunks, you might understand my jealousy. His name was Chris, and for whatever reason, he and I had become BFFs at the beginning of my sixth-grade year—always together at recess, always on the same team, etc.

That was before all the girls in school started drooling when we walked by—and it wasn't me they were looking at. They passed little notes to him during lunch, giggled and laughed when we walked down the hall, and after a while it just got to be kind of tiring to be around him. Then one day the girl in my class that I'd had a crush on for more than a year came up and handed *me* a note, almost sending me fainting to the floor in shock. I was so excited I could hardly open it up. Suddenly she snatched it away and looked at me, annoyed. "No, silly; it's for *Chris!* Go give it to him." Whatever friendship or bond that there had been between Chris and me disintegrated in the time it took to refold that piece of paper. No more BFF.

Surprisingly enough, the Bible records a time God was willing to make a sacred friendship agreement with a group of people. In Exodus, just before He gives Moses the Ten Commandments, God speaks to the people and tells them that they will be His best friends out of everyone on the earth, if only they'll commit to living in harmony with His laws. And they said they would, binding themselves to Him, and He to them; best of friends. But it wasn't going to last, because within days they'd turned their backs on Him and were praying to the statue of a cow, the same way they'd worshipped in Egypt. By all rights God could have rejected them then and there, saying, "You broke your promise, so I don't have to keep My end either." But unlike us humans, God doesn't let go so easily. The rest of the Old Testament is all about how God tried in so many ways to keep the promise alive, to keep the covenant. And thankfully, He's still that kind of God today. God keeps His end of a promise even if we fail on ours.

—GH

Desiderata: God's Greatest Desire

Let them make Me a sanctuary, that I may dwell among them. Exodus 25:8, NKJV.

They circled and descended on our household in droves. They moved in. They brought luggage and garbage and everything but the kitchen sink. When Greg's relatives arrived from the East to visit for nine days, I was completely overwhelmed—what would we do with them all that time? How would we entertain them? What would we talk about? How could I feed all these people three times a day? We made menus. We planned outings. We found several places to take them all each day. But to my surprise, they didn't seem to care about that. They weren't particularly interested in the Space Needle or the Pacific Science Center with its IMAX theater and tropical butterfly house.

All they really wanted to do was hang around the house. "We just want to be with you guys!" they would say. I thought that that would get old after two or three days, but they were true to their word. They didn't care what we ate or when. It didn't matter if entire days went by without anyone leaving the house. They simply chatted and visited and enjoyed our presence. At the end of the week I began to realize they had meant what they said. They didn't come to tour Seattle or be waited on hand and foot. Their greatest desire was to just be around us.

That just so happens to be God's greatest desire too. In Exodus we have seen God desiring to free the people from slavery, and we've seen Him teaching them how to worship Him, but we come to see that it was all for one purpose—He wanted to dwell among them. He was a holy God, and they were sinful people, but He still wanted to hang out with them. In order for Him to be able to do this—to mix holy with sinful—He had to teach them how to be holy. Thus the laws, the regulations, the commandments, and the sanctuary. In fact the entire point of the sanctuary was so that God could have a place to physically come down to earth and dwell among His people.

This is still His greatest desire today—to dwell among us. But He won't come uninvited. Is it your desire to be with Him? Realize today that God puts all His efforts toward the chance of just being near you, and decide to make space in your life for Him.

—MH

Afraid of the Dark?

Keep the lamps burning before the Lord from evening till morning. Exodus 27:21.

I don't know if anything ever lived under your bed as a child, but there were wolves under mine. Seriously—wolves. Under my bed. We lived at the base of the foothills, and so late at night we could hear the coyotes howling from our house. From this howling I developed a fear of wolves, and became convinced that they were lurking under my bed, waiting to snatch me when the lights went off. My poor mom tried for months to tell me it wasn't so. Just when I was starting to believe her, one night my dad launched an evil plan of his own. He decided to hide under my bed at bedtime, and once the lights were out and I came close enough, he reached out his arm and grabbed my ankle, letting out a piercing, beastly "Rraaahh!" I screamed and shrieked and sobbed. My dad no doubt shrieked and sobbed later when my mom finally got hold of him.

Now that we're grown up, most of us lie awake at night with fears and thoughts far scarier than wolves. We wonder why we feel so alone, why our lives are spinning out of control, what the point of our lives is anyway, and if there's any purpose or reason to it all. Questions, doubts, fears, and insecurities—they stalk us like predators in the night.

That's why I think it would have been cool to be an Israelite teenager camping in the Sinai desert. I've been there—it is one of the most desolate places on earth. When the Israelites camped there, the priests had strict orders from the Lord to leave the oil lamps in the sanctuary burning all night long. Why waste oil when everybody was asleep? Because the lamps represented the presence of the Lord's Spirit. And it was super important to God for His children to know that He was available all night long. Through the darkest hours and the most desolate watches, God was awake. Any kid could wake in a sweat from a nightmare and simply peek outside his or her tent to see the warm comforting glow from the sanctuary in the middle of the camp, and be reminded, "My God is standing by." This is how God developed the reputation for being the God who neither slumbers nor sleeps (see Psalm 121:4). So next time you find yourself struggling through the middle of a dark night, remember that your God is awake too. He doesn't sleep or slumber. The lights are burning in heaven, and you are not alone in this darkness.

—MH

A Divine Temper Tantrum

> When Moses approached the camp and saw the calf and the dancing, his anger burned and he threw the tablets out of his hands, breaking them to pieces at the foot of the mountain. Exodus 32:19.

When my son is having a tantrum, he throws things. Sometimes I'll come into his room to find every single book from his bookshelf thrown madly across the floor. Other times I will find all his toys thrown to the bottom of the stairs, or—if I've taken too long in coming to get him—every stuffed animal thrown out of his crib. While this type of behavior is perhaps to be expected in a little toddler, it's alarming to find tantrum tendencies still around in some adults I know. One of my friends throws punches at walls when he is mad. Another girl I knew broke the windows in her apartment when she was angry— that got expensive. One friend has a designated doll she repeatedly slams against the wall when she is irked. I even knew a guy who threw a lamp—an entire lamp—at his girlfriend when he lost control of his temper.

I had always thought that Moses just threw a fit and broke the stones when he came down from Mount Sinai. He had just spent days with the Lord, and was carrying the Ten Commandments written on stone by the finger of God Himself. But when he came upon the scene in the camp—the Israelites dancing wildly before the golden calf Aaron had made—his anger burned, and he threw down the stone tablets, breaking them to pieces. But this was not a tantrum. It was symbolic. The people had broken the covenant they'd just recently vowed to obey, promising God to do everything He'd said. And Moses literally broke the commandments to symbolize the fact that they had already broken the covenant.

You might not throw and break things when you get mad—and I don't suggest you do—but like Moses, all of us have broken God's laws. There is no excuse for it—we have done it intentionally, sometimes even after swearing we would keep them. But the pieces aren't shattered forever. God is as patient today as He was back then. If you've done some damage and need to come back to God, don't wait another minute. He's waiting for you.

—MH

Your Face Is Glowing!

When Moses came down from Mount Sinai with the two tablets of the Testimony in his hands, he was not aware that his face was radiant because he had spoken with the Lord. Exodus 34:29.

My boyfriend took one look at my beaming face through the window and immediately knew I was on the phone with another guy. It was late at night at summer camp, and I'd left my boyfriend hours before, saying I was headed off to bed. Which I'd planned to do. But just as I was turning out the light, my best friend (a guy on whom I also had a huge crush) called me. I'd been standing at the lobby pay phone talking to him ever since.

I was shocked to learn that my boyfriend knew exactly whom I was talking to. He had gone back to his camp station late that night to check some gear, and as he passed by the window of the girls' lodge he saw me at the only phone. He said his heart just sank in his chest at the sight of my shining eyes and the smile jumping off my face. He knew it could only be one person—my best friend—and he also knew I was falling in love with someone who wasn't him. I didn't realize that my face changed when I talked to my best friend, but I guess it still does—he's my husband now, and some people claim that my eyes still shine when my cell phone lights up with his number.

In the same way, the people of Israel didn't have to wonder whom Moses had been talking to when he came down from Mount Sinai. They knew exactly who it was, because his face was "radiant" from speaking with the Lord. The text says that Moses was not aware of it, but everyone else was. It was obvious. They couldn't miss it. In fact, they asked him to cover his radiant face because it made them afraid. (Check out Exodus 34:29-35.)

When we spend time with someone we love, it shows. By the way, it works this way when you spend time with God as well. When you spend time in His presence, it will show not only on your face but also in your life. It starts to become obvious that there is something different about you, and whether you recognize it in yourself or not, other people do. So get in the habit of spending regular time with God. You will grow to love Him more and more. And when people take a look at your life, they will know that you have been with Jesus.

—MH

You Think You Know a Guy

When any of you brings an offering to the Lord, bring as your offering an animal from either the herd or the flock. Leviticus 1:2.

When I married him, I didn't realize that my husband does laundry only twice a year. This handsome, clean, well-dressed and well-put-together man secretly cannot muster up the courage to drag himself and his dirty clothes to the washing machine more often than every six months. Once married, apparently ashamed of this inadequacy, he took to hiding the clothes in various nooks and crannies of his closet. I finally discovered his little habit the day I stuck my hand in for a shoe and a small avalanche of dirty clothes fell at my feet. I wondered just how many clothes were in there, so I went on an excavation. I uncovered more than nine loads of laundry. It was July, but I found clothes in there that he hadn't worn since New Year's Day.

Every day I learn new things about the man I married. I thought I knew him really well when we married, but now I realize that I'll never stop learning. It truly takes a lifetime to know a person completely. And that reminds me of Leviticus.

The first time I read through the book of Leviticus I felt disgusted and repulsed by the sheer number of sacrifices that God required. Why would He ask for so much killing of so many innocent animals? Surprisingly enough, God was just trying to be user-friendly. For starters, at that time in the ancient world you learned about a god and his character from the sacrifices he required. It helped you understand who the god was. God Himself may not have chosen this idea if His people didn't already understand the world in those terms. He came to their level. Second, the plan of salvation God was trying to teach His children was kind of like my marriage. There was always more to learn. Jesus' sacrifice of Himself on the cross is so multifaceted that one single sacrifice wouldn't explain all the aspects of it. Even 20 didn't cover all that He would do, but it brought the Israelites closer to understanding how God would deal with sin, with guilt, with law, and more.

Don't ever get trapped into thinking that you already know everything about God, or that you already understand everything about Jesus' sacrifice. If we can never fully know each other here on earth, we will surely never run out of things to learn about God.

—MH

The Human Cannonball

If the whole Israelite community sins unintentionally . . . even though the community is unaware of the matter, they are guilty. Leviticus 4:13.

You have to believe me when I say that I didn't break his arm on purpose. It was one of those mornings that you get up way before your parents and find there's absolutely nothing to do. My brother and I were trying to come up with something to pass the time when all of a sudden inspiration struck. A human cannonball! I lay down on my back with my feet up, and told him to sit on my feet like a chair. Then I would suddenly launch him across the room without any warning. He absolutely loved the idea.

After several initial launches, I started getting the hang of it and going for distance. I launched him higher and farther, one time almost hitting the ceiling fan with my human cannonball. After about the tenth time something happened. When I launched him, he somehow rotated backwards in the air and landed, with a sickening crack, on his outstretched arm. We both stared in shock, knowing that something was very, very bad. But it wasn't until Mom woke up and confirmed the broken arm that he started crying—which I've always thought was rather strange. In any case, the entire incident was quite innocent. I didn't start out *intending* to break my brother's arm; it just happened.

Is a sin still a sin even if you didn't mean to do it? What about accidents and mistakes? I'm sure my brother would say that I should be held accountable for his broken arm, even if it wasn't my intention to break it. Strangely enough, in Leviticus God says the same thing. Is this fair?

We read that the Israelites had to make offerings even when they sinned unintentionally. That seems pretty harsh, until we realize that all sin is detestable to God, and all sin separates us from Him. It gets in the way of the relationship. Even sin that we don't commit on purpose breaks His holy law and puts us in need of a Savior. Which makes me so very thankful that we have a Savior, because I think I sin "by accident" quite a lot. I wouldn't waste a lot of time trying to think about *my* accidental sins if I were you. No—instead, spend your time better by thanking God today that He has made provision through Jesus for any sin you commit—accidental or not!

—GH and MH

Return Fire

> Aaron's sons Nadab and Abihu each took his own firepan, put fire in it, placed incense on it, and presented unauthorized [strange] fire before the Lord, which He had not commanded them to do. Then flames leaped from the Lord's presence and burned them to death before the Lord. Leviticus 10:1, 2, HCSB.

Every other time I go through the drive-through at a local fast-food establishment I'm led to question the ability of the human race to carry out simple instructions. On a recent adventure to Burger King I ordered a vanilla shake, a well-known culinary delight featuring milk, ice, and sugar. But upon my arrival at the second window to pick up my treat I received a little surprise. A young adult (someone who presumably passed at least fourth grade) handed me my shake and asked, "Would you like salt or ketchup with this?" Maybe the rest of the world enjoys salt and ketchup mixed in with their shakes, but I am the odd one who thinks that mixture would induce rampant vomiting. At first I was speechless, unsure how to respond. I finally overcame my shock and said, "No!" Taking my untainted order, I moved along, allowing the person behind me to deal with whatever strange mixture the man in the window would suggest.

In the Old Testament, God had very specific orders for what He wanted to be served with—and some people either didn't take Him seriously or really didn't pay attention. Nadab and Abihu offered fire to God that He didn't order . . . and God sent it back. It is a rare thing to offer strange fire in church nowadays—as a matter of fact, I don't recommend it. But what is common is mixing together in our lives things that God likes with things that He doesn't. For example, we'll attend church on Sabbath but ignore God the rest of the week. I remember hearing one girl laugh about how she'd party the night before church and then show up to worship service and participate as if it didn't matter what she'd done the night before.

This isn't to say that we don't have room to grow or that God doesn't give us grace when we struggle. But too many times we think that if we mix a few religious services, a few devotional readings, and a handful of prayers in with a couldn't-care-less-what-God-thinks life, we're serving God. But God asks for our entire life. Those of us who think we can get by with a halfhearted mix of religion and sin may find ourselves not going anywhere.

—SP

Why Should I Be Pure?

I am the Lord your God; consecrate yourselves and be holy, because I am holy.
Leviticus 11:44.

What about those times we really want to do the wrong thing? In high school I heard a lot of chapel and vespers talks about how and why we should be pure and holy and good boys and girls. But I just gotta say, I didn't always want to be pure, you know? I mean, sure, it's a really nice idea, and I loved God and all that, but when it came down to daily living, there were often things I wanted to do that just weren't very pure or holy. Sometimes it seemed so much more enticing or exciting or, I don't know, worth it! You're only young once; why not live it up?

The fact of the matter is that if any of us are going to decide to be pure, we need a really good reason. We need motivation that is bigger than "God said so" or simply "I *should* be pure and holy." We need something that actually benefits us. Doesn't God still love and forgive us even when we don't choose the right things? So what's in it for us? What can we get out of walking in God's ways and being pure?

I think that the answer to that question—what's in it for me?—shows up in Leviticus, of all places. God tells the Israelite people that they need to consecrate themselves and be holy. Why? Because He is holy. He gave them directions on how to live, because they'd left their lives of slavery in Egypt and truly didn't know how to be free. They didn't know much about Him, either. And He told them how to run the sanctuary—the place He actually came to live in among them, saying basically, "You need to be pure because I am pure. Because I am going to be in your midst." (Humans are strange. The Israelites had been saying, "Yes, sir," and "No, sir," to the Egyptians for 400 years, so why did they have such a hard time doing what the God of heaven asked of them?) This comes back to the fact that if we want our lives to be full of the presence of God— and I know I do—then we need to make an effort to be pure people. I have always wanted more of God in my life—I wanted to feel Him more and experience Him vividly and sense His presence. Those were the things I craved! I wanted Him to be real to me. And I've learned that one of the best ways to make God real is to consecrate myself and be holy. Why? Because He is holy. If I want a holy God hanging around with me, it makes good sense that I at least ought to try to be holy myself.

—MH

Birthdays and Bathwater

Because on this day atonement will be made for you, to cleanse you. Then, before the Lord, you will be clean from all your sins. Leviticus 16:30.

When I was a kid, the most important day of the year for me was Christmas. It seemed as if I waited all year for it to come, and when it finally did it was magical. Then in high school, when Christmas had lost its charm, my birthday became the most important day of the year—an entire day that was all about me! In college the last day of finals became the most important day of the year, because I was free from sleepless nights of studying for three whole months. Then, once I married, it was my anniversary that was the most important day—we celebrated another wonderful year of marriage. But when I had my first son, that day changed again—suddenly the day I gave birth to him was the most important day of the whole year, and when it would come, my husband and I would marvel at how much he had grown and how fast the time was flying.

In the Israelite community the most important day of the year never changed—it was always the Day of Atonement. On this day the high priest went into the Most Holy Place and made atonement for the sins of the people. The people were cleansed, and then the sanctuary was cleansed. This day was a day of judgment, and it is symbolic of the final judgment at the end of time. All year long the sins of the people had been forgiven, but on this day the sanctuary needed to be cleansed. There was nothing wrong with the sanctuary itself, but like the clean and clear bathwater we use for cleansing ourselves, all year the sanctuary had done its job of cleansing dirty people of sin, and was now infected with sin itself, like the murky water at the end of a bath. Why did sin need to be taken care of twice?

Because it affects God's reputation. Part of the judgment is about God—is it fair that He has forgiven guilty people and thereby broken His own law? A righteous judge cannot do this. But the symbolic sacrifices on the Day of Atonement, and the literal sacrifice of Christ on the cross, vindicate God's forgiveness, and therefore vindicate those of us He has forgiven. If all this sounds too complicated for you, let's just break it down: God has thought of everything, down to the very last detail, for how to see you saved and in heaven with Him someday.

—MH

The Sight of Blood

For the life of a creature is in the blood, and I have given it to you to make atonement for yourselves . . . ; it is the blood that makes atonement for one's life. Leviticus 17:11.

My husband will never live down the day that he fainted dead away and landed on top of me. He was standing at the kitchen sink washing dishes when he accidentally cut his finger on a sharp knife. Immediately the blood started gushing out and running down his hand, and the next thing he knew, he was waking up on the floor with me, smashed and screaming, underneath him.

I'd been standing behind him drying dishes, and I had no idea what was happening. Suddenly I saw him start to collapse, so I reached out and tried to catch him—bad logistical idea. He is much larger than I am! Before I could yell, I was pinned to the floor, his whole limp body sprawled on top of me. I was unable to move even an inch! When he came to, I remember yelling, "What just happened here? I was drying dishes, and the next thing I know, I'm trapped on the floor!"

Later my husband explained that it was the sight of the blood that had caused the sudden fainting. Of course, he wasn't totally aware of what was going on. He's not usually affected by blood at all, but it was the sight of it running down his hand when he didn't even know he had cut himself that caused such a shock. The sight of your own bright-red blood spilling can be pretty sobering.

In Bible times people had a healthy respect for blood as well, but it was for a far different purpose. They had been taught by the Lord that blood is the only thing that can make atonement for a person's life. The Bible tells us a simple fact: the wages of sin is death. Sin separates us from God, and separated from God, we will die. We have sinned, and in order for us to be saved, blood must be shed. We praise God that Jesus shed His blood in order to fulfill that law so that we don't have to. The next time you see blood, remember that it represents your very life, and that your life has been paid for, ransomed, by the blood of Jesus Himself.

—MH

Why Can't the Chicken Cross the Road?

You must not live according to the customs of the nations I am going to drive out before you. . . . [I have] set you apart from the nations. Leviticus 20:23, 24.

If you drive blindfolded or flick boogers to the wind as you drive in Alabama, you are breaking a state law. Have you ever read some of the crazy old laws that are on the books in the U.S.? Did you know that moose are not permitted to have sex on the city streets in Alaska? (Who is going to stop them!) Michigan residents cannot put a skunk in their boss's desk, and nobody in Omaha, Nebraska, is allowed to burp in church. The poor men in Hartford, Connecticut, can't kiss their wives on Sunday, and Delaware men cannot go fishing on their honeymoon. Florida residents can't jog with their eyes closed or tie elephants to unpaid parking meters. In Indiana and Iowa it's illegal to bathe during winter; it's a crime to insert a penny into your ear in Hawaii; and in Quitman, Georgia, it is actually illegal for a chicken to cross a road—if that road is within city limits. Silly rules now, but they were once passed for a reason.

The book of Leviticus might at first seem like another list of silly rules such as the ones above, but the laws in the book were actually given in order to teach the Israelites how to live better than the wicked nations around them. You may think some of the rules are weird—such as being forbidden to wear clothes with mildew—but some other rules actually make really good sense in real life. For example, it's just mean to curse deaf people or put stumbling blocks in front of those who can't see. It's probably a good idea not to cut yourself or get tattoos. Other great ideas include not spreading slander, not hating your brother in your heart, not seeking revenge or bearing a grudge, and loving your neighbor as yourself. (Where have we heard these before!)

The point of every rule recorded in Leviticus is to set the people of Israel apart from the wicked nations around them. Today, it's still the same with God's rules. They are not there to ruin our lives or take away all our fun. They not only set us apart, make us different from the way much of the world is living, but simply make good sense. Today, try to think about the stark differences between God's way of living and the world's way of living, and ask yourself, Which one is truly a better life?

—MH

Inedible

No man of Aaron's descendants who has a skin disease or a discharge is to eat from the holy offerings until he is clean. Leviticus 22:4, HCSB.

Recently, on the way to speak at a youth rally in Kansas City, I passed a large rig pulling a giant chrome tank—the kind that usually contains chemicals. I've seen these tanks before, sporting signs that read "hazardous," "nitrogen," "flammable," etc. But the sign on this truck read "not edible." Now, you and I know very well that a warning like this is there only because some numbskull once tried to get a snack out of one of these tanks. I mean, who in their right mind looks at a truck like this and thinks, *Mmm, I bet whatever is in there would taste good?* As I passed the truck, another sign gave some more details. "Not edible by humans—animal food."

More questions came to mind: *What are they feeding animals that humans can't eat?* and *Who would want to taste it anyway?* And then I wondered if at the docking station where people hook up tubes and such to drain the stuff from the tank, they sat there saying, "Man, this smells JUST like my cat's food at home—I love that stuff."

Most people wouldn't have the slightest thought toward consuming whatever was in that tank. However, when it comes to how we approach God's "food"—which is supposed to be eaten by certain people—we treat it flippantly.

What do I mean? Take Communion, for example—a ritual designed for those who want to rededicate their hearts to God and acknowledge their need of a Savior. Have you ever eaten the unleavened wafer just because it was there? Or let's take it from a spiritual perspective. The Bible, God's Word, is likened to spiritual food. But many times, because we've become so used to it, we approach it as just another book. Instead of stopping to pray and ask God to fill us with His Spirit, we mindlessly read a verse or two and go about our business.

God has given us things to nurture and feed us spiritually, things that have great meaning. But too often we take them for granted. We don't prepare our hearts so that by His grace we are ready to consume them. So the next time you pick up a Bible or participate in church for your spiritual nourishment, don't do so without asking God to clean your heart and mind so that you can digest what He has provided.

—SP

Camping With God

Live in booths for seven days . . . so your descendants will know that I had the Israelites live in booths when I brought them out of Egypt. Leviticus 23:42, 43.

Jacques Doukhan, one of my seminary teachers, used to make fun of anyone who said they liked camping. "There's no way anyone could actually enjoy camping!" he'd say. "Just think about what you're doing. Sleeping on the hard ground, eating lousy food, sitting out in the heat or the cold all day, spending hours just to cook a meal, and going to the bathroom in places you'd avoid at all costs on any other normal day!"

I completely disagreed with this man, because I've always loved camping. I love the outdoors. I love sitting around a bright, crackling campfire and looking up at thousands of stars. I love the festivity of setting up a tent and cooking on a camp stove. However, the last time I went camping I was about six months pregnant, and I do have to admit that when I walked about a mile to the bathroom seven times each night, or simply tried to roll over in my sleeping bag, I began to think, *You know? Maybe that guy has a good point!*

Leviticus 23 tells us that God instructed His people to go camping. God set up a seven-day festival in the fall. During this time they were to live in tents because after He brought them out of Egypt they lived in tents in the desert. This happy festival enabled the Israelites to relive their rescue from 400 years of slavery in Egypt. Later, after they were in the land of Canaan, it continued to remind them that God had delivered them and put them in the land He had promised Abraham centuries before. Many Jews continue to celebrate this festival even now. It's called *Sukkot* in Hebrew, or Festival of Booths. They build shelters of trees and branches, sometimes in their front yards. Friends and family come by to sit in the "booth" and visit and eat with them. This is a hands-on reminder that the God of heaven came down to earth and brought His people out of slavery and into the Promised Land.

Next time you're camping, try to think of an entire nation of people living this way in the middle of a barren desert for 40 years. But also remember, as you set up your tent and build a fire, that God has rescued you from slavery—slavery to sin and death. So while you're lounging in the great outdoors, take a moment to remember that, and thank Him for your freedom.

—MH

The Middleman

And the tabernacle of meeting shall move out with the camp of the Levites in the middle of the camps; as they camp, so they shall move out, everyone in his place.
Numbers 2:17, NKJV.

Many times I have thought that some of the most boring parts of the Bible are its tedious details. I mean who really wants to read page after page of Ahaziah begat Methu-sa-shetha-what? But the crazy thing about all those details is sometimes they're secretly hiding some of the most fascinating things. For example, at first glance when you start reading through the second chapter of Numbers you can get bogged down quickly, as it describes where everyone's tent was supposed to go when the children of Israel set up camp in the desert. Judah goes to the north, Dan to the west, yada yada. Basically the formation of tents forms a perfect square with the tabernacle at the center. But when we compare these seemingly bland details to some hieroglyphics in the tomb of the Egyptian pharaoh Ramses II in Egypt, we actually come up with something that both proves the Bible to be trustworthy and also gives us some spiritual insight.

An ancient diagram of this Egyptian king's army was found on the walls of his tomb, showing how he organized his troops' encampment when they were going to war. Archers were on several sides, with the larger horses and chariots protecting the outskirts. All in all, it forms a perfect square, with the king's tent at the very center of the square. Sound familiar? It shouldn't surprise us, because Moses was brought up and trained in the house of Pharaoh, meaning he was also trained in the Egyptian methods and techniques of war. So when he takes a large group of people into the desert, he uses the knowledge and skills learned in Egypt to organize them. Even in small details such as this, the Bible is shown to be trustworthy. Notice again what he puts in the center of the encampment: the tent of God. *God is the center.* This is symbolic of the fact that God, not Moses and not any other man, was their king and leader.

What do you put in the center of your life these days—God, or something else? What do you give the most time and attention to? If it's not God, it may be time to rethink some priorities. The center of Jewish religion back then wasn't just dogma or a list of rules; it was a Person—God Himself—and He came and said, "I want to bring you back from the brink. I want to be what you value most in your life, because that's how I feel about you."

—GH

The Heart of a Daredevil

But because my servant Caleb has a different spirit and follows me wholeheartedly, I will bring him into the land he went to, and his descendants will inherit it. Numbers 14:24.

He lay there with all those broken bones after his motorcycle accident, and already he was talking about getting back on his bike just as soon as his body healed. My cousin Keith was the biggest daredevil I've ever known personally. He took risks. He rode too fast and was just generally reckless and wild. It seems as if every time we heard from him, he had broken more bones or gotten into more accidents. He broke his leg twice, his arm, both collarbones, and that's just the start. But it never stopped him—somehow he always healed and went back for more.

My favorite biblical daredevil is Caleb. When we first see him, he's sneaking through the Promised Land with a bunch of other spies—pretty gutsy, considering it's populated with a fair number of giants, as well as regular warriors. Most of the spies come back from that initial scouting mission scared out of their wits, yelling at Moses not to attempt anything crazy. But not Caleb. He shuts everyone up and encourages Moses to go for it!

Next we see him decades later, at age 85, asking permission to go and conquer some of that same land he crept through as a spy nearly 40 years before. Amazingly enough, he does it! The pagan land filled with "giants" that the entire army of Israel had been afraid to attack, Caleb conquers on his own, with just his family. "Here I am today, 85 years old," he said, "and I am still as strong today as the day Moses sent me out!"

What was it about Caleb that he was able to have such courage and do such daredevil things? I think his secret was serving the Lord wholeheartedly, having "a different spirit" than other people—a spirit of courage, and not of fear. (See Numbers 14:24.)

Because Caleb served the Lord wholeheartedly, he wasn't afraid of the things that frightened other people. I want that kind of courage. Wouldn't you like it too? I want to dare to serve the Lord with all my heart, even if it means I'll end up doing some frightening and risky things. If you want that too, ask the Lord to give you the courage of Caleb so that you can serve Him wholeheartedly. And prepare yourself by keeping close contact with Him every day of your life.

—MH

The Blue Circle of Love

[Then the Lord said,] "You are to make tassels on the corners of your garments, with a blue cord on each tassel. You will have these tassels to look at and so you will remember all the commands of the Lord, that you may obey them." Numbers 15:38, 39.

Some of the worst clothes I ever owned came from close relatives. You know the type—bright-orange sweaters with a giant bunny in the middle, or stars-and-stripes-patterned sweatpants with oversized pockets right at the knee—horrendous things! And Mom made us actually wear them so that so-and-so could see us in them. Each time I had to leave the house in one of those hideous garments, my belief grew firmer and firmer in the fact that nobody should ever pick out a teenager's clothes for them.

But it's interesting that God picked out the Israelites' clothes. He wanted them to dress in a really simple way to distinguish them from the wicked nations around them. One of the things He asked them to do was to place tassels on the corners of their garments with a blue cord on each tassel. Another was to put a ribbon of blue in the border of their garments, upon which a short version of the Ten Commandments was embroidered. Both of these were to remind them to keep God's commands. But there was a whole lot more symbolism going on than that.

The Ten Commandments are essentially laws on how to love God and other people. So when the blue ribbon made a circle that surrounded their feet, it represented this circle of commandments, or a circle of love. All of their steps were kept within this circle—their feet walked within the ribbon on the edge of the garment. Steps represent our thinking, our motives, our actions, and the ways we are walking. So God was illustrating the fact that He wanted all of their actions to be kept within this circle of love—everything they said and did should be done with love. Nobody could even touch an Israelite without first coming into contact with his "circle of love."

We don't dress like that anymore, but the symbolism is still supposed to carry on. People we come in contact with should feel as though they are entering an atmosphere of love. They should be able to sense the love of God radiating from us. Do we have that kind of love? If you don't feel as if you do, pray for it. Spend time with Jesus, and ask Him to fill you with the kind of love that touches the people you come in contact with.

—MH

He [Aaron] stood between the living and the dead, and the plague stopped.
Numbers 16:48.

Do you ever get overwhelmed with how much pain and suffering is going on around you? I mean, do you ever just take a look at the world and feel totally helpless? Even a short inventory of your friends and family would probably reveal people who are struggling and hurting right now. It feels so helpless just to watch them hurt, doesn't it? It's as though—you wish you could do something!

In Numbers 16 I found a random, obscure story about a whole lot of hurting people. It happened when a big revolt took place in the camps of Israel. Basically, a guy named Korah started a riot against Moses and Aaron. He was mad that they had authority above everyone else. Korah led 250 men to come to the tent of meeting with their own fire in their censers, rather than fire from God, to prove they didn't need priest Aaron burning incense for them. When Moses asked God to show who His chosen leaders were, the ground actually opened up and swallowed the rebels. Well, then the whole camp got angry at Moses, and that's when this huge deadly plague broke out.

Moses told Aaron to do something *now!* So Aaron grabbed one of the censers, put holy fire in it from the altar, put incense on it, and ran wildly through the camps. The smoke and sweet incense drifted from the censer, and get this— wherever Aaron and the incense went, the people lived. The incense actually halted the progress of death. But where it did not reach, people died. They needed the incense. It was a life-and-death matter.

So is prayer! The incense symbolized prayers of the people ascending up to God. Today when you see hurting people in your life, think of this scene with Aaron. He literally stood between the living and the dead, as the text says. Incense (symbolizing prayer) made the difference. And prayer can make the difference between life and death today. A lot of times the people we worry about most don't pray for themselves at all. But we can make the difference! We can, as did Aaron, actually stand between the living and the dead. What if it were your prayers that gave God permission to continue working in someone's life today? Who is God putting on your heart right now that you need to take a minute to pray for?

—MH

No Preparation Necessary?

Then Moses raised his arm and struck the rock twice with his staff. Water gushed out, and the community and their livestock drank. Numbers 20:11.

It worked out really well the first time. An elder in the small island church came to me only 20 minutes before the church service to say they had no preacher that day and would I mind giving the sermon? I was 19, and it was my first month as an excited young missionary, so naturally I said yes, even though I had no time to prepare at all. God would come through for me, wouldn't He? Well, He did. I stood up in front of the people with nothing, and a half hour later an entire, logical, sensible sermon had flowed from my mouth. I was amazed. And delighted! No preparation is needed—let the Spirit move!

So the next time I was asked to preach back at home, I decided to try the same tactic. I didn't prepare a thing. I didn't study, and I didn't worry. I expected to stand up in that pulpit and have the Lord bring me a sermon the way He did the last time I was asked to speak. But when I got up front, nothing came. I looked like a fool. Why didn't it work the second time?

I bet Moses was wondering the same exact thing at Kadesh in the Desert of Zin. It was the second time the entire Israelite community had run out of water, and they were grumbling, as always. The first time it happened, God had commanded Moses to strike a rock with his staff, and fresh water flowed out. But this time God told Moses to speak to the rock. Why come up with this whole speech when he could just hit the thing the way he did last time and have instant water? Moses thought he already knew how to get water, and besides, he was mad. He fell back on his old methodology instead of doing what God had asked. The water came, but because Moses defied God and did things his own way, he never got to see the Promised Land.

I always thought this punishment was kind of harsh until I learned that the rock represented Jesus, and the striking of it represented His death on the cross. Jesus died for all, for every person who ever lived. There was no need to strike the rock a second time. He doesn't need to die again every time we sin. When we sin, we need only to "speak" to Him, as Moses should have spoken to the second rock. If you know there are changes you need to make in your life, don't assume your old lazy ways are good enough. Make those changes today!

—MH

A Drunk Dog and a Reckless Path

Then the Lord opened the donkey's mouth, and she said to Balaam, "What have I done to you to make you beat me these three times?" Numbers 22:28.

The only time my dog ever "spoke" to me was the night I got her drunk. It was Thanksgiving, and she had raided the trash in search of the turkey, eating leftover skin, meat, and bones. I knew that fowl bones can splinter and lodge in the intestines of a dog, so I thought the best thing to do was to make her throw them up (wrong idea). When I was a child and my dog ate poisonous mushrooms, the woman next door poured a bottle of beer down his throat to make him throw up. Not knowing what else to do, I decided that was the best approach (worse idea). After two large cans of beer and a lot of wrestling on the dog's part, my husband, his brother Doug, and I were soaked and stinking, and the poor thing still hadn't thrown up. What's worse, she was drunk—totally and completely, stumbling-down drunk. She tripped over her own feet. She growled at the living room chair. Then she turned to me and howled a slow, sad melody at the very top of her doggy lungs that seemed to say, "How could you do this to me?"

When God gave Balaam's donkey the ability to speak, she said basically the same thing: "How could you do this to me?" He had beaten her three times because she'd veered off the path, run him into a wall, and then just flat-out lain down underneath him, refusing to move. The donkey had done all this after seeing something Balaam hadn't seen—the angel of the Lord, sword drawn and ready, standing ahead in the middle of the road. The angel had come to kill Balaam as he traveled to meet King Balak. Balaam knew better than to fool around with God, but he *so* wanted the money he'd get from Balak if he managed to curse the Israelites camped on the king's border. When Balaam's eyes were finally opened to see the armed angel, he realized that the donkey had saved his life. "Your path is a reckless one before me," warned the angel of the Lord (Numbers 22:32)..

What path are you traveling down today? Is it a reckless path before the Lord? Has the Lord put things in your way to try to turn you back? Take note of the paths your feet have chosen so far this year, and ask yourself today if it might be time to do some turning around. As you do, ask the Lord for His help and guidance.

—MH

You Are Your Own Twin Sister

God is not a man, that he should lie, nor a son of man, that he should change his mind. Does he speak and then not act? Does he promise and not fulfill? Numbers 23:19.

The cruelest trick I ever played on my brother, Russell, was telling him he had an identical twin sister who had been sent away to China. There was a picture of him at age 1, hanging in the hallway, and in it he had girlishly long, wavy, thick, curly hair. He didn't look like a boy. He honestly looked like a little girl. Apparently my mom just couldn't part with the beautiful curls and didn't cut his hair until he was fairly old. So when he asked us one day who it was in the picture, I just couldn't resist. "Oh, that?" I casually replied. "That's your twin sister, Susan."

"I have a twin!" he exclaimed. "But where is she?"

"Well, she has a growing disease, you see," I elaborated. "She's already 30 now, and we were embarrassed about her, so we sent her to the other side of the world. She lives in China."

He was devastated. Days and weeks went by. Sometimes I'd see him standing in the hallway, looking sadly at the photo. For me, the crowning moment was the day I caught him sobbing on the floor, cradling the picture in his lap, repeating "I love you, Susan! I miss you! Come home!" Russell admitted to me a few years ago that it wasn't until high school that the truth struck him, and he realized I'd lied. One day Mom stood in the hallway in front of the photo and sighed, "Oh, Russell, I miss your curly hair!"

A lot of us here on earth have been lied to, and often the lies are a lot more serious than the mean trick I played on my little brother. Often they are horrific, life-shattering, and completely devastating lies. And sometimes it's easy to become jaded, to stop trusting people; even to stop trusting God Himself. We start thinking that God is just like everyone else—people lie to us and let us down, so He probably will too. Fortunately for us, that's not the case at all. In the book of Numbers God spoke through Balaam to assure us that God is not like human beings. He doesn't change His mind, and He doesn't lie. So don't lose your trust in God over what someone has done to you. Don't confuse Him with those people—He's not the same. Friends and even family may let you down, but God is still in heaven, and you can trust Him.

—MH

Covered

Each day present two unblemished year-old male lambs as a regular burnt offering. Offer one lamb in the morning and the other lamb at twilight. . . . On the Sabbath day present two unblemished year-old male lambs. . . . It is the burnt offering for every Sabbath. Numbers 28:3-10, HCSB.

In ancient Israel there was never a time that something wasn't being killed, spilled, or grilled, in terms of sacrifices. But what was the point of this perpetual carnage?

A couple years ago after 10 days we came home, and saw our neighbors working on the fence we share. I had spoken to an "older" woman on their deck a couple weeks before, assuming she was the grandmother. This was a chance to meet the rest of the family, and I began chatting with a middle-aged man who appeared to be healthy. As we talked I asked about the elderly woman I'd met. He looked puzzled and said he wasn't sure what person I meant. So I persisted in saying that I'd talked with a very nice older woman, and was wondering if they had any extended family staying with them. "No, he said cheerfully, "just me and my wife."

Unfortunately, my mouth kept going, even though that part of my brain that *supposedly* connects neurons and forms coherent thoughts was missing in action. "Look, I *know* I saw *some* older woman here. This makes *no* sense." By this time my wife was giving me signals, but I had no time even to notice. Then just before I concluded that I had completely lost my mind, the "old" woman came out onto the deck. My neighbor said, "Hi, honey." At the same time I shouted, *"There she is!"* I shook her hand vigorously, living proof I wasn't crazy—just stupid—and I triumphantly announced that we'd met before. At last, when my wife and I were alone, she convinced me that the woman was his *wife*. Thankfully he either forgot, didn't notice, or was extremely gracious, and today we get on just fine.

There are times we make mistakes—we even sin—and don't know about it (see Leviticus 4), and we need to be covered by Christ's death until we have a chance to confess our sins and make things right. The reason for all the sacrifices made every day/week/month and even year (see Leviticus 16) was to provide forgiveness for all until they had a chance to realize what was going on.

Jesus covers us in the same way. We still need to repent when we realize we've made a mistake, but He covers us with His blood until we have the chance.

—SP

It's Because of Who He Is

I am the Lord your God, who brought you out of Egypt, out of the land of slavery. You shall have no other gods before me. Deuteronomy 5:6, 7.

The U.S. Midwest is ugly and boring and lame," I insisted. "I'll never get stuck there!" I used to tell everyone that I'd never even think of going to college in the Midwest—who in the world would want to waste away their college years in the middle of nowhere? Me? I had big plans to end up in beautiful northern California, but that was before I met Tonja. She was the Taskforce worker at our academy that year, and she just so happened to be from a quaint little college in the Midwest. And she had just so happened to plan a trip to this cute, quaint little Midwestern college. But even though she'd become a very close friend, and I'd grown to love and respect her tremendously, I still laughed at the trip and made fun of my friends who signed up to go on it. Many of them asked me to come too, but I loudly refused.

But when Tonja herself came to me and personally asked if I would please just come check it out, I did. In the end, it was because of who she was in my life— someone I trusted and respected—that I boarded that plane headed east to the Midwest. I went only because she meant so much to me. Admittedly, the entire course of my life may have been different had I not. You see, I did choose to go to college there, and I met my husband there as well.

I love it that the second list of the Ten Commandments, found in Deuteronomy, begins with God explaining Himself. He identifies Himself as the God who brought the people out of Egypt and out of slavery. This comes first—this reminder of who He is and what He's done for them in the past. He first gives them a *reason* they should keep His commandments. Then He asks them to serve Him and follow His laws. He doesn't ask for obedience until He has given them a reason to obey.

It's the same for us today. We were not rescued from Egypt, but we were rescued from sin. God doesn't expect us to keep His commandments "just because." Instead, He asks us to keep them out of thankfulness that He has already rescued us. We keep them because of who God is. I don't know how you feel about the big Ten, but try to see them this way: as a way to thank God for what He has already done for you.

—MH

No Such Thing as a Working Vacation

Observe the Sabbath day by keeping it holy, as the Lord your God has commanded you. Six days you shall labor and do all your work, but the seventh day is a Sabbath to the Lord your God. On it you shall not do any work. Deuteronomy 5:12-14.

For our second anniversary my husband took me on a cruise to Alaska. For a whole week we were on complete vacation—people made our beds, cooked our meals, provided entertainment options, and waited on us hand and foot. It was glorious—the ultimate getaway. Except . . . I ruined it. It was my first year teaching, and I just felt as if I had to take some lesson plans along with me or I would never catch up when I returned. My husband warned me not to bring them. "You won't relax!" he said. I told him I'd bring them just in case I had some free time, but I wouldn't plan on working on them.

And I didn't—work on them. The whole week I never touched them. They just sat in our room. But I thought about them. Everywhere we went—whether touring small mountain towns, or sitting on the deck drinking hot cocoa, I'd ask myself, "Should I be doing lesson plans now? Am I wasting time?" Even the day we cruised Glacier Bay I sat atop the ship in the all-window lounge and thought of my lesson plans. I never touched them, but they still managed to steal the freedom out of the vacation for me.

I think God knew that it's impossible to have a vacation and think about work at the same time. They kind of cancel each other out. In order to feel as though we're on vacation, in order to rest and relax and enjoy our free time, we have to stop working. In fact, we have to stop even thinking about work—and just *be*. That's why God gave us the Sabbath. It's supposed to be our weekly vacation from our work and worries. But the only way we can truly enjoy the vacation is to stop work completely. If we try to squeeze it in here or there, or try to justify it somehow, we're only cheating ourselves. We will ruin our own vacation. So this week, make it a point on Sabbath to stop all your work completely, and get ready to enjoy a real vacation.

—MH

Impossible to Forget

These commandments that I give you today are to be upon your hearts. . . . Talk about them when you sit at home and when you walk along the road, when you lie down and when you get up. Tie them as symbols on your hands and bind them on your foreheads. Write them on the doorframes of your houses and on your gates. Deuteronomy 6:6-9.

The first time I broke up with my husband (there were several times) was in the spring of our first year of dating. I had decided that I knew he was not the one for me and that it had to end. I explained how things could never work between us; how, in the long run, we were simply much better off as friends. He listened quietly, seeming to know something I didn't. He didn't say much. And then he let me go.

I returned to my dorm room determined to forget him forever and move on with my life, but to my horror he was everywhere. There were the dried daisies tied with a satiny yellow ribbon that he had given me on our first date. (By the way, a few years later I tied that yellow ribbon around my bouquet as I walked down the aisle toward him.) There was the pen-and-ink drawing of forget-me-nots that he had made for me. (A wise choice in flowers, don't you think?) A photo of us hiking in Colorado haunted me, and I kept smelling his empty cologne bottle 86 times a day. Even when I'd leave my room for class, "I Love Greg" was stenciled on the covers of my textbooks. I'd pass benches we'd sat on and trees that we'd climbed together, and I'd miss him. It was hopeless. There was no way on earth I could forget him, because aside from all the hundreds of reminders, I began to realize that he had actually become a part of me.

God wanted the Israelites to decorate their rooms and yards with His commandments. He wanted reminders of Himself to be everywhere—on their hands, foreheads, doors, and gates. He wanted His chosen people to talk about these reminders all the time. He knew that this was the way to make them become a part of their hearts, and it's still a good way to make His laws part of your life too. If you really want them to be part of your life and thus change your heart, then put them everywhere. Tape up verses, memorize favorite texts, set up reminders—make them impossible to forget. Talk about them and think about them, and slowly they'll become woven into the very fabric of your personality. They'll truly be part of your life.

—MH

When We Forget About God

Otherwise, when you eat and are satisfied, when you build fine houses and settle down, and when your herds and flocks grow large and your silver and gold increase . . . then your heart will become proud and you will forget the Lord your God. Deuteronomy 8:12-14.

When my husband and I were first married, we were as happy as could be, but we were as poor as bums. There actually came a time that we didn't even have the money to go out and buy groceries—we were really that poor. So instead of dressing in rags and trying to blend in at the local soup kitchen, I decided to call my mom and ask her to send money. Being the abundantly generous soul that she is, she was happy to send a pretty hefty check in the mail right away. We were so excited! We spent her money for weeks. It was in our wallets for so long that we pretty much forgot that it was even her money. It started to seem like our own. And then, after many days had passed, she called me. She was worried. Had I received the check, or had it been lost in the mail? It was then that I realized my horrible mistake—I hadn't even called to thank her. I was so thrilled to actually have money that I had totally forgotten where it had come from.

In Deuteronomy, when the Israelites are heading into the Promised Land, God warns the people that they are very likely to do the exact same thing I did to Mom. God knows that they are about to enter a life of luxury and abundance, free of worry, and this puts them in danger of forgetting Him. It's pretty funny to me that God knows us so well. He totally gets the fact that when life is going well and things are good, we often don't think about Him. It's somehow easy to forget Him when life is good. And not only do we forget Him—we actually go so far as to thank our own proud hearts for our lives being so great. Our blessings start to seem like the money in my wallet did—like our own, not really a gift from someone else.

If your life is going great right now, check yourself to make sure you aren't thanking your own efforts and totally forgetting about God. Do you seek Him only when times are bad? Do you talk to Him only when you need something? Try to keep your relationship with Him going when times are good as well! And take a moment today to acknowledge that all of your blessings originate with Him.

—MH

Speaking Through the Clutter

Hear, O Israel. You are now about to cross the Jordan to go in and dispossess nations greater and stronger than you, with large cities that have walls up to the sky. Deuteronomy 9:1.

When I finally stood up in front of the small Nicaraguan congregation to speak, it was all I could do to keep from stumbling over my translator. I'd been sleeping on a lousy cot for weeks, and a rooster had awakened me at 5:00 a.m. Then to top it all off, I heard someone coming down the road screaming through a megaphone. It got louder and louder, until I couldn't actually hear anything else except an incessant cacophony of jumbled Spanish words, repeated over and over. Finally I saw an old rusty minivan covered bumper to bumper with stereo speakers. A guy stood in the van's open doorway, screaming into a microphone at the top of his lungs. It was the most amazing portable speaking platform I've ever seen, even to this day. And the van just kept looping around the same three blocks again . . . and again . . . and . . . I could hardly get through one sermon story without having to pause—again—for three minutes as the blaring mobile stereo system slowly made its way through the street outside the church.

It's likely that Moses would understand my frustration, because his audience was much, much larger than mine, about 600,000 people. And even though he wasn't contending with a minivan full of speakers, he had to figure out how to give a speech to thousands of people with nothing more than his voice. The book of Deuteronomy, in fact, is a goodbye speech. It's the last chance that Moses had to speak to the people he led out of Egypt, those to whom he had literally given the last 40 years of his life. He wanted to remind them of their history, of all that God had done for them, and of the laws they had agreed to keep. It took him several days to give the whole speech. Have you ever wondered how all those people even heard him? Well, he had runners set up at intervals along sections of audience. They would hear his words, shout them to their section, then run to the next guy, who would shout to his section, then run to another, etc., all the way to the back of the crowd. Quite a process! God's laws were that important.

Is God's law that important to us now? How much does it matter to you? Would you sit for days or run for miles to hear it? As we move into Deuteronomy, ask yourselves what place you want the law of God to have in *your* life.

—GH

That Fateful Day

The Lord your God will circumcise your hearts and the hearts of your descendants, so that you may love him with all your heart and with all your soul, and live. Deuteronomy 30:6.

I watched my newborn son get circumcised last month. As a father, it was one of the most horrific things I've ever witnessed. At this moment, half of you are cringing and groaning with sympathetic feelings of pain (guys). The other half of you are never going to get it (ladies), but trust us, it's really a disturbing thought. The wound itself typically heals in about six days, but the change made is forever. There's no going back. They don't have circumcision reversal procedures; it's a permanent decision. And reading about it in the Bible, I wondered how the whole thing started in the first place. Why did God come up with this seemingly terrible idea?

Reading about circumcision in the Old Testament, I admit I can't understand what they were thinking. It was performed, not only on babies, but on men from their teens into adulthood—with no anesthetic or pain meds to take afterward. Everything had to be suffered through "for three or four days," according to the Bible passages. Circumcision was seen as a duty. But for the males who went through the surgery, it was also a sign that they were officially part of the Jewish nation—and accepted into the tribes like long-lost brothers. Nobody could take away this permanent mark of God's ownership.

Today's scripture says that God will circumcise the hearts of believers. Obviously this isn't physical cutting. Rather God uses the word to explain the change He will make in our heart and personality if we'll let Him. Just as circumcision made a permanent change in the physical body of Jewish men, God says He wants to make a permanent change in our hearts. The reason? So you and I may love Him with all our heart and soul.

God wants an experience with you that will forever change something on the inside. He wants to make sure that your believer status is forever. But the question is Do we let Him do that in our lives? Do we live in such a way that we stand out in public places as converted believers in Jesus? Do we exude a spirit of love and gentleness, or are we more the product of our worldly surroundings than of our heavenly Father? Do our actions show that God has selected us to be changed and circumcised in our hearts, so that we can love ourselves and each other as He does?

—GH

The Song Remembers When

Now write down for yourselves this song and teach it to the Israelites and have them sing it, so that it may be a witness for me against them. Deuteronomy 31:19.

Whenever I hear that Beach Boys song, no matter the outside temperature, I get a sudden urge to roll down the windows and sing at the top of my lungs. When I was a kid, my dad loved the Beach Boys, and we listened to their music almost every time we rode in the car with him. But one song in particular, "Fun, Fun, Fun," had to be experienced in a very specific way. Dad would crank up the volume as loud as we could stand it, roll down the windows so that the wind came blowing in, and whoop and yell and sing the words at the top of his lungs. I could never count how many times I heard him sing it like that. And today, no matter where I am, if "Fun, Fun, Fun" comes on the radio, it takes me back to being a little girl, riding in the car with Dad, the wind whipping my hair. It just doesn't seem right not to roll down the windows and sing.

Songs have a way of taking us back to the past, don't they? Music has a certain pull on our memories and sensory experiences, taking us back to the people we were when we first heard it. That's why God had Moses teach the Israelites a song before he died.

Everyone was excited. At last they were going to enter the Promised Land. But God, looking into the future, knew that they would turn away from Him—even offering their children to idols. He knew, too, that He'd beg them to return, and they would—for a while. But this would happen again and again, until at last He would allow their destruction. Even so, He wanted to help them remember His faithfulness and the covenant they had made with one another. So God chose a song. He knew they would remember the song for years to come, that their children's children would sing the song even as they were going into exile. When they were marched into exile, God wanted them to have something in their hearts so they would not doubt Him, something to help them remember He had been faithful.

If there are times in your life now that trust is hard and you need something to tell you that God is faithful, go back to the songs and stories of Him that you learned as a child. If you didn't learn any back then, learn some now and keep them with you. Let them remind you of a time when God was faithful, and trust that He will not forsake you now.

—MH

Pink Canoes and the Promised Land

I know what they are disposed to do, even before I bring them into the land I promised them on oath. Deuteronomy 31:21.

One of the best camp pranks I ever played was painting all the canoes pink. One of the staff members had gone out earlier that afternoon and purchased giant jugs of pink paint on the cheap, and we'd hidden them until our secretly arranged 2:00 a.m. meeting. Silently, one by one, a whole group of us sneaked out of our cabins and met at the waterfront. Dressed in old overalls and armed with paintbrushes, we painted canoe after canoe a bright, hideous pink. The prank was aimed at the waterfront director, who was the local villain of the camp that year and who also, incidentally, hated the color pink. We couldn't wait until morning when she would find the canoes and be appalled! As we snuck back to our cabins a few hours later, the job completed, each one of us vowed that we would never admit to being part of the prank.

The next morning the camp pastor approached me and asked if I'd been involved in painting the canoes pink. I acted dumb, faked shock. For weeks he continued to ask me if I knew anything about it, but I continued to play dumb. Finally, on the last night of camp, as we were all packing up and saying our goodbyes, the pastor found me. "You realize I knew the whole time that you were involved in the canoe painting, right?" Once again I began to protest, but he stopped me by touching a small spot on the bottom of my overalls—pink paint. I'd been wearing the overalls for weeks, unaware that I had dripped paint on them. Laughing, he explained that he had actually been the one who had purchased the paint for us. The whole time, he'd been in on the prank! I'd been denying it for weeks, but he had known about the prank before we had even done it.

God also knew what the Israelites would do before they did it. Though they had promised to keep all His commands, He said He knew they would turn away from Him in the end. But He cared for them anyway. He gave them the Promised Land, protected them, and fought for them, and when they left Him, He pleaded with them to repent. He never gave up on them. And God is the same today. He already knows what you are going to do before you do it. He knows what you love and what you hate. He knows your struggles and the decisions you will make. But no matter what you do or don't do, He's not going to give up on you.

—MH

The Secret of Success

Do not let this Book of the Law depart from your mouth; meditate on it day and night, so that you may be careful to do everything written in it. Then you will be prosperous and successful. Joshua 1:8.

One of the weirdest morning rituals I've ever heard of was practiced by an energetic woman speaker who came to Union College my senior year. Radiating confidence, capability, and strength, she shared with us the secret of all of her success. She told us how to have—and keep—a positive attitude, how to boost our own sense of confidence and learn to believe in ourselves. Upon awakening every morning, she ran to the mirror, looked herself right in the eye, and shouted at the very top of her lungs, "You sexy thing! Don't you ever die!" As the audience burst into laughter at such an absurd practice she assured us that it worked. "Tell yourself every single day that you are great and need to keep living, and it's not long at all before you believe it 100 percent. You feel good! You believe you look good! You believe your life is worthwhile, and you want to stay healthy and live long. It works!"

For many weeks after that talk students at Union College would pass on the sidewalks and shout to one another, "You sexy thing! Don't you *ever* die!" The phrase became a standard part of that school year. To this day two of my friends still greet each other with it. And you know what? After a year of using it, somehow we all felt a little better about ourselves. Did it work?

God knows that repetition matters. He knows that something doesn't start to sink into our hearts unless we say it or do it over and over and over. That's why He told Joshua that if he wanted to be a successful leader of Israel, he needed to meditate on God's law day and night—to never let it depart from his thoughts. God knows that for us to really buy into His laws and His ways, they need to be a regular part of our lives. Each and every day of our lives hundreds of things compete for our attention and allegiance. If we want God's ways to have a stronger pull on us than the world's ways, we have to keep His ways constantly in our minds and hearts.

Do you want that for your life? You can have it. A good way to start is to make it a priority every single morning of your life.

—MH

From Prostitute to Grandma

Then Joshua son of Nun secretly sent two spies from Shittim. "Go, look over the land," he said, "especially Jericho." So they went and entered the house of a prostitute named Rahab and stayed there. Joshua 2:1.

In high school I drove a teal-green 1997 Chevy Cavalier, and my favorite attribute of that trusty little car was that I could sneak my dorm friends off campus in its trunk. With the back seats folded down, the cab extended into the trunk, making it possible for people to lie down in the trunk and stretch their legs out, unseen, as I "innocently" drove right through the main front gates. I think the most I ever shoved into that trunk at one time was eight dorm students, lying all over each other in a tangled mess—but they thought it was worth it. The cafeteria was serving "leftover loaf" (all of the last week's leftovers mashed together and baked in a gaggy loaf), and those poor souls needed some Taco Bell! I never got caught, but looking back now, I realize my trunk wasn't the wisest or the safest place to hide my desperately hungry friends.

I like Rahab's idea better—hiding people under flax stalks on her roof. It was no secret that Rahab made her living sleeping with men. Her house was built into the wall of Jericho, and the two Israelite spies sent to scope out the city came to her place to hide for the night. Everyone in Jericho was terrified of the Israelites because they'd heard about the Red Sea drying up and the defeat of nearby kings, so the local cops came looking for the spies. But Rahab told them that they'd left the city at dusk and were headed to the Jordan. Then just before she dropped the spies down on a rope through her outer window, she asked them to remember her when they attacked the city. Even though she had a dishonorable profession, the Lord honored her because she trusted Him, and Rahab and her family were saved when Jericho was destroyed. But that's not the end of her story. Hundreds of pages later, in the book of Matthew, Rahab is listed in the genealogy of Jesus. You see, with God, it's never too late to become someone better. It doesn't matter who you are or what kind of person you've been before—God can rescue you from that life and bring you to a brand-new place if you're willing to let Him. If He can turn a prostitute into His own great-great-great-great-etc.-grandmother, He can do something great with your life, too.

—GH

Out of the Ashes

Joshua set up at Gilgal the twelve stones they had taken out of the Jordan. He said to the Israelites, "In the future when your descendants ask their fathers, 'What do these stones mean?' tell them, 'Israel crossed the Jordan on dry ground.'" Joshua 4:20-22.

The ashy blackened brick sits on my desk to this day, next to a warped stack of waterlogged pictures and a small set of keys. They are remnants of another time, some of the oldest things I own. They were mine before the fire. My husband and I lost just about everything we owned in the girls' dorm fire of 2003 at Auburn Adventist Academy. The few things we were able to save have become precious to us: three wedding photos, some knickknacks, and these items I keep on my desk. When I look at them, I remember the fire, but more specifically I remember the danger of it—how I, or others, could have been killed, but God kept us safe, and everyone made it out alive. The other day a friend was in my office and she asked me, "Why do you have an old black brick sitting on your desk?"

I smiled. "To remember," I stated simply. "I don't want to forget."

Most of the people who had crossed through the Red Sea on dry ground had died by the time Joshua led the Israelites into the Promised Land, so crossing the Jordan on dry ground—especially when it was at flood stage—was pretty exciting. When the feet of the priests touched the water's edge, the water from upstream stopped flowing and piled up in a heap a long distance away. Then thousands of people walked to the other side of the river on dry ground. From the riverbed Joshua had the priests collect 12 stones, then stacked them up on the bank to serve as a reminder of that day. He told the people that years later when their children asked about the stones, they were to share their experience of crossing the raging Jordan—on dry ground. From this their children would learn to trust in God to carry them through difficult times.

There is nothing like remembering the past to give us faith for the present. It's easy to forget about the things God has done for you when some new trial looms large ahead, but it's still important. Try to remember specific times in the past when God has been there for you, and hold on to these when the present is difficult. Have faith that He will carry you through now, just as He did back then.

—MH

Walking in Circles

And at the sound of the trumpet, when the people gave a loud shout, the wall collapsed, so every man charged straight in, and they took the city. Joshua 6:20.

They must have looked absolutely insane. Marching around an armed and fortified city like kids parading their special toys, blowing their little ram's horns. That's not a way to fight a battle! The people of Jericho must have peered down from their walls at the Israelites circling their city and shook their heads in confusion. Crazy ex-slaves . . . they had heard so much about these people, and now what a disappointing sight they were. Yes, their fighting men walked in front of the priests and behind them, but none said a word or even appeared threatening. The priests walked with trumpets instead of swords. And they carried on rods a golden box crowned with two angels—an ark, they called it. Jericho's residents had been frightened and awed by the dry path through the Jordan. But this silent marching army? How did these ex-slaves think they'd overcome a large, fortified city such as Jericho? But we know they did.

For six days they circled Jericho once a day, their feet throbbing on the ground, the trumpets sounding now and then. But on the seventh day they circled seven times. Then there was an ear-shattering blast of trumpets, a roar of voices, and, as the song says, the tall, wide city walls with their towers and battlements came a-tumbling down. I can only imagine the shock and terror of the city's residents as their lives collapsed around them. Did they even have time to understand how it happened? We don't know. All we know is that Israel did things God's way. They may have looked foolish, but marching around the city and shouting turned out to be so much better than a bloody battlefield confrontation.

I admit that doing things the Lord's way often sounds downright crazy. We're afraid of how stupid we might look if we do exactly as He says. We don't want to look like idiots to our friends. But God knows what He's doing. The way He asks us to live is so much better than going our own way. Obeying His commands leads to a much easier life: no going to jail for crimes, no cheating on your wife, no angry fights with your parents, a vacation every week—just a better way of living. So if you feel hesitant about doing things God's way, remember Jericho. Friends might think you're stupid, but in the end it will be clear that God's way was the best.

—MH

Taking God for a Fool

But the Israelites acted unfaithfully in regard to the devoted things; Achan son of Carmi . . . took some of them. Joshua 7:1.

He actually tried to play jokes on God. My friend Mike had heard somewhere that God knows everything we are thinking all the time, and that God always knows what we're going to do as well. Mike decided that God may know what other people were going to do, but he was sneakier. He was going to trick God! He decided he would change his thoughts suddenly in midthought and confuse God. Jumping on his bike, he rode down the street thinking only about bikes, when suddenly he switched his thoughts immediately to baseball. *Ha!* he thought smugly. *I'll bet God didn't see that one coming! That was totally unpredictable!*

As silly as Mike's game was, through the centuries many people have tried to trick God. Achan was one of them. Before the walls of Jericho fell, God had specifically told the Israelites that they were not to take for themselves any of the gold or silver that they found in the city. Instead it was all to go to the Lord's treasury. He warned that if anyone did, the entire Israelite camp would be made liable to destruction. So I don't know what Achan was thinking when he stole a beautiful robe, gold, and silver from Jericho and hid them in a hole in the ground under his tent. Did he actually think that God wouldn't see?

Sure enough, destruction came to Israel. They went out to conquer the small city of Ai, but 36 of their men were killed, and the rest were chased into retreat. When Joshua heard about this and asked the Lord why He wasn't fighting for them anymore, God made it plain: someone in your camp stole things from Jericho that were supposed to be Mine. Eventually, of course, they discovered that it was Achan and he was stoned, because we can't hide from God and we can't fool God either.

What about you? Have you been trying to fool God? It sounds silly, but we do it all the time. We try to sneak little sins past Him—He won't notice, will He? Or we try to pretend that it doesn't matter if we break His laws—does He really care that much? God is serious about sin and His law—so serious, in fact, that He went to the cross to rescue us from the result of disobedience. In that light we ought to take what He says seriously too!

—MH

Unexpected Defeat

After returning to Joshua they reported to him, "Don't send all the people, but send about 2,000 or 3,000 men to attack Ai. Since the people of Ai are so few, don't wear out all our people there." So about 3,000 men went up there, but they fled from the men of Ai. Joshua 7:3, 4, HCSB.

One of the worst defeats in my life came when the Minnesota Vikings lost to the Atlanta Falcons. The Vikings, although a superior team—my team—have never won a Super Bowl. But that year we were 16-1. One more win and we'd be in the Super Bowl. Everybody in Minnesota was abuzz, painting themselves purple and gold and salivating at the prospects of what it would actually feel like to finally see the Vikings become the best team in football.

At the time I was at a youth retreat watching the big game with a group from Wisconsin (the ultimate rival of Minnesota). The game came down to a kick. One simple field goal. And we had the man for the job—Gary Anderson, the first person in the NFL not to miss a kick all season! Victory was ours . . . until Anderson missed the field goal, giving the Falcons the chance to tie the game, and then to win it in overtime. The shock and awe that followed is unforgettable. Some wept, some shrieked, some just stared in abject horror, and the Wisconsin guys—they laughed and made fun of us.

This act of treason so upset the head pastor's wife that she chewed out the Wisconsin group, reminding them they wouldn't even be at the ski resort if we hadn't invited them, which really got the Spirit moving. It took an additional prayer meeting and worship service that day to help us cope with the loss.

Just after the famous battle of Jericho, Joshua was faced with a minor battle at Ai (which can be translated "the heap"), a ratty junkyard of ruins that should have been an easy defeat. Unfortunately, a man named Achan kept some of the spoils from the Jericho battle, something that God had expressly forbidden. Result? Defeat at Ai, and the death of 36 men, despite Israel's powerful army. One of our greatest temptations is to think that because we've had tremendous success in the past, we can coast in our relationship with God, and even take a few liberties in obedience to His commands. While God can forgive us of anything, often the results of disobedience make life miserable. The time to stick closer to God is after victories and success. Never think that you've become powerful enough on your own to do things your own way.

—SP

The Day That Never Was

Surely the Lord was fighting for Israel! Joshua 10:14.

We hid in the basement of the restaurant and hoped that the tornado would pass. When the tornado sirens sounded during our romantic dinner, the restaurant manager had encouraged customers to take their plates and drinks with them as we all filed downstairs, so Greg and I did. The servers came with baskets of bread and pitchers of water, trying to keep the atmosphere light and cheerful, though we were all afraid of what was happening above. There had been the most violent-sounding wind, and then an eerie, frightening silence, just before the sirens went off. I had experienced my share of natural disasters—I'd hid under my classroom desk as a child during earthquakes, I had lost possessions in several fires, and had waited out quite a few really terrible storms—but this was the time I was the most afraid, because nobody knew what was going on above.

A seemingly "natural" disaster in the Bible that we often overlook is found in the story of the day the sun stood still. The sun gets most of the attention in that story—how it stood still for an entire day because Joshua asked the Lord for more time to fight the Amorites. But did you know that on that same day the Lord sent a deadly hailstorm, too? We read that more of the Amorites were killed by the hurling hailstones than by the swords of the Israelites. So the Lord performed two miracles for the Israelites that day: He made the sun stand still in the sky, and He wiped out most of the enemy army. It was like the entire battle was essentially won by God.

Today it's hard to feel that God can truly "fight" for us. We don't see Him doing such dramatic things as making the sun stand still or using deadly hailstones to wipe out the people we hate.. He doesn't seem to take sides like that, or perform drastic visible miracles, either. I doubted that He still fights for us as He did in days of old, until I took a look at my own life and tallied up time after time after time that God showed up and rescued me in quiet, subtle ways. Sure, you could say it wasn't God but chance, but then you could also have just said the sun was in eclipse or there was just an unusually bad hailstorm that day the Israelites fought the Amorites. The point is that God's work is visible for people who choose to see it. Open your eyes today. Try to notice what God is doing in your life.

—MH

Knowing You're Going to Win

As the Lord commanded his servant Moses, so Moses commanded Joshua, and Joshua did it; he left nothing undone of all that the Lord commanded Moses. Joshua 11:15.

It was the chance at $400 cash that had us rising with the sun. That cold and blustery winter morning Seth and I weren't too worried about the weather—we were more worried about the crowds that would come to compete for the cash prize. Our school was putting on a version of *The Amazing Race*; we'd work as teams to run around campus finding clues and figuring out puzzles so that we could find the next clue, and the next, and the . . . Who in their right mind wouldn't at least try for all that cash?

But as we jogged over to the starting line that day, we were shocked to find only one other group standing there. They were freshmen—we were grad students. They looked like they had just rolled out of bed, all bleary-eyed and yawning—we had been up excited for hours. So far, our chances of winning were looking good. And by the 9:00 starting time, when only two more groups had showed up, both looking as sorry as the first one, Seth and I knew the money was ours. Which is why for the next three hours we took our sweet time. We watched the other groups run full speed in circles in all the wrong directions, and laughed as we ourselves leisurely jogged to clue after clue after clue. They never even got close to us, and in the end the money was indeed ours.

Joshua, like us, always knew he was going to win. Before every single fight and battle the Lord assured him, "I will give you the victory." Joshua overthrew 31 kings and countless cities and fearlessly kept on going. This military feat was truly a large conquest, but he was able to fight like this because God was with Him. He knew he was going to win.

You run the race and fight the fight differently when you know you're going to win, don't you? When you are assured of victory, it changes how you fight—you fight with confidence instead of fear. I don't know what you're fighting right now, but remember that the ultimate victory has already been won for you. Jesus conquered Satan at Calvary. Even if it seems as if evil is triumphing in the world and in your life, remember that the Winner has already been made clear.

—GH

No Girl Can Serve Two Boys

Choose for yourselves this day whom you will serve. . . . But as for me and my household, we will serve the Lord. Joshua 24:15.

Have you ever been in love with two people at the same time? It's easier to do than you might think. If it's happened to you, you know that in the end you have to choose one or the other. I had to make such a choice my sophomore year of high school. I was dating a guy whom I'd fallen for as we sat in math class together day after day, and we were quite happy. On Valentine's Day, at a romantic picnic dinner under the stars, he asked me to be his girlfriend, and I happily agreed. But little did he know that I'd been fostering a crush on a quieter guy whom I worked with in the mornings, someone a few years older than I who I didn't think would ever give me the time of day. He was so kind and smart and amazing and wonderful—almost every girl who got to know him had fallen for him! But then one day I found out, to my utter shock, that he was interested in me. I was elated, and devastated—for I had a terrible choice to make. I agonized and obsessed, but finally I chose the older guy. Was it the right choice? Maybe so, maybe not . . . he broke up with me only two months later. I cried all summer.

Just before he died, Joshua forced the Israelites to make a similar choice. He told them that it was time to decide whom they loved most—whom they were going to serve. Would it be the gods and idols of the pagan nations around them, or the God of heaven? We know that time and again in the past they'd promised to serve only God, but time and again they'd turned away. The lure of idol worship was so appealing to them, and as time proved, in the future they'd again turn from God. But on this day, before he left them, Joshua asked them to make a final choice: who would get their love and loyalty? As one voice, they chose the Lord.

Maybe several times in your past you have promised to serve God—maybe in your childhood, maybe at your baptism, or maybe just recently. Or perhaps you've never fully decided to serve Him at all. Maybe you're still checking out other gods to worship: yourself, your desires, the world. But at your age it's time to make a final choice.

Whom *will* you serve with your life? Remember that we make the choice every single day. Think about it. Right now, today, make your own choice of whom you will serve.

—MH

> Then Ehud closed and locked the doors of the room and escaped down the latrine. Judges 3:23, NLT.

I'm going to call this guy Maurice. To my ear it's a kind of weird name and seems to fit a weird guy, 'cause Maurice was anything but your typical teen. He was the type who would sit around in class dreaming up bizarre questions for the teacher, such as "Why doesn't your chalk make that screeching sound when you draw circles?" Everyone in school knew Maurice, and if you weren't rolling your eyes when you saw him, you usually just wanted him to go away.

My senior year rolled around, and I'd been voted the class president. We were working on fund-raising, and needed to keep track of our money. All of a sudden Maurice kind of came to mind, and I threw his name out there to my committee. They looked at me as if I had a third eye, but I pressed the issue, and ultimately we asked Maurice to come on board as our "technical consultant." And you know what? He did an amazing job! He happened to be awesome with spreadsheets and computer databases, and soon had a whole system set up that kept track of every-one's hours and all the money that was raised.

Never overlook someone's good qualities just because you find them a bit annoying or strange. The book of Judges relates a story about a lefty named Ehud. Being a lefty in Jewish society was especially bad, because the left hand was considered the "unclean" hand, since in those days there was no toilet paper. (Need I say more?) So being a lefty was already bad enough; then God showed up and wanted Ehud to be the one to dispatch a particular king who had been terrorizing the Israelites. Why Ehud? What did he have that others who were more capable didn't? One thing that made him different: when the palace guards checked messengers for weapons, such as knives or swords, they checked only their left side, since most people were (and still are) right-handed. So in went Ehud with the sword hidden on his right thigh, and Judges tells us that once in the palace, Ehud finished off King Eglon, then locked the door of the king's inner chamber and escaped through the latrine to the outer wall. Though it's a strange story, the big thing that jumps out here is that God wants to use everyone, and He will use their perceived weaknesses as well as their strengths. Think about yourself. No matter your strengths or weaknesses, you're valuable and useful to God if you choose to open up and give Him a chance to use you.

—GH

Failing the Test

Barak said to her, "If you go with me, I will go; but if you don't go with me, I won't go." "Very well," Deborah said, "I will go with you. But because of the way you are going about this, the honor will not be yours, for the Lord will hand Sisera over to a woman." Judges 4:8, 9.

I must have sat there for about 10 minutes waiting to pull out into traffic, with the police officer sitting next to me almost breathing down my neck. She was a big woman. Her breath smelled bad, and the perpetual scowl on her face made you think she was about to hit you upside the head with her gun or something. A number of the guys in my driver's ed class had had their driving test with her, and every single one of them had failed and been sent back through the course again. They said she hated guys and never passed any of them on the first try, just out of spite.

My palms were sweaty, and I was panicky thinking that she was going to fail me for being too timid or something. So when I finally saw an opening in the long line of cars, I zipped into line with the rest of the people stuck in traffic. I heard a small intake of breath from my official passenger, and suddenly the little notepad whipped out and her pen scribbled furiously. I knew it before I even got back to the Department of Motor Vehicles. When she stepped out of the car, she said, "You failed. Come back 30 days from now, and you can try again. But next time don't pull out in front of someone in the middle of traffic like that."

Timidity can sometimes save you from a bad situation, but many times it makes you just miss the boat. The story told in the book of Judges of the Israelite general Barak is just such an example. The prophet Deborah told Barak that God had ordered him to go fight the tyrant king who had been oppressing Israel for many years. She said that God would lead the way, and would give the king and his army into Barak's hands. But Barak's response was "I'm not going out there, unless you're going too." What's wrong with this? Nothing except the fact that in wanting the prophet there as insurance, he was saying that he didn't trust God to do what He said He'd do. And frankly, sometimes we treat God the same way. We're too timid to take God's promises at face value, and we end up missing out on what God has wanted to give us all along. Are there things you could step out in faith on, and trust God in today? What opportunities aren't you taking because you're worried that He won't come through?

—GH

A Hundred Second Chances

Again the Israelites did evil in the eyes of the Lord. Judges 6:1.

Like a high-action adventure movie, the story of Gideon looms large in the book of Judges. Gideon lived during a pretty messed-up time. His own father had erected both an altar to Baal and an Asherah pole, which was where sex orgies and sacrifices (sometimes even human) took place. Of course this meant that Israel had abandoned God once again, and as a result they were literally starving. All the nations around them had been allowed to invade their land and plunder their crops and live-stock. When the Lord first found Gideon, he was threshing wheat in a winepress, hidden from view in an effort to keep anyone from finding and stealing the grain.

God chose Gideon for a reason: his clan was the weakest in Manasseh, and he was the least in his family. God commanded Gideon to tear down his father's altar and Asherah pole and build an altar to God instead, offering a sacrifice using wood from the pole as fuel. When the men of the town discovered Gideon's altar, they wanted to kill him, but his father defended him through this logic: "Let Baal defend himself, if he really is a god!" But God was not through with Gideon. Next His Spirit came upon Gideon, and he mustered up an army. In the meantime Gideon twice put out his infamous fleece to make *sure* the Lord had really called him to free his people from the Midianites. Twice God reassured him that He had truly called him, but said that 32,000 soldiers were far more than He needed. Then bit by bit God whittled the army down to only 300, so that "Israel may not boast against me that her own strength has saved her" (Judges 7:2).

In the middle of the night they surrounded their enemies. They shouted, blasted their trumpets, and uncovered their torches. God caused the Midianites to fall into confusion, turn on each other with their swords, and flee. Then Israel enjoyed 40 years of peace. But after Gideon died, one of his sons killed all but one of the rest of his sons and set up altars to Baal. God was forgotten again.

It blows my mind how many times these people turn away from God. I just don't understand—think of the miracles they witnessed! Then as soon as a strong "hea-then" leader takes charge, they turn from God to idols. And yet He seeks them—time after time. Throughout all of these miracles and wars and conquests, one picture emerges: a God who will not give up on His people. You are one of His peo-ple, too—and God will also never give up on you.

—MH

Gideon: The Rest of the Story

Gideon made the gold into an ephod, which he placed in Ophrah, his town. All Israel prostituted themselves by worshiping it there, and it became a snare to Gideon and his family. Judges 8:27.

The entire country wanted him to become king. Why did he refuse? Gideon, whom we read about yesterday, was a hero among the nation of Israel. He not only was a great guy, faithful believer, and wartime hero, but also had a penchant for innovative battle tactics. God used him and an army of only 300 men, with nothing more than trumpets and torches, to defeat thousands. Most of us know this story, but what people don't talk about is what happened to Gideon afterward. After returning from the battle, he was brought out before the people of Israel, who were itching to get him to do more. They cried out, "Rule over us as our king, you and your son and grandson, because you have rescued us from the Midianites!" But here we see that Gideon was still a pretty amazing guy, because he told them, "I will not rule over you; neither will my son rule over you. The Lord will rule over you!" Gideon understood that God Himself wanted to be their king and rule over them in fairness, wisdom, and generosity. Gideon refused to become their king, because that position belonged to God.

But unfortunately, he did want to be something else: the high priest. He rejected the throne, but he aimed for the next-highest position in Israel. He asked the people to bring the gold earrings they had plundered from the Midianites, and he formed an ephod from it. An ephod was the special gold tunic worn only by the Jewish high priest when coming before God in the tabernacle services. He took this sparkly ephod back to his hometown (where he was, of course, a celebrated hero) and, instead of using the tunic in the tabernacle services, set it up in the town. It became like an idol to the people there—they actually came and worshipped it.

So the whole story is that Gideon rescued his people from one oppressor only to saddle them with another—the curse of idolatry. They simply traded one enemy for another. Gideon had been a success while following God; then he went his own way and almost undid what had been accomplished. Don't just follow God's plans partway. Follow them *all* the way through! Especially after you experience success. That's perhaps when it's the easiest to go off on our own way. Decide today to follow God's plan for your life completely, without wavering.

—GH

A Sacrifice for God

And Jephthah made a vow to the Lord: "If you give the Ammonites into my hands, whatever comes out of the door of my house to meet me when I return in triumph from the Ammonites will be the Lord's, and I will sacrifice it as a burnt offering." Judges 11:30, 31.

The two most handsome men in the world just happen to live in my household. One is 2½ years old, and the other is a little more than a month. They are my two sons, and they are so beautiful to me because they are mine. I love them with all my heart—even more than I do my own life. So when I read the story of Jephthah, I was horrified beyond belief. I could never imagine doing what Jephthah did. Why would God ask that of him, anyway?

God didn't! When Jephthah was advancing against the Ammonites, he made a vow to the Lord. If God would give him victory, he promised to sacrifice whatever first came out of his house when he returned home. When he arrived home victorious, it was his only child—his daughter—who came dancing through the doorway, celebrating his victory. At this Jephthah tore his clothes in grief. "Oh! My daughter!" he cried. "I have made a vow to the Lord that I cannot break" (Judges 11:35). At that point I would have backed out of the vow, but Jephthah believed he needed to keep it. His daughter believed it too. She asked only for two months to visit her friends and mourn. And the text says that Jephthah did what he said he would do.

Now, we could start to get really angry at God about this, unless we realize that God did not ask Jephthah to make that vow. Moreover, the laws that God gave His people specifically say they were *not* to imitate the pagan nations. If Jephthah had known God well enough, he would have remembered this, but he had gotten God confused with Baal—a god whom you had to bribe for blessings, a god who demanded human sacrifices out of greed. Jephthah wasn't a bad guy—he was sincere. He thought he was doing what God would want. He had the best of intentions.

The point is that your good intentions are not enough. Your opinion is not enough. Your sincerity is not enough. Even your very best intentions are ultimately destructive if they aren't in line with God's commands. Don't rely on your own opinion of what is right—it's not enough. Learn instead what God says is right, and follow that.

—MH

The Rebel Who Forgot His Cause

He replied, "Out of the eater, something to eat; out of the strong, something sweet." For three days they could not give the answer. Judges 14:14.

He was a rebel. He liked to date women his parents didn't approve of, and he had a temper that flared up when people tried to push him around. Despite his parents' best efforts to hook him up with a nice local girl, he went off and found a foreign girl who not only didn't share his culture or his religious heritage. Obviously this didn't put him on a good footing with his family or hers, for that matter—but nobody wanted to tell him so. His wedding day was full of awkward moments, and to lighten it up a bit he challenged his guests to a riddle. If they could tell him the answer in seven days, he'd give each one a brand-new set of clothes. The offer was so enticing that they pressured his bride to find out the answer, going so far as threatening to kill her if she didn't. So when the guests came to him a week later with the right answer, he knew exactly where it had come from. In a rage he went out and single-handedly killed enough of his wife's countrymen to cover the clothing and cloaks he'd "lost," knowing that this would be the start of something that wouldn't end well. And in short order what started as a squabble about a riddle became an all-out war—one man versus an entire country.

To say the guy was physically strong is a vast understatement, and his amazing powers could have been given only by God. At various times whole armies were sent to capture him, but he fought them off—sometimes with stones, once with the fresh jawbone of a donkey. One night, when they tried to lock him in, he just picked up the city gates and carried them away. It seemed there was no way to stop him! When they finally did, it was because a girlfriend named Delilah was able to discover the one secret that would remove his amazing strength.

I have always read Samson's story as that of a real person who struggled with who he was and who he was supposed to be. Sent by God to be a judge over his people, he couldn't quite stick to the job assignment. Yet God never gave up on Samson. In the final moments of his life God renewed Samson's strength so that he pulled down a pagan temple around his enemies. That shows me that God is willing to work with each of us no matter how far we fall away. So take a lesson from Samson and turn to Him while you're young, instead of at your life's end.

—GH

Sin Makes You Stupid

Having put him to sleep on her lap, she called a man to shave off the seven braids of his hair, and so began to subdue him. And his strength left him. Judges 16:19.

The more I cheated, the easier it got. A friend of mine was failing history—a subject I excelled at—and would not be able to graduate. I decided to help him by copying my test answers down on very small pieces of paper and slipping them to him between classes. As his grades began to climb, I got careless. I felt invincible—the clueless old teacher would never catch me! I got more and more confident and less and less careful, until one day I wrote the answers on a shiny silver gum wrapper—about the least discreet thing you could find. The teacher's eye noticed the shimmer of silver, and we both were caught and promptly presented with a big fat F.

Now, you might be thinking that I'm dumb (well, yeah), but I have to say that I think Samson was even dumber. A judge who had led Israel for almost 20 years and a Nazirite from birth, his amazing strength was tied up with his long hair. No razor had ever touched his head. Until Delilah came along.

Delilah was a Philistine woman he never should have even been with. He should have chosen a woman from among his own people, the Israelites. The Philistines offered her ridiculous amounts of money if she could find out the secret of his strength, and so she began asking. He lied to her three times—telling her that if he was tied with leather thongs, then with new ropes . . . And each time, she tried it! Wouldn't you have become suspicious of her after the second time, or even the first! But Samson had gotten careless. He felt invincible, and his lust for her apparently clouded his brain. Finally, after "much nagging," he gave her the secret. It cost him his strength, his freedom, his eyesight, and then his life. He should have seen it coming.

The way I see it, the more time you spend living with sin, the stupider you get. You start to think you're invincible. You get careless, and you make really awful choices. Sin seems to have either a numbing or a dumbing effect on the mind, so that the longer you mess with it, the worse your decisions become. So don't lose your good sense by thinking you can mess around with sin. You will only get stupider when you do.

—MH

Hey, We Don't Need No God

In those days Israel had no king; everyone did as he saw fit. Judges 21:25.

It's like the worst horror movie ever. A man hands his concubine over to a mob of men. She is raped and so terribly abused throughout the night that she dies. Then the man cuts her into pieces and sends the grisly chunks to all the tribes of Israel to show the terrible evil that was done. Almost the entire tribe of Benjamin is wiped out because of this evil—thousands and thousands are killed, and the few men who are left kidnap and steal nonconsenting wives just to keep their tribe alive. But that's not all. A woman named Jael is a hero for killing a man by driving a tent spike into his head. Samson, who is always killing people (sometimes with the bones of dead animals), is finally caught, and his enemies gouge out his eyes and put him in prison. An obese king is fatally stabbed in the belly, and the knife disappears into his fat. Almost all the 70 sons of Gideon are murdered on the same day. Jephthah sacrifices his daughter to God.

Rape. Murder. Violence . What is going on here? Is this actually the Bible? These are stories we don't want to think about, stories I don't want my children to hear! So why are they included in God's holy Book, and how can we feel OK about it?

For a long time I struggled with the book of Judges, and with the God who allowed all this to happen. But then I came to the last sentence of the book: *In those days Israel had no king; everyone did as he saw fit.* Do you remember who was supposed to be Israel's king? It wasn't a man. It was God Himself. But when the people turned from God to serve the idols of the nations around them, they suddenly had no king. And with no king to tell them how to live, it was every man for himself. Everyone did what was "right" in their own eyes, and you read about the result in the book of Judges. That's what it looks like when there is no higher law. Judges is in the Bible to show us the kinds of things that happen when people try to live without God.

Today many believe that we don't need God or His laws—we can simply live good lives and be good people. Don't buy into this thinking. We all need a standard to live by, or things will start to look like the terrible things recorded in Judges. The next time you're tempted to make up your own ways and forget God, remember that that's already been tried, and remember how it turned out.

—MH

Engagements Then and Now

But Ruth replied, "Don't urge me to leave you or to turn back from you. Where you go I will go, and where you stay I will stay. Your people will be my people and your God my God." Ruth 1:16.

I knew exactly what my sneaky boyfriend was doing even from all the way across the crowded room. He was asking my parents for permission to marry me. I knew instantly because of the way my mom jumped off the ground ever so slightly and gave a joyful little clap of her hands. It was their surprise twenty-fifth anniversary party, and for reasons that I hadn't understood before, Greg had insisted on flying out with me for the occasion. I hadn't realized my parents or their anniversary mattered to him so much until I witnessed the scene across the banquet hall. He shook my father's hand as if they'd just made a business deal (had they?), my dad proudly patted him on the back, and they all hugged. I quickly turned away and pretended I hadn't seen the exchange, but in my heart I knew that Greg would soon ask me to marry him.

In the time of Ruth, during the period of the judges, the engagement process was a lot more complicated than just asking a father for permission. If a husband died, in certain situations a man called a kinsman-redeemer could take over the property of his deceased close male relative's property *and* marry his widow. When Ruth met Boaz and they wanted to marry, it was fortunate that Boaz had the relation of kinsman-redeemer. But another man was a closer kin to Naomi than he, so he had to give the other guy first chance. When the other man declined the property and so declined Ruth, Boaz happily received both as his own. They were married. Ruth gave birth to a son they named Obed. King David was Obed's grandson.

When Ruth and her mother-in-law, Naomi, became widowed and virtually helpless, she had no way of knowing that Boaz, a son, and a life of happiness lay before her. She went with Naomi, not in hopes of getting something in return, but because it was the right thing to do. She didn't want to abandon her mother-in-law in her old age. And God blessed her abundantly because she had been so faithful to Naomi.

Determine in your heart to do the right thing simply because it is the right thing. But don't be surprised if God ends up blessing you abundantly in the process.

—MH

Was It Love at First Sight?

Boaz asked the foreman of his harvesters, "Whose young woman is that?" Ruth 2:5.

My very first thoughts about him were *Wow, what a nerdy-looking guy.* He was wearing an ugly orange-and-red-plaid shirt. His hair was a wild mess. And he had a beard that belonged only on a caveman. We met in Greek class, and my husband will assure you that he wasn't too impressed with me, either. I sat at the desk in front of him, and he'd waited for days to see the face attached to the blond head he'd been staring at. When I finally turned around to look at him, he was disappointed. *Oh, she's not that pretty,* he thought. Neither of us would ever have expected to end up married to each other.

When Ruth first met Boaz, she was a penniless widow living with a depressed woman. They had arrived in Bethlehem from Moab with little more than what they wore. It was the beginning of the barley harvest, and Ruth asked her mother-in-law, Naomi, if she could pick up the leftovers in the field of Naomi's relative Boaz. Now, Ruth had one big thing against her in this Hebrew town—she was a Moabite. (Remember all the wars Israel fought with Moab?) But there were at least two good things going for her: she was loyal to Naomi *and* a hard worker. Ruth had what it takes, and if it was up to her they wouldn't starve.

Boaz noticed her the first day and asked his foreman who she was. She had worked steadily since early morning, the foreman said, taking only a short rest in the shade. Boaz was impressed and went to talk to her himself. He encouraged her to remain in his field and made sure none of the male workers tried anything with her. He gave her some lunch, and even sent food home for Naomi at day's end. When Naomi heard about Boaz, she set a plan in motion for Ruth to marry him. Ruth and Boaz could never have known that their "chance meeting" would end in marriage. God brought them together in a fitting and beautiful way.

Boaz first took notice of Ruth because he had heard about her commitment to taking care of her widowed mother-in-law, and he was impressed. He was also impressed with how hard she worked in his field. It just goes to show that when you are busy doing good, people will notice you. Today, do the kind of work that you would be proud of if your spouse-to-be was somewhere watching you. Because you never know . . . they could already be noticing you from afar!

—MH

It Wasn't the Food

And she made a vow, saying, "O Lord Almighty, if you will only look upon your servant's misery and remember me, and not forget your servant but give her a son, then I will give him to the Lord for all the days of his life." 1 Samuel 1:11.

I'd never been that sick in my life. We had just returned from Japan, and for some reason 10 days of eating Japanese food had done awful things to my stomach. Every day I woke up sicker than sick. And each day seemed worse than the one before. What's more, I was exhausted. After about a week of this I realized I must be fighting a really strong virus. So I drank gallons of water and went to bed and slept for a day and a night. And to my surprise, the next morning I was sick again! It hung on week after week . . . long enough, in fact, that I finally drove myself to the nearest drugstore and bought a pregnancy test—that announced a fat little blue positive sign. So it wasn't the Japanese food at all. As it turned out, it was my first son, Caleb.

Things weren't so easy for Hannah. She was one of the two wives of Elkanah, and she wanted children terribly, but could not have any. The other wife insulted her and made fun of her on a regular basis, and often Hannah wept all day and refused to eat. Her husband loved her with or without children. He wished she'd just get over the fact that she couldn't have kids, but she couldn't.

One day when they visited the tabernacle, Hannah poured out her troubles to the Lord. She told Him that if He would only give her a son, she would give that child to Him for all the days of his life. Eli the priest found Hannah in the middle of this prayer. Her lips were moving but she made no sound, and he thought she was drunk. When he went to her to rebuke her, she explained that she was pleading with God for a child. Eli answered her, "Go in peace, and may the God of Israel grant you what you have asked of him" (1 Samuel 1:17). And within due time a baby boy, who would become the great prophet of Israel, was born to Hannah. She named him Samuel, saying, "Because I asked the Lord for him."

Hannah dedicated Samuel to the Lord because she knew he belonged to God in the first place. She recognized that what good she had in her life was there because God put it there. Have you remembered this lately—that all the good things in your life are blessings from God? Stop today. Take a moment to recognize how much He has blessed you.

—MH

The Day My Husband Pretended to Be a Girl

So Eli told Samuel, "Go and lie down, and if he calls you, say, 'Speak, Lord, for your servant is listening.'" 1 Samuel 3:9.

I once thought my husband was a woman. It was the week before he asked me to marry him, and little did I know that he was making secret plans with my family to fly to Arizona for spring break and to surprise me there with a proposal. His flight had been delayed the day he arrived to propose, so he called my house to let my brother (who was picking him up at the airport—this had gotten complicated) know. Except that I answered the phone. Immediately he became a teenage girl. "She" asked if my brother was there, giggled and sighed, and consented just to call back later. "She" wouldn't give me her name. "She" was Greg! And the whole time I spoke to "her," I never recognized his voice at all.

One night when the little boy Samuel was asleep in the tabernacle, he heard Someone calling his name. Not surprisingly, Samuel didn't recognize the voice of God. First Samuel 3:7 tells us that Samuel didn't yet know the Lord, that God's word had not yet been revealed to him. So when he heard his name, he jumped up and ran in to Eli and asked why Eli had called him. Eli assured Samuel that he hadn't called, and sent him back to bed. Three times this happened, but by the third time Eli had figured out that God was calling his young helper. So Eli helped Samuel to prepare an answer. Sure enough, when God called his name again Samuel bravely answered, "Speak, for your servant is listening" (1 Samuel 5:10).

Would I recognize the voice of God if He called me today? Would you? Are we familiar with His voice? Are we close enough to Him to understand when He is calling?

I want to be the kind of person who recognizes God's voice among the rest of the clutter and worry in my own head. In order to be able to do that, we need to know a secret. Samuel's reply to God's call tells what it is. We have to listen. We need to have an awareness of God in our lives.

Listen for God today. Try to discern what He is saying to you amid all the noise of the rest of the world. Spend some quiet time getting to know His voice.

—MH

After the Philistines had captured the ark of God, they took it from Ebenezer to Ashdod. 1 Samuel 5:1.

When I was growing up, some of my favorite Disney movies were those of the classic Herbie, the Love Bug. In them a little white Volkswagen Beetle, with a life and personality of its own, raced around corners, opened its own doors, and generally caused a little chaos on any road it could find. The appeal was the idea that a car could drive itself and speak with quick little beeps on its horn. There was something about it that made me long to drive a little white VW bug with blue and red racing stripes.

First Samuel has its own version of *Herbie*, complete with a gold box that seemed to have a mind of its own, for it broke pagan idols and made a whole town sick. The story begins with the horrible defeat of the Israelites by the Philistines. So the Israelites decide they need a "good-luck charm." With all the stories they'd heard of their grandfathers carrying the ark of the covenant into battle, they figured that if they wanted to win, they should do the same. But when they pulled it out of mothballs and dusted it off for battle, the ark wouldn't cooperate. They were defeated again, and the ark was carted away by the enemy.

Then began an odd journey for the ark. First it was put in the Philistine temple of Dagon (half man, half fish), where morning after morning the priests discovered the large idol Dagon on the floor, and finally smashed to pieces. This wasn't going well, so they shipped the ark to the next town, but everyone there got sick with mysterious tumors. The same thing happened in the next town, until finally the Philistines sent the ark back to the Israelites on a cart with offerings of gold, hoping to apologize for messing with such a dangerous article. God didn't encourage the Israelites' belief that the ark itself was capable of helping them win battles. But in the presence of nonbelievers God took action and made the ark seem responsible for miraculous things.

God seems willing to work with people where they are. He showed the Israelites that the ark itself wasn't powerful, so that they'd stop treating it like a good-luck charm. He showed the Philistines that it was more powerful than their idols or gods. He works with all of us where we are in our lives and understanding. Maybe He's trying to get through to you. Are you listening?

—GH

The Grass Is Always Greener Syndrome

They said to him, "You are old, and your sons do not walk in your ways; now appoint a king to lead us, such as all the other nations have." 1 Samuel 8:5.

I wanted to drive so badly. Think of a continual itch you can't stop yourself from scratching. I had waited and waited to get to the place where I could drive without an adult sitting next to me in the passenger seat. I knew the feeling of autonomy would open up a whole new experience of life—one full of freedom and blowing wind in my hair. But after I finally got my license and began driving everywhere, the excitement began to fade just a little. The costs of driving a car started to add up a lot faster than I realized they would. The gas was expensive, and I realized I was working hard to pay for the gas it took to take me to and from work (kind of a crazy circle of money in and money out). Then there was the first of what would be many tickets from staunch old police officers who insisted I was driving too fast. And car insurance! Soon the excitement of having my license faded away into nothing, as I experienced the real cost of driving. The reality wasn't as exciting as the dream itself.

The Israelites had a similar problem. They'd been settled in the Promised Land for quite a few years, and even though they had God-appointed judges and rulers to keep the peace, they wanted what all the nations around them had—a king. Samuel, the prophet and current judge, was angry with their request, but still took it to God to see if He would give any feedback. God said, "Go ahead; give them a king. But be sure to tell them what's going to happen as a result." Samuel told them that taxes would increase, that the king would demand the best of their crops and fields, and, on top of that, that he would forcefully recruit all young men to join his army when there was a battle to be fought. In the end, the thing they wanted so badly turned out to be not so great.

Sometimes the things we think we'd almost die for turn out to be something we don't really want after all. God's commandments tell us how to live, including things we should not do. But sometimes we feel that these 10 rules are taking away our fun. Usually it's quite the opposite—God calls things bad because they really are bad. Go your own way, and things won't be so great after all. The next time you catch yourself thinking that God's rules will take away all your fun, remember that this isn't about Him. It's to make your own life better.

—GH

Bench-lifting the Fat Kid

Then Saul said to Samuel, "I have sinned. I violated the Lord's command and your instructions. I was afraid of the people and so I gave in to them. 1 Samuel 15:24.

If it hasn't happened to you yet, it probably will. There'll be things you did that, years later, still make you cringe with shame. For me that cringe goes up for a guy I haven't seen since sixth grade. Bob was new at school, and just happened to be the heaviest kid in the class. Not just pudgy, but fat. Not just fat. Huge. Naturally he was the target of many a joke, but somehow he kept a sheepish grin on his face through them all. Lunchtime was the worst for poor Bob. He had no friends to sit with, and the few kids he did sit near taunted him with such questions as "Hey, Bob, how many kindergartners did you eat today?" or "Didn't anyone ever tell you there's more to life than Twinkies, Blobbert?" Doomed to eat alone, inevitably he was like kryptonite in the friend market, too—hang with him, and you'd be made fun of with him.

One day we found Bob sitting in the hall, and before the clever "Blobbert" jokes began I decided to get a good laugh out of the guys. So I ran over to Bob and called, "Five bucks to anyone who can lift Bob off the ground for 10 seconds!" I then tried picking him up, exaggerating the extreme exertion it would take. My ingenious wit prompted peals of laughter, with several of the students falling to the floor holding their stomachs. Then I turned and looked at Bob, really looked at him. His face was red, but not with anger; red with embarrassment and sadness. My heart silently broke. I never apologized. I still want to.

Peer pressure and the desire to fit in can make us do things we're not proud of, but we do them because of our need to be liked. Israel's first king fell prey to the same thing when he went to war. Saul was told not to take anything as plunder, not even livestock. And when his soldiers brought back the best of the oxen and cattle, instead of standing up to them Saul caved and did what they wanted him to do. Then he lied to the prophet Samuel about it. This eventually cost him the loss of his throne to a young man named David. In the end Saul knew good and well that peer pressure is just not worth it. Sure, it's important to be liked and accepted, but sometimes the cost is too great. So don't give in to things that you know good and well aren't right. You might end up like me, years later, still wishing you could apologize to poor ole Bob.

—GH

Jessie and Jesse's Son

"The Lord does not look at the things man looks at. Man looks at the outward appearance, but the Lord looks at the heart." 1 Samuel 16:7.

Jessie was the only student I was ever completely wrong about. After years of working with teenagers, I have developed a certain knack for being able to tell almost immediately what sort of person someone is. I am almost never wrong—I can spot the good kids, the bad kids, the cool kids, the deceptive kids, the leaders and the followers long before they realize that I have them figured out. But not Jessie.

When I first met her, she was wearing all black—black fishnet stockings under a three-and-a-half-inch miniskirt with 10 chains hanging clear down to her legs. Her short spiked hair was dyed black. She had on black makeup and was wearing a crazy two-foot-high pink top hat. She was also carrying a giant rubber rat she called "Mr. Squeakers." She was jumping and laughing and talking so fast, and making so little sense, that I just knew she was on drugs. I had her grouped in with the "bad kids" and didn't give it a second thought.

That's why it was so surprising when she turned out to be one of the kindest, most admirable and upstanding girls in my entire dorm. Come to find out, she had never touched drugs in her life. She was not swayed by what was popular—she was her own person and stood her own ground. And she was so honest and trustworthy that I ended up hiring her to be my reader, the person in charge of my grades, my files, and the very key to my office. Today she remains a close friend of mine. I'm so glad I was wrong about her.

Samuel was wrong about the kid David, too. When God told him to go to the house of Jesse to anoint the future king, Samuel saw Jesse's strong, handsome older sons and thought surely one of them would be God's choice. But God reminded Samuel that He doesn't look at the kinds of things people look at. Rather, God looks at the heart. Though on the "outside" David's older brothers seemed more suited to rule a nation, God knew that David was the one with the heart of a king. It's easy to sum up people by their outward appearance, but challenge yourself to go beyond that. You might be missing out on some really great friends. Try to see people the way God sees them. Try to see their hearts.

—MH

Get Your Own Clothes!

Then Saul dressed David in his own tunic. He put a coat of armor on him and a bronze helmet on his head. David fastened on his sword over the tunic and tried walking around, because he was not used to them. "I cannot go in these," he said to Saul. . . . So he took them off. 1 Samuel 17:38, 39.

I tried to steal an entire sermon one time. The sermon began its life as a chapter in a Max Lucado book, and I took every piece of it, even his personal stories, and used it as my own, not just for a preaching class, but before an actual congregation of 300 people. It was not pretty. Not only had most of them already read the popular book the sermon was lifted from—they didn't have a hard time figuring out that I wasn't even old enough to have experienced all those mission stories from Africa. But it wasn't that I was trying to steal. It was that I was trying to be great. At the time I didn't realize that I had my own armor—words and stories of my own that were actually pretty powerful. I thought I had to use someone else's armor to be great.

Luckily for Israel, the young shepherd David didn't make the same mistake. When he showed up in front of King Saul and asked permission to fight Goliath, Saul was so desperate for victory that he let David go—but first he dressed him in his kingly armor. David put on the cumbersome suit, tried walking around a bit, and right off he knew it wasn't going to work. It wasn't his armor; it was someone else's. David knew that we all fight best in our own armor, so he shook off the fancy gear and, slingshot in hand, challenged—and defeated—the giant.

I don't know who you're trying to be, or be like. I don't know the people you want to look like and sound like and imitate, but I bet there are several in your life. I bet there are a lot of people's "armor" you'd rather wear around than your own, and I bet there are many days you'd so much rather be anyone other than yourself. But that kind of thinking is a mistake.

You were made exactly the way you are for a reason, and the best way to face life is just like that—in your very own armor, in your very own skin, trying to be none other than just yourself. Take a moment today and ask God to help you learn to trust that He has made you enough, just as you are.

—MH

My Husband the Cheapskate

David said to the Philistine, "You come against me with sword and spear and javelin, but I come against you in the name of the Lord Almighty, the God of the armies of Israel, whom you have defied." 1 Samuel 17:45.

My cheapskate husband always tries to save money by making his own photography equipment. Once at a restaurant he talked the server into giving him a giant handful of black straws because he was making a device that would restrict light to a beam so that he could direct it where he wanted it. He made a "beauty dish" (look it up) out of a $4 plastic garden pot and an old CD stack case. He even made a macro extension tube for his lens with PVC pipe and duct tape—I told him he's not allowed to take that one out in public when I'm around. Surprisingly enough, though, not only do all of his contraptions work, but he takes absolutely gorgeous pictures with them.

The tools that David used in battle against Goliath probably seemed incredibly cheap and shabby compared to the giant's classy metal armor. Goliath had a sword, a spear, and a javelin plus a shield bearer who went before him. All David had was a much-used slingshot, a shepherd's bag, and five smooth stones. But after years of protecting his sheep it's likely that David could sling a stone at 60 miles an hour, and with that unsophisticated weapon he took down the champion giant warrior. Then in one quick move he cut off Goliath's head with the giant's own sword—and the Philistine army fled. The men of Judah and Israel took off running, chasing them all the way to the entrance of Gath and the gates of Ekron. Then they came back and plundered the Philistine camp.

It's not that David's weapons were "good" enough to kill a giant. In fact, it's not about the weapons at all. Goliath had the height, the heavy armor, and the weapons. There wasn't a warrior in Israel's army willing to take him on. But David accepted Goliath's challenge in the name of the Lord Almighty. That was his power, and the secret of his success.

What giants are you fighting in your life today? What problems loom large and impossible to conquer? Are you fighting them with your own weapons, or are you coming against them in the name of God?

—MH

My Wife, the Food Greed

"Saul has slain his thousands, and David his tens of thousands." Saul was very angry.
. . . "They have credited David with tens of thousands," he thought, "but me with only
thousands. What more can he get but the kingdom?" 1 Samuel 18:7, 8.

It was one of those lovely times that I came home to the scent of something amazing. This particular evening it was the rich, spicy smell of homemade enchiladas baking in the oven. And then I saw my wife busily whipping up a bowl of fresh guacamole. Ah, avocados! I was making a dive at the bowl with a tortilla chip when my hand was playfully slapped. So I retreated while the enchiladas finished their tedious cooking. My wife is passionate about food, both eating and making it, so I've been a bit spoiled. However, a unique quality has joined her love of cooking and eating: greed.

When everything was ready, I scooped a huge pile of guacamole onto my plate. I noticed my wife glancing sideways at me, but didn't think much of it. I added salad, enchiladas, salsa, and sour cream, then took another stab at the guacamole—only to be slapped again. I looked up and saw a greedy beast holding a butter knife. "You've already had too much! This side is yours, and this is mine!" My wife drew an uneven line through the guacamole with the knife, giving herself the far more generous portion to equal out the "too much" I'd already given myself. That was the night I realized I had married not only a wonderful cook but also a strange creature that greedily watched how much food was being taken from her.

King Saul had a similar Jekyll and Hyde living in him. By this time Saul and David had teamed up in many battles, and their fame had spread throughout the kingdom. The people rejoiced when they came home victorious, singing that Saul had slain his thousands, but David his ten thousands. This ate into Saul's pride. Soon it became jealousy, and finally it festered into open hatred of his faithful servant. Saul began plotting to kill him. But nothing was ever said between the two, so everything seemed fine.

Jealousy has a way of digging in deep, and the best way to keep jealous feelings from growing is first to pray about them, then to talk and get it out in the open. Don't let this stuff get bigger than it should, or you'll be dealing with your own greedy monster someday.

—GH

To Kill, or Not to Kill—That Is the Question

The men said, "This is the day the Lord spoke of when he said to you, 'I will give your enemy into your hands for you to deal with as you wish.'" Then David crept up unnoticed and cut off a corner of Saul's robe. 1 Samuel 24:4.

The bills were piling up, and the money was long gone. I listened to a very worried member of my church as he related the financial situation his family now faced. He asked if I'd come and pray with him about the bills, asking God to step in and make something work out. He said he knew that God would take care of them, as He had promised, but he didn't know how. I was struck first of all by his faith, but also his complete honesty. He knew that he had nowhere to go. The money was gone, and if they didn't pay their bills, things were going to unravel.

So I went to his house and prayed with him about their bills, which were even larger than I expected. He showed me five cars in his yard that he'd been trying to sell. He thought that maybe God would bring in some buyers for them, but who could tell? He only hoped God would see fit to help him out of the hole he was rapidly spiraling into. As I drove away from the house I wondered if God was going to say yes. Nobody really knew how his problems would be fixed, but he hoped and prayed they would. Two days later I got a phone call. "Two of them sold today—and for more than I had originally asked! I was able to pay off everything!"

When he was confronted with the opportunity to kill King Saul, David showed a similar faith in God. Saul had been chasing him through the desert trying to kill him, but so far had been unable to find him. One day Saul paused at a cave to use the "men's room." And it just happened to be the cave in which David and his men were camping. David's men urged him to kill Saul and be done with it, but David refused. "Am I to kill God's anointed?" he asked. He believed that God would make him king someday, and he refused to jump ahead and take matters into his own hands. He preferred to let God work it out in His own way, and ultimately David had both the throne of Israel and a clear conscience. We too have the same kinds of choices. We can follow God's way, or we can jump ahead and take over ourselves. But if we stick with God's way, it'll always come out better than anything we could come up with. Next time you have a chance, choose God's way and trust the outcome to Him.

—GH

B-I-B-L-E—Basic Instructions Before Leaving Earth

Then David said to Abiathar the priest, the son of Ahimelech, "Bring me the ephod." Abiathar brought it to him, and David inquired of the Lord, "Shall I pursue this raiding party? Will I overtake them?" 1 Samuel 30:7, 8.

Instructions are for sissies, low-intelligence guys who don't know a Phillips from a flathead. This has been my belief for some time, but I can't say it has always served me well. I had just bought a cool new bookcase that bolted to the wall. There were lots of brackets, screws, and bolts, but overall the design was fairly simple. I drilled a few holes, used some anchors, and voilà: new cool shelf! I had positioned these shelves over a futon in my office that was even-spaced and complemented the feng shui in the room quite nicely. Then I smugly stacked dozens of my favorite books on the shelf.

A few days later my brother-in-law Josh was staying with us and slept on the futon under that shelf. The next morning I wandered in to check my e-mail and found him sleeping soundly underneath a large pile of books *and* the shelf that now had a big piece of drywall stuck on its back. A gaping hole marred the wall. Instantly I knew what was wrong: way too much weight and no anchors in the wall's studs. If only I'd read the instructions!

While flipping through 1 Samuel, I noticed a trend in almost all of the major decisions or battles that David made or fought. His first response was to "inquire of the Lord," to ask for instructions, typically through a priest that traveled with him. Even when a raiding party kidnapped his wives and the families of the 600 men who were with him, before he just ran off to rescue them he stopped and asked God, "Shall I pursue this raiding party?"

Sometimes I wish that I had access to that kind of thing. I'd love to just ask a question of God and get direct answers, as David did. But don't we have something better than that? We have the whole Bible, written by God through men, which records details, stories, and wise instruction to deal with all our problems and issues. But do we turn to the Bible? Do we stop and study and ask God, "What should I do?" Like the instruction book that I never seem to pick up, I'm sometimes guilty of not reading God's instruction book enough. That's how God is trying to speak to all of us. Don't try to put your life together without consulting it first.

—GH

The Domino Effect

When they came to the threshing floor of Nacon, Uzzah reached out and took hold of the ark of God, because the oxen stumbled. The Lord's anger burned against Uzzah because of his irreverent act; therefore God struck him down and he died there beside the ark of God. 2 Samuel 6:6, 7.

It seems like one of the most unfair deaths in all Scripture. I mean, what if Uzzah was just trying to be a good guy? David was leading a joyful procession toward Jerusalem (where they were taking the ark of God), when the oxen stumbled. Uzzah was one of the men guiding the cart that held the ark, so when the oxen stumbled he might have reached out without thinking to steady the wobbling ark. Certainly everyone in Israel knew not to touch the ark for fear of death, but did Uzzah think about this, or did he just react? Did he think he must not let something so precious and sacred fall to the ground? Was he trying to be a hero, instead of trusting that God would save the ark Himself? The Bible doesn't tell us. All we know is that God had said that if you touch the ark you will die. Uzzah touched it. And he fell to the ground, dead.

This is a hard one. Some have taken this story and accused God of being an arbitrary murderer. Others say His ark mattered more than His people. I don't know what to say . . . except . . . let's imagine for a minute . . . what if people had been allowed to touch the ark? What would that have meant? They would have been able to touch the stones on which the Ten Commandments were written. And if they'd been able to touch the commandments, they could have changed them at some point, if they wanted to. God and the nation of Israel had sworn sacred promises to each other based on those very commandments and laws. If the commandments were changed, the covenant was null. Their entire society would fall to pieces.

So maybe it makes a little bit of sense that no one was allowed to touch the ark. The people had full assurance that the commandments of God could never be changed. They were that important! Many today say that they are not relevant anymore, or that it's OK to change one or two, such as the Sabbath, but don't buy it. God protected the commandments from change at all costs, and therefore so should we.

—MH

Mephibo-who?

"Don't be afraid," David said to him, "for I will surely show you kindness for the sake of your father Jonathan. I will restore to you all the land that belonged to your grandfather Saul, and you will always eat at my table." 2 Samuel 9:7.

I stood on the open-air deck overlooking a pungent forest of pine trees winding down the hillside to the ocean below. The vacation home had an all-wood interior, a woodstove with a pipe that ran from the first floor through the second-floor ceiling, and even an observation tower that gave you a higher view across the bay. No, we didn't make tons of money writing this book! A few times a year we come and stay in this beautiful home only because my wife's mother and the house's owner were college roommates—very good friends back in the day. It's because of their friendship that the offer to stay in their summer home in the San Juan Islands of northern Washington State was opened to us. Sometimes you get hooked up, not because of anything you yourself have done, but because of what people have done before you.

David and Jonathan were just such friends, and one of the last times they saw one another Jonathan asked David to be kind to his family and descendants when he came into power. In the years after Jonathan's death, David (now the ruling king in Israel) looked for surviving relatives of Jonathan's family. David's servants told him that a son of Jonathan's was still alive, but crippled in both feet and could not walk. His name was a mouthful—Mephibosheth. As he shuffled his way toward David on his crutches, the king's heart went out to him, the only living connection he had to his long-lost friend. Mephibosheth understandably was afraid for his life, knowing that it was his family who had tried to kill David years before. But David remembered his promise. Even though he didn't know the lame man, he knew his father. Because of Jonathan, David extended a helping hand to him. Then he gave Mephibosheth a seat at his royal table plus all the lands that had belonged both to his father, Jonathan, and his grandfather, King Saul.

This secondhand generosity isn't foreign in our time, either. Even though none of us have even seen God the Father directly, He extends the offer of salvation to each of us because of our connection to Jesus. What Jesus has already done allows you and me to reap the benefits of His perfect life, which is mainly all of heaven itself.

—GH

Naked in the Onsen

One evening David got up from his bed and walked around on the roof of the palace. From the roof he saw a woman bathing. The woman was very beautiful. 2 Samuel 11:2.

I've taken a bath in some pretty strange places. In Japan I went to the public bathhouse (an onsen), where everyone gets naked in a big swimming pool and rub-a-dub-dubs without a care in the world. And if that wasn't weird enough for a shy little Westerner, the little hot-tub-style baths had electric current running through them that twitched every muscle in one's body, supposedly to help heart and blood circulation, but I bailed when things began feeling like a heart attack revving up.

The fastest bath I ever took was in a lake fed by glacial runoff in northern Washington. The water temperature wasn't much warmer than an almost-melted slushie. I scrubbed body and hair in one huge swipe and practically walked on water all the way to the shore. I've even taken a shower in an outdoor stall with a tarp thrown around it. It had no floor, so I had to wear shoes and stand ankle-deep in mud while attempting to get clean (a exercise in futility, let me tell you).

But I've never taken a bath on the roof of my house; to me it's a no-brainer. Of course I don't live in the Kidron Valley in 900 B.C. The floors of their homes were packed dirt—pretty sloppy when wet. Besides, local culture demanded that you *never* looked down from your house to the rooftop of a house across or below you. (It seems that King David had no trouble ignoring that social nicety.) As the story unfolds, David compounds trouble with trouble as he first sleeps with Bathsheba, then tries to trick her husband into spending the night with her to cover up any clues of his indiscretion. When that fails, he conveniently has Uriah killed on the battlefield. But the part that blows me away is the prophet Nathan telling David about a rich man who steals a poor man's only possession, a small ewe lamb, and serves it to dinner guests. David is furious at such a barbarous act, and declares that the man should die! In an almost perfect Hollywood moment, Nathan points his finger in David's face and cries, *"You are the man!"* Sometimes we can clearly see the error in someone else's way but be blind to the same thing in ourselves. But we really can't justify criticizing anyone else until we've taken a long hard look at ourselves. And really, cleaning up our own act could take a lifetime anyway.

—GH

O my son Absalom! My son, my son Absalom! If only I had died instead of you—O Absalom, my son, my son! 2 Samuel 18:33.

It began when they were teens. They watched their dad initiate an affair with a stunningly gorgeous woman, then discovered that he had also killed her husband so that he could marry her. Dad brought her home and thought he could quickly patch things up, but we know that these two sons never forgot it. It messed them up for the rest of their lives, and the "sword never left his house," as God had predicted.

Their names were Absalom and Amnon. They were the sons of King David. Teens during his affair with Bathsheba, they grew up to model his reckless sexual behavior. Amnon was so attracted to his half sister Tamar that he captured and raped her—following after his lust as Dad had, instead of restraining himself. When older brother Absalom found this out, he so hated Amnon that years later he killed him. Though he knew this would grieve his father, he didn't care. He'd lost respect for *him* long before.

After this murder Absalom and David don't see each other for five years, but finally David goes to him and welcomes him home with kisses. Absalom, however, is not softened. He spends the next four years gaining the allegiance of the people to himself, then tries to declare himself king. Eventually war begins, and when David's men find Absalom hanging by his hair from a tree, they kill him. Instead of being relieved that the threat against himself is gone, David is heartbroken, sobbing for his son. You can read above that he wished he had died instead.

The story sounds more like a soap opera than the family history of the greatest king of Israel. And even though David was a godly king before and after his affair with Bathsheba, he was never able to erase the consequences of that sin. And Absalom, who had several chances to start over, never could quite recover from the bitterness he carried as a teenager. While the mistake started out as his father's, in the end it was his own—we can blame our parents for only so long. The choices you make today in your teenage life can follow you for a long, long time. Be careful what you choose, because with each choice you come closer and closer to the person you will be someday.

—MH

Give God Something of Value

But the king replied to Araunah, "No, I insist on paying you for it. I will not sacrifice to the Lord my God burnt offerings that cost me nothing." 2 Samuel 24:24.

I think it's cruel and unusual to make your child choose their own punishment. My parents used to play this sick game every now and again. "Would you rather be grounded, do the dishes for a month, or lose your allowance?" The meanest form of this punishment tactic, in my opinion, is the open-ended choice: "Well, what do YOU think your punishment should be?" I had always had half a mind to say, "Nothing! Ha!"

In the very last story of Second Samuel we read about David; he has sinned again, and this time God gave him the chance to choose his own punishment. The prophet Gad came to David and said that the Lord was giving him three options: three years of famine, three months of fleeing under enemy pursuit, or three days of plague. Which one would you choose?

David didn't know what to pick—each one was horrible in its own way, and each one would bring about deaths of the people he was sworn to protect. So instead of choosing himself, he tells the prophet, "Let us fall into the hands of the Lord, for His mercy is great." And then, we are told, the Lord sent a plague on Israel. Many people were dying from the plague, so David asks to be punished for them. Instead, the prophet instructs David to build an altar and make a sacrifice. Then the plague will stop.

Mere verses before the end of the book, we see David asking to buy a threshing floor on which to build this altar, so that God will stop the plague. The man who owns it wants to give it to the king, but David refuses. He says he absolutely will not give God a sacrifice that cost him nothing at all.

Intrinsic to a sacrifice is the fact that it costs something. It is expensive in some way. Someone has to pay for it. Jesus had to pay for our sins. It cost Him dearly—it cost Him His life. But today we don't want to make big sacrifices of ourselves or of our time. We don't want sacrifice to be costly, but that's just what it is. So don't try to skimp on God. Don't try to offer Him things that cost you nothing—that is not a real offering. Instead, give Him what is valuable: your time, your devotion, your future.

—MH

Christmas With the Homeless

So give your servant a discerning heart to govern your people and to distinguish between right and wrong. For who is able to govern this great people of yours? 1 Kings 3:9.

I can remember the first Christmas I gave gifts to the homeless. Up until that point Christmas was all about me and how much loot was waiting for me under the tree. I could hardly keep my little hands off all the boxes and ribbons, and finally when Christmas morning came I dove into the pile like a rabid animal, squealing and squirming. But this year, in the midst of my crazed and self-absorbed moment of glory, we were suddenly bundled up and stuffed into the minivan. After driving for quite a while, we pulled in under a big neon sign that read "Come all you are who heavy-burdened," and saw a line of bedraggled, shaggy-looking people standing out in the icy winter air. As we got out of the car Mom handed me a box and said, "You need to choose someone to give this to." I remember rushing over to the first person I saw and handing him the gift. His eyes filled with tears, and he nodded as we ran back to the van. Learning what really matters in life is something that is a sign of both maturity and responsibility.

This is all the more reason I would've expected King Solomon to be a little more arrogant and self-absorbed. As we see him come on the scene he has had to have his father fight to get him on the throne, alienating his own brothers and others in the government. The Bible says that at the beginning of his rule God came to him in a dream and said, "I will give you whatever you ask for." You would expect him, as a brand-new king, to say something like "Give me all the money in the world" or "Destroy all those who are plotting against me." Instead, Solomon asked for an extra dose of wisdom so that he could be a fair and understanding ruler. Not even a new gold-covered chariot or the destruction of some oppressive nation. Just wisdom. God was so impressed with his request that He said, "Since you wanted wisdom, I will also give you all the other things you might have asked for."

When we're willing to look beyond ourselves, we get more than we could've asked for. When I got home from giving the gifts to those homeless guys, the presents under the tree meant quite a bit more. How lucky we were to have such blessings! Is this how you see the world around you? Or do you focus so much on your own life that you miss what's most important?

—GH

Cut the Baby in Half

Then the king said, "Bring me a sword." So they brought a sword for the king. He then gave an order: "Cut the living child in two and give half to one and half to the other." 1 Kings 3:24, 25.

Yes, it's true. King Solomon actually decided a dispute by ordering that a baby be cut in half. Two women lived in the same house together, and both gave birth three days apart. During the night one of the women apparently rolled over onto her baby and killed him. Seeing that he was dead, she got up and switched the babies. She exchanged her dead baby for her friend's living baby, then went back to sleep as though nothing had happened.

In the morning the other woman awoke to find the cold blue body of a dead baby beside her, but when she looked closer she recognized that this baby was not her son! An argument broke out between the two women, both claiming that the living baby was their own. So they came before King Solomon for a decision to be made. It is the first story recorded after Solomon asked God for wisdom—the first official test of his wisdom. Nobody knew yet that he had received special wisdom from God.

Because there was nobody else in the house, it was one woman's word against the other's, but Solomon had an idea. He ordered a sword to be brought to cut the baby in half, and ordered that each woman would receive half of the baby. At this the first woman cried, "Please, my lord, give her the living baby! Don't kill him!" But the second woman said, "Neither I nor you shall have him. Cut him in two!" (1 Kings 3:26). Immediately Solomon recognized the true mother. No mother would agree to have her own infant killed, cut in half in front of her eyes. At this Scripture tells us, "They held the king in awe, because they saw that he had wisdom from God to administer justice" (verse 28).

God gave Solomon wisdom for a reason: He wanted the king to use it! With such wisdom Solomon's kingdom prospered beyond his wildest dreams. It is the same with the gifts and the talents that God has given you. He wants you to use them, not let them go to waste. Have you been using the abilities God has gifted you with, or are you hiding them? Are you perhaps using them for yourself, or for bad purposes? Bring them back in line with God's will today, and endeavor to use all you have to honor Him.

—MH

The Man With 700 Wives

King Solomon, however, loved many foreign women. . . . They were from nations about which the Lord had told the Israelites, "You must not intermarry with them, because they will surely turn your hearts after their gods." Nevertheless, Solomon held fast to them in love. He had seven hundred wives of royal birth and three hundred concubines, and his wives led him astray." 1 Kings 11:1-3.

It came as a surprise to all three of us that we were dating the same guy. My roommate and another best friend of mine had sat down to talk one night, updating each other on the details of our love life, when we started to realize there were some similarities between our stories. It turned out that the same guy was going out with each of us secretly, and we had been so busy keeping a secret from everyone else that we didn't share it with each other and so he was getting away with it. We were furious beyond belief! You can imagine his surprise the next morning when he found out that dating three women at the same time had caught up with him!

If you think being with three girls at the same time is bad, consider King Solomon for a moment. He had 700 wives and 300 concubines. Ladies and gentlemen, that is 1,000 women! Some of you might think that doesn't sound like a half-bad problem, but before you let your mind go to ridiculous places, look at where it took him.

Solomon had made a promise to the Lord that he would keep His laws and walk in His ways, as his father, David, had done. And he did a very good job of that, until all those women came into his life. Women have a strange way of influencing a guy, don't they? The Bible tells us that as Solomon grew older, his wives slowly turned his own heart away from God, until he built places of worship and sacrifice for the gods of all his wives—including the gods that required child sacrifice. Never underestimate where turning away from God can take you.

Be careful whom you let yourself love—and that includes you guys, too. You think your girlfriends or boyfriends don't influence you? Take a look at Solomon. Slowly, over time, the people you love shape and form your character. The people you give your heart to receive the power to turn your heart. If you want your heart to stay true to God, then limit your romantic involvement to those who also love and serve the Lord.

—MH

Girl Wars I, II, III, . . . VIII

In the fifth year of King Rehoboam, Shishak king of Egypt attacked Jerusalem. He carried off the treasures of the temple of the Lord and the treasures of the royal palace. He took everything, including all the gold shields Solomon had made. 1 Kings 14:25, 26.

Ever heard of the Girl Wars? The "wars" took place so often that we had to go into multiples, just like World War I and II. During the Thanksgiving party or the annual trip to a park to see the Christmas tree lighting, or even just during a daily recess, one of the girls would hear that someone had been trash-talking about her. Then that girl would snoop around, rallying her friends, until her group was just as angry about the attack as were the first trash-talkers. Then the gossiper rallied her own troops—and the female fighting tactics came out in full force. Unlike guys, who usually just knock each other down and move on, the girls destroyed each other socially and emotionally. Gossip and lies shot around like missiles and bombs. Intricately folded paper notes flew like bullets between the girls, the angry, hateful words spreading like fire.

While all of this was going on, we guys pulled out the popcorn to watch the show. In fact, we soon found that the girls were so concerned with the battle that they were lax in other areas. So we started "collecting," intercepting their notes and reading them to the rest of the class, causing much hilarity and laughing at the girls' expense.

The sad story of how Israel broke into two separate kingdoms illustrates this foolishness perfectly. Jeroboam broke off from King Solomon's royal palace and started his own nation, taking 10 of the tribes with him, leaving only Judah and Benjamin in the hands of Solomon and his sons. When Solomon died, his son Rehoboam came to power and spent the next 15 years battling Jeroboam in the north. So intense and vicious was their fighting that the kingdoms became vulnerable to outside attack. The Egyptian pharaoh, Shishak, attacked Jerusalem and looted both the city and the exquisite Temple Solomon had built. Neither Judah or Israel had been ready for such an attack. As a result, they had left themselves wide open to the real enemy.

If you're too busy fighting each other, you forget to watch for the real enemy at your door. This can go for your personal life as much as for the life of a school, church, or family. Satan will take whatever opening he can get. Don't give him a chance.

—GH

Meals on Wheels, Paws, and Wings

You will drink from the brook, and I have ordered the ravens to feed you there.
1 Kings 17:4.

The pastor stood in the small cell, imprisoned under Stalin's rule because of his faith in God. The warden himself had escorted him there, slamming the door behind him. The warden's last words were a challenge: "You think there's a god? Then let your god feed you. You'll get nothing from us."

"My God will feed me," the prisoner had calmly replied. But now, in the darkness, he knelt by the bed and prayed for God to strengthen his faith. He awoke before dawn, stiff with cold, and tried to find sleep again. But soon he got up and paced the cell, trying to get warm. A sound by the high narrow window drew his attention, but he could see nothing. He sang and prayed as he paced, as much to keep up his courage as for warmth, and then curiosity drew him back to the window. Standing his bed on edge, using the slats as a ladder, he could just reach it. There was no covering, only closely spaced bars. And against a bar lay a thick slice of bread.

Oh, he was hungry. But as he held the bread and smelled it, it felt almost sacred, and he could not eat it. He decided to place it under his mattress to show the warden that his God had sent him bread. And so he spent the day in praise, singing, recalling biblical passages, and praying for his family and church members. About dusk he again heard a sound against the window. Excited, he tipped up the bed— and found another slice of bread. Again he drank in the aroma, but could not bring himself to eat it. He saved it, too, to show the warden.

This happened the next day, and the next. When the warden returned the fourth day, he was greeted by the pastor's joyful face. "My God has fed me!" he cried, lifting the mattress. "I saved the bread, so you could see the truth of it and believe."

Moments later a sound at the window drew their attention, and both men looked up to see a black cat with a slice of bread in its mouth. "That's my cat!" the warden bellowed. "My cat has been feeding you from my table!"

I don't know why we worry about the Lord providing for us. If He can feed people through cats and ravens, He can surely find a way to meet all of our needs, too. What are your needs and worries? The Lord can provide for them, in ways that you could never even guess.   —MH

Old Desert Pete

For this is what the Lord, the God of Israel, says: "The jar of flour will not be used up and the jug of oil will not run dry until the day the Lord gives rain on the land." 1 Kings 17:14.

One of my favorite Arizona desert legends is the story of Desert Pete, a hermit who mysteriously lived alone in the wild dry desert. One day a weary traveler was lost in the desert. Parched, dehydrated, and almost dead, he came upon a water pump standing on the dry, cracked ground. Water! At last! He grabbed the pump handle and pushed it up and down, but no water came. Then nearby he saw a jar of water with a note signed by Desert Pete. It said to pour the water into the pump to get it started. Then it would produce an unlimited supply of water. The man suddenly had a dilemma of trust—if this was a joke and Desert Pete was a myth, then after pouring out the water, he would die of thirst. If he drank the water, he'd live a while longer, but that small amount would not be enough to get him out of the desert alive. He decided to trust Desert Pete, so he poured the precious water into the dusty metal pump. Then grabbing the handle, he pumped as fast and as hard as he could. The pump sprang to life, and gallons of cool, clear water poured out, more than he could ever have imagined lying beneath the dry desert dust.

The story of Desert Pete reminds me of Elijah and the widow at Zarephath. The drought was so great that people were dying from lack of food and water. God sent Elijah to this woman for food, but she had only enough flour and oil to make one last meal for herself and her son. Then they would die. Elijah claimed to be from the Lord and promised that if she fed him first, her flour and oil would not run out until the drought was over. Like the desert traveler, she was faced with a trust dilemma, and she chose to trust. Then, no matter how much flour and oil she used, there was always more. Later her son died, but through Elijah God brought him back to life. The small meal the widow made for Elijah brought her much more than she could have guessed!

Deciding to serve God is still a trust dilemma. Will it be worth it? You'll have to turn your back on some of the "fun" and "exciting" things life has to offer. But think of it this way: what do you have to lose? When you serve God, you have everything to gain. When you choose another way, you end up with experiences you'll regret. It happened to King David. It happened to Solomon. Stick with God. He'll give you much, much more than you could ever have imagined.

—MH

Not Choosing *Is* a Choice

Elijah went before the people and said, "How long will you waver between two opinions? If the Lord is God, follow him; but if Baal is God, follow him." But the people said nothing. 1 Kings 18:21.

My wife can't make a decision between two conflicting choices to save her life. She'll literally sit for hours agonizing about two colors of the same sweater. It's gotten to the point that I can't waste my days shopping with her, so now I avoid the entire process. One of the worst times was painting our new house. We had never lived in a house that we were allowed to paint, so we went a little crazy. Who knew there were so many different shades and variations of yellow, blue, red, and green? I always thought colors had only one name—the ones I learned in kindergarten. But sometime later such names as burnt umber, Tuscan sun, and dozens of others were added to the basic colors brown and yellow. This, of course, was like kryptonite for my wife. With so many choices and color options she was frozen in a paroxysm of indecision. She'd take home 15 or 20 shades of each color on small cards, taping them to the walls and belaboring their slightest differences. I don't think my eyes were even capable of telling the difference between the ones she agonized over, but we spent mind-numbing hours debating the pluses and minuses of each one.

Elijah must have felt the way I did as he stood atop Mount Carmel, the entire nation of Israel surrounding him. He had called them together at a time that the worship of the foreign gods Baal and Ashtoreth was rampant among God's chosen people. However, they still claimed to worship Yahweh, the God of Abraham, too. So his question "How long will you waver between two opinions?" shows us that staying in the middle, wavering between two decisions, is never as good as simply choosing one or the other. In the book of Revelation Jesus says something similar about the church of Laodicea, that it is neither hot nor cold. And so, like lukewarm water, He spits it out.

Are there conflicting things in your life that you know aren't compatible but you haven't taken the necessary steps to choose between them? Pray for courage and God's guidance, and get rid of one or the other—otherwise, your lack of a decision will end up making itself for you.

—GH

The Sound Without Sound

Then a great and powerful wind tore the mountains apart and shattered the rocks before the Lord, but the Lord was not in the wind. After the wind there was an earthquake, but the Lord was not in the earthquake. After the earthquake came a fire, but the Lord was not in the fire. And after the fire came a gentle whisper. 1 Kings 19:11, 12.

Choosing which college I should go to was a terrible decision process for me—one of the biggest questions I faced my entire senior year. All my life I had planned to go to beautiful Pacific Union College, and I had a job, a room, and even a roommate waiting there. Then I visited Union College and fell in love with it. For days I agonized over the options. Where could I save more money? Where could I grow spiritually? Where did I want to live? On and on the battle raged, until a trusted friend told me simply to clear my mind of all the questions and listen for God's leading. This seemed impossible, but I tried. Every time the frantic thoughts rose up, I spoke out loud: "God, just make it clear." I can still see that couch in Barnes and Noble where I was sitting when I heard, felt, or was impressed by the first whisper: "Union College." Over the days and weeks it grew and grew into a strong, steadfast certainty, and I knew He'd led me to it.

What does God's voice actually sound like? Elijah knew. He had a huge success at Mount Carmel, where he challenged the prophets of Baal to a duel and they danced around their altar all day, but no fire came down from heaven. Elijah drenched his altar seven times, and it burned up completely, vindicating the Lord as the true God. Then when evil Jezebel threatened to kill him, Elijah ran for his life and ended up in a cave, where the Lord met him in a strange way. (See today's text.) There was a wind, an earthquake, and a fire, but God was not in any of them. Then there was a gentle whisper. Some languages have translated this as "a sound without sound." Many have called it the "still small voice." It was God. He told Elijah to get up and go home.

We often pray for things and wait to hear God's voice. One way to discover it is to remember ways He led you in the past, for He often speaks to you in similar ways. But when you are listening for the Lord, remember that He is not in the noise. If there is a lot of noise in your life and clutter in your mind, you may not be able to hear His quiet voice. Make it a point to clear some space and time that belong only to Him, and listen.

—MH

No Pain, No Gain

And a certain man of the sons of the prophets said unto his neighbour in the word of the Lord, Smite me, I pray thee. 1 Kings 20:35, KJV.

There is no doubt about it—this is a weird verse and an even weirder story. Apparently a prophet received instructions from God to have someone punch him in the face. The idea was to provide a disguise and an object lesson for a king who had not done what was right. With the bruised face, the prophet looked like a soldier and snuck into the king's army to confront him. But what's the lesson for us?

The second book I was asked to write carried a deadline of about two and a half months. That one, *What We Believe for Teens*, was an exposition of our church's theology. It's taken our church 150 years to come up with our statement of 28 beliefs, and I had only three months to describe and explain them. I felt God speaking to my heart that I needed to take on this task for Him, but quite frankly, getting punched in the face would have been easier.

To make matters worse, I was entering finals season of seminary (including Hebrew finals). In order to complete the task, I had to get up at abysmal hours (anything before 7:00 a.m.) and write. And I had to stay up all hours of the night to write. I interviewed seminary professors and scribbled detailed notes—then spent hours deciphering what I'd scribbled. I wrote while others had fun. I wrote while others slept. I wrote while other people enjoyed Thanksgiving and Christmas vacation. It was a ton of hard work—but I made the deadline.

But the project wasn't over, and neither was the stress. The edited version came for me to check, and its illustrations were for 6-year-olds! They had been put in for layout purposes, but hadn't been checked at the last minute. Just weeks before the book went to print, I frantically called and pointed this out. The publisher corrected the problem, and the book has sold thousands of copies. Praise God.

God has wonderful plans for each of us, but accomplishing them isn't always free of stress and pain—even Jesus had to die to accomplish the salvation of humanity. Even so, He can bring us through them and use us to do great things.

—SP

The Teacher's Pet

The king of Israel answered Jehoshaphat, "There is still one man through whom we can inquire of the Lord, but I hate him because he never prophesies anything good about me, but always bad. He is Micaiah son of Imlah." 1 Kings 22:8.

Nothing made me angrier than having to sit next to the teacher's pet. Every time this kid raised his hand you knew he was going to slobber out some ridiculous kiss-up phrase such as "Oh, Teacher, you make it so easy to understand!" or "Teacher, you're really the best teacher I've ever had!" I usually wanted to punch this kid before he even got out of his chair. Then one day I realized that whatever he was doing was working. We'd spent more than a month creating science fair projects. The presentations ran the gamut from "How to Make Maple Syrup" to "My Happy Ant Colony," and the teacher's pet had made what I thought was a pretty lame setup: "Volcanoes, and How They Erupt." H'mmm. They make lots of noise, and lava comes out. Pretty simple in my book. He'd set it up with illustrations pasted on a big piece of cardboard, but he misspelled "volcano," and some of the illustrations looked as if he'd drawn them with his kid sister's broken crayons. To top it off, he'd made a crazy little clay volcano that had baking soda and vinegar in it, which bubbled and fizzed. And the teacher just gushed and gushed about it, and gave him an A for his "amazingly creative presentation." And for what? Bubbles?

As unfair as it seemed to me, it was definitely not a new phenomenon. A story about a king in Israel tells that the king had hundreds of so-called prophets at his beck and call. Whenever he wanted to know if a battle would be successful, or if a business venture would succeed, he'd call these guys, and they'd give him glowing reports about his amazing prowess in battle or the heights of his genius in financial affairs. But when King Jehoshaphat from Judah came in to ally with him for a battle against the king of Aram he didn't want to hear from the kiss-up prophets. He wanted the real deal. When Jehoshaphat asked if there were any *real* prophets around, the king of Israel said, "Yeah, but he never has anything good to say about me."

Truth is, we don't always need verbal back rubs. Sometimes it's the people who are willing to tell us the bad things about us that we need to listen to the most. If we're always surrounding ourselves with people who think we're great, we'll never grow beyond their praise.

—GH

Playing the Comparison Game

When they had crossed, Elijah said to Elisha, "Tell me, what can I do for you before I am taken from you?" "Let me inherit a double portion of your spirit," Elisha replied. 2 Kings 2:9.

One of the scariest job offers I ever received was to take the place of a woman who had been excellent at her job. Because I knew what big shoes I had to fill, I was stressed and afraid. I worried that I'd never measure up. I doubted myself and constantly reviewed all my shortcomings. And I expected everyone to compare me to her and be disappointed. But when I finally started working, I had more success than I ever could have dreamed. I realized I didn't need to be the other woman—God had blessed me with talents and gifts too!

It must have been intimidating for Elisha to take Elijah's place. He probably felt very small as he watched his predecessor ride to heaven in a fiery chariot. He knew what big shoes he had to fill. I wonder if he felt stressed out or afraid of his new position. We don't know. All we know is the amazing things he did.

A town's water was bad, so he poured salt in it, and suddenly the entire water supply became useful. A bunch of prophets who were cooking a large stew accidentally put poisoned gourds in it, but Elisha added some flour, and it became edible. He told Captain Naaman to bathe in the Jordan, and sure enough, his deadly leprosy was cured. A student who borrowed an ax lost the metal axhead in deep water, and Elisha made it rise to the top. A widow who was about to lose her two sons to a creditor's slavery asked for help, and he had her collect as many empty jars as she could get. She began pouring oil from her near-empty oil jar into the jars, and soon every single jar was filled to the top. She was able to sell the oil, pay her debts, and keep her sons. Then there was his greatest miracle. A rich older woman who had provided a home for Elisha—building him a room and cooking for him—longed for a son, and one day she miraculously had one. But years later the boy died. She hurried to find Elisha. He came at once, and brought the boy back to life! Obviously Elisha's career as a prophet was just as blessed as, if not more blessed than, that of Elijah.

It's really easy to compare yourself to other people, especially good-looking, well-liked, successful ones. It's easy to doubt yourself, and to feel inadequate. Don't do it! God has blessed you with your own set of gifts and talents. Trust Him to use your life for His honor and glory.

—MH

The Invisible Basketball Game

From there Elisha went up to Bethel. As he was walking along the road, some youths came out of the town and jeered at him. "Go on up, you baldhead!" they said. "Go on up, you baldhead!" He turned around, looked at them and called down a curse on them in the name of the Lord. Then two bears came out of the woods and mauled forty-two of the youths. 2 Kings 2:23, 24.

Eighth-grade year . . . the year of crazy people. For whatever reason, my class of fairly reasonable, courteous seventh graders came back from summer break as wild, uncontrollable eighth-grade wackos. And it was the substitute teachers that got the worst of us. One morning as we walked in, we saw a younger substitute standing at the front of the room. She was writing on the chalkboard "My name is Esther" as a quick visual cue that we could call her Miss Esther. She turned around and began flipping through a stack of papers, and someone walking by added "the Molester" to the end of her sentence. The teacher sheepishly tried to play it off—"Ha, ha, guys. Nice one." Then we pulled out the "invisible basketball game," as we liked to call it. One of the guys who always brought a basketball would wait until the teacher turned. Then they'd chuck the ball across the room to someone who hopefully caught it as soundlessly as possible and got it out of sight. But this day an errant throw nailed the ceiling fan and almost brought the whole thing crashing to the floor. As everyone in the class cringed, we saw the sub turn slowly around. She looked up at the mangled fan, broke down crying, and rushed from the room.

Rarely is respect simply given. It's always earned, and if you don't get it at the beginning, sometimes you never will. Elisha was returning home after witnessing Elijah whisked out of sight in a fiery chariot. (Think about *that* for a moment.) He came upon a mob of young men who jeered, "Go on up like Elijah, old baldy," showing disrespect for God as well as him. Elisha yelled a curse at them, and a pair of bears came flying out the woods and mauled 42 of the young men. Their lack of respect for the new man God appointed to be His mouthpiece to the nation was shocking, but after this incident no one dared confront Elisha again. It was painful. It was violent. But was it necessary? This tells me that God takes seriously disrespect toward people who work for Him. We need to respect those whom God has put in positions of authority, because really any disrespect we show them is actually aimed at God Himself.

—GH

"Engrish" Saves the Day!

Now bands from Aram had gone out and had taken captive a young girl from Israel, and she served Naaman's wife. She said to her mistress, "If only my master would see the prophet who is in Samaria! He would cure him of his leprosy." 2 Kings 5:2, 3.

I can't think of a time I underestimated anyone more than I did the day a Korean student saved my hide in class. It was one of those days everything was going along great. But as I slid into my desk and began to look around, I become a little puzzled. Everyone had their noses in books, which seemed odd. No banter, no preclass rowdiness. And then it dawned on me. I nearly grabbed the collar of the guy next to me and screamed in his face, "Is the midterm test today?" I hadn't studied a millisecond for it, and when the teacher told us to get into groups (it was going to be a group test), I didn't feel much better. My group consisted of one guy who slept through class, a Korean student who could hardly speak English, and another guy like me who may or may not have actually studied. But as we worked through each question, the Korean student said, "Let see me, please." Then he'd take the paper, scribble down an answer, and slide it back to us. "I don't know what say that, but it's the answer." He had gone through the notes and memorized the shapes and letters of the words so that he could recognize the questions and write the answers! We passed this test with an A, and all because a Korean student who couldn't speak much English had spent hours and hours memorizing the material. Sometimes it's the people you wouldn't suspect who can help you the most.

Have you noticed that Naaman's skin was literally saved because of a young servant girl? And when you read "servant," think "slave." She was a Hebrew who had been kidnapped and hauled away from her home a few years before by Naaman and his soldiers, for he was the commander of the army of Aram. The last person you'd expect to help him would be this girl, but here we see that she had compassion and pity on her captor, and told his wife that if only he could see the prophet back in her homeland he would be cured.

Never feel that anyone is insignificant. You can't know how God will use them for His purposes. And that goes for you, too. No matter what your skills or failings, keep an open mind. Be willing to expect the unexpected. God may have something in mind just for you.

—GH

Healthy Habits

Elisha sent a messenger to say to him, "Go, wash yourself seven times in the Jordan, and your flesh will be restored and you will be cleansed." But Naaman went away angry and said, "I thought that he would surely come out to me and stand and call on the name of the Lord his God, wave his hand over the spot and cure me of my leprosy." 2 Kings 5:10, 11.

Recently the youth group at my church decided to play a game of flag football. In addition to several youthful participants, those of us in our young adult years—lamenting the loss of the days when we played neighborhood games— also jumped at the chance to participate. While everyone played their best, I, as the quarterback, delivered an impressive performance in my Vikings thermal T-shirt, leaving a lasting impression in the minds of all involved.

However, one ambitious member of the other team had the audacity to rush me. *Me! An ordained minister!* I leaped into action and ran 60 yards for a touchdown before they even knew what had happened. The youth tried again. And again I scored. And again, and again.

Coupled with two spectacular touchdown passes by yours truly, my team won, and the other team was left bamboozled as to what went wrong. However, their pain soon became mine.

The next morning—actually, the next week—proved a devastating testimony to how out of shape I was. My performance on Sunday revealed the next day that I may have the moves of a cheetah, but I have the muscle of a beached jellyfish. The soreness that plagued me, and the repeated references by my wife to "grandpa," have inspired me to start working out again. But it isn't going to be easy. To get the results I want is going to take time, effort, and habit—no magic pills or formulas will make it happen.

Naaman wanted to be healed by having the prophet say some special words or making a special gesture. Instead he had to dip down seven times in a dirty river in order to be healed. You and I may struggle with health, bad grades, and any number of things. And while God can give us instant victory, most often He gives us victory though our being willing to do hard work and cultivate good habits. He is there to give us strength and encouragement while we do it. So don't be discouraged if you don't excel immediately. Dedicate yourself to God and keep trying.

—SP

That Which Lies Behind

And Elisha prayed, "O Lord, open his eyes so he may see." Then the Lord opened the servant's eyes, and he looked and saw the hills full of horses and chariots of fire all around Elisha. 2 Kings 6:17.

I had stars in my eyes this final evening of my senior year. It was my job to introduce the guest speaker, a popular school coach everyone loved. I determined not to do a usual introduction; I wanted to say something witty, do something impressive. So I worked hard all week. To me the final product seemed almost Shakespearean in its quality—the jokes were punchy; the one-liners had depth. It was going to be a speech worth remembering forever!

The whole crowd felt electric with excitement when I ascended the platform. As I dove into my prepared lines they seemed to be leaning forward, listening to my every word. Then as I started to wrap it up, I saw the audience stand to their feet and break into spontaneous applause! Overcome with the moment, I stepped back from the podium smiling and raising one hand in acknowledgment. I even began to take a bow. It was then that I felt a hand on my shoulder. It was the coach. He had come up from behind a little earlier than expected, and it was for him that the applause had begun. Not for me.

Sometimes we forget that there's a force behind us greater than ourselves. Elisha's servant found this out in a dramatic way. The city in Samaria in which Elisha was staying was surrounded by an enemy army intent on capturing him. His servant rushed to the city walls and saw hundreds of chariots, archers, and soldiers surrounding them on every side. "What are we to do now?" he cried. His response seems fairly reasonable, considering the circumstances, but strangely enough Elisha told him, "Those who are with us are more than those who are with them" (2 Kings 6:16). And at this Elisha prayed for his servant's eyes to be opened. They were, and he saw a heavenly army surrounding the human one outside the city walls. These angelic warriors were standing in flaming chariots of fire, and by sheer numbers and power they dwarfed the rest.

No matter what things may seem like in life, we too have at our disposal an army of warriors, if only we ask for God's protection. Remember this, and take heart, when the world seems to threaten—and when it applauds.

—GH

The Dumbest Fight We Ever Had

The Lord removed them from his presence, as he had warned through all his servants the prophets. So the people of Israel were taken from their homeland into exile in Assyria, and they are still there. 2 Kings 17:23.

All day we had been crabby with each other, but things finally blew up over a stupid $12 painting of the Eiffel Tower. We had been traveling through Europe for more than three weeks, and the joys of living out of a backpack and missing trains, showers, and sleep had begun to catch up with us. But it was that stupid painting that did it. From a vendor's cart overlooking the Seine, Greg had made a hideous choice of paint slopped on canvas, and I hated it. We argued and yelled, and while he stomped off to return it, I went into the Notre Dame Cathedral without him. Down the aisles I stomped, mad as a hen under the blue stained-glass light, brooding and stewing about our fight. He came in and did the same. There I was in Paris, and I missed out on Notre Dame—one of the most beautiful cathedrals in the world—because I was so busy focusing on stupid things.

The people of Israel did essentially the same thing. They were not in Paris, of course. Rather, they had the chance to live in the very presence of God Himself. Instead of enjoying that, they got sidetracked. They followed the gods and wicked practices of the nations around them. Ahaz, king of Judah, sacrificed his own son in the fire to other gods. Hoshea, the last king of Israel, set up high places for pagan worship, Asherah poles for sexual orgies, and worshipped idols, as had so many kings before him. And their faithful old God—He sent prophet after prophet and miracle after miracle to bring them back. He chased them and pursued them, but still they left Him time and time again until finally, we are told, God removed them from His presence. The king of Assyria attacked and laid siege to Samaria for three years, then finally conquered the city and marched all its people to Assyria. These foolish people had one of the most beautiful chances of all time—to live in a God-protected society forever. But they were too busy focusing on other stupid things, and they missed out. They ruined it for themselves.

It's a sad story, but before you judge them, look at yourself. Are you missing out on the best life has to offer—salvation and a walk with God—because you're busy being sidetracked by stupid things? I like the way a popular bumper sticker puts it: Don't miss heaven for the world!

—MH

Ramona the Bus Driver

They worshiped the Lord, but they also served their own gods in accordance with the customs of the nations from which they had been brought. 2 Kings 17:33.

I had the meanest bus driver on the face of this earth. She stopped at our school to pick up four of us. It was a major detour in her route, and the way things were scheduled, she had to wait 30 minutes every day before we even got out of class to get on her bus. Needless to say, she hated the whole situation, and us, too. She was always in a sour mood, and used to scare us to death with her crazy driving. No matter how tightly you held on to the seat in front of you when she hit speed bumps and hills going 50 miles per hour, it always sent one or more of the unlucky souls in the rear of the bus flying through the air and careening into the roof or another passenger. And I am positive that those were the only times I ever saw Ramona smile.

Then one day I decided I was going to be fake nice to her, just to try to make her feel bad for being so mean to us. For several days I went out of my way to say hi. I thanked her for the ride and in general tried to ingratiate myself to her. And surprisingly, it started making a difference! I was so excited that my plan was working that I let a friend in on the ruse, gloating over how Ramona had swallowed my "niceness" hook, line, and sinker. We were both laughing, when suddenly Ramona's head reared up over one of the nearby seats. She'd been cleaning away some gum, and had heard my every word. Glaring at me, she stalked back to the front of the bus, and ever after seemed twice as angry as before. (Can you blame her?)

Insincerity can sometimes mask the reality, but it will never change the state of things inside of us. The Bible tells that after the nation of Israel had been conquered and its people deported to Assyria, the king of Assyria filled Israel's land with foreigners from the surrounding nations. These foreigners brought their own gods with them to worship, but also tried to appease the God of the Israelites by offering sacrifices to Him as well. But they didn't stop worshipping their own gods, so any benefit or blessings that God had promised never materialized. Even though their outward actions of worship said one thing, their hearts had never come to God. To God outward appearances will never mask the true nature of our hearts. What does your heart look like these days?

—GH

Let's All Ditch Spanish Class

He held fast to the Lord and did not cease to follow him; he kept the commands the Lord had given Moses. And the Lord was with him; he was successful in whatever he undertook. 2 Kings 18:6, 7.

One year on my birthday I talked my entire Spanish class into ditching that afternoon as a birthday present to me because I was mad at the teacher. I don't think everybody wanted to do it, but there was a lot of peer pressure going on—if only half of us ditched and the other half showed up, they'd be traitors and make us look like the bad kids. We all had to do it together. Somehow I put enough pressure on everyone to agree, and we left the teacher standing up front speaking to the walls that day. It was a hit on campus—the event was celebrated by everyone who found out about it, and oh, how smug we were, until we had to show our faces in class after the blatant defiance. We all almost lost out on a whole semester of Spanish credit. I'll never forget the teacher's opening line: "Do it again, and I'll drop you all!"

When Hezekiah became king of Judah at age 25, he faced a lot of peer pressure. The nation of Israel had split in two. Israel had been carried off to Assyria, and the people of Judah who were still left wanted to worship idols. King Hezekiah followed a long line of kings who had encouraged idol worship, and there was a lot of pressure on him to continue the evil practices of the nations around them. It would have been easy for Hezekiah to give in, but he chose differently. He decided to do what was right. He trusted in the Lord, "held fast" to Him, and followed *all* of His commands. Because of this, he was successful, and the Lord blessed everything he undertook. Imagine—every single thing!

Can this formula still work today? If we trust in the Lord, hold fast to Him, and follow every one of His commands, will we also be successful in everything we do? Was that blessing just for the kings of Israel back in the day, or is it for us as well? God doesn't promise to give us everything we want, but He does guarantee that following His commands is a better way of living. Think about each one—they lead to a more successful life! So I suggest that this year you put God's old success formula to the test in your life. Trust Him, hold fast to Him, and follow His commands to the best of your ability. See if you don't have more success than ever before.

—MH

Facing Death and Jellyfish

I have heard your prayer and seen your tears; I will heal you. 2 Kings 20:5.

On the fourth day of our honeymoon I thought I was going to watch my husband die. We had been snorkeling at sunset in Tahiti, and I was quietly enjoying a serene coral reef when Greg started screaming and bellowing through the tube of his snorkel. By the time I got a good look at him, he was flailing in the water like a madman—throwing off fins and mask, beating his arm wildly and frantically. And then I saw them: tiny blue tentacles burning into his flesh like embers from a fire. He had been stung by a Portuguese man-of-war.

We swam to shore in a panic and got him into the hotel lobby to call for a doctor. As I tried to pantomime "jellyfish" to the receptionist, who spoke only French, Greg began shaking. Then his body went into spasms, convulsing uncontrollably again and again and again. He said that he felt the poison traveling up his arm and into his chest, and then, he said, he felt his heart hurting terribly. I had never been so scared in my life. I was afraid that the poison would stop his heart and that I was watching his last moments. What I remember vividly as he thrashed on the floor is that we both didn't say much. What do you say when you are possibly facing death?

King Hezekiah knew exactly what to say when faced with his own death. God sent the prophet Isaiah to tell him to put his house in order because he was going to die. Immediately Hezekiah turned his face to the wall and cried to the Lord. "Remember, O Lord, how I have walked before you faithfully and with wholehearted devotion!" he said, weeping bitterly (2 Kings 20:3). And before Isaiah had even gotten out the palace door, God sent him back to give a new message: Hezekiah would live 15 years longer. A fig poultice was put on his boil. God turned the sun shadow backwards to guarantee the miracle, and he lived. (Thankfully, Greg lived too, of course, after a doctor gave him two injections that stopped the convulsions.)

So many people throughout history have asked God for healing or for longer life. Sometimes He says yes, and sometimes He doesn't. I can't tell you how or why God makes those choices. All we know is that God is able to heal, that He hears us (see above), and that He is faithful to His people, even if His faithfulness looks differently than we might want. Ask God to teach you to trust Him—both when He does as you wish, and when He doesn't.

—MH

Matthew Suggests Betty Lou Lane

Neither before nor after Josiah was there a king like him who turned to the Lord as he did—with all his heart and with all his soul and with all his strength. 2 Kings 23:25.

My mom has the worst sense of direction of anybody I've ever met in my entire life. She cannot read a map to save her life. She gets lost in the same town she's lived in for 20 years. A simple detour sign can send her into fits of panic, and any type of extended road construction can shut her down completely, leaving her on the side of the road hyperventilating. I was just a little kid when I first realized this paralysis. She was driving my friend Matthew home from kindergarten, and as we approached his neighborhood we came upon entire streets coned off for construction, one street after another. Mom was about to mentally collapse when Matthew pointed out a narrow, dusty, shabby old alley called Betty Lou Lane. He explained that sometimes his dad took this winding little alleyway home instead of using the main roads. Lost and terrified, Mom had no other choice than to trust a 5-year-old child for directions. And the alley led us straight through the construction maze, right to his street.

It's not always a bad idea to trust a child. King Josiah was only 8 years old when he became king in Jerusalem, but he made one of the most important discoveries of his time. He had ordered the Temple to be repaired, and in the process one of the priests found a strange book, a book of the Law. When it was read to Josiah, he actually tore his clothes, because he realized his people hadn't been following the commands of God as they had promised to do years before. They'd been away from God so long that they didn't even know His laws anymore! So Josiah got all the leaders together, read the law to them, and they renewed the promise their ancestors had made to God to keep His ways. Then Josiah had every altar and shrine to other gods torn down, and got rid of all the mediums, spiritists, and idols in the land. We're told that never before was there a king like him who turned to the Lord "with all his heart, soul, and strength."

You are never too young to know the right way. And you are never too young to lead others in the right way either. If there are some people in your life who are headed for disaster, ask the Lord for an opportunity to help set them on a better path. You are never too young or too old to turn to the Lord with all your heart and soul and strength.

—MH

Who's in the Driver's Seat?

Jabez was more honorable than his brothers. . . . Jabez cried out to the God of Israel, "Oh, that you would bless me and enlarge my territory! Let your hand be with me, and keep me from harm so that I will be free from pain." And God granted his request. 1 Chronicles 4:9, 10.

Don't we always want to be the one in the driver's seat? I couldn't wait till my parents stopped ferrying me around and handed over the keys to the car, and when the day finally arrived, it was such a sense of freedom. I could go anywhere and do anything! Nothing was going to stop me anymore (well, until the first speeding ticket, but that doesn't count). The sense of mobile independence was one of the best moments of my teenage years.

Jabez, a man mentioned briefly in 1 Chronicles, probably felt a little bit the same, though he didn't let it go to his head. The first sentence of the story says, "Jabez was more honorable than his brothers." Then Jabez prays for an expansion of his territory, through peaceful means. The first question I had was If this is about getting more land, why this talk about Jabez being more honorable? This was answered soon, in the next section of stories in chapters 4 and 5. Here it talks about people from the other tribes expanding their borders and taking territory through warfare and force. Even though God Himself had said they could do this, it wasn't His original plan. Originally God had told the Israelites that *He* would go before them, driving the nations out with hornets. But the Israelites wanted to get in the driver's seat, so they pushed out the tribes by force. In light of this scenario the sentence above makes more sense. Jabez asked God for more land, and he didn't feel the need to use force to get it. Jabez was "more honorable" because He was willing to let God use His original plan rather than one of his own, even though he technically was allowed to do it just as his brothers around him had done.

And we're still faced with a similar choice in our own lives today. Do we take over the controls and run our life the way we want to, or do we let God guide and direct us? He's given us free will, and allows us to drive if we choose, but He also says that He has a better way. If every day when you woke up you consciously said, "Today, God, whatever happens, I want You to be in control. Show me where I should go, whom I should talk with, and what I should do," how different might your life be?

—GH

He-Man and She-Ra Grow Up

All Israel was listed in the genealogies recorded in the book of the kings of Israel. The people of Judah were taken captive to Babylon because of their unfaithfulness.
1 Chronicles 9:1.

There was a time, circa kindergarten, when I thought I was She-Ra the warrior princess. My best friend, Matthew, was He-Man, her twin brother, and together, plastic golden swords in hand, we tried to conquer the evil worlds of the playground and the backyard. We dubbed Matthew's little brother Skeletor, and since we were always able to capture and overcome him, we believed this was proof of the courage and power of He-Man and She-Ra residing within us. Well, we got older, and life got harder, and I learned there was in fact a whole lot I couldn't do. I struggled with school, friends, family, and myself. I forgot about He-Man and She-Ra until one night when I was a high school freshman. Depressed and discouraged, I came upon my old She-Ra sword, bent and cracked, the golden plastic looking a little worse for wear. The whole game seemed silly now—for now I didn't have any courage or power at all. Back then, when I was so young, I'd thought I was somebody special, but now I didn't even know who I was.

When the exiles returned to Israel after their Babylonian captivity, they felt the same way. They used to think they were someone special—God's chosen people, the apple of His eye, more powerful and courageous than any other nation around them. But time had passed, and life had gotten hard. They were taken to Babylon as slaves and captives, and when they returned they needed to know a few things: Was God still interested in them? Did the old covenants still matter? Did His promises to David still have meaning? That's why the Chronicles were written—to remind them that they were still God's chosen people. By remembering their past and all that God had done for them and their ancestors, and by reviewing God's promises, they found hope that He still had a plan for their lives.

What about you? Have you been feeling as if you don't know who you are anymore? Perhaps you used to know you were someone special, but now life is harder and everything seems unclear. If you're questioning life's meaning today, do what the exiles did: take some time and revisit God's faithfulness and what He has done for you in the past. You can also review His promises to you in the Scriptures. Be reminded that He still has a plan for your life.

—MH

David's Mighty Men

*And David became more and more powerful, because the Lord Almighty was with him.
1 Chronicles 11:9.*

I remember them as the Mailbox Men. They were a group of my students—all boys—who made it their secret mission to go through the neighborhoods and destroy mailboxes. It began "innocently"—throwing large rocks, bricks, or pumpkins to knock down the boxes. Sometimes they kicked them down. I believe a potato gun was put to use a time or two. But then the sabotage evolved into bombings. They put firecrackers inside the mailboxes and actually exploded them, sending fiery pieces of personal letters, bills, and advertising parachuting in all directions. (This is not only mean, it's illegal and subject to high fines, so don't even think of it.) Though we knew this was going on, the Mailbox Men were never caught. It's still a mystery to me how they were so successful time and time again.

The Mailbox Men of David's day were called "David's mighty men," but unlike the Mailbox Men, they were nothing short of true valiant war heroes. They are listed both in 1 Kings and 1 Chronicles, and they did some amazing stuff in the height of Israel's glory days. In one single encounter Jashobeam killed 300 men with only a spear, and later Abishai did the same. The famous trio—"the Three," as the Bible calls them—once broke through heavy enemy lines to raid a well and bring water back for the king. A man named Benaiah went into a pit on a snowy day and killed a lion. With only a club as his weapon, he also killed a spear-wielding Egyptian who was seven and a half feet tall.

It seems there was nothing David and his infamous mighty men could not do. What was their secret? I found it tucked in among the stories, and it is written above: David was powerful because the Lord Almighty was with him.

Are there areas in your life that need some real power? Are there battles you need to fight and win? You may not have mighty men fighting on your side; in fact, you may be fighting all alone. But David's battle secret will still work for you. Ask the Lord to be with you! Invite His presence into your life, invite His company along your way, and choose to serve Him to the best of your ability. When you walk with God, powerful, good things will happen in your life.

—MH

The Bedouins Have My Underwear

King David dedicated these articles to the Lord, as he had done with the silver and gold he had taken from all these nations. . . . The Lord gave David victory everywhere he went. 1 Chronicles 18:11-13.

I accidentally descended Mount Sinai without my underwear. When my husband and I visited Egypt a few years ago, a crowning moment of our trip was climbing to the top of Mount Sinai to watch the sunrise. In order to make it to the summit in time, however, we had to begin hiking in the deep dark middle of the night, and of course the air was freezing. I set out in layers upon layers of clothes, but the longer we hiked and the steeper we climbed, the hotter I got. I started peeling off the layers, one by one, and pretty soon I was carrying an armful of jackets, shirts, and long underwear.

When we reached the top, I set down my clothes and became preoccupied with collecting giant pocketfuls of rocks "from the top of Sinai" to take home as gifts for people. My hands were so full of rocks that I forgot to pick up my clothes. The clothes are still up there somewhere—I hope some Bedouin is enjoying that expensive RCI long underwear, because I still miss it. I don't, however, know where any of those rocks are today. I made a bad choice up there. I clung to the wrong thing when I should have remembered what was more important.

King David didn't make this same mistake. He could have clung to the piles of silver and gold he had acquired from every town he conquered, and it would have been easy to do so. Who doesn't want to hang on to silver and gold! But he knew what was most important. He dedicated it all to God—not just 10 percent, but every last bit of it. It was really as though he just gave it back, because God had made it possible for him to get it in the first place. And the result? God gave David victory every single place he went. It was as if David could not fail.

I wonder what it is that you're clinging to today. Is it the right thing, the most important thing? Or is it as worthless as were my rocks? Could it be time to let go of some of the things you're clinging to, and grab on to the things that matter more instead? The most important thing you can cling to is your relationship with Jesus. Don't let go of that for anything else on earth.

—MH

War Heroes Now and Then

Be strong and let us fight bravely for our people and the cities of our God. The Lord will do what is good in his sight. 1 Chronicles 19:13.

Desmond Doss is one of my favorite war heroes. A Seventh-day Adventist, he served as a medic during World War II. Because he refused to carry a weapon or to work on the Sabbath, he was shamed and ridiculed by everybody around him. Soldiers treated him terribly, but he stood firm. One fateful day the Americans invaded Okinawa, and the Japanese were waiting for them. The only possible access was up the side of a steep cliff, and the Japanese stood at the top and fired down, killing hundreds. But when others turned and ran out, Desmond ran in. Under heavy fire he returned repeatedly to the cliff to rescue wounded soldiers—some of them the very men that had treated him so badly. At the risk of his own life he lowered them down the cliff with ropes, saving the lives of more than 75 men, though he almost lost his in the process. Not only was he fearless—he entrusted his life to the Lord. Whether he lived or died was in God's hands. He simply continued to do what was right in his heart, no matter the personal cost. He knew that God would take care of him if He saw fit, and sure enough, Doss lived to be an old man.

When the Chronicles retell the stories of David's battles for the exiles to remember, Joab stands out from the crowd the same way Doss did thousands of years later. Joab was the commander in chief of David's army, the rank that David offered to the first man who would lead the attack on the Jebusites in Jerusalem. Chronicles is a war buff's dream, filled with war and battle stories, and Joab appears in most of them. He is always leading the Israelites to win another battle. He wasn't perfect, and not every decision he made was right, but I like what he said during the battle against the Ammonites. He wasn't sure if they could win, but he made this statement of faith: The Lord will do what is good in His sight. Like Doss, he was determined to go into battle, and he left his life in the hands of the Lord. That day he more than won the fight.

Do you trust that God will do what is good in His sight now? Would you entrust your life to God for the sake of doing what's right? You may not be on a battlefield, but don't forget that a fight exists each and every moment for your soul. You are part of a supernatural war called the great controversy, in which the strength of the warriors lies only in their trust in Jesus.

—GH and MH

Twenty-three Blankets

But who am I, and who are my people, that we should be able to give as generously as this? Everything comes from you, and we have given you only what comes from your hand. 1 Chronicles 29:14.

A few weeks after our first wedding anniversary, my husband and I lost everything we owned in the dorm fire at Auburn Academy where I was the Taskforce girls' dean. Can you imagine owning nothing in the world except what you are wearing right now? I'll never forget waking up the morning after the fire and feeling totally helpless—no toothbrush, no comb, no change of clothes, no makeup, no bags to take to the hotel where we'd gone to spend the night.

But it wasn't that way for long. Within days, donations started coming in from all over the country. Almost every Adventist college and academy sent gifts. One woman volunteered to take me shopping for an entire new wardrobe. Another Christian couple, whom I still have never met, sent us a check for $1,000. A retired pastor gave my husband half of his library. People sent blankets, socks, slippers, toiletries, and more. The donations kept coming and coming, until finally we had to start turning them away. There were just too many. Today I have about 16 sets of towels and 23 blankets in my linen closet—all donated by people I still remember.

This is what it was like when the people of Israel brought gifts for building the great Temple in Jerusalem. They brought everything they had—gold, silver, bronze, iron, and any valuable stone they owned. And they gave happily, wholeheartedly. Chronicles records this event because the exiles were now looking at rebuilding the old Temple—a daunting task, to be sure. How would they ever acquire all the riches of the past? But an important reminder is slipped into the story, which I believe was written just for those who worried about such things. It is written above, and basically says this: everything the people donated came from God in the first place. They gave only what He had first given them.

I bet this gave the exiles a little boost of faith—knowing that God would and could provide anything they needed, and that all riches and wealth come straight from Him in the first place. It's a good reminder for us, too. Everything you have came from God in the first place. And everything else you need, God is more than able to provide for you.

—MH

I Dumped Him . . . Four Times? Maybe Five?

Solomon son of David established himself firmly over his kingdom, for the Lord his God was with him and made him exceedingly great. 2 Chronicles 1:1.

At first you would think ours was the perfect love story—two young kids who met on the first day of class, dated all the way through college, wrote love letters daily when they were separated by an ocean, married in the fall of their senior year, traveled the world together, and then finally settled down to have a little family. That is the bare-bones skeleton story of our marriage—the one Greg and I like for people to know. But unfortunately there's more. . . .

During the four years we dated I actually broke up with him more times than either of us can remember. I left him twice for two other guys. He kissed one of my best friends behind my back. He stopped speaking to me for an entire summer. He bought my engagement gift, then held on to it for months because I wasn't sure I wanted to marry him. After we were married, there were days we both wondered if we'd made a mistake, if we'd married the wrong person. All of that seems like a long time ago now, because we've been so happy together these seven years, but it's all really part of our story. It's ugly, but it really happened. And we usually leave it out.

I think the author of 2 Chronicles must have felt the same way Greg and I do, because when I read through it, I noticed a lot of ugly details from the original stories that had been left out. Second Chronicles was originally part of 1 Chronicles, and remember—all this was written after the exiles had returned from Babylon, to remind them of their history and rich heritage: Israel's glory days of David, Solomon, and others. Evidently the author thought the people would take more pride in their forebears if some of the bad details weren't included.

But when I look back on my own story, I think it's the bad things that make our love seem more real. We came through all that mess, and we are still in love with each other today. And it can be the same with you and your walk with Jesus. The bad details don't mean your relationship with Him is lousy or your love for Him is fake. Sometimes the fact that bad things happened, but you kept on going, makes the story a whole lot better. So if you want to keep your relationship with God real, persevere with Him through good times, and especially the bad.

—MH

The Treasure of Random Details

Then Solomon began to build the temple of the Lord in Jerusalem on Mount Moriah, where the Lord had appeared to his father David. It was on the threshing floor of Araunah the Jebusite, the place provided by David. 2 Chronicles 3:1.

A professor of mine once told me that the Old Testament has a funny quirk about it. It never gives you the details you think it should. He said that during the big exciting things, such as a battle, it glosses over details and simply says, "David fought them from dusk until the evening of the next day" (1 Samuel 30:17). But in other, unexpected places it turns on the critical eye: "So she quickly emptied her jar into the trough, ran back to the well to draw more water, and drew enough for all his camels" (Genesis 24:20). Bible writers find importance in places we may not see—the real meat of the story may be hiding in the details, if you know where to look.

Here is a great example: the story of Solomon building the new Temple in Jerusalem. It began with some details that don't seem to matter much at all: Solomon built the Temple on Mount Moriah, on the threshing floor of Araunah the Jebusite. Now, if you were too excited to read on about all the gold and silver or marble that was used in the Temple, you might miss something in those details. But instead, stop to think a minute. Where have we heard of those places before?

The threshing floor of Araunah the Jebusite on Mount Moriah was part of one of the last stories recorded about King David. This is the place he made a sacrifice to the Lord to stop the plague on his land, brought on by his own mistake against God. But that's not the only sacrifice that was ever made there, was it? Hundreds and hundreds of years earlier a man fully dedicated to God prepared to sacrifice his only son, Isaac, on this very mountain. God had told him to do it. (You may remember the story from Genesis.) Just as Abraham was about to plunge the knife into Isaac, the Lord stopped him, commending him on his faithfulness, and providing a ram for the sacrifice. This is one of the earliest symbolic events that point toward the death of Jesus on the cross for our sins. This mountain is on which God chose to have Solomon build His Temple.

What's the point of all this? That God is in the details, and that hundreds of years before we may see the significance of them, God sets plans into place. Realize that this same God who orchestrated everything so perfectly back then is still the God behind the scenes of your life now.

— GH

A Formula for Prayer?

If my people, who are called by my name, will humble themselves and pray and seek my face and turn from their wicked ways, then will I hear from heaven and will forgive their sin and will heal their land. 2 Chronicles 7:14.

The first time I realized that God actually answered our prayers came about over a lost pet rat in our backyard fort. She had escaped into a giant ivy patch, and everyone said I'd never see her again. But when I asked Jesus to send her back, no sooner had I opened my eyes than she came walking right out of the ivy and into my hands. I was also wowed by the power of prayer when I was in high school. A close friend of mine was in some real personal trouble. I stayed up for hours into the night, praying for him. The very next day he came to find me and asked if I would pray for him, because he wanted to turn his life back to the Lord. I was amazed! Just recently a friend of mine in another country got involved in a cult type of situation. A group of us met every night to pray for her deliverance. It was only after she was on a plane for home that we discovered she had made the decision to leave one certain night at the very moment we were gathered in prayer for her. Prayer has truly worked in my life!

There are many more stories I could tell about prayer—some as silly as a pet rat, and others as serious as life or death—and I'm sure you have some stories of your own as well. Unfortunately, I bet you also have some stories of times your prayers did not get answered the way you wanted. I have those stories, too. I don't like to tell those as much as the others. Did God ever say anything in the Old Testament about how we should pray if we want Him to listen?

When Solomon dedicated the brand-new Temple he built to the Lord, God actually appeared to him at night and talked about prayer. You can read God's outline above, but here are the basics of what people are to do: humble themselves, seek God's face, and turn from their wicked ways. God promises that He then will do three things: hear, forgive sin, and heal the land. think it's wise to still use the formula today.

Who and what are you praying for in your life? Do you need to see the power of prayer at work in the world right now? Humble yourself before God and seek His face. And remember that God wants to do more than just give you an answer—He also wants to forgive and heal.

—MH

My Stinky, Embarrassing, Annoying Family

They will, however, become subject to him, so that they may learn the difference between serving me and serving the kings of other lands. 2 Chronicles 12:8.

"Chaotic" was the word my teacher used to describe my family after she came to visit, and I think it fit just perfectly. My family was too loud and too messy, and there were too many of us! My complaint list was long. I had to share a bathroom with two stinky brothers who always left the toilet seat up, as if they had no memory whatsoever for this elementary-simple task. They ate all the good food out of the fridge almost as soon as Mom brought it home, and they played the TV too loud. My sister never wanted to do anything fun. My dad wore neon baggy pants from the 1980s when he picked me up at school. Mom always pointed out to my friends that my ears stick straight out through my hair. Thanks, Mom! I wanted to be rid of all of them.

Then I got a family of my own. My amazing husband leaves the seat up too; and as for my two sons—they don't even *use* the toilet yet! Greg doesn't have baggy neon pants, but he has a lot of ugly shirts that I hate, and he wears them all the time with pride. Besides all this, nobody fills the fridge full of food anymore—I have to do that myself. Nobody comes to pick me up, either. I have to drive myself where I go. I have to clean and budget, and basically I have to do everything. Life wasn't so bad living with my family—I just didn't realize it at the time.

Sometimes we don't realize how good we have it until it's too late. God knew this truth, and He said so when he allowed King Shishak of Egypt to attack Jerusalem. The people became subject to him, and God said that *now* they could see the difference between serving the Lord and serving kings of other lands. The Israelites realized pretty quick that serving God was a whole lot better than serving foreign kings. They just hadn't known it before.

We get to thinking that sometimes life would be a whole lot better without God—without all His strict rules and expectations and prohibitions. But those who have tried life the other way can tell you straight from the school of hard knocks that God made commands for a good reason: to make your life better, not worse. Serving God is actually the best way to live, and those rules are part of that. Don't find out the hard way—choose the better life now, while you are young.

—MH

For the eyes of the Lord range throughout the earth to strengthen those whose hearts are fully committed to him. 2 Chronicles 16:9.

My mom once dressed up like a guy and sneaked into the boys' dorm to see her boyfriend. Disguised in a large shirt, baggy jeans, and a ball cap, nobody ever suspected she was a girl. And as for Dad, he once painted an enormous "73 RULES!" on the blacktop by the picnic tables and on the wall in the breezeway between the classrooms, which is still there to this day. Nobody ever caught him. These "wild" teens became my parents! I love finding out crazy stories I've never heard before about people I know well.

If you're ever bored, grab a Bible and read some of the fascinating stories and random details written in the last half of 2 Chronicles. King Rehoboam's subjects asked him to lighten the load his father had put on them. He replied, "My little finger is thicker than my father's waist. . . . My father scourged you with whips; I will scourge you with scorpions" (2 Chronicles 10:10, 11). What an angry, sick man. Then there was King Asa, who deposed his own grandmother because she made an Asherah pole, but in his last years failed to rely on God. Despite the prophet's warning, King Ahab of Israel went to war, dressed in the clothes of a commoner so he wouldn't be attacked. Nevertheless, a random arrow pierced between his armor plates. Ahab propped himself up on his chariot and watched the battle until sunset, when he died. To remind people of God's ways, Jehoshaphat, the first king to send missionaries, sent Levites into Judah with the Book of the Law. When he asked God to help him fight Moab and Ammon, God had the armies turn on each other. By the time the king arrived, he found a field full of dead bodies. When Jehoram became king of Judah, he killed all his brothers and led his subjects to idol worship. He got a disease that caused his bowels to *come out, a*nd died in great pain, to no one's regret (2 Chronicles 21:20).

As I read through the recounts of the kings, I started seeing a very clear trend: those who followed God's ways were successful. Those who didn't brought evil upon themselves. It's that simple. Why? Today's verse gives the secret: God is looking for people with hearts fully committed to Him, and He strengthens them. Do you want to be one of those people today? If you do, take a moment now and recommit your heart and life fully to Jesus.

—MH

Selective Memory

King Joash did not remember the kindness Zechariah's father Jehoiada had shown him but killed his son, who said as he lay dying, "May the Lord see this and call you to account." 2 Chronicles 24:22.

I guess you could say it was because he was so young. After all, he was only a baby when he went into hiding with his nurse. His father was dead, and his father's mother, Athaliah, was killing the entire royal family of the house of Judah. He alone was saved, and only because his aunt Jehosheba took him to the Temple and hid him there. For six entire years she and her husband, Jehoiada the priest, took care of him. It wasn't until he was 7 years old that Joash was finally crowned king and placed on the throne to rule. And even this happened only because Jehoiada the priest rallied all the Levites and the heads of Israelite families and launched a great campaign. He stationed them all around the Temple, crowned Joash king and put a copy of the covenant in his hands, and then led the people to cheer and accept him. So Jehoiada not only helped save Joash's life, but put him on the throne as well. And then later he chose wives for him! Everything Joash had he had because of Jehoiada.

But Joash forgot. Many years went by, and Jehoiada died. After his death, Joash got a little sidetracked—he turned to the gods and idols of other nations. God sent prophets to Joash to bring him back, but he would not listen. Finally God sent a special man to warn him: Zechariah, who was the son of Jehoiada himself. You would think that after everything Jehoiada had done for him years ago, Joash would honor his old friend's son, but no. The Bible tells us that he did not remember all the kindness Jehoiada had shown him. Instead of accepting Zechariah's warning, Joash got really angry at him and had him stoned to death. Can you believe it? He actually killed the son of the man who had given him everything.

There may be people in your life that you're angry at right now—possibly friends, parents, teachers, maybe an old love interest who hurt you terribly. Sometimes we are so angry in the present that we completely forget the kindness these people have shown us in the past. It's hard to remember the past when you're angry, but try not to make the same mistake Joash did. Don't ever let anger erase your memory of the kindnesses shown and good deeds done for you.

—MH

In the Zone of Stink

But Hezekiah prayed for them, saying, "May the Lord, who is good, pardon everyone who sets his heart on seeking God—the Lord, the God of his fathers—even if he is not clean according to the rules of the sanctuary." And the Lord heard Hezekiah and healed the people. 2 Chronicles 30:18-20.

I couldn't tell where the awful smell was coming from in the classroom. Depending on which person you sat next to, you knew there'd be a distinct personal odor, but I had never yet sat next to anyone that smelled strongly like a urinal. After several minutes of looking around with mild disgust, I finally decided to move to a different desk. Choosing a place sufficiently removed from the previous "zone of stink," I settled myself in and began to take notes while the teacher lectured. However, every time I bent down to write I smelled the same terrible smell, only stronger! I subtly leaned from one side to the other, testing the air next to my closest companions; nary a pungent odor to be found. Again I bent down to take some more notes, and there was the awful stink. Now I realized the source. It was coming from me! I quickly vacated the room and examined myself thoroughly. I found my boxers were crusty with some ammonia-smelling stuff. Apparently my dear old cat had used my stack of freshly washed boxers for his cat box, and all of them had dried before I dressed. I had been walking around all day in litter box boxers! It's really lousy to be dirty when you know you're supposed to be clean.

The people of Israel in the days of King Hezekiah knew about feeling dirty. Hezekiah wanted to start a revival and bring people back to a true understanding of who God was and why life was better when they served Him, so he started up the old holidays, such as Passover and the feasts. When the people began coming together, Hezekiah realized that the descendants of the original priests, who were supposed to run the services, hadn't followed the rules for ceremonial cleanliness for a long time, so technically they couldn't offer the sacrifices or lead out in the ceremonies. They were "dirty." But Hezekiah knew the people's sincere desire to come back, and when he prayed for a pardon, God too saw their sincerity and offered grace. It's more important to God that you are sincere than that you are "clean." Don't let the dirty things in your life keep you from coming back to God. He's ready and willing to take you back as you are.

—GH

The History of Promises Fulfilled

This is what Cyrus king of Persia says: "The Lord, the God of heaven, has . . . appointed me to build a temple for him at Jerusalem in Judah. Anyone of his people among you— may his God be with him, and let him go up to Jerusalem in Judah and build the temple of the Lord, the God of Israel, the God who is in Jerusalem." Ezra 1:2, 3.

I am 24 years of age right now and don't expect to live through the end of this book. I thought I should at least make some attempt to let the world know what Jim Jones and the Peoples Temple is—OR WAS—all about." This is the beginning of a letter written by Anne Moore, probably one of the last members of the Peoples Temple alive when more than 900 of its members committed mass suicide in 1978. In this final letter she says that she's not sure why she's writing, but that she hopes that maybe someone will read and understand. The desire to leave something behind, to record what happened, is a strong one, and just like people today the Bible writers recorded important events for the benefit of those who would come later.

The books of Ezra and Nehemiah are just such books. They, along with Chronicles, were probably written by the Jewish scribe Ezra, after the return of the Jewish people from exile in Babylon. They are purely historical books, record-ing how God's people returned to their decimated homeland and tried to rebuild their own lives from the rubble of their parents' former ones. But these books are not all about a sad group of people picking through a destroyed land. The book of Ezra is about an excited group of people who are living out the predic-tions of the prophets Isaiah and Jeremiah when they prophesied that God would bring His people back and restore their land and their cities to them. In this sense the books are all about God fulfilling His promises, and bringing the Jews back to the favored status of "God's chosen people." On top of that, these books also point us to the fact that the prophecies of Daniel 8 and 9 are beginning their fulfillment, just as He had predicted during the exile itself. So instead of dry history, these books are teeming with the stories of lives rebuilt, and of God doing exactly what He had promised He would do. As you read through these two books, remember that the God who held up His promise back then will also hold up His promises to each of you. And His promise to *you* is that He will be coming back soon, "that where I am, there ye may be also" (John 14:3 KJV).

—GH

The Gestapo Came Knocking

Despite their fear of the peoples around them, they built the altar on its foundation and sacrificed burnt offerings on it to the Lord, both the morning and evening sacrifices. Ezra 3:3.

The lights burned brightly over the small desk in the German Gestapo officer's office. He'd been interrogating various members of the Dutch Resistance all day, but the elderly father of the ten Boom family he knew personally. He had been surprised when his officers brought the family in as suspected harborers of Jews, not because he didn't think they were members of the Resistance, but because they had been caught. They had been watched for several years, but had always been meticulous and detailed in their preparations for police raids. Now as he looked at the tired watchmaker he shook his head. "I'd like to send you home, old fellow," the interrogator said with a soft voice. "I'll take your word that you won't cause any more trouble."

"If I go home today," the weary response came, "tomorrow I will open my door again to any man who knocks." The steely gaze that met the officer's was not that of a broken man, but that of a man whose mind had been made up long before this sleepless night. People aren't brave just on the spur of the moment. They're brave because of convictions made ahead of time.

The Jews returning from exile had had 70 years to build up lost convictions, and when they began the process of rebuilding the Temple, people in surrounding countries didn't like what they saw. Uprisings seemed virtually assured, but the Jews refused to back down and went right on rebuilding. First they built the main altar in the courtyard of what had been Solomon's Temple. They located the descendants of the former priests and outfitted them in clothing and robes brought in for the ceremony. More threats came, until all the returning Jews gathered in the ruined city for fear of violent outbreaks. Instead of debating about whether or not they should cave in to local pressure, they finished the new altar and for the first time in 70 years worshipped and performed the ceremonies as God had commanded Moses. Their bravery and strength came out of 70 long years of knowing that they had turned their backs on God, and they were determined to make things right. Prepare now for those times that may come in your life that call for bravery. Don't put it off, and don't assume you'll make the right choices. Conviction and bravery are cultivated in the peaceful times, and they're harvested when things get tough.

—GH

Pulling Your Hair Out

And when I heard this thing, I rent my garment and my mantle, and plucked off the hair of my head and of my beard, and sat down astonied. Ezra 9:3, KJV.

Ezra, a prophet, was busily trying to rebuild the house of the Lord. His people were supposed to keep themselves out of trouble. And one of the main ways to do that was by not marrying into the surrounding cultures, for this inevitably led God's chosen people away from Him.

So you can imagine Ezra's "delight" in the midst of this holy work to have some of the common people tell him that "everyone," including prominent leaders, had hooked up with the women of the lands around them. So delighted was he that he yanked out handfuls of his hair and beard, ripped off his clothes, and sat down in a stupor.

Ever had a day like that? A day nobody does what they're supposed to do?

I remember planning a youth event that was to be hosted by a family in my church. The youth had all the information and were looking forward to the event, and everything was set up and ready to go. Then less than a week beforehand I got a call from the host family. Apparently there was to be a parade that evening, and they couldn't possibly host the event.

Now, I must admit that *my* reaction was not to pull out my own hair. My personality rather mirrors Nehemiah's, who pulled out other people's hair (see tomorrow's devotional). I secretly wished the sky would rain on the parade—or better yet, some float carrying the bumpkin princess of their little town would lose all control and run over them. No, no! Not to kill them. Just bump them a little so they'd realize the error they had made. But God doesn't call us to wish harm on people who harm us.

We are called to pray for our enemies (Luke 6:28). And once Ezra comes out of his shock at the stupidity of his coworkers, that is exactly what he does. He takes their sin upon himself—as though he was one of the offenders—and asks God for forgiveness on their behalf. Today if there is anyone who makes you want to rip out your hair, tear off your clothes, and sit in shock for the rest of the day, go ahead and express yourself . . . but just make sure that when you're finished you pray for them.

—SP

Pulling Other People's Hair Out

I rebuked them, cursed them, beat some of their men, and pulled out their hair. I forced them to take an oath before God and said: "You must not give your daughters in marriage to their sons or take their daughters as wives for your sons or yourselves." Nehemiah 13:25, HCSB.

Now, that's what I'm talking about. That is a prophet in action. But we have to ask why he used such manly tactics when Ezra made himself the object of abuse. Chronologically speaking, Ezra dealt with this problem 30 years prior to this. So right off, we see that this is not the first time God's people had fallen into this trap. Second, if you read early on, the Israelite children were not speaking Hebrew anymore (the language of Scripture); they were picking up other dialects, which was one of the chief identifiers of a foreigner.

So what does God have against foreigners? Well, nothing except that these particular people (the Moabites and the Ammonites) served a god named Molech. Worship services among Molech's followers did not involve children's stories—they involved child sacrifice. Excavations have shown thousands of little skeletons burned to a crisp, all in the name of this foreign god. So when Ezra saw the beautiful Israelite children speaking the language of this religion, he lost it.

I have a hairy Alaskan malamute named Winston. Winston by all accounts is a good dog. However, there are times I tell Winston "No," or "Drop it," or "Stop," and he defies me. He tests me even though he knows better. And these are the special times I grab him by his hairy hide and put him on the ground to communicate, in a tangible way, my displeasure at his disobedience. Then once I sense his repentance, I let him up, and we play. And so it goes every now and then that I have to instill in him that I am Alpha, and he isn't. That my way—not his—is best.

Now, before you exercise your ability to pull the hair of, curse, or beat senseless the object of your irritation, let me give you the principle. There are times we intercede for people (all the time, actually); but there are also times we confront. Confronting someone's bad behavior isn't always pleasant, but if done in love (see Ephesians 4:15), it can lead to healing and deeper friendships. If you've been praying for someone who has hurt you—and if you've been praying for a long time with no results, and you haven't spoken to them about your concerns—maybe now is the time for that confrontation.

—SP

Waiting, Waiting . . . Still Waiting

They said to me, "Those who survived the exile and are back in the province are in great trouble and disgrace. The wall of Jerusalem is broken down, and its gates have been burned with fire." Nehemiah 1:3.

It's been almost five years, and I still don't have my two-year degree. Most people in my life are beginning to wonder if I'll ever graduate. I'm beginning to wonder myself. When my husband and I first enrolled at the seminary, we both planned to finish in two and a half years. But 10 months into my first year of study I found out I was pregnant. When Caleb was born, I took a whole semester off to be with him, figuring I'd return and finish up the next semester. However, since Greg and I had to take turns being at home with the baby, scheduling wasn't easy. By the time we left the seminary, Greg had his degree, but I had several classes still to take. So I flew back to take some that were condensed into a week, did some online, and did a lot of home study work. I was almost finished—when I became pregnant with Toby Jacob, our second. I planned to finish my classes by the time he was born, but I just didn't get it done. As I write this I have exactly one half of a class to go. I just can't seem to finish.

I would have been in good company with the exiles in Nehemiah's day. They couldn't seem to finish either. Nehemiah picks up almost exactly where Ezra left off, like any good sequel in the movies. The action has hardly stopped from Ezra 10, where Ezra is trying to bring spiritual reform to the returning exiles, who no longer understand what it means to be God's chosen people. Enter Nehemiah, the royal cupbearer of Artaxerxes, king of Persia. He brings word that Ezra's attempt at rebuilding the city wall has been halted. The walls have been torn down and the gates have been burned by the same people who'd been threatening Ezra and his workers in the last book. So King Artaxerxes gives Nehemiah special permission to return with soldiers and official papers, allowing him to begin a thorough reconstruction. Without this essential protection in place, the exiles are left open to the treachery of the surrounding nations. As in any good sequel, God has the next hero ready, to make sure His promise of restoring the Jewish nation comes true.

Don't ever doubt that God *will* do something, even if He takes longer than you might expect.

—MH and GH

Maybe I Should Have Kissed Her

Moreover, in those days I saw men of Judah who had married women from Ashdod, Ammon and Moab. . . . Was it not because of marriages like these that Solomon king of Israel sinned? Nehemiah 13:23-26.

I stood in the doorway of the girl's house thinking I should just go ahead and kiss her; it's what we were both wanting. But I was a senior, and moving on to college. She was a year behind me, and had a pretty big crush on me. Kissing her would've been fun, and I could've told the guys about it later, but it just didn't seem right to get her hopes up and then leave her stranded. But she was petite, blond, and drop-dead gorgeous, so why not? Just as I was about to give in, a car horn blared from the driveway. My buddy, who was driving, must've been able to read my mind. He laid on the horn again. Still I wavered, looking into her eyes and thinking, Just a quick good-night kiss—or two? Then the horn blasted and kept going. He wasn't letting me open up this can of worms—he knew the ramifications. And ultimately, for fear of his waking up the whole house, I blurted out a "Good night!" and left.

Nehemiah and Ezra could have used a friend like mine. Unfortunately for them, the returning exiles come home not only to a destroyed city, but also to lots of exotic, beautiful women from the surrounding nations. Even though God had prohibited their marrying foreign women, they'd gone ahead and done it. The can of worms this opened up was that when you married a woman from another culture, you didn't marry just her, you married her *and* her religion; and she brought all her idols and pagan worship with her. This was the very thing that had started the downfall of Israel when Solomon was king, and ultimately it's what brought about God's punishment and the exile to Babylon. Nehemiah and Ezra weren't about to let this happen again, and they put a stop to it by ordering all of the men who had married these women to return them to their own countries.

I guess God knows that being in romantic relationships can cause people to bend their principles and change their actions. He also knows what will keep us from suffering, both today as well as tomorrow. So keep God in mind when dating around. The ones you choose will play a large part in your life. Never let them play a larger part than He does.

—GH

For Such a Time as This

And who knows but that you have come to royal position for such a time as this?
Esther 4:14.

As we leave this house, let it be with the purpose to be grateful to God for having brought Abraham Lincoln to the kingdom for such a time as this; for having endowed him so plentifully with wisdom from on high, for his great trust; for having preserved his life so long through so many dangers; and for giving us such sure hope in his death."

These are the closing remarks given at one of the funerals of President Abraham Lincoln, who, even in his own time, was seen as one who had accepted a call to stand before a mighty storm that had broken on a young nation. Lincoln's life as president was filled with a multitude of personal anxiety and fear over countless grievous decisions. He hated the war, the knifepoint on which his time as president balanced itself. He thought of slavery as a "monstrous injustice" and a "cancer." But even then he couldn't bring himself to hate his Southern brothers, saying, "They are just what we would be in their situation." His was an untiring commitment and sense of purpose both to end the war and to begin the process of reconciliation,

The book of Esther paints a strikingly similar picture of, not a man, but a young woman who is perilously placed in the Persian royal house "for such a time as this." As queen to King Xerxes, Esther was brought to one of the highest positions in Persia when those in Xerxes' court were plotting the genocide of Persia's entire Jewish population. These were the Jews who'd chosen to remain there instead of returning to their homeland with Ezra and Nehemiah. You would expect this kind of story to be full of references to God, but it's interesting that this is the one book in the Bible in which God is never actually mentioned. Only in today's verse do we get a hint that someone like God might be working behind the scenes. Though God remains hidden in this book, we find a beautiful young Jewish woman placed as queen at just the perfect time—when all her people have been condemned to die.

God's plans are always running, whether we are able to see them or not. And if God was able to engineer things for the Jews in Persia, He's certainly still working things out for you. God has placed you, too, here on earth for a specific purpose—for such a time as this. Consider today what God's plans for your life might be at this time in history.

—GH

God Knows How to Show Up

For if you remain silent at this time, relief and deliverance for the Jews will arise from another place, but you and your father's family will perish. Esther 4:14.

When I finally made the decision to go, I had just three short weeks to come up with almost $3,000. I felt God calling me to be a student missionary on the tiny, bustling little island of Ebeye in the Marshalls, and since they had recently lost a teacher, there was no time to lose. Everyone told me that my plan was insane, that there was no way I could come up with that kind of money in a few weeks, even if I wrote letters to everybody I'd ever known! But I had this quiet peace in my heart, this feeling that somehow something would work out, because God was impressing me to go. After the first two weeks went by and no money had come in, some encouraged me to give up my plans. I couldn't explain anything to them, except to say that I knew God would work it out. Sure enough, only a few days before I was to leave, a man in my parents' Sabbath school class whom I had never even met decided to transfer his thousands of frequent flyer miles into my name, and within no time I was on a plane headed across the sea.

When God tells you He's going to show up, that means one very specific thing: that He's going to show up! The Jews who lived scattered throughout Persia in Esther's time had been unfaithful to the Lord, but they knew He would not be unfaithful to them—He had promised that He would rescue His people and bring them home again one day. So when King Xerxes, persuaded by Haman, issued a decree to kill off every Jew in the land, Esther's uncle Mordecai did not give up. Many may have thought that it was finally their end, but we know Mordecai didn't, because of what he says in the verse above. As he is trying to persuade Esther to help, he states that even if she doesn't, help *will* come from some other place. He doesn't know how. He can't explain where. But he knows that somehow, some way, God will show up to save them, because God is faithful.

God is still faithful. Just because He may not be showing up in the ways that you expect Him to, don't lose heart. His help may come from another place that you never even imagined. Just trust that one thing is certain: His help *will* come.

—MH

Insomnia

That night the king could not sleep; so he ordered the book of the chronicles, the record of his reign, to be brought in and read to him. Esther 6:1.

When I woke up, I found myself lying cheek down in the middle of the sidewalk as busy students passed by on either side. I had somehow fallen asleep waiting for the bell to ring—I lay down right outside the classroom door and slept on the pavement. You are thinking I must have been terribly tired, but that's not it. Actually, I have a strange "talent" that allows me to sleep just about anywhere on earth. I've fallen asleep in treetops and on rooftops. One time I napped while swimming—a complicated story to explain. Occasionally I've put my head down on a lunch table only to awaken refreshed 20 minutes later. I've slept through flights during which people all around me retched into barf bags because the turbulence was so horrible. I've slept in elevators and buses and boats and against a hundred car windows. In college I could sleep through any class and not miss a thing, because the teacher's words were part of my dreams!

So the night I awoke at 3:00 a.m. and couldn't return to my dreams seemed pretty strange indeed. I tossed, I turned, and I counted sheep. I thought about math to bore myself, but nothing worked. I had never in my life experienced this! Slowly, as the dark night hours wore on, I began to feel impressed that I was awake for a purpose. A certain friend kept returning to my thoughts, so I began to pray for that person. I prayed long into the night, and continued to pray until, at long last, sleep finally came. That afternoon (that's when I woke up) I called my friend right away to see what was going on. Apparently it had been the absolutely most pivotal night of this person's entire life.

In Esther we read that King Xerxes couldn't sleep. I believe that God kept him up all night for a reason, too. It was the night before the evil Haman was going to ask for Mordecai to be hung on the gallows he had built. Unable to sleep, the king decided to read through the entire history of his kingdom. He stumbled upon a story of Mordecai's bravery and decided to reward him in the morning, not knowing that in the process he had just saved his life.

If God ever keeps you up into the night, it's for a good reason. Be still and listen to His leading. You never know when you might be needed to intervene for another life.

—MH

Cruel Intentions and Poetic Justice

So they hanged Haman on the gallows he had prepared for Mordecai.
Esther 7:10.

If I could make a movie out of just one book of the Bible, it would be the book of Esther. It could win an award for the most fitting and ironic ending ever written.

Esther, a Jewish orphan, had been raised by her uncle Mordecai. When King Xerxes deposes Queen Vashti for defying him in public, he has the most beautiful women in the land (no doubt, mostly teens) brought to his palace, and gives them beauty treatments for a year. Then he chooses his favorite—Esther. Jealousy and intrigue seem to be part of palace life, and soon the king's top official, Haman, has a run-in with Esther's uncle. When Mordecai refuses to bow to him, Haman talks the king into issuing a decree that all Jews in Persia will be killed on a certain day. Of course they are terrified. Esther risks her own life to approach the king, uninvited, to invite him and Haman to a banquet. Xerxes knows she wants something, but she doesn't tell. Instead, she invites them to a second banquet. She will ask him then.

But the plot thickens. The night after the first banquet Haman decides he will kill Mordecai in the morning and has a 75-foot gallows built by his house. That same night the king can't sleep, so he asks for the history books to be brought in and read to him. He learns that some time before, Mordecai reported an assassination plot on his life but was never rewarded. So in the morning, just as Haman comes to ask permission to hang Mordecai, the king tells Haman to parade Mordecai as a hero through the streets on his own horse! Shame! But it gets better . . .

Later that night, at Esther's second banquet, she exposes that "this vile Haman" (Esther 7:6) is trying to kill all her people. The king is so angry that he leaves the room, but Haman stays to beg Esther for his life. Just as the king returns, Haman has fallen onto the couch where Esther is reclining. "Will he even molest the queen while she is with me in the house?" the king roars (verse 8), and has Haman hanged. Where? You guessed it—on the very gallows he built for Mordecai. Oh, the irony! Xerxes decrees that the Jews can defend their lives, and they are victorious. What a story! Though unmentioned by name, you can see that God stepped in at all the right places, just in the nick of time. So if you're in a situation in which you need God to intervene, ask for His help today. Then count on Him to show up at exactly the right moment.

—MH

The Claims of a Crook

One day the angels came to present themselves before the Lord, and Satan also came with them. The Lord said to Satan, "Where have you come from?" Satan answered the Lord, "From roaming through the earth and going back and forth in it." Job 1:6, 7.

It's not easy to spot a crook. They pretty much tend to look just like everyone else. That's the problem my dad ran into many years back when he entered into a business deal with a crook. The man didn't look shady . . . he didn't smell shady . . . he didn't even act shady! He invited my dad and mom to an impressive home one night to talk shop and seal a deal. The large home had beautiful rooms, lovely decorating, spacious grounds, and a swimming pool. Expensive cars were parked in the driveway. This man assured them that he owned all these nice things because his business was so incredibly successful. It was only many months later, after learning that this guy was a liar and a crook, that my dad discovered that the house wasn't even his. He had invited them over and given them a tour of someone else's home, a place he didn't own, all the while acting as if it were his and he were the owner of everything they saw. Unbelievable!

In the beginning of the book of Job we see Satan doing the exact same thing. There is an important meeting in heaven, and Satan shows up as if he's been invited. When God asks him where he's come from, he says that he's been roaming throughout the earth and going back and forth in it. While this may just sound like wandering to us, that phrase actually has a far deeper meaning—it is a way of claiming ownership. Satan is actually claiming that the earth is his. That's why he has showed up at the meeting. He is claiming that he's the owner of Planet Earth, that he can walk back and forth in it as he pleases. This is a pretty large claim—the claim of a crook.

Because God knows that *He* is the rightful owner of the earth, He immediately points to Job as an example of a life that Satan doesn't own. Job's life of obedience to God is proof that Satan is not in control of the whole earth. Isn't that a cool thought? When we live as obedient examples of God's followers, we are proof to the world and to the universe that God is still in control. It's true that there's a crook afoot and that he'd like you to help him in his cause, but we know better. Step up to the challenge of Job and use your life to show that God is still in control of the earth—that no matter how many others have gone astray, He still has a servant in you.

—MH

The Unexpected

"Does Job fear God for nothing?" Satan replied. "Have you not put a hedge around him and his household and everything he has? . . . Stretch out your hand and strike everything he has, and he will surely curse you to your face." Job 1:9-11.

As I slowly bit through the fudgy warm chocolate topping and crispy, crunchy caramel coating, my teeth sank into something surprisingly unfamiliar. It felt like chicken. It tasted like chicken. When I spit it out, disgusted, it even looked like chicken. Come to find out—it was chicken! A huge, gristly chunk of chicken meat right in the middle of my warm gooey chocolate dessert, where soft creamy vanilla ice cream should have been. Gross! Maybe you'd enjoy this, but it's not my personal preference. I don't like expecting one thing and then getting another!

But the book of Job does that to us. We expect one thing from God, and instead get something very different. Thus far, all the way through the Old Testament, a clear pattern has been set up. When you follow God's ways, you live a blessed life. When you turn from God, prepare for trouble. It's simple. But that's not what we see happening in Job. Job himself is blameless and upright, a man who has followed every last command and decree of the Lord. Things should have gone well for him, right? I mean, isn't that the way it works? Instead, he loses everything in four successive fell swoops—all his livestock, all his servants attending them, and all his sons and daughters—one right after the other. As if this weren't devastating enough, Job is then inflicted with painful sores from head to toe. And God allows this? It doesn't seem right.

Apparently, Job himself didn't understand either. He kept saying that he wanted to plead his case before God. Maybe he didn't realize that there's a true cosmic battle (otherwise known as the great controversy) being waged between God and Satan. Satan had accused Job of serving God only because he got good stuff out of it. If there were nothing in it for Job, Satan taunted God, Job would turn from Him. But God knew Job's heart, and He knew that though Job did live a blessed life, he served God out of love. When God let Satan destroy and kill all his blessings, Job's relationship with God was still left intact (though confused). What is your relationship with God based on? On what He gives you? what He does for you? Or would you love Him no matter what?

—MH

An Enemy Has Done This

So Satan went out from the presence of the Lord and afflicted Job with painful sores from the soles of his feet to the top of his head. Job 2:7.

We awoke in the night to an ominous pounding on our front door. Greg stumbled downstairs and found a uniformed man standing on our porch, clipboard in hand. At the end of the driveway his tow truck flashed its frantic lights. "I'm here to impound your car, sir," the man said. "You haven't made a payment in more then a year. You should have paid your bills!" We were speechless. We'd never missed a payment, and furthermore, we hadn't even owned our car for a full year! The man checked his papers again, and checked our address. Sure enough, he had the right house. "I have to take your car. I'm sorry!" he apologized. It was only when he checked the make and model of our car that he realized he had the wrong people. Apparently the car he'd come for belonged to the people who had lived in the house just before us. He made a note on his clipboard, and we returned to the status of people who do, in fact, pay their bills.

It sure feels lousy, and even scary at times, to get blamed for something you didn't do. But that's how God must feel all the time, isn't it? I mean, just think about how many things God gets blamed for, and all because He "has the power" to stop them from happening. He gets blamed for all our bad choices, the bad choices of other people, and the effects of the sins we choose. What's more, He even gets blamed for the things that Satan does. Even in the book of Job, when Satan is clearly named as the cause of Job's pain, Job questions God instead.

When we feel like blaming God, my college chaplain Pastor Rich taught us to say instead, "An enemy has done this." When we see fires and floods and job loss happen to good people, when we see pain and suffering, disease and hardship, or even when we see death, we often blame God. But instead we should blame the enemy—he, not God, is the one who causes the suffering and death. The enemy is responsible for all of it, and has been from the very beginning. Next time something in your life goes wrong, resist the temptation to blame God, whose only responsibility lies in allowing us freedom of choice. The rest of the blame falls on our poor choices, the poor choices of others, and on the enemy. So put the blame where the blame belongs. Instead of accusing God for the wrong, learn to say, "An enemy has done this."

—MH

For Better or for Worse

Shall we accept the good from God, and not trouble? Job 2:10.

I used to think Greg got a pretty good deal when he chose me to be his wife. I mean—I'm energetic, outgoing, spontaneous, fun to be around, confident, smart. What's not to love? But then a few years later, about six months into my first pregnancy, I became deeply depressed. I wasn't energetic or fun anymore. I didn't want to leave the house. My confidence had vanished. And I became afraid that Greg would stop loving me. One night I shared this fear with him, and he said something I'll never forget. He told me that he didn't sign up for the marriage only when times were good. He had promised to love me forever—even when things were really bad. I still remember how relieved I was to hear him say that. It's an amazing feeling to know that you don't have to earn love, that you are loved no matter what happens.

I think that Job must have loved God this way, because of the response he gives his wife when she begs him just to curse God and die. Job says, "Shall we accept the good from God, and not trouble?" We're told that throughout the entire ordeal, Job did not sin once by charging God with wrongdoing. Instead, he conceded, "The Lord gave and the Lord has taken away; may the name of the Lord be praised" (Job 1:21). This is amazing faith and amazing love. It seems that, like Greg, Job had signed up to love God not only during the good times, when things were going well and he was blessed. He also was prepared to love God during the worst of times, even after he had lost everything he owned on earth.

Instead of asking if you love God this way, I'd rather point out the fact that God loves YOU this way. He loves you no matter what. You don't have to earn it. You don't have to deserve it. He loves you through the absolute worst times of your life, through the most terrible choices you have ever made. And He will always love you this way—He too signed up for forever. It's an amazing feeling, isn't it? It is this feeling that helps us love God in return. It's really hard to think of loving God no matter what, until we realize that He loves us no matter what. Then our love for Him is simply a response of gratitude. So let the reality of God's love truly sink into your heart and soul, and suddenly you may find that loving Him in return is easier than you ever thought.

—MH

It's Not Time for the Fat Lady Yet

Why did I not perish at birth, and die as I came from the womb? Job 3:11.

Please, God—I want to die. The words were scratched in thick, dark letters across the entire page of the black leather-bound journal, forming a desperate plea to the Lord. Obviously the person who owned the journal didn't seem to believe that life was worth living anymore. The journal was almost 15 years old, and it was mine. I wrote those words as a teenager, on a night I didn't feel as if I could face life anymore. I meant them too.

I am so full of joy and happiness I could just burst. These words were penned in purple ink, in cute curly letters, at the top of a flowery green "Journal of Motherhood." This is also my journal, almost 15 years later. On this page, in an entry from just a few weeks ago, I expressed how amazing it felt to be a mother of two beautiful little boys, and wife to such a wonderful husband; how sweet and full my life had become. So when I think about the entry in that other journal all those years ago, it seems very far away and silly. Just think what I would have missed! Just think of all the joy and beauty that is mine now! How sad it would have been if I had never gotten to meet Greg, or if my two sons had never existed.

Job also wanted to die. Did you know that? We see him as a great man of faith, but we hear him saying such things as "Why didn't I die at birth?" or "If I were dead, I could be at peace" or "I wish I was buried in the ground like a stillborn child." Harsh words, aren't they? He was thinking that it would have been better if he had never been born, that death would be better than his suffering. But what I love about Job is that these cries are not the end of the story.

The end of the story comes many chapters later, where we learn that God blessed the second half of Job's life more than twice as much as the first. Job has double the possessions and wealth, 10 more children for him and his wife to love, and among them the most beautiful daughters in all the land. The story ends with happiness—a whole lot of it.

What I learned from reading Job is that even in your worst pain and sorrow it's not the end. Life can always begin again, and hold more beauty, wonder, and blessings. If you've ever felt like Job—or me—hang in there. Don't give up yet, because your present suffering is not the end of the story. God has so much happiness prepared ahead for you. You don't want to miss it!

—MH

Apostasy Is All They Require

Though he slay me, yet will I hope in him. Job 13:15.

The slow shuffle of a condemned man was the only sound in the courtyard of the Dublin Castle. A large audience came to see him hanged that day, not for any crimes against the people or the state, but for being what everyone else in that Protestant town was not—a Catholic. Two documents were brought to the condemned man, one the order for his execution, the other a document of pardon if he recanted. He grabbed the document of pardon and held it over his head.

"See you here the condition on which I might save my life? Apostasy is all they require; but before high heaven, I spurn their offers, and with my last breath will glorify God for the honor he has done me, in allowing me thus to suffer for his name." With these words Peter O'Higgins dropped the pardon to the ground and stepped forward toward the executioner and the waiting rope. Those standing closest to the gallows before the trapdoor was sprung could hear Peter thanking God with his last breaths. His hope was in God, even if God let him die.

This one man's example is an echo of a similar statement of faith spoken by a man suffering in his own right. Job spoke out as one who had fallen to a fate he couldn't begin to fathom. His children were dead, his earthly possessions were gone, his wife had turned her back on him and demanded that he curse God for all the hardship, and leave her as a widow who would be thankful to be done with him. And in spite of all this, Job still had the audacity to say, "Even if God chooses to kill me, I will still put my hope in Him." There's a faith in this that bears closer inspection, because it's when things are really tough that the true nature of our relationships is tested. We look to those who suffer, and wonder how they will handle it, wonder how they will cope. We wonder and watch, because deep down we wonder how we ourselves would handle such problems. Would we cash in our chips and say, "Forget about God. He's obviously no help here." Or would we stand up and face the threats around us with a faith that says, "Let God's will be done"?

In my heart of hearts I hope that I, in my darkest days, will be able to echo the words of Job and the countless others who have given their lives for Jesus: "Though he slay me, yet will I hope in Him." Would you put your trust in God, even in the face of death?

—GH

Because I Said So

Where were you when I laid the earth's foundation? Tell me, if you understand. Job 38:4.

"Because I said so" has got to be the absolute worst parentism on the planet, and a sorry, lame excuse for an answer as well. What kid hasn't experienced being told no after asking their parents for something, and the only explanation given is "Because I said so"? In my book this is a nonanswer. It's a cop-out for uncreative parents who can't find a good explanation for their weak rules. I hated receiving this pathetic excuse as a reason from people.

I am a better parent than all the folks out there who use this tired out old line. That is, I *was* a better parent—until this afternoon. I came downstairs to find my entire kitchen floor, living room floor, dining area, and the dog all covered in globs of butter. My 2 ½-year-old had apparently flung handfuls of butter everywhere and then waltzed through the entire thing. I tried to retain my Christianity as I cleaned up the mess, but it was hard. Hours later he had the absolute nerve to ask me if he could have some butter. I said "*NO!*" When he pressed me as to why, I did it. I said it. I'm ashamed, but I shot back at him, "Because I said so!" (Don't tell anyone.)

Job got more or less a because-I-said-so from God. All through the book he asks God for permission to plead his case—he doesn't deserve this; he wants to defend himself. Why has God allowed such terrible things to happen to someone who has served Him faithfully? "Why, God? Why?" God doesn't answer the "why" question—He skips it completely. I like that. Instead, He begins to fire questions back at Job, one after another. Where was Job when He laid the foundations of the earth? Did Job give the ocean its limits? Does Job send the lightning bolts on their way? Did Job give the horse its strength? And on and on. Basically, what God is doing is reminding Job of who He is: He is God. He knows the end from the beginning, and if He has chosen to allow something to happen, it was the right choice, whether we can see that or not. Why was Satan allowed to test Job? God reminds Job that He is master of things that we can't even begin to understand. He is in charge. God's answer is simply this: Remember whom you are questioning. Remember who I am. Do you have questions for God, things you want explained? Next time you question God (and that's OK to do), keep in mind who He is. Because we have limited understanding, there will be times that we just have to trust Him.

—MH

The First Time You Met

My ears had heard of you but now my eyes have seen you. Job 42:5.

Try to think of someone in your life that you love with all your heart—maybe your best friend, your secret crush, an admirable mentor, or the love of your life—and then do your best to remember the first time you met that person. Was it magical, was it love at first sight, or at least friendship at first sight? Do you remember your first thoughts and feelings about the individual? Do you remember the first words you said?

As I ask you these questions, I'm thinking of my son. You could say that I met him in stages. The first time I heard him, he was only the rhythmic *pound-pound-pound* of a heartbeat through the monitor. Then the first time I saw him, he was a tiny little squiggle on the ultrasound machine that kicked his little feet and rubbed his cheeks with his tiny little fists. The first time I felt him, he was like a flutter in my stomach—I hardly even knew what it was. So I was kind of like Job in the verse above—my ears had heard about him, but I hadn't literally seen him yet. When I did finally meet him, he was wrinkly and gray and crying, and I loved him immediately and completely.

Job really thought he knew God well—thought he understood all the ins and outs of how God worked and operated. He even told his friends that he had God figured out. But he still had much to learn. When God finally showed up and talked about the many things He had done and was responsible for, Job saw God in a new light. He probably had never before considered the vastness of God's job. It was as if He were seeing God for the very first time. That's when Job made the statement: "My ears had heard of you, but now my eyes have seen you." Apparently it's when we take time to consider who God is and just how much He has done that we finally begin to see Him well.

Have you only heard of God, or do you feel as though you have actually seen Him—at work in the world, in the Bible, in your own life? If you need a new experience with Him, if your eyes could use some new sights of Him, then I suggest spending time considering all that He has done. Read through the last five chapters of Job, and see if you don't come away with a whole new picture of your Lord and Maker.

—MH

Those Who Save Us

My servant Job will pray for you, and I will accept his prayer and not deal with you according to your folly. You have not spoken of me what is right, as my servant Job has. Job 42:8.

For most of the night I had been making fun of him to his face, and I wasn't planning on stopping anytime soon. My friend Sheldon and I were in the gym watching a basketball game, and I had been criticizing and shaming him throughout the whole first half. He wasn't saying much. Suddenly his hand shot out right at my face. I froze—would he actually hit me? A heartbeat later I heard it—the sharp smack of a fast-flying basketball hitting his palm. I hadn't been facing the game, so I didn't see the ball zoom across the court. It would have slammed me square in the head if Sheldon hadn't stopped it. Slowly it sank in—as I was in the very act of making fun of him and criticizing him, he was saving me.

The three friends of Job—Eliphaz, Bildad, and Zophar—had a similar experience. They had spent a good long time criticizing Job, but in the end it was Job who had to step in and save them. Because of the way they understood God, they were certain that Job had to have sinned, or such disaster would never have happened to him. So they accused him and criticized him, begging him to admit to faults. The entire time Job defended himself, saying that he was innocent. Job assured them that his feet had closely kept to God's steps, and he had kept to God's ways without turning aside (see Job 23:10, 11). But his friends would not hear of it. They insisted that bad things happened only to bad people.

In the end God showed up "out of the storm" (Job 38:1), and after He questioned Job, God turned to Job's three friends. He was angry with them, saying they hadn't spoken rightly of Him. Strangely, what God asks is that Job pray for his friends, saying He'll accept Job's prayer on their behalf. After all the misery they had brought on Job in his already-miserable state, blaming and accusing him, now Job is asked to stand in the gap and save them. And he does! What's interesting is that it is only after Job prays for his friends that God begins to restore all his former blessings to him.

You might not realize it, but some of the people you treat the worst could be the very ones who pray for you and stand in the gap for you each day. Be careful whom you criticize, make fun of, or take for granted. You never know whom you may need to rely on in trouble.

—MH

Lightsaber

How happy is the man who does not follow the advice of the wicked, or take the path of sinners, or join a group of mockers! Psalm 1:1, HCSB.

I remember the day I walked into Barnes and Noble shortly after George Lucas released his latest nerdfest, *Revenge of the Sith*. Amid the candy, pocket-sized notebooks, and general miscellanea that nobody buys at the checkout counter stood a box of elaborately designed lightsabers of various makes and models. I looked at it in awe. Then I saw something better: a lightsaber out of the box—on display—and available for use. I touched the metal handle and ran my fingers over the fiberglass tube that contained dazzling LED lights that glowed Jedi green. Before long before the weapon was in hand, and I held it aloft and flipped the switch. With a peal of sound, known very well to *Star Wars* nerds, the light blade came to life. It hummed in my hands as I wove it back and forth, fighting the urge to strike something or someone in the store. Sensing my delight at this $100 marvel, the store clerk came over nodding enthusiastically.

"Pretty sweet, huh? They make crashing sounds when you strike things. Last night a bunch of us had duels in the dark after closing the store down—they're pretty durable." After briefly considering applying to work at this particular Barnes and Noble so that I might join in the midnight lightsaber wars, I relented, and simply purchased the lightsaber instead.

The first psalm describes a progression. First is a man who follows the advice of the wicked, then he walks their path, and finally he joins their company. So, simply speaking, sin is a flirt. It tempts us with thoughts, leads us to meditate on those thoughts, and eventually leads us to take actions that can lead to destruction. That expensive toy is still in my office—but after considering my budget and what's important, I'm going to sell it. I don't need it, of course, and I am in need of other things. It would have been better had I not bought it at all. Thankfully the lightsaber has retained its value. However, when it comes to sin, the consequences are much harder to return once you walk its path and join the company of those who embrace it. Instead of allowing sin to take you down a destructive path, take David's advice in verse 2. Spend time meditating on God's Word. That will lead you to a progression of being firmly rooted in the right place—like a tree by water able to produce fruit (see verse 3).

—SP

I Want That Avocado Sandwich

Taste and see that the Lord is good. Psalm 34:8.

When I threw the sandwich across the bus, I truly didn't mean to hit Shannon in the face. In fact, I threw it in my sleep, if you can believe that. Two caring students, Ashley and Harmony, had bought some of Peru's most delicious giant avocados that day on our mission trip, and had lovingly saved a few pieces for a sandwich for me. Knowing I'd be delighted with the snack, they quietly placed the sandwich in my lap as I dozed in my bus seat.

But the feeling of something randomly dropping into my lap on a crowded stinky bus apparently didn't sit well with my subconscious mind. And so in that halfway-in-between-sleep-and-awake place I instantly picked up whatever parcel had been placed on me and chucked it as far away as possible. The bewildered students around me stared in horror as the messy avocado sandwich hit poor Shannon square in the eyeball at the front of the bus. The wasted precious avocados fell to the floor, and Shannon was left to wonder why her seemingly sweet Bible teacher had just thrown her lunch at her.

When I finally did wake up, I just couldn't understand why my students were giving me such dirty looks. I didn't believe them when they told me the story—actually, I still sort of think they made the whole thing up. I do get to thinking about that sandwich, though, whenever someone mentions how famous Peru is for their amazing avocados. They're supposed to be the best in the world, but I never got even a taste.

It would be a shame to have those sorts of regrets about God, wouldn't it? When David wrote Psalm 34, he didn't just *look* insane in his sleep, the way I did. He actually pretended to be insane. On purpose! He did this in order to escape from King Abimelech, and it worked. Overjoyed at how God rescued him, he then encouraged people to "taste and see" that God is good. Taste God? It really means to give Him a try, see what you think, get a taste of a life lived God's way! And this line was written with confidence—David was sure that when we try God out, we'll certainly find that He is very good indeed. But many people never give Him a try at all, assuming He's a burden, a trick, or a trial. Don't you miss out on the very best way to live your life! Get a taste of God, and you will find He makes your life pretty delicious.

—MH

The Greased Widow Maker

He lifted me out of the slimy pit, out of the mud and mire; he set my feet on a rock and gave me a firm place to stand. Psalm 40:2.

If you are not entirely covered in slippery, slimy soap by the end of the night, then you probably didn't try very hard to make it to the top of the Greased Widow Maker. It's a Union College tradition, and it's likely to land you flat on your backside floating in film. Each fall, on the first weekend of school, after the handshake, the willing and the brave make their way to a hillside that's been completely covered in giant tarps. The tarps have been doused with bottles upon bottles of soap, and students armed with hoses stand on the sides to keep the soap sudsy. At the top of the hill the tarps cascade up and over a stack of old mattresses. An extra dozen bottles of soap have been emptied here. As the rule goes, the student who makes it to the top of the hill first and can actually stand up on the mattress stack gets a large cash prize. You have never seen so many college students covered in soap, sliding down a hill on top of each other. Maybe it sounds simple to you, but unless you've tried it, you have no idea how hard it is to climb up a soap-coated tarp. It's practically impossible to manage just a few steps, even if you get a running start. Half the fun is watching people flail and fall and roll down the hill.

Whenever I read Psalm 40, I think of the Greased Widow Maker. David claims that God lifted him out of a slimy pit and set him on firm ground. I imagine this metaphorical pit to be somewhat like the Widow Maker—impossible to surmount, dangerous even to try. I can picture David in this muddy, miry hole in the ground, covered in slime, trying to climb out. That's how he felt about his life. Have you ever felt like that? Are there places in your life that have you stuck? Are there things you can't free yourself from? At times, does even a small step seem next to impossible? David says that God is capable in these situations. Most of us waste a lot of effort trying to climb out on our own, only to end up covered in filth. It's not the best strategy for reaching the top.

Realize today that God is able to lift you out of even the dirtiest, messiest, slimiest places in your life. No pit is too deep for Him. No dirt is too dirty. There is nothing you can do that He cannot rescue you from. Nothing! So instead of slipping and sliding on your own, reach your hand up and let Him lift you back out and onto solid ground.

—MH

As the Camel

As the deer pants for streams of water, so my soul pants for you, O God. My soul thirsts for God, for the living God. Psalm 42:1, 2.

The thirstiest person I have ever known was my brother Josh, on the day when my entire family, like idiots, went hiking through the Arizona desert in the summer —without water. Well, one person had water, and that was me. I alone brought a single bottle of water. The day was scorching and the hike was a long one, through the brush and rock and dust, and the air was so hot it felt as if we'd opened an oven door and climbed inside. Poor thirsty Josh followed me throughout the entire hike, crying "Just a swig! Just a swig!" My water was gone in the first 20 minutes, except an inch or two at the bottom that I was saving for dire emergency, but still Josh persisted with every sweaty step: "Just a swig!"

The thirstiest animal I ever encountered was a wild camel in the Sinai desert. Our jeep caravan had stopped so some of us could find a private spot to go to the bathroom. You cannot imagine how terrifying it is to be discreetly doing what you're doing only to look up and see a wild camel charging toward you. He was thirsty—terribly thirsty. That's the only thing I can imagine. He must have thought I was pouring water on the ground. I bet he was really disappointed when he got there—I didn't stay to see, though. It kind of scared me!

It's one thing to thirst for water, but have you ever thirsted for God? Psalm 42 talks about thirsting for the Lord in the same way an animal thirsts for water. Think for a minute about the feeling of being terribly thirsty. Your throat is parched. You can hardly swallow. An hour passes. You feel dizzy. You're getting desperate. Frantic. Your body needs water right away, and you can hardly think of anything else until you get it. You're willing to pay any amount (think airport prices) for a few ounces of that measly little drink. That's how the writer feels about God. Desperate for Him, frantic to find Him, willing to do whatever it takes to get Him.

When was the last time your need for God was this strong? If you're like me, your soul thirsts for God when things have been rough or when you need extra help. But wouldn't it be nice to seek God this determinedly all the time? Don't wait until your soul is thirsting and panting for God to go looking for Him. Instead, take time each day and have your fill of Him.

—MH

You Come *to* Me

Create in me a clean heart, O God; and renew a right spirit within me.
Psalm 51:10, KJV.

Apparently they were pretending to be zombies awakened from the dead when they bumped into the precious vase. My good friend Lhamo and her brother stared at the pieces in shock and horror, realizing that their mother would be home soon. It's the classic childhood dilemma, isn't it? They pieced the vase back together well enough, but while they were applying the glue, Lhamo got cut by one of the broken shards. She wrapped and bandaged her arm as her brother finished with the glue; then they sat and waited for the worst. Mom never did notice the vase, but she noticed the cut on Lhamo's arm. When she questioned her, Lhamo had to tell the whole story. What I liked the most, though, was that instead of lecturing her and giving her the classic line "your sins will find you out," Lhamo's mother gave this shocking order: "When you get hurt, you come *to* me. When you need help, when you're in pain, come to me. I don't care how it happened—don't hide it. You come to me." Lhamo says that for the first time she realized a mother isn't someone you hide from when you're in trouble, but someone you go to.

King David decided that God is that kind of person. First, he slept with another man's wife, then sent the man to the front lines of battle to get him out of the picture. God sent the prophet Nathan to confront King David, who knew he'd sinned and felt pretty lousy. So he wrote out his feelings in Psalm 51. He doesn't try to hide his sin, explain himself, or defend his actions. Instead, he has learned the lesson Lhamo learned that day: When you are in trouble, come *to* God. It's the opposite of our first instinct: to hide from Him or drift away from Him when we sin. Instead, we ought to come straight to Him as soon as possible.

My favorite verse in this psalm is the one written above, David's plea for God to create a clean heart in him in place of the wicked heart he has. You see, this is something we cannot do for ourselves, and that's why hiding from God is futile. If we really want a changed heart, if we want freedom from that sin, we have to come to Him. He's the only place that that can happen.

Have you been hiding? Have you been trying to cover up some wrong? Try running to God, instead of away from Him. You can't erase your sin or change your heart on your own.

—MH

Who Wants to Kill Hitler?

Strangers are attacking me; ruthless men seek my life—men without regard for God. Psalm 54:3.

All day long they twist my words; they are always plotting to harm me. Psalm 56:5.

One of the most amazing statistics of World War II is the number of people who tried to kill Hitler. Recently declassified German reports, along with many other international sources, give us a confirmed number of 42 assassination attempts on Hitler's life, with the possibility of many more undocumented ones. Among these were attempts from an angry student whose three pathetic tries were easily thwarted by Hitler's guards early in his career (consequently getting the student sent to the guillotine) to James Bond-like missions during which three well-trained and -equipped secret agents were sent in with poison and "exploding rats." One of the most intense attempts on Hitler's life was organized and implemented by generals and members of his own military. They used a bomb in a briefcase left in his main conference room headquarters, known as the Wolf's Lair. The bomb went off on July 20, 1944, killing eight and wounding many others. But Hitler was not killed in the blast—the heavy wooden conference table support had acted as a shield. Believing that he was invincible, and under "divine protection" after so many failed attempts, Hitler openly scoffed at and jeered all who might try to kill him. But after this final attempt, he purged and executed all those in the military whom he feared might want to get rid of him.

In many of the writings throughout the book of Psalms David is bemoaning that his enemies have surrounded him and hope to bring about his ruin or death. The funny thing, though, is that David doesn't respond by killing off his enemies. He simply brings his fears to God and asks for *His* divine protection. He doesn't rely on human plans or protection, but seeks God as his Protector and Savior. Sometimes it's almost funny that the first thing we want to do when we're in trouble is look for ways to get ourselves out, when the most reliable source of help at our disposal is nothing more than a prayer away. So take David's response to heart. Remember that when you face enemies or when things around you are going against you at every turn, your best source of protection is going to be from God. He's promised to help and protect, so we should take our fears and concerns to Him first.

—GH

Find rest, O my soul, in God alone; my hope comes from him. He alone is my rock and my salvation; he is my fortress, I will not be shaken. Psalm 62:5, 6.

No army has ever bothered to attack the stronghold fortress in Salzburg, Austria, simply because there would be no point. I've been there and seen how it sits like an unruly bear atop the jagged stone cliffs overlooking the whole city. The Hohensalzburg Castle is one of the largest medieval castles in all of Europe. Measuring more than 800 feet long and about 500 feet wide, the castle has always cast a long shadow not only over the city it protects but also over any who choose to hide within its walls. Many a bishop and king, as well as residents of the town, fled to its impenetrable walls when an intruding army happened to pass by the city. Salzburg itself was a major place of trade and industry, centering on its winding river and the abundant salt mines found in the nearby Alpine mountains. Among its more famous home-grown residents are Mozart and Maria von Trapp (of *The Sound of Music* fame), both of whom turned and looked at the stalwart protector of their fair city on a daily basis. With a castle that had never been overcome, who wouldn't feel safe?

This feeling of security is echoed in Psalm 62. David croons on about God in a somewhat curious allusion. In verse 5 he says his very soul finds rest in God only, and his hope for the future comes from Him. Then he paints a word picture of God as a solid rock, and a fortress that will never be shaken. This song passes on to its listeners the idea that God is a constant source of security in a world that doesn't have much of it to go around. David doesn't say he just runs away from problems, but he knows that when he needs protection he can call on God. It's as if God is his lifeline, the backup plan when everything else in life seems to be losing ground. But beyond this "call in an emergency" aspect, he also says that his soul finds rest, and his hope comes from God. That means that even in regular life, when he isn't feeling desperate, he goes through it without fear or anxiety because he can always turn and look up at the "fortress" that can't be shaken. It's a secure feeling to know that you always have a place to run to when things get bad. Just like those residents of Salzburg who live in the shadow of that impenetrable castle, we believers too stand in the shadow of a God whose protection of us will never be overcome.

—GH

Those People Who Have It All

For you have been my hope, O Sovereign Lord, my confidence since my youth.
Psalm 71:5.

There was that sickeningly typical girl in high school that I was insanely jealous of because everything always seemed to work out for her. It didn't matter which guy she liked. If she wanted him, he was as good as hers—she always got the guys everyone else only dreamed of. She had all the cutest clothes to complete her perfect face, perfect hair, and perfect body. She was sporty, confident, smart, and sweet. It was hard to know whether you should hate her or love her, but one thing was sure: she had it all.

David has often been painted as one of those same types of people—everything always seems to work out for him. He wins almost every battle he enters and succeeds at almost everything he puts his hand to. It's amazing when you read the accounts of his story—everything always goes his way! What's his secret?

I've always wondered why he lived such a blessed life and why the Lord's favor rested so strongly on David. When I came upon Psalm 71, I felt as though I'd found the answer. David's secret of success is written above, and it is this: The Lord had been his confidence since his youth. He had walked with God and depended on God since he was a child, and because of this, God never let Him down. God blessed just about everything David ever attempted. While other kings wasted years of their lives following after other gods and methods, David, despite his many mistakes, never turned away from God. He always walked with the Lord.

You are still young enough that almost your whole life stretches out ahead of you. Now is the time to decide whom you will walk with. Some of your largest life decisions are made in your youth, and the choices you choose today will greatly affect where you find yourself years from now down the road. Big choices such as what you'll do to make a living and the person you marry, and so-called small ones, such as the video games you play and the food you eat. So choose wisely! Adopt the success secret of David, and decide to walk with the Lord from your youth and onward. That way, when you look back years from now, you will, instead of regretting your choices, marvel at the great happiness that has been yours.

—MH

A Town Called Vernazza

Better is one day in your courts than a thousand elsewhere. Psalm 84:10.

Maybe it was because we missed so many trains that day. Maybe it was because we didn't speak a lick of Italian and that's all the stationmaster could communicate with, or perhaps it was because of the really big argument we had on the railway platform about which train was, in fact, the one we should take. In any case, we ended up in Vernazza—a miniature, quintessential Italian village tucked serenely into a cleft of the Cinque Terre. In my memory Vernazza is the most perfect place in all the world. Its one main street winds through the colorful buildings that climb the cliffs above on either side, and the street ends at a cozy little Mediterranean bay. The entire town marches to the beat of a single church bell tolling the lazy hours.

When Greg and I arrived here after our ragged nightmare train experience, we never wanted to leave. We rented a villa overlooking the sea, and we stayed for days and days. We were supposed to cross the border the next morning and spend the week touring the magnificent castles of Germany, but we somehow couldn't bring ourselves to leave this quiet, beautiful place. In the town where pesto was invented, we ate pizza at the water's edge, slept side by side in the afternoon sun, and held hands on moonlit walks through the cobblestone alleys. Vernazza worked its magic on us, and we left Europe without ever seeing those castles. We decided it was better to stay as long as we could in this town we fell in love with than to go anywhere else at all. Even today, if I could choose one place on earth to revisit before I die, you'd find me in dreamy, sweet Vernazza.

You may feel this way about your favorite place on earth, but have you ever felt this way about God? The Psalms tell us that one single day with God is better than a thousand other days anywhere else on earth. They claim that God's company is really that valuable—it is more enjoyable than anywhere else you could possibly be. If you are prone to doubt whether or not this is true, then I encourage you to give Him a try today. Spend this one day as completely in the presence of God as possible—think about Him, read about Him, speak about Him, look for Him and notice Him, and talk to Him constantly. The day won't be without problems, but I guarantee you that you'll experience a companionship you won't soon want to leave.

—MH

Near-Death Experiences

Teach us to number our days aright, that we may gain a heart of wisdom. Psalm 90:12.

Several times during my life I escaped serious injury or death. My childhood home almost burned down one Thanksgiving because of a grease fire in the oven, but an unseen hand miraculously turned off the stove as we all slept soundly in rooms with no smoke detectors. When my old ghetto van overheated returning to college one afternoon, I had an unshakably strong urge to flee the vehicle. Seconds later the entire cab filled with flames. My airplane caught on fire on my way overseas—luckily we were still on the runway and not in the air, so everyone got off the plane safely. A dorm fire started in the walls and floors of the room directly under my bed. Had the fire started in the night, I would have burned or died of smoke inhalation before I ever knew what was going on. (Are you noticing the fire theme here?) I have also had my share of accidents—spinning across four lanes of heavy freeway traffic without being touched, getting my neck wrapped in the rope as I fell rappelling, being thrown from a moving vehicle.

After each of these near-death experiences I marveled at the phenomenon of the "next-day syndrome." You wake up the next morning and realize with full certainty that you are fortunate to be alive! Life takes on new meaning. It has a precious quality to it, and you feel thankful for everything because you realize with stark clarity that you almost didn't get to see this day. Each time we have a brush with death it tends to put the priorities in our lives back into perspective. Suddenly we're not worried about the silly details anymore— we are just thankful to be alive. But the truth is that none of us are guaranteed tomorrow. Each and every day is a gift. If you knew the date and time of your death, would it change the way you lived today?

The psalmist asks the Lord to teach us to number our days aright—meaning teach us to live well. Teach us to appreciate life and live as if tomorrow is not guaranteed. Help us understand that life is something we shouldn't take for granted. This helps us gain a heart of wisdom—giving us the perspective to make better choices. Try to see today for what it is: a gift. Try to live in such a way today that, were it to be your last day on earth, you would be happy with the choices you made.

—MH

The Sand Cave Grave

Unless the Lord had given me help, I would soon have dwelt in the silence of death. When I said, "My foot is slipping," your love, O Lord, supported me. Psalm 94:17, 18.

It was Pathfinder campout at McGrath Beach, and the plan for the afternoon was to tunnel deep into one of the many sand dunes that covered the windy shore. Just as we began digging our masterfully planned tunnel, my dad made this annoying rule: "You have to leave your feet sticking out!" Everyone seemed peeved because duh! You can dig only so far into a tunnel if your feet have to be sticking out. Certain that my dad was lame and ridiculous, I watched my friends take turns digging farther and farther in and bided my time.

When my turn finally came, I scrambled into the tunnel as quickly as I could, but Dad's knowing hands caught my ankles. I dug as deep and as fast as I could into the damp sand, all the while resenting his hands wrapped tightly around my ankles. Then suddenly I couldn't move, and everything went black. I couldn't breathe. A tremendous weight crushed me to the ground. The tunnel had collapsed, and I was buried alive under a mountain of sand. For a moment I was terrified of dying there, but that's when I felt Dad's hands tighten firmly around my ankles. He was holding on to me! There was one tug, and I felt myself come loose. Two tugs, and I was free. Gasping for breath through the sand in my nostrils, I fell into Dad's arms. Everyone crowded around and asked if I was afraid for my life. As my dad tells the story, he remembers I said, "When I felt his hands, I wasn't afraid. I knew he'd pull me out."

I wish I could tell you why life caves in on us sometimes. I wish I could explain why we're crushed under tremendous burdens of pain and suffering and grief. But I can't. I don't know why you have to go through some of the trials you face, but I do know this: when your life falls down around you, there will be hands on your ankles. God will be holding you; His grip will tighten, and He will pull you out, one way or another. We are assured of it in Psalm 94, when the writer admits that without God's help he would have met with death. But as his foot was slipping, it was God's love that supported him.

God's love is still holding on to you, and it is strong enough today to pull you out from under whatever weights may be crushing your life.

—MH

Reasons Not to Marry Greg

Praise the Lord, O my soul, and forget not all his benefits. Psalm 103:2.

As fourth-grade as this might sound, before I decided to marry Greg I really did sit down and make a "pros" and "cons" list of reasons I should, or should not, marry him. On the "pro" side, of course, were all his charming qualities and attributes: he's my best friend; he's committed to God; he's loyal, honest, loving, sensitive, wonderful, and amazing, etc. You don't want to hear all that sappy stuff, but you might be interested in the "cons" list: I hate chest hair, or hair of any sort that is not on a person's head, where hair belongs. And Greg is covered with it, from ear tips to toe tips. I wanted to marry someone outgoing. Greg prefers to keep to himself. I wanted to marry a man who was tall, blond, and blue-eyed. Greg is my exact height, has dark hair, and brown eyes. I don't like his teeth. I'm afraid he'll be fat one day. He doesn't exercise.

What you are probably thinking is that the "cons" list seems very shallow in comparison to the "pros" list—and you are right. Ultimately, I saw that myself, because I obviously married him. But those things on the "cons" list were a really big deal at one time. They were (extremely silly) things that I really wanted to have, things that I would need to let go of if I were to marry Greg. But the fact is that they truly paled in comparison to all his many good qualities.

David encourages the reader of his psalm to make a "pros" list for serving the Lord. Have you ever done such a thing—made a list of all the reasons to serve God? We often think about why we don't want to serve Him, but what are the reasons in favor of it? David's list includes some of the following: He forgives all your sins, heals all your diseases, redeems your life, lavishes love and compassion on you, satisfies your desires with good things. And He is slow to anger, abounding in love; He does not treat our sins as we deserve, or repay us for them; His love is as high as the heavens, and He has removed our sins as far as the east is from the west, and more.

Your reasons against serving God might seem a bit shallow when you take all that into consideration. God's benefits far outweigh any sacrifice we might make. In short, serving God is worth it! Take some time today to think about why *you* serve the Lord. What are the benefits it has added to your life? What are the blessings and joys it has brought you?

—MH

The Ride of His Life

I am passing like a shadow when it lengthens; I am shaken off like the locust. My knees are weak from fasting, and my flesh has grown lean, without fatness. . . . Help me, O Lord my God; save me according to Your lovingkindness. Psalm 109:23-26, NASB.

Twenty-one-year-old Ben Carpenter, of Paw Paw, Michigan, had dealt with the problems of muscular dystrophy for quite a while. But now he could get around with the new electric wheelchair his parents had purchased for him. On this day, as he was crossing an intersection with the protection of a red light, he wheeled in front of a large semi that was pulling out of a gas station. As the truck rolled forward, it struck Ben's wheelchair. But instead of knocking him over and crushing him, it pushed the chair forward, and the handlebars on the back of the chair became lodged in the grill of the truck. The truck driver couldn't see it, so for the next four miles the truck hurtled along at 50 miles per hour, taking Ben on the wildest ride of his life. No one was able to flag down or make contact with the semi's driver until state troopers pulled him over and walked him around to the front of the cab, where they pried Ben's wheelchair out of his grill.

"It was very scary," said Ben in an interview shortly after the incident. "I'm not [religious], but I, uh, somebody was watching over me." Ben survived his ride without a scratch, and the only thing wrong with the wheelchair afterward was that it needed a new set of tires. The rough ride had worn down the old ones to little eraser nubs.

Sometimes life can kind of feel that way. You're going along OK, and suddenly *Whamo!* you're hit by a semi and doing 50 miles per hour with no way of stopping yourself. Many of David's songs and poems that are collected in the book of Psalms show that he felt that way a lot! They are David's cries to God about his trouble and pain. He always sounds as if things will never get any better, but the amazing thing is that God is always just around the corner, both for David and for you and me. Often we can't see that the crazy things happening in our lives will later prove to be the times we most clearly saw God's work on our behalf. It doesn't mean that God sends the bad things; it means that *when* bad things happen, God is going to be on the phone calling 911 and sending His angels to guide and comfort us. Keep your eyes and ears open. God isn't going to let you get run over by that semi called life.

—GH

Men: The Great Disappointment

It is better to take refuge in the Lord than to trust in man. Psalm 118:8.

It didn't make sense—there were the poems he had written for me, beautifully composed poems, lines and lines of love and devotion for me, but that wasn't my name at the top. Instead, this exact same poem that he'd written to me was addressed to a cute little blond girl in the dorm, signed with love from him, and tacked up to her wall for all to see. I was devastated. And to think he had just asked me to be his girlfriend! How could I have been so blind?

More guys have let me down or disappointed me over the years than I could ever begin to tell you about. During my junior year an old flame was returning from college to spend the weekend with me, and I waited by the phone, literally, all weekend long, but he never came. His friends told me later he had been "detained" in Texas with an old flame of his own. That same year my boyfriend left me for one of my best friends. One guy left me to join the Army. Another took me out on dates only to talk about his ex-girlfriend and all their past drama. Still another broke up with me on our one-year anniversary. Even the boy I "dated" in eighth grade ran against me for class president and won. The other boy I liked that year chose my best friend instead of me.

So when I read the verse above, the verse that is the exact center verse of the Bible, it really rang true in my heart: It is better to trust in God than in man! The Bible obviously doesn't mean men as an entire gender, though—it means any human being. The basic idea here is one we have all probably learned well: that people will let you down. People will break your trust. Even the best people will still disappoint you at times.

We put our trust in all kinds of other things, don't we? We depend on things and people and circumstances to make us happy. We expect relationships to fulfill us, and we hope that life will be kind to us. But the only true source of happiness and safety is God.

Learn to put your trust in the only Man that you can trust at all times. Depend on Him for your happiness and fulfillment, because He alone can promise to always hold you up when life's inevitable disappointments come your way.

—MH

The Dark Game

Your word is a lamp to my feet and a light for my path. Psalm 119:105.

The "dark game" was one of the dumbest games I have ever played in my life, and I'm embarrassed to admit that I'm actually the one who made it up. The rules for the game were simple: turn out all the lights in any room, shut the doors, and roll around in the dark like blind idiots. My cousins and I played this; one person was always "it," and the object of the game was just to touch someone—anyone—randomly in the dark. Then that person would be "it." We would jump over tables and beds, roll onto couches and over legs, crash into corners, and bump into walls. Inevitably, someone always got hurt—either from being stepped on, or from running smack-dab into a sharp object lurking in the shadows. One time Angel fell off the bed. Another time Avri ran into someone's teeth. Miki's fingernails left multiple incisions on my arms, and I think Heather used to crash into me on purpose.

I haven't played that silly old game in years, but so often now as an adult I still feel like I'm stumbling around in the darkness of my own life. When I'm faced with tough decisions, it's really hard to know what path to choose or which way to go. The author of Psalm 119 must have understood this feeling when he wrote about God's law. He compared the Word of God to a lamp for feet walking on a dark path. He realized that walking through life often feels like walking without a lamp on a dark night, so he suggested God's law as a lamp.

How could laws be like a lamp? Simple—they tell us which way to go. They keep us from stumbling into stupid sins or from getting lost and thrown off course. They let us know which route is the best one to take. God's laws help us make better choices about the direction our life is heading. If you ignore them or turn your back on them, it's like switching the light off again—you're left in the dark, and who knows where you'll eventually end up?

Today, are you walking through life on a clear and lighted path, or have you been stumbling around in the dark for quite some time? If you need some illumination or guidance, take some time and think about the lights that God has given you: His laws. Let them lead you back onto a safe path, and allow them to improve the quality of your journey.

—MH

Someone Who Knows Me

O Lord, you have searched me and you know me. . . . You are familiar with all my ways.
Psalm 139:1-3.

Do you have a friend who knows you better sometimes than you know yourself . . . someone who can almost predict your every move and word and thought? My best friend Greg is like this. (Actually, he's my husband, too.) If we walk into a store and see 10 sweaters hanging on the wall, he immediately knows which one I'm going to buy—and that's way before I know. I have to try on six of them before I know! If we go to the library, he can predict which book I'm going to check out. He knows which woman in a room of strangers I'd most likely be friends with. He has sent e-mails from my account for me a time or two because he knows exactly how I'd respond—and he's right! If I've lost my keys in the house, he can guess where I've put them. Most of the time, he can even guess what I'm thinking and how I got there. He knows when I'm mad before I've said anything. He remembers my dreams and goals, sometimes long after I myself have given up on them. If only everyone had a friend like this!

But we *do*! Psalm 139 describes a God who has searched us, who knows us. Someone who knows our thoughts. Even before a word is on our tongue He already knows it completely. He is familiar with all our ways—all the days of our lives were written in His book before even one of them came to be. Think about that for a while! I mean, my husband knows my habits and preferences, but God knows all the days of my life! That's beyond even Greg's expertise.

Life can be pretty lonely when we don't feel as if there are people who get us or understand us. And sometimes God just doesn't feel like enough. We want real friends who know us, not just a God up in heaven somewhere. But He can be enough. In fact, He can be even better than that. Even the people who know you best actually only know you in part. They don't know all of you. There are still deep, dark secrets in every heart that get shared with no one. Nobody can love you *completely*, because nobody knows you completely. But God knows even these things, and He loves you anyway. To be known completely and still loved in spite of it is the most wonderful feeling in all the world. Today, enjoy the knowledge that God really does know you. He knows all the little details of your life—and He loves you anyway.

—MH

Brandon, the Accidental Desert Guide

When my spirit grows faint within me, it is you who know my way.
Psalm 142:3.

It was the walkie-talkie that saved her in the end. My sister Heather was camping with some friends and family in the Arizona desert when she decided to wander off for a special little time of solitude and silence. Enjoying the scenery and the chance to get away from the crowd, she wound her way deeper and deeper into the desert, and farther and farther away from camp. I'm not sure how long it was before she realized she was lost, but suddenly she did. She tried to retrace her steps, but most of the desert looks the same. She tried to look for familiar land-marks—stones, bushes, hills—but each one blended into another.

That's when she remembered the walkie-talkie she'd brought along with her. Frantically radioing back to camp, she hoped that she had not walked too far out of range to be heard. Lucky for her, though most of the others had left the camp, Brandon was near enough to a radio to hear her cry for help. He picked up and was able to understand her story. Then he slowly began talking her back to camp. Though he couldn't see where she was, he knew the way she needed to go, and he led her safely out of the desert and into the campsite.

You may not always feel lost, and that's good. But if at this point in your life you do feel lost and don't know which way to go, remember that Somebody else out there knows what you should do. God assures us in the Psalms that when our spirits grow faint and we forget our own way, He still remembers. He knows which way we ought to go, even when we don't. So it's important to seek His input once in awhile, and ask for His leading.

If you haven't done that lately, today may be the perfect day for it. Explain to God which areas of your life you're feeling lost in, then ask Him to lead you through and show you the way out. Have confidence that God knows the path for your life, even long after you have lost your own way.

—MH

Firecrackers and Fingers Don't Mix

Can a man scoop fire into his lap without his clothes being burned? Can a man walk on hot coals without his feet being scorched? Proverbs 6:27, 28.

Firecrackers and guys just seem to go hand in hand. It was one of those lazy summer afternoons when you don't have much to do except look for trouble. While rummaging around in the garage I'd run across a box half full of firecrackers that had been left over from the Fourth of July a few weeks before. I brought the box out to the deck on the back of my house and ran over the possibilities with my friend Matt. Suddenly my old slingshot came to mind. Not just one of those generic Y-shaped sticks, but the metal ones (with the arm brace) that are used for hunting—a serious slingshot for serious people! With this new, amazing implement we proceeded to take our mundane firecracker exploits to a whole new level. I'd place a firecracker in the pouch and pull back the rubber cords. Matt would quickly light the fuse, and a split second later I'd send the cracker on its merry way. However, on one of those times the fuse burned much faster than usual, and before I could even lose the slingshot it exploded with a deafening *kablam!* My ears were ringing oddly, my two fingers felt as if they'd been smashed by a hammer, and I smelled burning skin—my fingertips were black with exploded gunpowder. When I look back on this experience, the phrase "when you play with fire, you get burned" comes to mind. In today's verse Solomon said a similar thing in a different way—which shows me the concept isn't new.

Solomon knew the dangers that came from playing around with potentially dangerous situations. He'd been through a variety of marriages, political intrigues, and ultimately the degradation of the entire Jewish culture mainly because he chose to mess around with things he knew he shouldn't. Allowing his foreign wives to bring their gods and idol worship to his doorstep had introduced pagan worship to the Jewish nation—and it seems they never met an idol they didn't like. From this point on we see the Jewish monarchy falling into a downward spiral of idol worship and tyrannical policies, and worship of the true God was forgotten or ignored. So when Solomon speaks of fire in a man's lap, he's speaking from personal experience. Each of us knows what kind of fire we're playing with in our lives. The question is Will we be smart enough to put it down when we hear God warning our consciences to tell us to let it go?

—GH

The Seductive Woman of the Night

Do not let your heart turn to her ways or stray into her paths. Many are the victims she has brought down; her slain are a mighty throng. Proverbs 7:25, 26.

A man is walking down the street at dusk—just a young guy who doesn't have much sense—when around the corner a woman dressed like a prostitute comes to meet him. She is loud and defiant, and she takes hold of the young man and kisses him "with a brazen face" (Proverbs 7:13). Proverbs 7 continues to paint this picture of this woman, "the adulteress," seducing some poor young fellow. She tempts him with the fact that her bed is covered in the finest linens from Egypt, and her sheets are perfumed with myrrh, aloes, and cinnamon—apparently the choice seduction tools of the times. Her husband is away on a long journey, and he won't return until the full moon. In fact, he has taken his entire purse full of money—that's how long he'll be gone. She invites him to drink deep of love with her until the morning, and like an ox on its way to the slaughter, Solomon says, the daft young lad follows her. Solomon begs his own sons, to whom he is writing, not to fall victim to this type of woman, for she has "slain . . . a mighty throng" of men, and her house is a "highway to the grave" (verses 26, 27).

These are some pretty harsh words! But adultery has some pretty harsh consequences, too, as some of you have learned the hard way. How many have thought they would just toy with it for a time, only to lose their spouse, their family, their career, and everything they held precious and dear? Like the woman painted in the picture above, it's not something to play with. Just a simple stray into her path can send you on your way to the grave—it's that serious!

At this age you may think that it's not time yet to think about adultery, since you're not married yet, but guess again. The choices you make today, right now, are shaping you into the type of person you are going to be! When you give in to temptations today, it just makes it that much more likely that you'll give in at some time in the future, too, possibly when the stakes are a lot higher. When you give in, you are conditioning yourself to become a certain type of person. Each decision you make, however small it seems now, is leading you down a very specific path. Ask the Lord today to make you strong enough and wise enough to see temptation coming around the corner and, instead of following it, to turn and run in the other direction.

—MH

Women Driver Awards

Pride goes before destruction, and a haughty spirit before a fall. Proverbs 16:18, NRSV.

One of my good friends just e-mailed me the old "2006 Women Driver Awards" (photos included), and I'm still laughing. Tenth place went to a woman (in a jeans skirt, mind you) standing knee-deep in a mud hole, with her car knee-deep, as well. (I don't know which is more stupid: driving your car into a mud hole, or wearing a jeans skirt to go mudding.) The eighth-place winner was a woman in a red miniskirt, who had gotten her VW bug stuck parallel on the train tracks, meaning she had had to have been driving straight down the tracks. Fifth place went to a woman in a blue Dodge who was trailing a gasoline hose behind her. Apparently she'd forgotten she'd just filled her car with gas, and had driven right on out of the gas station without unhooking the nozzle. Brilliant! Fourth place had driven her car through six-inch-deep wet cement, becoming permanently stuck, of course. First place—and this is amazing—had driven her car right off a boat dock. However, the front bumper had landed on a yacht, and the back bumper was resting on the dock, leaving the car miraculously suspended above the water in midair. How had that happened? But my personal favorite, the picture that made me laugh so hard I almost cried, was of a girl on a moped. She's wearing a helmet, but her face is sticking through the neck hole, and her neck is sticking through the face hole. The strap is tightened securely across the dead center of her face, and she is riding happily down the street. I don't understand—can she even see?

I was feeling pretty smug about what a good woman driver I am, until the dark and stormy night I backed my own car out of a driveway and ended up stuck in a ditch. My friend Mary Ellen and I couldn't figure out why every car that drove past us stopped to stare, until we tried to get out of the car and fell about two feet into the mud. The car was balanced on three wheels, with one wheel spinning free up in the air. I thought immediately of the Women Driver Awards e-mail, and both my heart and my pride sank. I was one of those women I'd laughed at.

The Bible says that pride goes before a fall. Sometimes that means a literal fall, but I think it can mean a fall of your ego as well. So the next time you start feeling prideful—whether it's how great you look, how smart you are, or how well you drive—eat a slice of humble pie before you end up in a ditch!

—MH

The words of a gossip are like choice morsels; they go down to a man's inmost parts. Proverbs 18:8.

If you found out that a story about you was circulating through the camp staff, you could be sure it started with Joe. Joe was one of those guys who just loves gossip. He lived off of it, and he absolutely could not stop himself from sharing whatever anybody had told him—with the entire world. One day I and some of the other girls on the camp staff got sick of all Joe's gossiping, so we decided to play a trick on him. We'd invent a wild story, see how long it took for the story to come straight back to us, and then tell everyone it was a hoax meant to expose the gossip king.

We started a rumor that three of us had left our campers alone and snuck out of our cabins at midnight to the horse stables. Once there, we tore off all our clothes, hopped on the horses bareback (and bare-bottomed), and sped off riding wildly into the night. We begged Joe to promise not to tell a soul, but this ludicrously made-up story was simply too much for him—he couldn't resist. He told every single person he came in contact with that morning, and by 11:00 a.m., a whole hour before lunchtime, the story had circulated all over camp and come straight back to us. We had some explaining to do when the camp director found out, but he had a good laugh when he realized that our intent was simply to expose Joe for the gossip that he was.

To be fair to Joe, I guess we ought to admit that everyone likes gossip, don't we? Proverbs calls us all out on the fact that some good gossip is just as satisfying as tasty food that fills our bellies. We eat it up. We love it. And it's oh, so easy to do.

Today, as hard as it seems, try not to give in to the gossip game. When a "choice morsel" of gossip comes your way, instead of sharing it (as we all want to), be different. Let the gossip die with you, and you will likely save some reputations and some feelings along the way. You might even save your own name somehow. Who knows—when people see that you won't participate in gossip, they might even be moved to give it up themselves.

Don't spread stories, true or not. Pray for the strength to do the right thing.

—MH

That Beer Bottle Is Laughing at You

Wine is a mocker and beer a brawler; whoever is led astray by them is not wise.
Proverbs 20:1.

In 2006 there were 17,941 driving fatalities that were directly related to alcohol consumption, making them 41 percent of the total number of driving deaths that year. Surprisingly, most people with DUIs (a conviction for "driving under the influence") are not actually alcoholics but merely people who drank before getting behind the wheel. And 80 percent of these alcohol-related fatalities were because of beer, one of the most readily available and popular alcoholic beverages today. Thirty-one percent of average Americans are involved in an alcohol-related car crash at least once in their lifetime. Even if you don't wind up killing someone, if you're ever pulled over and convicted of a DUI (or a DWI, "driving while intoxicated"), you will face possible jail time and extensive fines. Also, your insurance will be revoked, with any future rates skyrocketing.

In many cases convicted drivers are required to carry an SR-22 insurance policy, a hard-to-get form from your insurance company to the state saying that they will insure you regardless of your previous conviction and the resulting risk factors. And that's just the statistics involved, which has nothing to do with the pain of real people who lose loved ones just because someone chose to kick back a few before driving home. Thousands of Web sites are dedicated to victims of drunk driving—the lives and dreams that were instantly snuffed out. What's interesting is that Solomon wouldn't be surprised at any of this, even if today's transportation differed from his.

So why did Solomon talk about alcohol so long ago? Because alcohol affects people today in the same way it did back then. Solomon didn't say drinking wasn't fun, but what he did say is more creative—that alcohol mocks you. In other words, it makes a fool out of you! If it had a voice, it would be laughing at you for drinking it. Talk to the families of people who started out as "social drinkers" and became alcoholics. See if they have any problem with Solomon's assessment: "Whoever is led astray by [alcohol] is not wise." Even though he says it in a kind of understatement, the message really means this: if you choose to fall into the trap of alcohol and everything it involves, you're stupid. The short version? If you've thought about drinking, *don't*. If you're currently drinking, *stop!* Or get some help from someone you trust.

—GH

Walk Softly and Carry a Big Saltshaker

Train a child in the way he should go, and when he is old he will not turn from it.
Proverbs 22:6.

The bird was gently pecking at something in the grass as I stealthily crept up behind it. This time there was no breeze, no sound, and no shadow to spook the bird into flying away, but as I lunged, saltshaker in hand, it somehow knew I was coming. A split second before my wildly shaking hand careened down toward it, the little sparrow took flight and headed for the highest power line it could find. I'd been hunting sparrows for an hour at least, and my stalking skills had increased considerably. I was certain that I had almost gotten the salt crystals on its tail feathers that time, and one more perfectly timed move on my part would certainly bag me a new pet. The thought of questioning my father's earlier lesson about birds and salt never crossed my young mind. "If you can get salt on the tail or wings of a bird, it can't fly anymore, and you can pick it right up off the ground." So there I was, stalking around the yard with a large saltshaker and a hoped-for cloak of invisibility. Finally another victim flew into my zone, and I carefully crept up from behind. Only inches away I raised the shaker in my hand and violently sprayed the bird with as much of the granulated sodium crystals as I could, only to see it shake off the fine dust and spring into the air yet again. I hurled the saltshaker to the ground, and turned to see my father rocking in his chair on the deck, laughing merrily at my antics. He told me later that his father had done it to him, and that he was passing on the tradition.

I tell you what, as soon as my son is able to understand what a saltshaker is really for, I'll have him in the backyard eyeing his first bird. What we pass on as traditions and beliefs are important. Part of our role as fathers is to learn and to pass it on to children so that they can learn from us. When Solomon speaks of training up a child, I think not only of saltshakers but also of all the really important things my parents taught me that have saved me from pain and heartache. They taught me right and wrong. They gave me priorities and a sense of honor. And like our parents here on earth, God is trying to pass along things that will keep us from falling prey to life problems that will cause suffering. His goal is to teach and to rescue, so that we don't have to lie as people do who don't know any better. His idea is to give us a sense of what life *could* be like, in the hopes that we choose wisely when the time comes. Will you listen?

—GH

Greg's Wife-Swap Offer

A wife of noble character who can find? She is worth far more than rubies. . . . Charm is deceptive, and beauty is fleeting; but a woman who fears the Lord is to be praised. Proverbs 31:10-30.

We were in Egypt, just outside the great pyramids, looking for Christmas gifts and souvenirs for our families. It was the man who ran the perfume and Egyptian oils shop that gave Greg the offer of trading me for 1,000 camels. I came through the door in my tank top and shorts (scanty dress for a woman in that part of the world), and apparently he decided right then and there that I would make a good wife and immediately began bartering with Greg. At first he offered Greg 100 camels for me. Greg laughed, assuming it was a joke. But the man took this to mean I was worth far more than that, so he upped his offer to 1,000 camels. Greg loves to remind me of this little exchange when we have an argument. "Woman, I could have gotten 1,000 camels for you!" he'll exclaim. (What would Greg do with one camel, let alone 1,000?)

Apparently a good wife has always been hard to find. The last chapter of Proverbs states that when you do find one, she's worth far more than rubies, and probably more than 1,000 camels, too. Then it goes on to outline what a good wife looks like. Girls and guys alike can learn a thing or two about the perfect mate from this chapter. The perfect wife in that long-ago day and age gets up before dawn, cooks for her family, makes linen garments, and then sells them at the city gate. She also works long into the night as well. But she does other noble things, too—such as extending help to the needy, faithfully instructing her children, preparing for hard times, and refraining from laziness. Her most important trait, however, is written in the verse above: she lives in respect for the Lord.

Half of you reading this are going to be looking for the perfect wife in the near future, and the other half of you will be trying to be that perfect wife for someone. Instead of expecting perfection in all areas, though, search for the quality that matters most—honor for God—and then cultivate it in your own life as well. Remember that if you expect to find a godly person, they will be looking for a godly person in you. Become the type of person you are searching for.

—MH

The Dude With 20 Different Majors

To the man who pleases him, God gives wisdom, knowledge and happiness, but to the sinner he gives the task of gathering and storing up wealth to hand it over to the one who pleases God. This too is meaningless, a chasing after the wind. Ecclesiastes 2:26.

The guy I sat next to in class was outright crazy. He hadn't yet declared a college major, and he was already in his junior year, well on his way to becoming a career student with no discernible completion date in sight—and it didn't seem to bother him a bit. He started out as a political science major because he liked talking on and on about politics. When this got tiring, he moved on to literature, and then to the arts. He was an art major for the majority of the time I knew him, but when he realized that he couldn't "find his expression" in any of the formal mediums, such as painting and sculpture, he moved on to philosophy. We took a philosophy course in a basement room of the main administration building, where he sat enthralled by the lecture the German professor was giving. Not that I didn't find a discussion of whether or not I existed to be fascinating, but it didn't have much real relevance to my life. According to my credit card company, I existed; and I'm pretty sure the school thought I did too, for they kept charging me tuition. So all in all, there didn't seem to be much point in debating it. I just wanted to get a degree, make some money, and get on with "real life."

But now that I've been engaged in "real life" for a while, I'm wondering if that crazy guy back in college wasn't on to something. Sure, he never actually graduated with anything, and I doubt he landed some high-paying job on the stock exchange, but I think he's been enjoying the ride a lot more than I did. I wonder what Solomon would have to say to me if he could reach out and speak. He says that to those who please Him, God gives wisdom, knowledge, and happiness, but to the sinners, He lets them toil and store up money so that He can give it to the ones who please Him. That means the guy who's more concerned with wisdom and knowledge gets all the stuff that I've been working for, and he's happier on top of it all! If nothing else, the book of Ecclesiastes can help us to step back and take a new perspective on the things that we want most. And in case you're obsessing about that high-paying job or new car, Solomon's got a few things to say about that kind of stuff, too. Vanity of vanities, anyone?

—GH

Neck-deep in Pond Slime

So I saw that there is nothing better for a man than to enjoy his work, because that is his lot. For who can bring him to see what will happen after him? Ecclesiastes 3:22.

Over the course of 15 years I've worked in 23 different jobs and have never been fired from any of them. (That's a little more than two per year, which doesn't necessarily look good on a résumé. But whoever puts down all their jobs, anyway?) The first seven or eight jobs were doing manual labor—mowing fields of hay, digging ditches for irrigation installations, or up to my neck in pond muck while clearing a truckload of dead and decaying weed slime from a pond.

The weed slime job was probably the one I hated most, because you could hardly breathe on account of the foul, choking smell that came up from this stuff. The weeds were actually long bulrushes that would crumple into the water and wrap around your legs and hands, and they decayed into a smashy pulp that somehow clung to the slick, muddy bottom of the pond no matter how hard you pulled. As I mentioned, the smell was overpowering. It had that sickening, makes-you-want-to-throw-up odor that anything organic gets when it's been left to sit in pond water for several months. I spent the better part of two days at this endeavor, just so the pond could be presentable for its owners and not spread its stench all over the estate. In future years, whenever I got tired of whatever current job I held, I'd always think back to that nasty pond and thank my lucky stars I wasn't doing *that* anymore.

I think Solomon could relate to my experience somewhat, for he takes a long look back over his lifetime and looks to see if anything he's done has been of lasting benefit to anyone. He spends much of Ecclesiastes describing how, throughout his life, he methodically looked for things that made him happy, for endeavors that would cause him to be remembered, for *anything* that held true meaning. And at the end of chapter 3 he sums things up by saying that in the end there is nothing better for a man to do than to enjoy his work in the here and now.

That gives some clarity to things, because we spend so much of our time living in the future or in the past. Solomon says you need to enjoy what you do *today*, not what you did in the past or will do someday. And through Solomon, God calls us to live in the here and now of our daily lives, promising that He will take care of the past and the future if we let Him.

—GH

Only Morons Steal Road Signs

Be happy . . . while you are young, and let your heart give you joy in the days of your youth. . . . But know that for all these things God will bring you to judgment. Ecclesiastes 11:9.

It's hard to explain what got into us that Sunday afternoon. Penny, Leiana, and I were bored out of our wits, bemoaning that there was nothing at all in the entire world to do. Yearning for some type of entertainment or adrenaline rush as we drove through an area of road construction, someone had the (not so) bright idea that we should snitch something. No sooner were the words said than my eyes fell upon the gem of the entire street—a large orange-and-white-striped barricade with a massive blinking light on the top. What a beauty! While Penny and Leiana stuffed the back seat with orange road cones, I dragged my precious barricade to the trunk and somehow shoved it inside. Once back at school, I proudly set it up in my dorm room for all to admire. I loved it! But there was just one problem. That blinking light . . . never . . . stopped . . . blinking. You couldn't turn it off, not ever, not until the battery wore totally down, and that would take weeks, some said. My prized possession began to keep me up at night, blinking nonstop. I covered it with blankets and jackets, but its relentless blink-blink-blink from underneath them still filled the room with an orange heartbeat. And with each blink the barricade seemed to jeer, "Stupid! Stupid! Stupid!" I grew to hate the thing, regretted terribly the day I took it, and eventually dumped it in a back desert alley. It was still blinking "Stupid! Stupid! Stupid!" at me as I drove away.

What a terrible idea sin—and stealing—always are. Our decisions follow us long after we have made them. Solomon cautions us about this. He suggests that we follow our heart and enjoy life as best we can, but whatever we decide to do, he says, God will hold us accountable for. Sin might seem funny in the beginning, but it haunts us and taunts us, and in the end it's just *never worth it*. What's more, you can't get away from it. You try to cover it up, but it'll still be there, flashing in your face. So the best way to avoid "Stupid! Stupid! Stupid!" ringing in your memory is to make good decisions today.

—MH

Remembering Tanya

Here is the conclusion of the matter: Fear God and keep his commandments, for this is the whole duty of man. Ecclesiastes 12:13.

My new baby and I were to play the parts of Mary and Baby Jesus for our church's annual "Journey to Bethlehem" Christmas production. My mood was anything but festive. I was starving because I'd missed dinner. My toddler had been repeating the same whiny phrase for about two hours. It was a bad hair day. And I had gotten too big for my jeans—again. Plus, who wants to play Jesus' mother out in the freezing cold when they're in a crabby mood?

But as I entered the church, it became immediately clear to me that something was very wrong. Everywhere, scattered in corners of various hallways and offices, were pockets of people crying and hugging. I soon discovered that the cause of their grief was Tanya, the beautiful, kindhearted, talented piano teacher at our school. She had just died. Only minutes before I had arrived. I stood there stunned, remembering her, so full of life and joy—how could she be gone? She was my age! I thought of the three beautiful little boys and loving husband she had left behind, no doubt in utter anguish at that moment. And suddenly the perspective in my life came into a real sharp focus—like a slap. I realized what really mattered, and what really didn't.

We spend a whole lot of time worrying over, and chasing after, so many meaningless things, don't we? I know I do. And I know Solomon concluded that almost everyone does. We chase possessions, power, pleasures, and people. We chase wisdom and work and wealth. We even chase after good things, such as relationships or causes. But Solomon says that in the end everything is meaningless—you can't take any of it with you. Even after death, where some believe we can look down on others, Solomon assures us that we won't know anything at all—we'll only sleep. So in that case, what is the purpose of our meaningless lives? What should we focus on? The answer is summed up above into two single purposes: Fear God. Keep His laws.

You see, it is our relationship with God that is the true meaning of our lives—how we serve Him, how we walk with Him. It's the only thing that will last into eternity. Ask yourself today—have you been spending your time and energy on things that matter, or on things that are meaningless? Choose to throw yourself into the thing that lasts: your friendship with Jesus.

—MH

For Mature Eyes Only

Let him kiss me with the kisses of his mouth—for your love is more delightful than wine. Pleasing is the fragrance of your perfumes; your name is like perfume poured out. No wonder the maidens love you! Song of Solomon 1:2, 3.

It's one of those books of the Bible that you hardly ever hear a sermon on. It's one that you've maybe browsed through, only to wind up a little confused and wondering if those sexual innuendos are actually there or if your mind is just in the gutter. Or perhaps you've read through it and thought, *What's with this guy's obsession with pomegranates?* Regardless of your reaction, there have been many before you that have wondered the same things and more. People have actually been arguing for centuries over what it all means, and according to a rabbinical tradition Jewish males weren't even allowed to read it until the age of 30, because of its erotic nature.

Various groups fall into several main camps when interpreting the Song of Solomon. The first group says that the whole thing is an allegory, or a symbolic story in which all the characters and elements in the plot are symbolic of something else. They see the character of the king (assumed to be Solomon) as representing God, or even Jesus, courting and marrying the woman, which represents God's people, or the church. This becomes a little more problematic when you consider that Solomon was quite the ladies' man and that this woman in the story would have had to be one of his 700 wives and 300 concubines. Any direct comparison between him and God seems kind of wrong. The other side says it's a poetic retelling of a time in Solomon's life in which he seems truly to have experienced some sort of monogamous love for one of his wives.

Regardless of these two ideas, the fact is that it's a very detailed and private look at relational love between a man and a woman. The story walks you through all the passion, feelings, and joy that can be experienced in a committed relationship. It's also interesting to notice that despite the prevalence of premarital sex in Solomon's world, this story very clearly affirms the joy he experiences when he waits until the wedding night. For a man who clearly had a wide variety of sexual experiences, it says a lot that his greatest experience of love and physical satisfaction is found in simply waiting for the mutual commitment of marriage.

—GH

Sappy Old Love Letters

Promise me, O women of Jerusalem, by the gazelles and wild deer, not to awaken love until the time is right. Song of Solomon 2:7, NLT.

Dear Greg, I love you! How many times a day do I say that—to you, to myself, to the other student missionaries, to God, to anyone who wants to know?" "Dear Melissa, You asked recently what we are now, who we have become. Well, I can only answer with this: you are my best friend. And I love you. And I guess you have the power to make me the happiest or the saddest man alive. I don't know if we'll ever be able to date each other and I don't know what the future holds, but today, knowing this is enough."

"Dear Greg, I think of you often. I used to wonder if it was a smart idea to let myself start loving you, because I don't even know if we'll be together or not, but it doesn't matter now. I love you, and that's how it is."

"Dear Melissa, I've never met someone who worked their way into my heart so quickly! I'm excited about our future together, though we don't even know whether or not there is one. I want to marry you! It seems like we dream a lot, but who knows, someday maybe it will all come true."

These are real excerpts from the love letters Greg and I sent each other more than 10 years ago while I was a missionary overseas. Though these letters are sappy and silly, there are other letters about private, personal things that I wouldn't want anybody to read. That's why it's confusing to me that Song of Solomon actually ended up in the Bible. It's pretty personal stuff! It's so "personal" that technically I'm not even supposed to read it, let alone write about it, because I'm not yet 30 years old. (As Greg mentioned yesterday, an ancient Jewish rabbinical tradition prohibited people under age 30 from reading the book because of its sexual content.) So what can we learn from all this stuff? One phrase stands out to me above all the rest: *Do not awaken love until the time is right.* This is the key phrase in the book, and that's because it's the key secret to a happy love life. Solomon makes it plain and simple: Be careful until the proper time. It may be difficult to wait until marriage, but God guarantees that it's absolutely worth it. Think about what this phrase means for you today in your relationships, and ask the Lord to lead and guide your choices and your timing.

—MH

You Have a Calling

Then I heard the voice of the Lord saying, "Whom shall I send? And who will go for us?" And I said, "Here am I. Send me!" Isaiah 6:8.

My calling in high school was to clean animal cages, dozens and dozens of them, for dogs, cats, turtles, rats, rabbits, snakes, lizards, fish, birds, etc. This may not sound like a very high calling, but I can assure you that the animals who lived in those cages would disagree. By the end of the week, if you had to sleep in your own mess, you can believe you'd be pretty thankful to have someone clean your cage regularly! Not only did I work for a vet—I wanted to be a vet myself, and my parents humored this dream by letting me buy and bring home somewhere in the neighborhood of 45 pets. I'm not exaggerating. But it was my job to care for them. I remember late evenings in my teens, while my friends were at home in their warm rooms doing homework like normal kids, I was in the backyard in the dark, scrubbing litter boxes and scooping wood shavings. Then on weekends at the vet, for hours on end I'd scrub and scrub dog doo-doo and cat barf out of the metal boarding cages. You can see how I didn't have a lot of competition for the position—it wasn't a very popular job.

The prophet Isaiah didn't have a very popular calling either. Being a prophet was akin to being a telemarketer or a burger flipper today—something nobody wanted to be! It was a pretty bum job. Who wants to be constantly talking about all the bad things that are coming? So when the Lord first comes to Isaiah to call him to this position, I'm a little surprised at what happens. God tells Isaiah that He needs someone, and Isaiah's response to this very undesirable job offer is surprising. He actually exclaims, "Here am I. Send me!" Why did he want the job?

All I can figure is that it had something to do with him being in the actual presence of the Lord. Sometimes volunteering to work for God sounds like a bum deal, but maybe it doesn't seem that way when you're in His presence—when you hang out with Him and spend time with Him a lot. Maybe there's something about being around Him that makes you *want* to go.

So if you're wrestling with giving your life over to God, up the amount of time you're spending with Him. He still calls people today, and He's calling you, too, for a very specific purpose. Answer His call, gladly saying, "Here I am! Send me!"

—MH

Tooting His Own Horn

At that time Merodach-Baladan son of Baladan king of Babylon sent Hezekiah letters and a gift, because he had heard of his illness and recovery. Hezekiah received the envoys gladly and showed them what was in his storehouses. Isaiah 39:1, 2.

If my brother-in-law Josh were given a choice between being called a show-off or an unknown, he'd choose the latter. If there's one thing he can't stand, it is people who toot their own horn and announce to the world how great, talented, lucky, smart—whatever—they are. He despises the need to lift oneself up in a desperate attempt for public recognition. Josh is actually a smart, talented, amazing guy, but you won't hear that from him. He keeps on the down low. Even though he could, he doesn't flaunt his humor or his wit, because he hates show-offs so much.

This may sound extreme to you, but I think King Hezekiah could have used a healthy dose of Josh's perspective. Hezekiah was one of the biggest show-offs of all time, and when he had the chance with this group from Babylon he couldn't resist strutting his stuff (literally!). This whole episode came on the heels of Hezekiah's miraculous healing and God's promising him 15 more years of life. The healing was accompanied by the sign that Hezekiah requested—the sun moved backward in its path 10 steps. Naturally, such a huge astronomical sign didn't go unnoticed, especially by the astrologers of the neighboring country of Babylon. So the king of Babylon sent delegates with gifts and a message asking Hezekiah what had happened. King Solomon had foreseen this kind of opportunity years and years before, and it had always been expected that when foreign officials came questioning, the kingdom of Israel would be an example of what God can and will do for a nation that follows Him. But instead of introducing Babylon's elite to the true God, Hezekiah took them around and showed off all of his toys. He wowed them with the royal treasury, his entire armory, and everything else impressive in his palace.

They returned home dazzled, but unwittingly Hezekiah had put in place the idea that Judah was ripe for the picking. In less than 100 years Babylon came knocking again, but this time with siege machines and armies. This long-ago lesson is still relevant. When people come into our lives, will they see evidence of God—or mainly ourselves?

—GH

Better Than Energizer

> Even youths grow tired and weary, and young men stumble and fall; but those who hope in the Lord will renew their strength. They will soar on wings like eagles; they will run and not grow weary, they will walk and not be faint. Isaiah 40:30, 31.

I can still remember the feeling of that grainy, cool cement floor against my cheek as I lay sprawled across the floor. It was the way every 12-minute run ended in freshman PE class. Our gym teacher was insane, making us run around the track on days when the Arizona heat was hotter than blazes. The unbending rule was that unless the temps climbed to 100 degrees, we had to run. Many a day, when it was 98 degrees by 10:00 a.m., I found myself panting and wheezing my way around that track, praying both for some semblance of a passing grade and for the will not to pass out cold. Students running around the track dropped like flies, staggering to the bleachers in a dizzy zigzag line, mumbling something about heat exhaustion as the rest of us ran on. I would close my eyes and plead with myself, "Just one more cone, just one more cone . . ."

When it was finally over, we would drag ourselves into the locker rooms, strip down as much as we dared, and spread out flat against that heavenly floor, ruing the day we had joined freshman PE class. One day, about 30 minutes after dropping there, I suddenly woke up lying on that floor, mostly naked. I don't know how I would have explained that to the janitors had they found me there, except to say that I was absolutely and completely exhausted.

Though in our teen years we're known for our energy and stamina, some things, like the 12-minute run, can take the wind out of even a teenager's sails. "Even youths grow tired and weary," Isaiah says. I'd bet he's not just talking about physical tiredness. If I had to guess, I'd say he's also thinking of the fact that life wears us out as well. We lose heart. Our souls get weary. Our hearts feel weak. We want to give up. But Isaiah promises us that those who put their hope in God don't have to feel this tired—whether physically, mentally, emotionally, or spiritually. He says that they'll actually be able to run without even getting tired. More than a workout secret, this can be a way of life. Put your hope in the Lord today, and watch how things that would normally knock you down somehow become manageable and bearable.

—MH

Right Hand, Left Hand

So do not fear, for I am with you; do not be dismayed, for I am your God. I will strengthen you and help you; I will uphold you with my righteous right hand. Isaiah 41:10.

Hardly anything is designed for left-handed people. From a purely selfish and convenience-oriented perspective, I'm glad that I'm right-handed, but it still seems as if these right-handed devices would be annoying for those who aren't. The cultural bent toward "rightism" (which, I'm told by lefties, is up there with racism and sexism) seems to be fairly deep-seated. In our cultural subconscious we have reserved the right hand for things such as handshakes, saluting, raising the hand to take an oath at court, and even for making the sign of the cross. And we're not the only ones who favor the right hand. In 1789 the nobility in the French National Assembly seated themselves on the right-hand side of the president, leaving the left side for the commoners—hence our political terms of right-wing and left-wing. McDonald's company had a bit of a shock when their sales in the Middle East took a nosedive after an ad that showed a man eating a Big Mac with both hands was posted in all its major cities. The reason? There the left hand is used for cleaning up in the restroom; the right is reserved for eating. Nobody wants burgers that have been handled like that!

So is the Bible participating in this "rightism" when it speaks of God offering us help and salvation with His "righteous right hand"? I'm pretty sure that God is ambidextrous, if in fact He even has hands, per se. But the fact of the matter is that Isaiah was writing in a time and culture (not so far removed from current-day Middle Eastern culture in this respect) that saw the left hand as unclean or dirty. In fact, there was a sense that the left hand was weak and unfitted for any noteworthy endeavors. So of course, to offer hope to a culture of people who thought that way, God represented Himself through His prophet as a Savior who comes with a righteous right hand. To have said that He came with a righteous left hand would have been like a local pastor getting up to wave to the church one morning with his middle finger extended rather than an open hand! The great thing that this passage tells me is twofold; God is here to save us, and He meets people where they are, culturally speaking or otherwise. So if you feel as if you can't quite make it to where He is today—don't worry. He'll make it to where you are instead.

—GH

When you pass through the waters, I will be with you; and when you pass through the rivers, they will not sweep over you. When you walk through the fire, you will not be burned; the flames will not set you ablaze. For I am the Lord, your God. Isaiah 43:2, 3.

You just had to love the guy, because he was always failing, forgetting, or the butt of every joke: Charlie Brown. He is still one of my all-time favorite cartoon characters, but the poor guy gets some pretty tough breaks. For Halloween he spends all night trick-or-treating, and every single person at every single house gives him a rock. At the end of the night, he just has a big sack full of rocks! Or how about that infamous sickly Christmas tree he picks out, and he becomes the laughingstock of the pageant. He never gets invited to parties. He can't even grow any hair. Poor kiddo—nothing ever works out for good ole Charlie Brown!

But he was a cartoon. Stacy is not. She is my real-life Charlie Brown friend that just randomly has bizarre bad things happening to her all the time—stuff that just doesn't normally happen to other people! There was the day she was walking through the camping section at Walmart, and out of nowhere, from a top shelf, a giant cooler suddenly fell directly onto her head and gave her a concussion. Then there was the time she was a bridesmaid at a wedding, and her dress caught on fire—imagine! Most horrible of all was the night she was home alone, and the police called to tell her that someone was making calls to them from inside her house. She was terrified! It turned out to be the wrong number, but of course, it would happen to her!

When really and truly bad things happen to us, the kinds of things that aren't funny at all, we wonder if God shouldn't stop them somehow. Didn't He say He would? Not according to today's verse. It talks about several pretty difficult situations, such as passing through a river or walking through fire. But do you notice what word keeps occurring throughout? God doesn't say *if* those bad things happen—He says *when*! He knows bad things are going to happen. It's a guarantee, because we live on a sinful earth. However, God also wants us to realize that when the bad times do come, as they most certainly will, He will be there for us. The bad times won't overcome us; we'll make it through. And why? Because He's our God. He's bigger than all of the big bad things that can happen at any time, including today.

—MH

Rockets + Gunpowder + Guys = Bad Combo

[It is I] who says of Cyrus, "He is my shepherd and will accomplish all that I please; he will say of Jerusalem, 'Let it be rebuilt,' and of the temple, 'Let its foundations be laid.'" Isaiah 44:28.

I'm pretty sure this is a bad idea," my friend said with a worried look. Most of the time, my buddy Steve was right. He just had a knack for knowing things. So while we stuffed a model rocket with firecrackers, gunpowder, and three additional model rocket engines, he stood off to the side shaking his head. As we all stood a respectful distance from the launchpad in a field behind the school and watched the cardboard tube shoot off like a missile, Steve looked downright scared. For good reason, it turned out. The flaming debris of the rocket finally landed in a dry field of grass near an expensive housing development and caught half the field on fire.

As we grew older Steve's uncanny ability shifted, and he started predicting when some guy and his girlfriend would break up. "They're not going to make it past the week," he'd predict with solemn tones during lunch. And sure enough, in a day or two the couple had called things off, citing "irreconcilable differences" or the like. So why didn't Steve become a modern-day prophet with TV ads, books, and celebrities knocking at his door? Because probably Steve was simply observant, and plans involving fireworks and guys never equal a good thing. But the fact is that when your predictions come true, people start to listen.

In the prophecies of Isaiah we see a prediction that is pretty rare, even in terms of biblical prophecy: a name. In the middle of the book of Isaiah God gives the name of a future king that He will direct to rebuild Jerusalem after its destruction by Babylon. What's funny to me is that this prediction comes after somewhat of a tirade. God is almost laughing at His people who chop down trees, take the wood for cooking their food, and then use the leftover pieces to fashion wooden images that they pray to for safety. Then He says, "I am the Lord, who has made all things . . . and fulfills the predictions of his messengers" (Isaiah 44:24-26). And He goes on to prove it by setting out a prophecy with the name of a king who wouldn't show up in world history for another 150 years. God knew that when you set out a prediction and it comes true, people will listen, the way my friends and I started listening to Steve. Since God has been willing to prove Himself like this, we should listen closely to the rest of what He has to say.

—GH

Have You Been Missing Him?

He grew up before him like a tender shoot, and like a root out of dry ground. He had no beauty or majesty to attract us to him, nothing in his appearance that we should desire him. Isaiah 53:2.

From uptown to underground . . . the experiment appealed to him, but of course the young virtuoso didn't know how it would turn out. Joshua Bell donned a baseball cap and strode down the tunnel toward the metro, hoping that no one would recognize him. Two nights before, he had played to a full theater in Boston, where each seat cost about $100. Now he slid his precious cargo out of the velvet-lined case. The 294-year-old Stradivarius violin was one of the finest of its kind, its sound superior to anything Bell ever played. He just knew that with this instrument he could awaken even the most hard-hearted commuter into at least stopping for a minute or two. But the crowds hurrying past him kept up their frantic pace, hardly noticing.

Clink, fell some change, and later on again, *clink*. Joshua Bell, one of the most skilled musicians in the world, played for 45 minutes. Only seven commuters stopped to listen, each for less than a minute. Twenty-seven people had tossed money into his open violin case. When a reporter asked how his social experiment had gone, Bell looked frustrated. "You can't blame the quality of the sound!" he said. Sometimes we can walk right past a once-in-a-lifetime event.

We're told in Isaiah that Jesus wasn't the kind of guy that stuck out in the crowd. He wasn't the star of the basketball team, or the valedictorian, or even the class clown. Until He began His ministry most people thought of Him as simply average. Jesus chose to come to this world as just an ordinary guy, and for this reason people didn't take notice. They walked right on past God Himself, without knowing how close they'd just come. And today He still does that. Matthew records Jesus saying, "Whatever you do to those who are least in society, you have done it to Me" (see Matthew 25:40). This means that Jesus still relates to those who are struggling and who are hurting. He relates with them so much that He takes personally any actions for or against them; it's as if we are doing, or *not* doing, it to Him. That's a sobering thought, but it's also a comforting one, because each of us has been just that "normal" guy or girl at some point. We've all felt common, or sometimes even less, and Jesus relates to us where we are at, because He's been there Himself. Don't simply pass Him by. Because He's anything but ordinary.

—GH

The Orphaned Baby and the Police That Brought Him

"For my thoughts are not your thoughts, neither are your ways my ways," declares the Lord. "As the heavens are higher than the earth, so are my ways higher than your ways and my thoughts than your thoughts." Isaiah 55:8, 9.

He was running around the living room with the TV remote control yelling, "You'll never catch me!" He was right—for the short term. There was no catching the scrawny little brat that had commandeered the morning's choice of entertainment. My little brother scrambled over couches, skidded around coffee tables, and managed to stay just out of my reach for a good 10 minutes before I finally succeeded in launching a well-placed couch cushion that sent him sprawling. In seconds I had him pinned to the floor, but the remote was nowhere in sight. I let him up slowly, and the pride of victory welled up in his face. Heading for my room, I noticed his baby book on a shelf, and a wonderful plan hit me. I opened it quickly and slipped his birth certificate into another book on the shelf. Then I triumphantly marched out to the living room.

"Doug! Did Mom and Dad ever tell you how we got you?" I looked at him slyly.

"Yeah, the hospital or something."

"No! You were a stranded orphan, brought to the door in a basket by a policeman. See? There's no birth certificate here 'cause we never had one!" I gingerly handed him the book.

He quickly rifled through the pages; a look of fear and then panic crossed his face. As he rushed to the bookshelf crying, I calmly took my seat with the whole TV to myself.

When I think back on moments like this, I realize how grateful I am that God is not like us. Isaiah said it so well: "God's ways are not our ways." So many times we attach human characteristics to God when there really is no comparison. Sure, God has feelings, but the motives that we sometimes try to pin on God's feelings aren't even in the same ballpark. Isaiah's message here as well as in the rest of the book puts God in a light that shows us His primary function is that of a caregiver and a parent. So many times the Jewish nation goes astray, and there is God sometimes punishing, but always rushing to bring them back. So keep this in mind: unlike most people in this world, the God we serve has nothing but the best of intentions, and desires our well-being in every interaction with us that He has.

—GH

Dirt and Barf and Doo-doo

As a mother comforts her child, so will I comfort you. Isaiah 66:13.

What used to make you cry as a child? Spiders? Spanks? Lima beans for dinner? Perhaps when you read the verse above you have tender images pop into your mind of sitting on your mommy's lap after you have just scraped your knee, or after someone in first grade called you a poo-poo head. Certainly you remember how, when you were a little kid and got hurt, there was nobody who could "make it all better" the way your mom could. I used to think of soft words, kind pats, and a gentle hand wiping tears away when I read today's verse. But not anymore.

I have my own kids now, so when I read "As a mother comforts her child, so will I comfort you," I think of my 2-year-old screaming and slapping and spitting in my face. I think of pulling him out of that wet muddy hole in the yard he always falls into. Then I think of my infant slashing at my neck with his razor-sharp fingernails as he wails like a wild beast about 3:00 a.m., or I think of being thrown up on and wet on, and middle-of-the-night fevers. That's what real Mom-comforting is, folks!

The scene is not so dreamy anymore, but this makes me like the word picture of God a whole lot better. It's one thing to think of God sweetly cradling a crying child on His knee or gently wiping away a dripping tear from a downcast eye. But that's not always how our sadness goes, is it? Sometimes we are kicking and screaming and spitting. Sometimes we're slashing at anything within arm's reach. Sometimes we are so mad we would throw up on God if we could! It's during those times that it's neat to think of Him still comforting us, still hanging in there with us, holding us in His arms even as we fight Him. He doesn't just want to comfort us when we're softly crying. He is ready to comfort us when we're screaming at the top of our lungs, too, when we are mean, or messy, or both. I like that. I respect a God who's bigger than my tantrums.

Today, remember that God is not afraid to get down in the dirt of your life with you. If He has to wade through some of your ugliest, dirtiest moments in order to comfort you, He will. We know just how messy of a situation He will go through in order to comfort us, because we saw Him hanging on that cross. If He did that back then, don't doubt His devotion now.

—MH

The Prophet Who Wept for 40 Years

The word of the Lord came to me, saying, "Before I formed you in the womb I knew you, before you were born I set you apart; I appointed you as a prophet to the nations." "Ah, Sovereign Lord," I said, "I do not know how to speak; I am only a child." Jeremiah 1:4-6.

With every football, basketball, or baseball game there is one linking factor that serves to captivate the audience: the question Who will win? The fact that you don't know is what keeps you watching, checking the scores, following every play in detail. You want to see the end, the final score, and hopefully your team come to victory. But what would it be like if you always knew, before the game started, that you were going to be the loser? No matter how hard you practiced, no matter how much money or talent you had, you knew that through some sick twist of fate you were going to lose. Eventually, after you'd convinced yourself that these feelings were more than just nervousness or fear, I'm betting you'd just give up playing. Who wants to keep playing a game you know you're doomed to fail?

Well, that's exactly the situation Jeremiah was in after God called him to be a prophet only 40 years before He allowed the destruction of Jerusalem by the Babylonian Empire. Jeremiah, born into a family of priests, lived just outside the capital city of Jerusalem. He lived happily through the early part of his life, but when God called him to speak to the nation as His prophet he cringed with doubt and fear. "I'm only a child!" he cried, hoping that God had made a mistake. For the next 40 years Jeremiah went through so many struggles, pain, and rejection that he became known as the "weeping prophet." This didn't make him a wimp—a lesser man would've quit long before. He even escaped death at the hands of Nebuchadnezzar when Jerusalem was destroyed. What makes me so interested in Jeremiah is that in spite of hardship, his whole message was that we need to enter into a heart relationship with God, not a formalistic ceremony. He said that God wants to meet with us where we are now, and that He desires a two-way relationship, not just a religious robot. Jeremiah lived on the edge of God's punishment against his people, so his message isn't bogged down with fluff. He cuts to the chase, and gives things straight. He gives us a refreshing picture of God. Sometimes we're tempted to feel as if God is distant and uninvolved; Jeremiah's story shows He is anything but.

—GH

The Ancient Paths

This is what the Lord says: "Stand at the crossroads and look; ask for the ancient paths, ask where the good way is, and walk in it, and you will find rest for your souls. But you said, 'We will not walk in it.'" Jeremiah 6:16.

There's just something about walking down ancient roads that gives me goose bumps. I'm not talking old dusty roads that lead through farmland or fields; I mean really ancient roads. While visiting the ancient Incan city of Machu Picchu high up in the Peruvian mountains, I decided to take a little stroll above the city. I came across a well-worn pathway that wound its way around down the side of a steep cliff that had been converted into terraces for growing food in the rugged mountain crags. I asked one of the Incan guides where the old pathway led.

"That will take you all the way back to Cuzco, the old Incan capital." He smiled widely. "But you'll have to walk for four days before you arrive."

The pathway wound in and out, and ultimately disappeared around a small bend. As I rounded this corner I was confronted with an amazing view of the surrounding mountain range and a tiny little trail that headed off into the vast wilderness that surrounded the Incan stronghold. The pathway was small and crooked, but you could tell it was just as old as the city it led to. I thought of all the hundreds—maybe thousands—of feet that had walked this path before me, climbing up the mountainside in search of this city and its inhabitants. I was only one in a vast crowd that had been drawn up this pathway.

Sometimes as I browse through the Bible and its various lessons and stories I start to get a similar feeling. Throughout the Bible I am confronted with a vast array of people, all who experienced God in some way. Perhaps I read stories about prophets who were called to deliver God's messages, or maybe it's just a simple shepherd boy who is made into a king. Regardless of the circumstances, they're all headed for the same destination; a Being rather than a place. They tread the same ancient paths again and again, some of them arriving, while others give up before they arrive. But the ancient paths, the experiences and the quest for a relationship with this Creator of humanity itself, seem always to be at the heart of the Bible's narrative. And hopefully as *you* read these stories, you will find that relationship as well.

—GH

Swedish Brides Have More Fun

From the time your forefathers left Egypt until now, day after day, again and again I sent you my servants the prophets. But they did not listen to me or pay attention.
Jeremiah 7:25, 26.

Several years ago when we were backpacking across Europe, my husband and I attended the wedding of our friends Bjorn and Petra in Sweden. One single moment has stood out in our memories: the moment the groom left the room. Suddenly, from all corners and tables, boys and men, young and old, were out of their seats, making a beeline for the bride. One by one, they ran up and kissed Petra on the cheek while her groom was "away." Then Petra left the room, and all the women ran to the front to plant one on Bjorn's cheek while his bride's back was turned. It was funny to watch the mad dash and scramble—and we didn't have to speak a lick of Swedish to participate! I'll admit, I had no complaints about kissing the blue-eyed Swedish groom, and I noticed that Greg was perhaps a little too eager to run up and kiss that gorgeous brunette bride!

Reading through the Old Testament sometimes feels as if I'm at a Swedish wedding again. Every single time God turns around, the Israelites are sneaking kisses behind His back—to foreign women that God has forbidden them to touch. Without fail, these idol-worshipping women lead the men of Israel back into idol worship and away from God. (Though it surely doesn't seem like the men object.) Time and time again, Israel forgets God. He sends prophets, warnings, messengers, and signs, but it doesn't matter. He pleads with them to return to Him, and sometimes they do—but they always leave again. This happens for literally hundreds and hundreds of years. Finally, the inevitable happens—God allows them to fall. He would have been a laughingstock if He hadn't, because it was part of the old, old covenant: Live in My ways and prosper, or leave Me and come to ruin. He had to keep His end of the deal.

Two things about the fall of the Israelite nation interest me: why they kept leaving God even when they knew the outcome, and how faithfully God tried for centuries to win them back. And then I think of us today—are we working really, really hard to leave God, messing around every time His back is turned? Are you? If you are, have you stopped to think lately about how hard He's working to win you back?

—MH

A Fire in My Bones

But if I say, "I will not mention him or speak any more in his name," his word is in my heart like a fire, a fire shut up in my bones. I am weary of holding it in; indeed, I cannot. Jeremiah 20:9.

She just wouldn't shut up! He sat there for 20 minutes, saying absolutely nothing, and she kept chattering on like a little bird. I'm guessing it was only their first date, and even though I'd been trying politely to ignore the conversation at the Italian outdoor restaurant's adjoining table, I just couldn't. By the end of the appetizer I was wondering how much longer I could take the incessant yammering, but the poor fellow seated in front of her was having an even worse time. I shifted my attention from her mile-a-minute verbal acrobatics and watched as he slowly slumped lower and lower in his chair. The look on his face told me that he wanted to be anywhere but there. Finally I saw him take a breath, and he mentioned something about his neighbor's dog. Success! She paused, and it looked as if he might be able to steer the conversation a little, but suddenly she came back with renewed vigor and went on a 15-minute tirade, in gruesome detail, about how she had been trying to teach her new puppy where to do his business. It was awful. The only thing I can think of that's worse than wishing someone else would stop talking is wishing that you yourself would stop talking!

That's the situation poor old Jeremiah found himself in as he reflected on several years of preaching God's messages to an angry and resistant people. They had threatened him, imprisoned him, and even thrown him into an abandoned cistern, hoping that he would just die and leave them alone. But the irony was that nobody wished his silence more than Jeremiah himself. He gets angry with the messages God keeps giving him, and longs just to stop speaking altogether! But then he describes how he simply can't; how if he tries to stop, the message burns like a fire in his very bones. Even though he is given a message that's hard to deliver, he knows that the God behind the message is trying to warn a people who are in danger of destruction. Love is pushing this message, and Jeremiah can't turn his back on that. So he turns again to the angry mobs, and he once more speaks of their need to repent and get a heart relationship with their Creator.

God will do whatever it takes to get His message through to people—including using you.

—GH

How to Have It All

"For I know the plans I have for you," declares the Lord, "plans to prosper you and not to harm you, plans to give you hope and a future. Then you will call upon me . . . and I will listen to you. You will seek me and find me when you seek me with all your heart." Jeremiah 29:11-13.

The greedy crowd gathered in eager anticipation of the estate auction, dreaming of the riches that would soon be theirs. The estate had belonged to none other than the richest man in the entire region, a man with neither living relatives nor heirs. Every fine and costly thing he had ever owned was up for grabs. Quieting the bustling mob, the auctioneer held up an old, worn painting of the millionaire's feeble son who had died of polio years before. The crowd yelled angrily at the sight of the painting. Just when it seemed there would be no bid, the crowd parted for the elderly gardener of the estate. He hobbled slowly to the front of the room, lovingly stroked the painting, and bid a dollar.

There were no other bids, so the auctioneer declared the item sold. Then the unthinkable happened. With great show, the auctioneer turned the portrait around, tore off a golden-sealed envelope from its back, opened it, and read aloud the words written by the millionaire himself: "To whoever buys this painting of my son I leave my entire estate and all my belongings." The crowd gasped in horrified disbelief. The auction was over. The old gardener had just inherited everything.

This fable illustrates a beautiful truth that many people don't know: God has promised us something quite similar. Whoever gets His Son gets everything. The verse above was written to those who had just gone into exile, and though false prophets said it would last only a few years, through Jeremiah God told His people to settle down and build houses—their exile would last a good 70 years. However, God assured them that He still had plans for them, plans to give them an even better future. In the original Hebrew the verse reads, "You will seek me and you will find, when you seek me with all your heart." The second "me" was added in English to make the sentence read well. The fact that God doesn't *say* what they will find is a literary tool, a way of saying they will find *everything*. They will find all. When they seek God, they will find everything else they've been looking for as well. It's as true today as it was for the exiles and the auction-goers: Whoever seeks the Son ends up with everything. So seek God, and end up with not only Him but also the best life has to offer. He who gets the Son gets all.

—MH

People We Hate

*They were angry with Jeremiah and had him beaten and imprisoned.
Jeremiah 37:15.*

Maybe we shouldn't have taken her bike, now that I look back on it. And even if we did, maybe we really shouldn't have wheeled it across campus and thrown it over the wall into the street. But we did. Andrea and I hated Mrs. Albertsen, our freshman English teacher, so much that we were just itching for ways to be mean. I don't even remember now why I hated her. I seem to hate people either because they are just plain mean, and she was not, or because they called me out on something I didn't want to admit to—the more likely of the two choices. Because I hated her, I went out of my way that year to be rude to her. I cut up in class. I wrote nasty notes. And every time I saw her riding by on that bike, I began to loudly hum the Wicked Witch of the West theme music.

But then something funny happened as my sophomore, junior, and senior years went by. I started to like that woman. Her dry sense of humor was quirky and funny, and she was really sweet, too. She worked so hard for the students, and she truly cared about us as well. I grew to like her so much that I actually started joining her classes on purpose. I ended up learning a whole lot from that nice woman. Today she is a good friend of mine. In fact, this evening I just eagerly added her to my Facebook. Funny how your opinion of someone can change so much.

Jeremiah was one of the most hated prophets of all time—though most prophets are not particularly popular. The people of his day absolutely detested the things he had to say, because they were being called out on their sins. They didn't want to hear it! But I wonder how they felt about him later, after being dragged into captivity, when they realized he had been right all along. I bet they felt pretty bad about how they had treated the last person who had tried to warn them.

I don't know if there's someone you hate and despise, or if there's anyone you're mean to on purpose. If there is—watch out. Live long enough, and you will probably come to regret your behavior. And who knows, God may have placed that person in your life as a learning opportunity for you. So don't waste it being a jerk. Get to know the people you dislike; give them a second look. You may be in for some really great surprises and friends.

—MH

He Has Broken My Teeth With Gravel

How deserted lies the city, once so full of people! How like a widow is she, who once was great among the nations! She who was queen among the provinces has now become a slave. Lamentations 1:1.

I sat on the metal girders of the partially constructed building, looking down at the ground. Every night after dinner I and the other student missionaries would gather on the roof and watch the sun set over this small town of 10,000 in rural Nicaragua. But this night I was overcome by something I hadn't noticed until now. As dusk settled I noticed the light of a TV coming from a curious little shanty that had been set up just outside the church property. As I looked closer I saw that the little house was actually constructed of just four sticks and pieces of cardboard. Inside this tiny room were four people, all family, gathered around a small television that was getting power directly from an exposed power line that ran overhead. I pointed this out to the others around me, and we all just kind of gawked, not knowing what to make of it. How do people live like this? What is it like? What happens to the cardboard when it rains? The next morning I went to check on our new neighbors, only to find a single stick where the shack had been. Obviously someone had run them off, so they packed the house and left for the next spot.

When I read through Lamentations, I feel similar to how I felt watching this family in their cardboard shack. I can't imagine what it must have been like to watch your home destroyed and your family and friends killed or chained and marched to another country as slaves. Jeremiah has just been forced to watch as the judgment of God that he's predicted for 40 years finally comes. He knew it would, but this foreknowledge doesn't help in the long run. At one point he even says it feels as if his teeth have been knocked out with rocks! It's not possible for me to relate to how he felt as he watched his country and his people literally burn to the ground.

But even in the midst of all this Jeremiah looks to the other promises of God. He knows that God came through on the punishment; now he begins looking at the God's promises to bring His people back home. Jeremiah moves on, just as the people did with their sticks and cardboard, knowing there would be yet another place to go. Maybe we can't relate to Jeremiah's tragedy, but we can always put our trust in his God when things in our own lives get tough.

—GH

The Book of Depression

My eyes fail from weeping, I am in torment within, my heart is poured out on the ground because my people are destroyed. Lamentations 2:11.

Back in the day, when it was considered reasonably safe for 8-year-olds to go door to door selling things, my brother, Matthew, and I once became trapped in the house of the craziest old woman ever. Well, it's not that she was crazy per se; it's more that she was totally downright depressed. I'll never forget her—old May Hate. We knocked on her door to ask if she'd like to buy a magazine subscription and, like fools, accepted her offer to come in and sit for a while. For the next two hours this woman who was older than the hills proceeded to tell us everything that was wrong in her poor depressing life—from her son's job to her bad health—in excruciating detail. Being fairly polite 8-year-olds, we didn't know how to escape until two hours later when she finally took a breath. We vowed never to knock on her door again for any reason whatsoever.

Whenever I read Lamentations, I feel as if I'm spending an afternoon listening to poor old May Hate again. Bitterly distressed, Jeremiah laments for verse after verse about the sorry state of his depressing, meaningless life. He has just watched Jerusalem fall and the Temple burn to the ground, while his people are ravaged and murdered or carried off into exile. He continues to watch women, children, and infants left in the city to starve to death. It's a terrible time.

My husband says that if he had to choose any one book to cut completely out of the Bible, Lamentations would be it. It's the only book in the entire Bible that is made up solely of laments, meaning it's chock-full of complaining and that's all. Why is this seemingly pointless book of depressing wailings included in our Bibles? Of what good is this downer to us?

Maybe not much on a happy day, but on a really bad day you can turn to Lamentations and find that God understands your depression and grief. He's big enough to handle them too—He doesn't mind it if you pour out even your worst thoughts and feelings to Him. Even if you're angry at God—in fact, especially if you're angry—go ahead and tell Him so. Jeremiah showed us that He can take it. Don't ever feel as if you can come to God only when you're happy and thankful to be alive. When you're really down, remember Lamentations. God wants to hear your depression so that you don't have to stay there. He wants to bring you through it.

—MH

He Needed a Chiropractor After That

Then lie on your left side and put the sin of the house of Israel upon yourself. . . . I have assigned you the same number of days as the years of their sin. So for 390 days you will bear the sin of the house of Israel. Ezekiel 4:4, 5.

The most uncomfortable place I've ever fallen asleep was in the luggage rack of a tour bus. We were on an academy band tour, and after sleeping on gym floors and in church hallways for almost a week, I was exhausted. Finally I couldn't take it anymore; I had to sleep. We had a long way to go that day and had gotten up before dawn. All the good floor spaces and extra seats were covered with sprawling, sleeping band members. I looked high and low for a place to snatch some shut-eye and noticed the empty luggage rack. It was long, and just wide enough for a girl like me. I climbed from armrest to headrest and through the bars, and in no time I was happily stretched out, inches away from the bus ceiling. I realized it wasn't such a clever idea when the bus turned its first corner and I almost rolled out of the rack. Soon after that, I noticed it was hot up there—stiflingly hot! After two hours I'd slept only about 15 minutes.

But that sleeping/not sleeping experience was nothing compared to what Ezekiel had to endure. God told him to lie on his left side for 390 days—a day for each year of Israel's sin against God, and when that finally ended, he was to lie on his right side another 40 days—this time for Judah's years of sin! Try to imagine what that would be like—more than a year, just lying on your side? While he was lying on his side, he was to face a little model he had built of the city of Jerusalem under siege. All of this symbolized the fact that the city would soon be in this condition—completely cut off from food, rationing its water, growing thin, and starving. God is taking drastic measures in this acted-out prophecy! Because all His other warnings have failed, He's pulling out all the stops in hopes of reaching His people before it's too late.

I hope God doesn't have to send someone lying on their side for a year into your life before you take notice of Him and listen to His warnings. Has He been trying to get through to you in subtle ways? Have you been listening to that still, pleading voice, or have you been ignoring it? God will go to drastic measures for you if He has to, but wouldn't it be simpler if you chose just to heed His warnings and hear His calling today?

—MH

Strange Fire Fuel

Eat the food as you would a barley cake; bake it in the sight of the people, using human excrement for fuel. Ezekiel 4:12.

Now, that just seems like going too far to me—cooking your food over a pile of human excrement? Don't get me wrong—I've made some strange fires in my time. I've made fires of trash, and burned old pieces of furniture. I've cooked over coconut husk fires, and I've enjoyed many a dead Christmas tree fire. I even used to burn pencil shavings in my dorm room late at night and roast almonds over them (they didn't taste so great). But I've never, ever even thought of cooking anything over that. Quite honestly, if that was the only means of fire fuel, I'd rather just not eat at all.

But this is exactly what God told Ezekiel to do. While he was lying on his side (for the 390 days, no less—see yesterday's story) he was to have two storage jars: one of mixed grains and the other of water. From these God told him to make cakes and cook them over a fire of human excrement. All of this was to symbolize to the people that when they went into exile among the foreign nations, they would surely be eating defiled food.

Even Ezekiel found this request too disgusting, and he had the nerve to argue with God. "Not so, Sovereign Lord! I have never defiled myself!" he gasped (Ezekiel 4:14). Because Ezekiel was so appalled, the Lord ended up letting him bake his bread over a fire of cow dung instead of human. It just goes to show how important it was to Ezekiel, and all the people back then, not to defile themselves.

Do we even care about "defiling" ourselves today? Do we even give much thought as to what goes into our bodies and minds, how we use them, and what we do with them? We all might object to cooking our food over a dung fire, but do we heartily embrace other things that are just as disgusting for our bodies, if not worse? Take some time today to think about how you treat your body, and see if you need to make some changes. If you do, come to the Lord and seek His help. Ask Him to grow disgust in you toward a habit you can't seem to shake. The very same God that heard Ezekiel's disgust and allowed another way can also make a way out for you.

—MH

Reasons to Shave Your Head

Now, son of man, take a sharp sword and use it as a barber's razor to shave your head and your beard. Then take a set of scales and divide up the hair. When the days of your siege come to an end, burn a third of the hair with fire inside the city. Take a third and strike it with the sword all around the city. And scatter a third to the wind. For I will pursue them with drawn sword. Ezekiel 5:1, 2.

I sat on a stool in the middle of a mocking, yelling, laughing crowd of kids and teachers. They hooted and hollered as the buzz of the electric hair trimmer whirred somewhere just behind my head. When the cold steel finally connected with my skull, a chill ran down my spine. I smiled as if I were in on the joke and weren't the joke, but I wondered if the money was worth all this. For several months I'd been working to help fund a mission trip to Nicaragua, and at the school auction someone came up with the brilliant idea of auctioning off my hair. *Why not?* I thought. *Who would ever buy my hair?* Well, it just so happened that the little old woman in the back row had been planning to donate money anyway, and this novel idea struck her fancy. She bought my hair that night for $500. The deed was to be done the next Monday during schooltime, and that is how I came to be sitting on a stool in the middle of the playground. And they weren't satisfied with only a buzz cut; they went all the way down to the skin and razored it all off, leaving a smooth shiny scalp to brave the elements for several weeks to come.

I'm pretty sure Ezekiel could feel my pain here, because God required him to do something quite similar, except he had to dispose of his hair in some weird ways as well. To help get people's attention Ezekiel had to act out the prophecies and warnings that God was giving him, and in chapter 5 he's instructed to cut his hair with a sword, and then burn some, toss some to the wind, throw some of it around the city and hit it with a sword, and tuck the last little stray remnant into his tunic. Sometimes God asks people to do things that seem a little crazy to the rest of the world, things that don't make total sense at first. But the big problem we have with these kinds of things is that we can't see the end the way God can. Trusting God's instructions, even when we don't understand them, has a purpose. I'm not suggesting that you shave your head, but I am saying that you should trust Him even when you can't see the end.

—GH

Big Prophets Don't Cry

Ezekiel will be a sign to you; you will do just as he has done. When this happens, you will know that I am the Sovereign Lord. Ezekiel 24:24.

Even though he knew she was already dead, he just couldn't bring himself to leave her side. Instead of running to save his own life, he stayed there with her dead body, kneeling beside her and cradling the body of his beloved so long that the enemy soldiers finally captured him and hauled him off to jail. Robert Fulghum tells this story about a young Russian man in his book *All I Really Need to Know I Learned in Kindergarten*, and as I read it I thought of how deeply the man must have loved his wife, and, how deeply he must have grieved her death.

All of us would grieve if the person we loved most suddenly died, but Ezekiel wasn't allowed to when his wife, the "delight of his eyes" (see Ezekiel 24:16), was found dead. The Lord instructed him not to mourn, not to take off his turban or his sandals, and even not to eat the customary food of mourners. When the people of Israel asked him why he was behaving this way, he told them it was symbolic of how they would respond when Jerusalem, the delight of their eyes, fell into enemy hands. Their sons and daughters would be killed in the attack, and when they were carried into exile they would not even be allowed to mourn their deaths. God said that when it happened just as Ezekiel predicted, the people would know He was the Sovereign Lord.

This seems to be the single driving purpose behind the entire book of Ezekiel—that the people *finally* come to know that God is indeed the Sovereign Lord above all gods. All the prophecies and their fulfillments are sent in God's hope that when they are fulfilled, His chosen people will look back and remember Ezekiel's words and recognize that He was at work and involved. This stated purpose is repeated more than 65 times in Ezekiel, so you can see how important it was to God that His people know and acknowledge Him.

If it was that important back then, it's safe to say that it's still extremely important to God that we know and acknowledge Him. Sometimes we get lost in religion and start to think that the most important thing is keeping the rules, but it's not. The most important thing to God has always been relationship: that we know Him, that we walk with Him, and that He dwells with us as an integral part of our lives. Make knowing Him tops in priority in your life today.

—MH

One Reason Among Many

They will destroy the walls of Tyre and pull down her towers; I will scrape away her rubble and make her a bare rock. . . . They will plunder your wealth and loot your merchandise; they will break down your walls and demolish your fine houses and throw your stones, timber and rubble into the sea. Ezekiel 26:4-12.

It's almost eerie how amazingly accurate the fulfillment of every detail of Ezekiel's prophecy turned out to be. The city of Tyre was an ancient stronghold along the southern coast of modern Lebanon. What made this city unusual was that the older section was built just off the coast on an island, making it uniquely defensible from land-based invaders. A second portion of the city was built on the mainland, and the city's inhabitants frequently traveled between the two. Even before this particular prophecy, the Bible mentions Tyre many times. What is interesting about this city was the seeming impenetrability of its defenses. Any army coming to lay siege to Tyre was first confronted with the sprawling mainland city, and second with the 150-foot-high walls of the island portion as well. Abundant supplies and food were easily had in this open waterway, and nothing invaders did could starve the city during a siege.

Then Alexander the Great came along in 332 B.C. and, as many had done before him, including Nebuchadnezzar of Babylon, laid siege to Tyre. As always, the people fled to the island portion of the city and hid behind the massive walls. However, that didn't stop Alexander. He wasn't called "Great" for nothing. He simply demolished the entire mainland portion of Tyre and ordered his men to push all of the debris into the ocean and build a bridge through the water all the way to the island city. It took several months, but in the end the mainland portion of Tyre was literally scraped down to bedrock. All the available timber, rock, and rubble was formed into a causeway that led Alexander's army straight to the island city. It fell to his incredible onslaught not long after. Even today the part of the prophecy that says, "Out in the sea she will become a place to spread fishnets" (Ezekiel 26:5), is fulfilled, as every day dozens of fishers in this area of the coastline spread their nets out to dry on the flat patches of rock cleared by Alexander's army. So why is this important for us to know? I figure that if the Bible got right the exact details in this instance, how much more reason do we have to trust what it says in the rest of it!

—GH

"Not Gonna Do It!"

I will give you a new heart and put a new spirit in you; I will remove from you your heart of stone and give you a heart of flesh. And I will put my Spirit in you and move you to follow my decrees and be careful to keep my laws. Ezekiel 36:26, 27.

Not gonna do it! Not gonna do it!" he chanted at the top of his voice as he stomped around the classroom in defiance. Again and again, arms waving in wild gestures and eyes wide with purpose, he repeated, "Not gonna do it!" My college professor, Mr. Blake, tells this story about one of his wife's wildest and naughtiest elementary school students. The class had been instructed to use pencils to complete some sort of activity when this particular student flat-out decided he would not participate at all. And to make his point clear, he jumped out of his seat and began his booming demonstration. But in her wisdom, Yolanda ignored him. She focused on the other class members, quietly connecting the dots with their pencils, and let him fuss and fume. Finally, frustrated with being ignored, the little boy stopped at the front of the room and announced in only partial defeat, "I'm gonna use crayon!"

Don't we act like this with God? Aren't there so many times we stomp around in anger and defiance, refusing to do things His way, and making a loud show of it to anyone who will listen? Then even when we decide to relent, many times we still try to hang on to control and do it partially our way, using "crayon." But God knows this is our tendency. He knows we have evil, stubborn, defiant hearts, and He knows we need some help. That's why He makes the promise above— to give us a new heart and put a new spirit within us. Our old hearts are worthless and wicked, and beyond repair. We can't fix them. We can't take the stubborn sin out of them. Instead, we need a new heart with the Holy Spirit living inside, so that He can move us to make the right decisions and do the right things. Without Him, we are flat-out helpless on our own.

When's the last time you threw a fit with God? How long has it been since you stomped around Him in utter defiance? Have you realized lately just how sad and sorry the shape of your stubborn, stony heart really is? Are you frustrated with trying to be a better person? You realize, don't you, that you just can't change it on your own! Therefore, waste no time. Ask the Lord today to send His Spirit to live within you, and to give you a new heart with brand-new desires.

—MH

Awakening a Pile of Bones

These bones are the whole house of Israel. They say, "Our bones are dried up and our hope is gone; we are cut off." Ezekiel 37:11.

One of the saddest days of my life was the day Greg took a vow to stop speaking to me. We weren't dating at the time and my current boyfriend had it in for him, so Greg decided the wisest thing to do was to silently bow out of my life. Our friendship and our relationship were over, and because I secretly was still in love with him I mourned the loss of him as if he had died. What I didn't realize was that Greg knew all along that my boyfriend and I weren't right for each other, and that he was just biding his time until he could have a chance at me again! When I was grieving and had given up hope, Greg still believed in the possibilities.

The Israelite captives that lived during Ezekiel's day had basically given up hope of returning to their city and their land. They had also given up hope that they were the people who would carry out God's purpose for them in the world. They had been in captivity for so long that it felt as if God had left them to die and rot into a pile of dead, dry bones. Their hope was lost, and without hope they were as good as skeletons. That's why God took Ezekiel in vision to a valley of millions of dry, dusty bones. Ezekiel didn't know what the point was when God told him to speak to the pile of dry bones, but then, piece by piece, one by one, the bones began coming together! Bone to bone, muscle to joint, flesh grew and skin covered over, and finally breath came into them, and an army of people came to life. Though all hope seemed lost for the bones and for Israel, God knew He wasn't finished with them yet. Though in captivity, He knew what they could become in the future. He still saw all the possibility and hope. God had plans!

Sometimes we are like that pile of dry bones, aren't we? Our hope in God is dried up. We don't know where He is or what He's doing in the world and in our lives. It seems like a fairy tale that He will return to earth and rescue us. Maybe you even know some individuals who seem totally beyond hope, their spiritual lives resembling nothing more than a pile of dry bones. Don't give up! God sees things that we don't see. In a pile of dry bones He sees the possibility of a living multitude. And He is still working in your life—and in the lives of your family and friends—even when things seem the darkest.

—MH

Miracles From a Prophet's Bones

In the third year of the reign of Jehoiakim king of Judah, Nebuchadnezzar king of Babylon came to Jerusalem and besieged it. And the Lord delivered Jehoiakim king of Judah into his hand, along with some of the articles from the temple of God. These he carried off to the temple of his god in Babylonia and put in the treasure house of his god. Daniel 1:1, 2.

The people on both sides of the river were angry. The time for talk, for diplomacy, had passed, and now it was a question of survival. Neither side was willing to give up the bones of the prophet, and those who currently possessed them were doubly certain that they would keep them. The city of Khuzistan was about to begin a civil war, all because of the bones of this long-dead holy man, this exile prophet named Daniel. The Jews on one side of the river were prosperous and well off, while the people on the other side lived in poverty. Those in poverty believed the bones of the prophet blessed the ones who were closest to them, so they wanted Daniel's coffin brought to their side of the river. When the Jews refused, a civil war began with many casualties and much fighting. At last they tired of this. In the end the king of Persia came in and demanded that the coffin be chained underneath the bridge that linked the two cities, exactly in the middle, so that the people of both sides were equally close to it. He demanded that a new coffin of crystal be made to put the old one in, and a small chapel be built for any who wanted to come and worship at the grave of the great prophet. And so Daniel's bones finally came to rest, suspended by chains from a bridge, in the middle of a river, with people coming to them daily for healing, prosperity, and answers to prayers.

The crazy thing is that these people were missing out on the one thing about this old prophet that really had some power: his writings and prophecies. When you pick up the book of Daniel you have to be ready not only to see the classic stories like his night in a lions' den and the king's dream of the statue, but also the crazier stuff with monsters and flying beasts with 10 horns and claws made of iron. The book is full of mysteries and symbols that even today's Bible scholars wrestle with. The message, loud and clear, is that God wants to give us reasons to believe, to have verifiable evidence that the Bible predicts our future, so that we can share our beliefs with confidence. Keep this in mind as we explore this powerful and mysterious book.

—MH

The Abduction

But Daniel resolved not to defile himself. Daniel 1:8.

They came with nylon-covered faces, wearing black jackets and gloves, surrounding my friend Jeff, forcing him to the ground and yanking a black hood over his face. Then he was carried off and shoved into the trunk of a car that sped away, tires squealing. He was thrown from side to side in that dark trunk as the car careened around corners, stopping finally with a sudden jerk. The trunk was thrown open, and Jeff was roughly dragged into a building and up some stairs. When the hood was finally removed, he was facing a crowd of friends and family, all singing "Happy birthday to you" as candles flickered on cakes, and balloons on streamers danced near the ceiling. We all figured it would make him feel better about turning another year older to realize that, hey, at least he still had his freedom—he hadn't truly been abducted!

Poor Daniel didn't have this same comfort when he was carried into exile. We know that he was from one of the royal families or the nobility, so probably he was used to being cared for and waited on. He wasn't used to the long, chained-up march across the desert into Babylon— whips cracking, throat parched, legs aching, tears streaming down his face as he mourned the loss of so many things. He'd been ripped from his homeland, his country, the Temple, and all his friends and family—quite possibly he saw some murdered before his eyes. Imagine the anger, sadness, and despair you would feel to be marched off into exile. Imagine realizing this was the fate of the rest of your life! Would you want to die? Would you feel hopeless? When others would have given up, Daniel instead showed renewed courage, strength of character, and devotion to his God. From the very beginning, he resolved not to defile himself or to dishonor his God in any way, no matter the cost. He set himself to constant prayer, faith, and devotion, and as a result, by the end of his life he was practically a living legend. God blessed and honored Daniel in amazing ways. He was even called "highly esteemed" by God (Daniel 10:11). This captive teen, during his lifetime, single-handedly changed the history of an entire nation.

When times are darkest and you are tempted just to give up, remember Daniel. Turn to God instead of giving into discouragement and doubt. Ask Him for the courage to overcome hopelessness, and resolve to walk in His ways no matter what happens.

—GH

So the king summoned the magicians, enchanters, sorcerers and astrologers to tell him what he had dreamed. When they came in and stood before the king, he said to them, "I have had a dream that troubles me and I want to know what it means." Daniel 2:2, 3.

Have you ever awakened from a dream in a cold sweat, thankful that whatever it was that was chasing you wasn't real, only to feel your heart still racing as if it had been? Dreams are funny things, because sometimes they're great and other times we're just praying they end soon. But what about the ones you can't remember? You know you feel happy, sad, or scared just after you wake up, but you can't remember why. The ancient Babylonians took dreams, both remembered and forgotten, very seriously. They believed that dreams weren't just the result of that Taco Bell binge the night before, but special messages sent from the gods. They would even spend the night in temples waiting for a dream that later would be written down in the "books of dreams," as they were called. If you couldn't remember a dream, though, it was seen as an especially bad sign. According to their ancient manuscripts concerning dreams: "If a man forgets his dream, this signifies that his god is angry at him."

So it's no wonder that when King Nebuchadnezzar woke up with a forgotten dream (told in the second chapter of Daniel) he was just a little worried. In fact, he threatened his magicians and diviners with being cut into pieces if they didn't tell him the dream *and* its meaning. No small feat for a group of guys who always had to have something to work with when it came to dreams. "There is not a man on earth who can do as the king asks!" they pleaded, fearing for their lives (Daniel 2:10). All but one, that is. Daniel, the former slave brought to Babylon in chains, stepped up and said, "There is a God in heaven who reveals mysteries" (verse 28). Instead of making excuses, Daniel said that he knew a God who would not hide things from human beings. Daniel then retreated with his three friends, and they simply requested of God that He reveal the mystery behind this dream. Daniel didn't sacrifice anything—he didn't make strange incantations or stay up sleepless in a temple waiting for a response. He just asked God for help. And here we see that prayer isn't just a ritual or something that we're obligated to do. It's an encounter with a real Person, someone who will respond and who knows what we need. So if you haven't for a while, take a moment and talk with this same God that Daniel spoke to years ago. He still answers, just as He did back then.

—GH

A Military Coup on the Plain of Dura

King Nebuchadnezzar made an image of gold, ninety feet high and nine feet wide, and set it up on the plain of Dura in the province of Babylon. He then summoned the satraps, prefects, governors, advisers, treasurers, judges, magistrates and all the other provincial officials to come to the dedication of the image he had set up. Daniel 3:1, 2.

The whisperings and nervous glances around the king's palace had reached almost a state of paranoia. Rumblings of rebellion, treason, and a military uprising against the king had been floating around for months, but nothing had happened yet. The king had tried meetings, councils, threats, and bribery. But those in the army and the official governors and satraps were fed up, so late one night, while most of the palace was asleep, the guards of Nebuchadnezzar had been bribed to leave their post. A rush of soldiers led by the generals and high officials in the kingdom swarmed onto the palace grounds and secured the main hall, the court, and some of the private residences of the king and his family. But they didn't expect the king to be ready for them. He burst from his chamber, his sword slashing, killing anyone who stood in his way.

This account was found by archaeologists in what has become known as the "Babylonian Chronicles," which detail the rule of Nebuchadnezzar during Daniel's day. At first this just seems like an interesting side note, but when we realize that this occurred shortly before the events recorded in Daniel 3, the whole fiery furnace scene takes on new meaning. The Bible tells us that Nebuchadnezzar set up a statue and commanded all his nobles to bow down to it. I used to think that this was just some kind of weird thing kings did back then, but when we see that he had just fought down a military coup the whole event takes on new meaning. He was trying to regain his authority from men who had just tried to kill him. With this background it's amazing that Daniel's three friends refused to bow to the image. Even though it was going to make them look *really* bad, and possibly get them killed, they stood up for what they knew was right.

How many times in your own life have you had to stand up for something that's hard, even if it makes you look bad in front of others? This story and its background is in the Bible to encourage you to be true to your principles even when it seems crazy. In the end God stands by those who stand up for Him.

—GH

If we are thrown into the blazing furnace, the God we serve is able to save us from it. . . . But even if He does not, we want you to know, O king, that we will not serve your gods. Daniel 3:17, 18.

I was asked many bizarre questions as a 19-year-old missionary teacher: What does snow feel like? Are you friends with Brad Pitt? Why didn't you bring my car to the island? And one teenage boy wondered if I could I visit his house really late at night for a "Bible study." But the question I think of most since I've left the island is this one: "Miss, why do you worship God?"

It seems like a simple question, but think about it. Why do *you* worship God? Why do any of us? Why do we do all this? Actually, it's a hard question. You may not realize it, but many people worship God because of what they'll get out of it. They want blessings, good luck, safety, success, and ultimately a trip to heaven. Don't get me wrong—we do get a lot of great things when we worship God, but that's not the entire story. If the only reason we worship God is to get good stuff, then what happens when things go bad? when we don't get what we want—or even need? when He seems silent? If we're worshipping Him only for what we get out of it, then when we don't get what we want, we'll be in *serious danger* of turning our backs on God.

So how do we prevent this? The three young men in Daniel 3 have the answer. Shadrach, Meshach, and Abednego were asked to bow down to Nebuchadnezzar's giant golden image, and they refused out of loyalty to God. When brought before the furious king and told they would be thrown into the fire, they made one of the boldest faith statements of all time. They said that their God was able to save them, but, *even if He didn't* they were still gonna worship Him. And there it is! They would worship God no matter what—whether He saved them or didn't; whether He gave them stuff or not; whether He answered or remained silent.

When we decide that we'll serve God no matter what, then nothing in all the world can shake our faith—no hardships, no unanswered prayers, no doubts. Why do *I* worship God? Because He is God. He created me, and He died for me. I love Him, no matter what He does or doesn't do. Why do you worship Him? Are you brave enough to decide you will worship Him no matter what? If so, circumstances will never shake your faith or loyalty again.

—MH

Werewolves Do Exist

Immediately what had been said about Nebuchadnezzar was fulfilled. He was driven away from people and ate grass like cattle. His body was drenched with the dew of heaven until his hair grew like the feathers of an eagle and his nails like the claws of a bird. Daniel 4:33.

The woman began scratching the bed and growling at her husband, who jumped away in a panic. For days she'd been saying that she wasn't feeling right, that she was scared of something in the mirror. Now, though, she was slashing, clawing, and snarling at him like a wild animal. He tried to calm her down, but she would have none of it. She ran around the room in a wild frenzy, and finally when she stopped by the mirror she thought she saw the face of a wolf with fangs and a snout staring out at her. The woman was only 49 years old, had no history of drug use, and had been quite sane a day or two before. But now she was convinced that she had transformed into a wolf and needed to be let out to roam the hills in search of meat.

The psychiatric term for this illness is known as lycanthropy. It is considered to be a chronic form of schizophrenia and is still found in modern industrial cities today. The story above of Nebuchadnezzar shares many facets of similarity with this diagnosed illness, and even some ancient tablets found in 1975 seem to hint at the "illness" that struck Nebuchadnezzar while out on the wall of the city surveying his building projects. It said that he became unintelligible, not recognizing his wife or children, and had to be removed from society for a time. It says that the illness lasted for a while and the king's advisers had to run the kingdom while he was ill. This at first just seems like kind of a crazy story, except that it's couched in a prophetic dream in which God had warned Nebuchadnezzar of his fate. And of course it was left up to Daniel to explain things. The end result of Nebuchadnezzar's bout of lycanthropy was positive. At the end of seven years, just as the prophecy had said, his sanity returned. He looked up to heaven and finally realized where he stood in the grand scheme of things. God had been working with Nebuchadnezzar for years, but this final story is a conversion story, because in the end it says he praised and worshipped Daniel's God. I hope it won't take something as drastic as lycanthropy to get our attention, but God is trying just as hard to reach each of us today. Are you listening for Him? What do you think He wants to say to you right now?

—GH

The King Who Was Scared Spitless

> Suddenly the fingers of a human hand appeared and wrote on the plaster of the wall, near the lampstand in the royal palace. The king watched the hand as it wrote. His face turned pale and he was so frightened that his knees knocked together and his legs gave way. Daniel 5:5, 6

How often do you hear about a king in his own palace, in the midst of a gigantic banquet that he's thrown for all his governors and officials, getting so scared that he literally collapses? Probably not often, but that's exactly what happens to poor old Belshazzar in this story of the floating handwriting on the wall. The story itself is kind of miraculous all around. First off, the obvious event with the handwriting on the wall is miraculous and a little freaky all at the same time. The fact that Daniel can walk in and tell Belshazzar that the writing says that his kingdom is about to be divided up and that he has been weighed in the balances and found wanting is yet another amazing feat, though of course we expect it from a guy like Daniel.

The other thing that is amazing here is that at the very time Daniel predicted Babylon's fall, the Medo-Persian army was already making their way through the water tunnels beneath the city wall. According to historians, the generals and the army came to the gate where the city's water supply ran beneath the city walls, only to find no guards and the gate standing wide open. They simply walked into the city without a fight and took it over completely. That very night, what the hand wrote on the wall came true, but beyond this another prophecy, made 150 years earlier, was fulfilled as well. The book of Isaiah tells of a future King Cyrus who would conquer Babylon and return God's people to their homeland. It adds, "This is what the Lord says to his anointed, to Cyrus, whose right hand I take hold of to subdue nations before him and to strip kings of their armor, *to open doors before him so that gates will not be shut*" (Isaiah 45:1).

Two prophecies were fulfilled together that night. Belshazzar's final legacy in all this is that he thought he was bigger than God and could thumb his nose at the prophecies. But as Daniel told him that night: "You've been weighed and found wanting." If Daniel were to come to you today, would you be the man or woman God has called you to be, or would you too be weighed and found wanting?

—GH

Two Different Windows

Three times a day he got down on his knees and prayed, giving thanks to his God, just as he had done before. Then these men went as a group and found Daniel praying. Daniel 6:10, 11.

She was completely nude and had no idea that every single one of us could see her. The new housing development built beside my elementary school had chosen to put large picture windows in their bathrooms, opposite the showers. Not a wise choice, especially if you forget to close the window as you shower— as this poor woman did—and especially if your window looks down onto the lunch area, where dozens of middle school kids are lurking below. I don't know who saw her first, but within seconds every single seventh and eighth grader was on their feet, pointing and staring her direction. Imagine her shock the moment she looked out the window and saw her audience! She dropped in a heartbeat; then we saw a shaky hand creep up and grab the soap. For the rest of the school year that window was never opened again.

Sometimes I feel like that poor woman on display when I bow my head to pray in a restaurant, an airplane, or another public place. I feel conspicuous, exposed, as if everyone is watching me, judging me, thinking that I'm silly, or expecting great Christian things out of me now. I guess that means I'd have made a terrible Daniel, because Daniel didn't care who was watching him when he prayed or what the consequences could be. He put himself on display in quite a different window. Even when he knew that death by hungry lions might result, that faithful and fearless man stood in his window and prayed anyway. And God honored him. Not only did He shut the lions' mouths, but time and time again He raised Daniel up. Through a handful of different kings and monarchies, God distinguished Daniel and rewarded him for his faithfulness. The reason? Daniel put God first, even before his own personal safety. As a result, he led countless numbers of people to the worship of the true God of heaven.

Do you have the fear of the woman in the shower, or do you have the courage of Daniel? Are you willing to put yourself on display as a Christian, a follower of God, no matter who might be watching? Do you want to be a strong example of a praying believer? Then shrug off your fear of the crowd and decide that God's opinion matters most. Ask Him for the courage to bear his name into the world, and for the opportunities to lead people to the Lord by your example.

—MH

Better Than a Crystal Ball

I approached one of those standing there and asked him the true meaning of all this. So he told me and gave me the interpretation of these things: "The four great beasts are four kingdoms that will rise from the earth." Daniel 7:16, 17.

Ever wanted to see into the future? What would you look at first? Most people would love to see where they'll end up, where they'll live, how many kids they'll have—and with whom. The future is something almost all of us would just love to get our hands on, if for no other reason than it would be great to know how things turn out. But the problem with the future is that it seems as if it's always on the verge of being different. A truck driver's getting a good night's sleep or having a screaming baby in his ear all night will often dictate how quick his reflexes are when the spaced-out teen swerves his bike in front of the truck while trying to miss a dog racing across the street. Any number of scenarios is possible at any given moment, which could change the "future." It all depends on the choices that each of us is making right now.

That's why the prophecies of Daniel 7 are so amazing. When reading through, we see symbolic beasts that represent entire future societies and kingdoms, not just individual people. God seems to be able to see things coming down the pipeline long before there are people to choose the circumstances into existence. But this has always begged the question: If God knows the future, do we truly make choices, or is it all just going to happen anyway? We can look back at world history and verify that Daniel's dream of the beasts and the successive kingdoms they represent occurred just as predicted. So does the fact that God knew it would happen mean it couldn't have happened any other way? This sticky question comes down to a fundamental element set in place by God way back in the Garden of Eden. God allowed Adam and Eve the choice of doing what He said, or not. God told them the outcome of either choice: don't eat the special fruit and live, or eat it and die. God knew what would happen in both scenarios. And ever since then God has known the outcome to every set of choices ever made. We're free to choose, but He knows what choice we will make, and He prepares for it. So even though you're allowed to choose today, know that God is prepared to deal with the consequences; and He's already making plans to save you from mistakes you haven't even made.

—GH

A Beginning for the End

He said to me, "It will take 2,300 evenings and mornings; then the sanctuary will be re-consecrated." Daniel 8:14.

This is the verse that did it all—hearts beat faster, the crowd grew excited, then afraid, both at the same time. For several hours the preacher had been working through his canvas illustrations of beasts and mathematical calculations, and now he finally revealed the date that the world would end, based on today's verse: October 22, 1844. There was no way to refute what he said. The "sanctuary" represents the earth, and according to the prophecy this symbolic "sanctuary" would be cleansed of all sin and corruption. The preacher spoke with conviction as well as reverence, and the people felt the weight of knowing that in a few months the entire world would be reduced to ashes and they would go home to heaven.

October 22, 1844, has obviously come and gone. Seventh-day Adventists call that date the Great Disappointment, because the only thing reduced to nothing that day were the hopes of those sincere believers. Yet the beginning of the SDA Church came from the study of those discouraged people, because they refused to give up the belief that the Bible had something to tell them about the future. At last they realized that October 22, 1844, marked the *beginning* of the end. They also learned that the "cleansing of the sanctuary" referred to Jesus going into the Most Holy Place as our high priest in the real sanctuary in heaven. But you know what they didn't find? More predicted dates. Yes, some tried to predict new times for the end, and then the man who had started the excitement with his calculations in Daniel, William Miller, found a final time prediction for the discouraged believers: "I've been waiting and looking for the blessed hope, and although I've been twice disappointed, I am not yet cast down or discouraged. . . . I have fixed my mind on another time, and that is Today, Today, Today, until he comes."

Like Miller, we need to shift our emphasis. Rather than worrying about *when* Jesus will come, we need to put our attention on being ready *whenever* He does. That means we need to be ready today, every day. That's the message that this church has to pass on. So are you ready . . . today? And if so, are you helping anyone else get ready?

—GH

As soon as you began to pray, an answer was given, which I have come to tell you, for you are highly esteemed. Daniel 9:23.

It was the poison sumac that saved me in the end. That fateful afternoon I had walked happily through the woods near our new apartment complex, chatting on the phone with my friend Caitrin about my life-or-death upcoming Greek entrance exam. Caitrin volunteered to pray for me that I would somehow pass the test, though I hadn't looked at the Greek language or thought about it in years. When we got off the phone, I sat in the warm afternoon setting sun, brushing my hand absentmindedly across the leaves and plants around me, and asked the Lord again to please somehow, some way, help me pass that test.

I first noticed the bumps beginning to rise and itch on my back that night as I sat against the couch at Aunt Eleanor's. On the way home the bumps began forming on my arms, neck, and face. When we arrived at our apartment, they had made their way across my stomach, down my legs, and to my feet, so that I was covered head to toe in itchy red splotches. The splotches turned into giant welts, and the welts ushered me into one of the worst weeks of my entire life, for apparently I am highly, extremely allergic to the leaves and plants I was touching, otherwise known as poison sumac. My body was covered in welts and hives for more than a week, and during that time, as I lay stretched out on the kitchen floor covered in itch lotion, I missed my Greek exam. However, the department learned of my predicament and granted me an extra week. I studied like crazy, and somehow—I'll never know how—miraculously passed. Looking back at how God answered my prayer to pass the exam, I feel as if He sent me an answer the very moment I was praying, as I was touching the plants. Though an uncomfortable answer, the moment I asked He provided a way for that extra week of study so I'd make it.

We know that God gets to work on our prayers as soon as we utter them, because of what the angel said to Daniel in today's verse. Daniel was praying that his people would soon be delivered and the angel told Daniel that as soon as he began to pray, an answer was given. God wastes no time. Remember this today when you speak to Him, or next time you're waiting on an answer. He is a God of action—and He acts immediately on our behalf, just as soon as we ask.

—MH

How Many Times Do You Take a Girl Back?

The Lord said to me, "Go, show your love to your wife again, though she is loved by another and is an adulteress. Love her as the Lord loves the Israelites, though they turn to other gods." Hosea 3:1.

It's embarrassing to admit how many times I left Greg, certain he was wrong for me, before I finally figured out he was the one I wanted to marry. After our first couple of dates I decided we were all wrong for each other. We were just so different! I dated someone far away, then I dated one of Greg's friends, but he waited. Just days before I went overseas as a student missionary we decided to date again, but once there we really struggled, and I took it as evidence that we were wrong together. I fell head over heels for a European guy who was not so different from me. Greg . . . kept waiting, still certain I should be his wife. When I returned to the States, I gave persistent Greg "one more try," and this time it went well for quite a while. Then an old flame from high school confessed his undying love and left me confused again. Little did I know then that Greg was already planning for marriage, because he knew we were "meant to be." Eventually I figured out what he had known all along, and we married. It was the best decision of my life. What's crazy to me is that no matter how many times I left, lost faith, or turned to another, Greg still loved me. He saw possibilities in us that I couldn't see, and from the very beginning he was prepared to love me forever.

If one could travel through time, Greg and Hosea could have a long commiserating chat, because Hosea's woman kept leaving him too—over and over and over. She was a prostitute, yet God had commanded Hosea to marry her. Actually, Hosea really loved her, and it broke his heart when she kept going back to her wild ways. But every time, he took her back, just like who? Yes, like Greg. But also like God. No matter how many times Israel left God, He always, always took them back. Hosea was His living lesson. God will take you back too, you know, no matter how many times you've left, or why. He loves you more than you can understand, and He sees possibilities in you that you can't yet imagine. He's prepared to wait as long as it takes. He'll *never* stop waiting for you, never give up on you, and never, EVER stop loving you.

—MH

And Then the Floor Drops Out From Under You

When Israel was a child, I loved him, and out of Egypt I called my son. But the more I called Israel, the further they went from me. They sacrificed to the Baals and they burned incense to images. Hosea 11:1, 2.

We were on our way home from the best week the summer had to offer. I was only weeks away from going off to college, and we had taken one last adventure to the wilds of the Smoky Mountains in North Carolina. The whole week had been spent hiking and riding large inner tubes down bubbling rapids at a campground called Deep Creek. With bumps, bruises, and a hundred hilarious tales of our exploits along the river, we drove home laughing and reliving the whole week. We had no way of knowing what was happening as we were driving home. No sooner had we pulled into our driveway than my mom came out with a look on her face that I'd never seen before. With tears streaming down she said, "Your grandpa is dead. They found him this morning slumped against the side of the barn." And just like that the trip was forgotten, college was forgotten, and everything seemed to crumble down around me.

Unlike me, the people in the northern kingdom of Israel weren't blindsided. They'd known all along what tragedy was coming. The book of the prophet Hosea is all about how one man stood up during a time of prosperity and wealth and warned that in a few years it was all coming to a fiery end when the brutal kingdom of Assyria would batter them down into slavery. The Assyrians were known for mercilessly destroying the nations they conquered, impaling any survivors who opposed them on 20-foot spikes in open fields. All of this Hosea declared to the people, who jeered and mocked him for being overly dramatic and depressing. However, Hosea lived to see the beginning of this downward spiral. The last successful king of Israel, Jeroboam II, died and left a weak successor who was assassinated and gave way to a succession of five other weak kings, almost all of whom were, in turn, assassinated by each other. The book of Hosea ends with a warning for those who are wise to listen to what he says, and to walk in the ways of God.

Sometimes we live our lives the same ways as those people in Israel did. When things are good, it seems impossible to think of anything bad happening, and we don't think we need God. Don't get stuck in this trap. In good times as well as bad, stay close to God.

—GH

Braving the Swarms

What the locust swarm has left the great locusts have eaten; what the great locusts have left the young locusts have eaten; what the young locusts have left other locusts have eaten. Joel 1:4.

There were more cockroaches than I could even count; I'd say they were in the triple digits. In our little missionary island apartment, whenever the power would go out the invasions began. Dozens upon dozens of giant hairy cockroaches would creep out of our walls and floors and ceilings, out of the cracks and crevices where they hid during the day. They scurried like Christmas Eve shoppers across our apartment, and many times across us in our sleep. I'd lay in bed and listen to the eerie *scratch-scratch* of their little feet running on the walls beside me, or cower under my blankets and feel them pelting me as they fell from the ceiling. If I had the nerve to shine a flashlight on the dark walls, I could count more than 20 of the horrid things running through the single circle of light in a mere four or five seconds.

These were the conditions in the ancient Near East at the time of Joel. Both a massive locust plague and a severe drought were simultaneously devastating Judah. The locusts had moved in by swarms, and proceeded to eat everything in sight—vines, figs, pomegranates, palms, apples, grains, wheat, and barley. What the swarms of locusts did not eat, their babies after them devoured. The little varmints were everywhere!

Joel saw this plague as a judgment from God, and he put his heart and soul into begging his people to repent of their sins. He believed that they had brought the creatures on themselves because of their evil ways, and he knew that God could send them away if the people would only turn back to Him once again.

You may not have to deal with millions of starving locusts or even with clusters of creepy-crawly cockroaches, but there could still be several nasty things in your life that are there only because you brought them in. Sometimes the pains we deal with today are actually nothing more than the results of our own bad choices. If you turn from some of your less-intelligent decisions and follow in God's ways, you may find things in your life cleaning up quite a bit.

—MH

Age 17, and a Third-Grade Education

And afterward, I will pour out my Spirit on all people. Your sons and daughters will prophesy, your old men will dream dreams, your young men will see visions. Joel 2:28.

If I were God, and I wanted to get a special message out to the masses that the end of the world was near, whom would I send as my messenger? Probably someone who had lots of clout in society, maybe a well-known preacher with big radio and TV stations at his beck and call. Maybe I'd want a big-name politician who could call for a large fancy press release and set the world on fire with amazing rhetoric. But I seriously doubt that I'd pick some sickly little 17-year-old girl in a time when few women were well educated and none even had the right to vote, much less to carry a divine message. But that's exactly whom God chose.

"At this time I visited one of our Advent sisters, and in the morning we bowed around the family altar. . . . While I was praying, the power of God came upon me as I had never felt it before. I was wrapped in a vision of God's glory, and seemed to be rising higher and higher from the earth" (Ellen G. White, *Early Writings*, p. 13).

What's crazy is that this young girl, Ellen, who had only a third-grade education, would go on to write more than 100,000 pages (more than 25 million words) throughout her lifetime. Her books and writings have been translated into 148 languages, more than those of Karl Marx, Leo Tolstoy, or even William Shakespeare. Her leadership and spiritual connection helped start the Seventh-day Adventist Church, and her guidance in early leadership matters has kept it from many serious mistakes throughout its history. God seems to have a special desire to use people who don't seem to be likely candidates for such work. So ultimately I don't think God is looking at résumés or press conferences as much as He is looking for a person who is willing to be used by Him. A lot of times Ellen White gets a bad rap, either from people who misuse her or from people who have had her misused *on* them. But in the end she is best understood as a teenager who was willing to let God lead her in whatever path He chose; and for her that path included the gift of prophecy, just as Joel predicted it would in the final days of earth. God still wants to use young people for special missions and work around the world. Are you the kind of person He's looking for? More important, are you willing to be used by Him for His work and glory?

—GH

Seize the Day

Woe to you who are complacent in Zion, and to you who feel secure on Mount Samaria, you notable men of the foremost nation, to whom the people of Israel come! Amos 6:1.

Peanut butter is probably the worst item of choice to use for a food fight. I say this from personal experience, remembering the night my parents hired my older cousin Miki to babysit the four of us kids and we decided to have a food fight. I'm not sure whose bright idea it was to choose peanut butter, but it surely was fun to scoop up by sticky handfuls and fling everywhere. I especially liked the sound it made as huge clumps of it pelted onto walls, floors, tables, and furniture. Nobody was thinking about the end of the party, though, until Mom called and said they were on their way home. Ever tried to wipe splattered peanut butter off a wall or carpet? Yeah. Not the easiest thing in the world. The worst discovery was that it was plastered onto my expensive wooden harp! Sometimes when I play it I think I can still smell the peanut butter.

When you're having a good time, you really don't want to think much about how things will end—what the consequences will be, or how you'll have to clean up the mess you're making with your life. You just want to have fun and live for now! That's how the people who lived during the time of Amos felt. They were enjoying peace, health, and wealth, when this crazy shepherd, sycamore-fig-tree-growing farmer turned prophet named Amos came and tried to tell them that destruction and judgment loomed ahead of them. He condemned those who were getting rich or gaining power by taking advantage of others, and he tried to rally for social justice and right living. But people didn't want to think about those things—judgment, right living, or honest business. They just wanted to have fun. Today's *the* day. Unfortunately, that attitude sent them into death, despair, and exile in the not-so-distant future.

It's kind of a dangerous frame of mind to have, isn't it, this living just for today? While it's true that your teen years are some of the best years of your life, it's also true that you have to live with the choices you make during these years—for the rest of your life. So go ahead and live life to the fullest now, but do it in ways that honor God, yourself, and others around you. Then you won't have a giant mess to clean up somewhere down the road ahead of you.

—MH

The Longest Grudge Ever Held

As you have done, it will be done to you; your deeds will return upon your own head.
Obadiah 15.

From their hills and mountain homes they joked and jeered as the city of Jerusalem below them was attacked and ransacked. It's as though they wanted it to happen—were happy to see it happening! These people were the descendants of Esau, and they were still stuck on the fact that more than 1,000 years before, Esau had been cheated out of his birthright by Jacob, the father of the people now suffering in Jerusalem. They had held this grudge for more than a millennium, and they wouldn't let go. When the people of Jerusalem were pillaged, they rejoiced. They took the opportunity to boast and brag, to march through the city and take what wealth was left. Some even waited at the crossroads and handed over escaped fugitives and survivors to the enemy. Talk about having a thirst for revenge!

But God doesn't look kindly on this sort of behavior, this holding on to anger for years and years and years. He sent Obadiah to warn the people of Edom, Esau's descendents, that they themselves would soon be destroyed because of their shameful behavior against Jerusalem. In this short little book we read about how God feels about people who purposely hang on to anger and act out of it.

Revenge isn't a game that pays, and holding a grudge ends up hurting the holder the most of all. It's like clenching a razor in your fist—in the end you're the one bleeding. I don't know what hurts and wrongs you're holding on to today. But I do know that even if you deserve to be angry, holding on to the anger will do nothing good for you. Not only does it bring unnecessary negativity into your life—it keeps anger alive in your heart when forgiveness could put peace there instead. Take a lesson from those old descendants of Esau, and let your grudges go. Trust God to deal with the people who have hurt you, and let go of the need to make them pay. If it seems too difficult to do this immediately, begin today to ask God to start teaching you how to let go of your grudges. God is always eager to give as many lessons as necessary on one of the hardest subjects for human beings: forgiveness.

—MH

Running From God

But Jonah ran away from the Lord and headed for Tarshish. He went down to Joppa, where he found a ship bound for that port. After paying the fare, he went aboard and sailed for Tarshish to flee from the Lord. Jonah 1:3.

In my younger years the first item on my short list of "never do for fear of losing your life" was: if you're in trouble, don't ever, under any circumstances, run away from your parents. So there we were, my brother and I, innocently playing a rousing in-house game of kickball. Suddenly an overzealous dive on my part sent the ball sailing into a ceiling fan. As it shattered with an awesome crash, my mother yelled loudly, "What did you just break?" In that split second I broke my primary rule, turned tail, and fled the scene like a scared rabbit. My little brother, not wishing to be the only obvious culprit, followed as quickly as his little legs could go. We raced through the house several times, but Mom was gaining on us and getter madder with every lap. So I made another split-second decision, which should've also been on my short list of things not to do. As we passed by the open door of the bathroom I made a sudden turn and dove inside, slamming the door in my little brother's face, and locking it. He stood on the other side, squealing and pounding away like some demented animal, till finally he lost his grip and was dragged away to the inevitable (a spanking). It was only then that I wondered (with a shiver) what I'd been thinking I'd do once locked inside the bathroom.

When I read Jonah's story I have to wonder the same thing about him. What did he think he was going to do when he took to a *boat* to escape from *God*? At least he could do what I failed to do after locking the bathroom door. Jonah admitted his mistake and told the sailors on the boat to throw him into the water to let God deal with him.

How many things are we not willing to face up to? Sometimes I want to blame my lack of interest in church on a pastor's boring sermons, or I say I don't have time to study my Bible and pray because I must stay up late working on projects. But whatever the barriers are that keep me from doing these things, it's my responsibility to stop running and turn around and face them. And the amazing part is that if I'm willing to face up to these things, God is there to do the rest, just as He did for Jonah when he saved his life by sending the fish to keep him from drowning.

—GH

This One's Gruesome

But Jonah was greatly displeased and became angry. He prayed to the Lord, "O, Lord, is this not what I said when I was still at home? That is why I was so quick to flee to Tarshish. I knew that you are a gracious and compassionate God, slow to anger and abounding in love, a God who relents from sending calamity." Jonah 4:1, 2.

The trial began on January 30, 1992, and already it had become a media sensation. People were clambering for the death sentence before a verdict had even been reached, simply because of the sheer horror of the crimes. Seventeen people had been murdered in gruesome and gut-wrenching ways, and not quickly or cleanly. Jeffrey Dahmer, the man on trial, was accused of killing, dissecting, and storing his victims' body parts in vats of acid in his home freezer. The evidence against him was so overwhelming that his trial lasted only two weeks, resulting in a guilty verdict for 15 counts of murder. Dahmer, who expressed remorse and said that he wished for his own death, was sentenced to 957 years in prison, 15 life sentences. Two years later, while serving his sentence, he claimed to have become a born-again Christian. He was baptized and attended the prison chapel services every week before another inmate beat him to death.

Frankly, the part of the story that gets me the most is the whole thing about his conversion. His crimes are so terrible that I have a hard time thinking, *Well, God loves him, and he'll go to heaven because he asked for forgiveness.* Jonah felt the same way because the people of Nineveh were Assyrian, an empire known everywhere for its brutal cruelty and destructive methods when attacking and subjugating neighboring people. Entire cities would hurriedly surrender to attacking Assyrians, only to have their families—women and children—impaled on 20-foot spikes in the surrounding fields. So really, it's no wonder that Jonah chose to run away and be thrown into the ocean than to go and offer Nineveh, the capital of Assyria, any sort of second chance. If God wanted to punish them, let Him! But God's justice and mercy are universal, not just for one or two special groups, but for everyone, regardless of their past or even their present. If He is going to bring about the destruction of a city, as He warns in the book of Jonah, God makes sure the people have a final chance to make things right and avert disaster. So I guess Mr. Dahmer, you, and I have an equal chance at God's grace. Thank God!

—GH

I Screamed at a Deaf Kid

But you, Bethlehem . . . , though you are small among the clans of Judah, out of you will come for me one who will be ruler over Israel, whose origins are from . . . ancient times. Micah 5:2.

It was when he looked me dead in the eye, took my son's ball after I had told him maybe four times not to touch it, and threw it into the street that I decided I couldn't stand this bratty kid. I asked him not to ride his bike on our grass, and what did he do? He pedaled right through it. I requested that he not grab toys right out of my son's hands, and he went right ahead and did it anyway. One day he came walking up the drive with a dog that was not our dog. No matter how many times I told him "Hey, that's not our dog!" he continued to tie up the dog on our lawn.

That night I was venting my frustration to my husband, saying that I just couldn't stand the stupid kid and wondering where his parents were and why he was such a naughty little boy, when suddenly Greg got the strangest look on his face. "Melissa," he began tentatively, "you know he's deaf, right?" The words hit me like a train. No, I had not known. That was the one thing I hadn't thought of. I had pinned him as being rude, obstinate, disobedient, and mean . . . but not deaf. Instantly I felt terrible. All those times I had yelled orders or reprimands at him, he hadn't heard a thing. The poor sweet little boy was just trying to play with another kid.

It's easy to misjudge people when you haven't taken enough time to really get to know them or to understand their situation. The book of Micah gives a prediction of two times that the people of God would misjudge—first with Bethlehem, and second with Jesus Himself. The city of Bethlehem was small among the other clans, and often it was looked at as nothing big, nothing special, the lowest of the low. But Micah predicted that out of little Bethlehem would come the One who would rule over Israel. But the real misjudging happened to Jesus Himself. People thought He was just another man, a crazy prophet, a troublemaker. Some even went so far as to say he was possessed. But Micah identifies Him as God Himself, by saying He existed even back in ancient times. Truly, Jesus was far more that what He first seemed to be.

Be careful when you are tempted to size someone up or judge them quickly, because too often this leads you to the wrong conclusion. Are there people in your life even right now that you may have seriously misjudged? Do you need to give someone a second chance today?   —MH

The Real Master Key

He has showed you, O man, what is good. And what does the Lord require of you? To act justly and to love mercy and to walk humbly with your God. Micah 6:8.

It does not seem wise to me to put a campus master key into the hands of any high school teenager, no matter how innocent and trusting that person may appear to be—and I'll tell you why. On a regular basis I'd use my "key of many doors" to sneak into empty buildings and kiss my boyfriend. I was Student Association religious vice president at my academy, in charge of planning all the spiritual activities for students on campus. So naturally I seemed like someone who could be trusted to do right and keep the rules. But when you think about it, a master key is just too much temptation for most 17-year-old kids. Besides, I didn't feel as though I was actually doing anything wrong. Didn't I lead out in services for Jesus several times a week? Wasn't I planning activities that helped other kids come to know Him? As long as I was doing good things, did it really matter so much that I sneaked around once in a while? I never got caught . . . but when I became an academy teacher I surely was suspicious of the kids with the big keys.

God's people pretty much thought they had a master key as well, because they did what they wanted but still assumed they were OK with God. Wealth and power belonged to a few, and these few used their privilege to take from others. If there was a field or house they wanted, they just took it—because they could. They drove women from their homes, bribed judges, had priests charge people for teaching them, and supported prophets who told fortunes for money. They were corrupt! Still, they thought they were all right because they made their sacrifices and kept up the Temple rituals. God Himself comes to them through Micah and tells them that He's not going to be pleased by their sacrifice of 1,000 rams, or even 10,000 rivers of oil. So what is it that God wants from us, if not just to keep His laws? It's written in the verse above: have good hearts; don't just do good deeds. Be people who are just, merciful, humble, and godly.

You see, there's a difference between doing the right thing and being the right person. Your actions matter, but not as much as the state of your heart. Who you are deep inside is what matters most to God. He doesn't want you to keep His laws but treat other people badly. Today, ask God to help you to get your heart in the right place.

—MH

Showing Your Underwear: The Sequel to Jonah

"I am against you," declares the Lord Almighty. "I will lift your skirts over your face. I will show the nations your nakedness and the kingdoms your shame." Nahum 3:5.

Go to any church on any given Saturday or Sunday, and you'll see her: the little girl who knows no shame. She'll parade proudly up to the front for the children's story in her sparkling dress and patent leather shoes, but instead of sitting with the other kids, she will stand and twirl. As she holds the edges of her beautiful little dress, you can almost see the desire spread across her face—she wants to raise it! Slowly, or sometimes suddenly, this angelic little being becomes a daring exhibitionist and pulls her dress right up over her head, leaving the entire audience to abandon all interest in the children's story and gawk at her frilly underwear.

Did you know that God once threatened to pull the skirts up over someone's face? Everybody who has spent any time in a Sabbath school class or a Christian school knows the story of Jonah and how it ends—stubborn guy has to get swallowed by a really big fish before he decides to go to Nineveh and warn them of the coming destruction. When the entire city repents, God saves them, and Jonah is all bent out of shape. That's where his story ends . . . but it's not the end of Nineveh's story. The book of Nahum is the rest of the story. Here we read that this important Assyrian city returned to their wicked, brutal ways. And God took notice. He sent Nahum to warn them, a second time, that they would be destroyed. In a random prophecy in the book of Nahum, God uses this mental image of pulling their skirts over their faces to warn Nineveh that they are soon headed for shame and ruin. In the end the city is ultimately destroyed because they didn't take God seriously, and God is once again shown to be the one in charge of history, of nations, and of the destinies of humanity.

Don't get caught with your skirts pulled over your face, in any meaning of the phrase! Don't wait until you are shamed and your reputation ruined before you start to take God seriously. He means what He says, and He is able to carry out His purposes in your life. It's far better to heed His warnings in the beginning than to look back in regret, picking up the pieces. Are you doing anything in your life right now that is kind of shameful? Is this really how you want to be living, or is it time to make some changes?

—MH

Questioning Authority

So there I was, standing in a pile of wood shavings, as angry as I've ever been at anything in my life. I had just one more chance, for I was holding the last piece of wood that would fit the plans. I'd worked out the woodworking project to build a custom chess set with my dad, who showed me how to shape the wood and get the box to fit together. It required several different cuts and runs through the planer. However, I felt that all those steps were unnecessary. So when he left me alone I took a few shortcuts that made sense to me at the time, only to find that my shortcuts gouged, slipped, and chopped the wood into unusable sticks. The last board I ran through the planer was ripped out of my hands, and a sickening whine and chunk told me I'd just ruined the last piece of wood, bringing my efforts to an inglorious end.

Sometimes we need to trust people who know more than we do. The prophet Habakkuk stands out among the Old Testament minor prophets as the only one who openly questions what God is doing. It's just a few years before the Babylonians will destroy Jerusalem, carting off its inhabitants to be slaves in Babylon. The entire first chapter is Habakkuk yelling, crying, and demanding an answer for what he sees as God's insane punishment. He doesn't deny that his people deserve punishment, but he doesn't get why God would have the Babylonians, the brutal heathens that they are, dish it out. God's response is twofold. He says that He will still punish the Babylonians for their own sins, but also that Habakkuk simply needs to trust that He knows the best thing to do. Ironically, Habakkuk takes this in stride and is able to write in 2:4, "But the righteous will live by . . . faith." The rest of the book, chapter 3, is written as a song that highlights Habakkuk's decision to trust in God's actions, even if he doesn't understand them.

And there it is, in simple terms. Trust God even when you don't understand everything He does. It's not always the answer we want, and frankly, we shouldn't always assume that bad things that happen are sent by God to mess up our lives. But in the grand scheme of things, whatever happens to us, our family, or even our country, Habakkuk would tell us that it's best simply to trust God even if you don't understand everything that is going on.

—GH

Information, Please

I will stand at my watch and station myself on the ramparts; I will look to see what he will say to me, and what answer I am to give to this complaint. Habakkuk 2:1.

The little boy had seen his mother do it a hundred times, so when he ran into problems on his homework he simply walked up to the phone and said to the operator, "Information, please!"

"How can I help you?" asked the operator. (This was back in the days when a live operator connected your calls.)

"What's the capital of New York?"

"Albany . . . How old are you, anyway?"

"Seven."

So began a relationship that spanned several years. The boy called when he needed help with homework, and sometimes when he needed to know what to do for a scraped knee. As he grew older the boy stopped calling and soon forgot about the woman who had helped him so many times. Then, years later as he was passing through his hometown on a break from college, he picked up the phone and said, "Information, please." The voice on the other end of the line was familiar. "What's the capital of New York?" he asked.

"It's still Albany! How old are you now?" she replied with a smile in her voice.

"Twenty-two. Thanks for humoring a little boy. It really meant a lot to me back then."

Some of us don't feel we can talk to God like this—start a prayer at any time, on any subject, and say anything we want. But we can! Habakkuk is proof that a conversational relationship with God is completely acceptable. Habakkuk was mad at God and asked Him some tough, accusatory questions. It was OK. God answered. They talked. God didn't strike him dead. This tells me that God wants to communicate with us in this way! He wants us to talk to Him as we would any trusted, close friend—to give Him a call anytime we have something to say.

Maybe you aren't in the habit of having this kind of close talking relationship with God, but today's a perfect day to try it out. Treat prayer like a conversation with someone you simply want to talk to. Don't stress about it. Your prayers don't have to be perfect—just honest and real. Talk to God as though He's your best friend, and then watch Him turn into exactly that.

—GH and MH

Mighty to Break a Car Window

The Lord your God is with you, he is mighty to save. He will take great delight in you, he will quiet you with his love, he will rejoice over you with singing. Zephaniah 3:17.

Last week I smashed a window of my car with my own fist . . . and a rock. My baby was trapped inside, and I had to get to him. We were driving home from church, and the poor little guy was screaming his head off. I turned on music, drove fast, reached back and patted him, but nothing soothed him, so I finally just pulled the car to the side of the road. As I stepped out, closed my door, and reached for his, the automatic locks of my very smart car flashed and locked on me—with all doors closed and my keys and cell phone inside. My car has a feature that's not supposed to allow this, but there I was—in a church dress and heels, stranded on the side of the road, with my desperate, screaming baby trapped inside.

I tried all the doors. I tried the windows. I tried to flag someone down to use a phone, but then I became afraid of what type of person might stop to help. Then something came over me—I can't explain it—call it Mom instinct? fear? I knew I'd do whatever it took to rescue my panicking baby. Hardly even thinking (maybe that was the problem), as if I were temporarily without reason, I picked up a big rock and frantically pounded on my own car window. It took six or seven hard hits before the glass shattered with a terrible popping sound. I found my hand inside the car, glass embedded in it and bleeding profusely. Instantly I picked up my sobbing child, wrapped his shaking little body in my arms, and sang to him until he was quiet. Someday, when he asks me about the strange scars on my left hand, I'll tell him this story.

I'd never understood what the Bible meant when it called God "mighty to save," but that day I felt pretty mighty breaking thick glass and rescuing my baby. But think of God's might. He is able to save us from *anything*. He breaks through our struggles, our habits, even the separation of sin itself. It's not hard to be saved—God makes it happen. He is mighty! Even as we cry and scream in anger, He is already on the way to help. And when He gets to us, there won't be scolding or head-shaking. Look above. He will not only quiet you with His love, but actually rejoice over you with *singing*. He cheers for you! He celebrates and delights in you. And He will do whatever it takes to save you—just think of *His own* scarred hands.

—MH

Greg's Disgusting, Stinky, Stuffed Armadillo

At that time I will gather you; at that time I will bring you home. Zephaniah 3:20.

The nastiest, most stinky, foul, and repulsive thing my husband ever brought into our home was a dead, stuffed armadillo from Nicaragua. This thing smelled like a sack of death, and it was disgusting to look at besides. Whoever had killed it must have also stuffed it and sold it only minutes later, because it actually had fleas shellacked onto the underside of its glazed, hairy tummy. I don't know what he saw in this horrendous excuse for a souvenir, but he loved that thing. It would stink up the entire room of any place he put it in. People would walk into his apartment and exclaim, "Oh, man, something died in here!" and he would retort proudly, "Oh no, that's my armadillo!" Each time we moved I tried to hide the creature or mysteriously make it disappear somehow, but he kept finding it and setting it out in a place of honor. If it hadn't burned with all of our other belongings in our fire six years ago, he'd probably still have it stinking up his office, because he simply adored that dead animal's carcass.

Israel, in many ways, was just like that shabby, smelly armadillo. It's hard to imagine what God saw in them. They were always leaving Him, shunning Him, and deliberately disobeying Him by participating in horrific rituals and idol worship. But He kept chasing them, pursuing them, trying to get them back. He loved those disgusting people! Even in the books of the Bible that contain the judgment warnings God gave the prophets, such as Zephaniah, His anger and punishment are not the last word. I absolutely love how Zephaniah ends—not with stern warnings or fearsome consequences, but with redemption, desire, and love. That is God's last word—that He'll never give up. That He'll always come after us, always gather us, always try to bring us home. The end is not punishment—the end is love. He cherishes us! *He cherishes you.*

Are you safe at "home" with God today, or are you running, fleeing, wandering away? You may look at yourself and wonder how God could ever love someone as messed up as you, but remember Israel. He loved them no matter what, and He feels the same way about you. You don't have to understand it. Just believe it, embrace it, and be thankful for it—that God could love even the most disgusting of us. He always loved Israel, and He'll always love you.

—MH

A Twice-broken Nose With No Painkillers

Then Haggai, the Lord's messenger, gave this message of the Lord to the people: "I am with you," declares the Lord. Haggai 1:13. "This is what I covenanted with you when you came out of Egypt. And my Spirit remains among you. Do not fear." Haggai 2:5.

It was just about the worst possible scenario I could imagine. In the course of a single accident I had broken both my left arm and my nose. My face had a kind of flattened look to it, with the cartilage and bone of my nose smashed into little crumbly pieces. It had been two weeks since the accident, and my nose had started to heal in the shape that it was smashed. I knew that the doctor needed to do something drastic, but I didn't know exactly what. As I sat back in the dentist-type chair, he peered casually through his glasses at my busted schnoz.

"Hold on to something. This is going to hurt quite a bit."

And suddenly his hand was reaching for my face, his fingers poised like he was going to playfully pinch my nose. Instinctively I grabbed for the armrest, realizing that whatever was happening would happen without any painkiller. Instead of cold metal I found my mother's hand firmly grabbing mine with all the love that could be communicated through fingers alone. I'll leave out the gruesome details, but suffice it to say that with all the awful crunching and popping, the feel of my mom's support got me through the haze of pain the way nothing else could have.

Haggai's book is only two chapters long, but in those few words he calls the people to look through their pain and start the process of rebuilding their faith and their lives. By then 18 years had passed since they'd returned to rebuild Jerusalem, but the Temple itself—the house that symbolized their true source of healing and protection—still lay in the pile of rubble left by Nebuchadnezzar and his armies. People were distraught. Twice in his message Haggai tells the people that God is saying to them, "I am with you!" as He'd said to their ancestors just days after their liberation from Egypt. All through these minor prophets God assures both them and us that He is with us, no matter what circumstances surround our lives. If you get nothing else from these prophets, the thing they practically scream is that God is always present, always loving through the pain, and always reaching out to people who may or may not even be paying attention.

—GH

When Forgiveness Runs Out

The Lord was very angry with your forefathers. Therefore tell the people: This is what the Lord Almighty says: "Return to me," declares the Lord Almighty, "and I will return to you," says the Lord Almighty. Zechariah 1:2, 3.

It began to click when I checked out his story with a few people. My best friend went to a different church on the other side of town. Sometimes I'd go with his youth group to events, but mostly it was to check out the women. After hanging out a few times with one girl I was interested in, I asked him if he thought I should just go ahead and ask her out on a date. He'd known this girl most of his life, and I figured he'd be the best person to ask about what my chances were. He said he'd find out for me later that night and would give me a call. I anxiously waited for any word from him, and finally he did call—late that night. He told me that she was sorry but thought that it probably wasn't a good idea because she'd been wanting to go out with him for a while. Admittedly a red flag should've gone up in my mind, but he was my best friend, after all, and would never pull anything like that on me. Then when I started asking around, I found out from other people that he had gone up to her with a big bunch of flowers and asked her out himself. He intentionally went behind my back. He betrayed me. We had a big blowup about it later. He came clean, and as I struggled to forgive him I quickly found out that my forgiveness has limits.

But if anyone had tested the limits of forgiveness, it was the Israelites. By the time the prophet Zechariah came on the scene, they had rejected God dozens of times over hundreds of years. Today's scripture says that God was very angry with the forefathers of these people, but that if they would turn back to Him, He would return to them as well. It's this kind of thing that always astounds me about God. In the face of way more broken promises and outright rejection God says that He's still willing to come back to these people. The book of Zechariah goes on to describe how the Temple that these returning exiles would build would be greater than the previous, and that He Himself would visit it to restore and cleanse the people from all sin—a prediction of Jesus Himself. Ultimately this book vividly points out that God is the kind of God who will take us back when we ask Him. No matter how far you've gone or what things you've done, He's always ready to start over with you. There's nothing you can do to escape His love.

—GH

Listen, O high priest Joshua and your associates seated before you, who are men symbolic of things to come: I am going to bring my servant, the Branch. Zechariah 3:8.

Several people claimed to have seen the book, although no one knew for sure it existed. But Mr. Allen, the physics teacher in the high school in which my wife taught, created a tradition based on the mysterious little black book. Throughout the year he'd make observations about who was dating whom, and which senior would marry which other senior in the future. He'd pair up everyone from the senior class and write it down in his little book. He never showed it publicly, but would refer to it every once in a while. Rumor had it that he was right more often than not, but how could you ever be sure if you couldn't get your hands on the book? Many a senior had tried, but no one truly knew where he kept it. Only when one or another of the students got married would he confess that he'd predicted it long before.

The book of Zechariah makes a lot of predictions about events in the Messiah's life, but you don't have to wonder what they were or hunt in a locked desk somewhere. Zechariah was trying to get the word out because he wanted everyone to know what and who was coming along down the line. The returning exiles from Babylon had to deal with the fact that their lives had been torn apart, and that it seemed God had completely rejected them. But His message is quite the opposite. In fact, He says that they will be blessed more than those who came before.

Here Zechariah paints one of the most vivid pictures in the entire Bible of Jesus' life, death, and resurrection. The verse above describes the high priest Joshua and his associates, "who are men symbolic of things to come." In the Hebrew language the name Joshua is *Yehoshua,* which is sometimes shortened in form to the name *Yeshua,* or Jesus, our high priest in heaven. This servant, the Branch, that God promised to send was the one thing that would bring all the other prophecies and predictions to fulfillment. It's fitting, then, that in almost the last book of the Old Testament we see again the promise that was given to Adam and Eve on the day they were forced from the Garden of Eden: *I will send a Savior to you who will bring you back home.* That's the overarching theme of the Bible: we have left God, but God will not leave us. And today, if you're hearing His voice calling you home, don't ignore it. Just come home.

—GH

Change Is Good?

I am the Lord, I do not change. Malachi 3:6, NKJV.

I hate change. I hate change in every way possible. I know some people thrive and excel with change, but I do not think I'm one of them. I like for my clothes to stay in the same order in the closet (maybe that's a different problem!), and I like to order the same meals at restaurants. I get very upset when a favorite drink of mine is discontinued at Starbucks. I like to visit the same old places. I get attached to things—I got terribly sad as a child when my dad would sell the car or throw out an old broken toy. I have always hated it terribly when people I love have to move away. But I hate it even more when I myself have to move away, and start over somewhere new, which I've had to do often. Usually I have a hard time the first few months or so; I get depressed and don't thrive, don't make friends, don't leave the house—that type of thing. Everyone tells me that change is a natural part of life and you just have to accept it, but that doesn't mean I have to like it. I have several friends who say that they actually look forward to such big changes as moving and starting over. They say they get bored with life, and it gives them a lot of excitement to be able to do different things all the time. I can see their side—excitement is good—but the old things are just so much more comfortable!

If you're like me and don't like change, or even if you are like my friends and welcome change—whichever you prefer—I don't think any of us would say that we want a God who changes all the time. No matter how much we love or hate change, there are some things in life that we need to stay constant, and God happens to be one of them. That's why it's such a relief to me when He assures us in the last book of the Old Testament that He does not change.

Think what it would be like if God changed all the time. You couldn't count on His rules, you couldn't invest in His purposes, and you couldn't bank on His love. You couldn't trust Him either. One day He could say one thing, and the next day it might be different. So it's wonderful to know that in a changing world we have something that is constant. We have a North Star in the midst of the black night that can always guide us home.

Our God does not change. Even if all of life is falling down around you, He is the same. For all of us, but especially for me—that's a great big sigh of relief!

—MH

"Bring the whole tithe into the storehouse, that there may be food in my house. Test me in this," says the Lord Almighty, "and see if I will not throw open the floodgates of heaven and pour out so much blessing that you will not have room enough for it." Malachi 3:10.

With a shaky hand Dad slowly wrote out the tithe check for a little more than $100—the last money the family had until payday, but he and Mom knew they were going to pay tithe, no questions asked. They didn't know how they'd buy groceries to last the rest of the week for themselves and four kids, but they had faith. They had started a new business that was, so far, not making any money, and we'd moved to another state and left all we knew. I remember Dad mentioning the verse above, and telling us that God is true to His word. We were worried about starving, but Dad claimed that God would somehow come through. I went off to my room to think about these things, but within just a few minutes my thoughts were interrupted by a knock at the door. It was my grandparents from out of town—unexpectedly dropping in on us. That was not so remarkable in itself. But the remarkable thing was that in their arms they held bags and bags and bags of groceries. My grandpa had the trunk of the car open, where more groceries were waiting, and he was yelling, "Come on, kids! Help me carry some of this in!" I tear up even now when I think about the fact that before my dad even signed the check, our grandparents were at the store, buying the food. Before Dad even put God's name on trial before his little family, they were on their way to our house, supplies abundantly filling their car. God is faithful.

Tithes and offerings can be a sticky subject these days. Some say the practice can only be supported in Old Testament times. Others say the precedent isn't really in the Bible at all. Still others think it's mean of God to ask us to put our families at risk in hard times in order to give money to His church. All I can say is this: *God is true to His word.* He asks us to give, and promises blessing. Sometimes the blessings arrive immediately, sometimes they're delayed, but God keeps His promises. This is one of the only clear times in the Bible in which the Lord actually challenges us to put Him to the test—with tithes and offerings. Are you in the habit of giving money to God? It can feel hard to do, but I challenge you to put God to the test. See if He won't open the floodgates of heaven, and bless you more than you ever dreamed possible.

—MH

A God for Everyone

"And they will call him Immanuel"—which means, "God with us." Matthew 1:23.

My ridiculously large wedding party was quite possibly the most giant one in history. Because I didn't want to choose between my closest friends, I simply decided to have everyone. I had nine bridesmaids, and Greg had nine groomsmen. Then I had two candle lighters, a procession of six (or was it eight?) candle holders, an usher, a Bible boy, and two flower girls. In addition to all these folks, I also had every relative seated to music—not just mothers, but aunts, grandmothers, people who had acted as mothers in my life, etc. It just went on and on forever! But that's because it was so important to me that nobody be left out. I wanted everyone included.

Matthew had the same idea as I had, when he began the Gospel that now opens the New Testament. He wanted to make sure everyone knew they were included. You see, the genealogy of Jesus is somewhat peculiar. Genealogies usually include only men, but Matthew throws women in—Gentile women, ones with some blatant sexual issues, too (think Rahab, Tamar, Bathsheba). Why include these women? He is writing to Jews, but he wants to make it clear that Jesus is not just for the Jews; He is for all people, all kinds. Everyone is included! Matthew goes on to tell the story of the Magi's visit—Gentiles again—and he also tells the story of the angel announcing Jesus' name: "Immanuel, God with us." This is how the Gospel starts, with the clear picture that God is coming to be with us, with all of us. Did you know this is also how it ends? Jesus' last words in Matthew are "I am with you always."

Why does Matthew care so much about this emphasis on God being with us? Because the Jews had known this was God's desire for thousands and thousands of years when, at the foot of Mount Sinai, God asked them to build Him a sanctuary so that He could dwell among them; so that He could be with them. For thousands of years prophets had been predicting the coming of a Savior: God with us. Truly Jesus was the fulfillment of God's greatest desire: to be with us. All of us.

Now that He isn't still here in person, it can be hard to feel that God is actually "with" us in our day-to-day lives. But His company and His presence are still for everyone, just as it was back then. He's not available to only the holy and best— He is for everyone; all are included. Whether you feel it or not, He wants to be with you. Invite Him to be with you in your life!

—MH

More Than a Dream

After Herod died, an angel of the Lord appeared in a dream to Joseph in Egypt.
Matthew 2:19.

The horrid black creature was as real as life, and I was terrified. Though it was a dream, I'll never forget how I felt as it stood over me and snickered wickedly. That night I had been praying for help in forgiving someone whom I'd been angry with for years, a woman who had hurt me again and again. When my dream began, I was standing in the hallway of my school, outside my classroom door. Students were coming and going, but they were not alone. Each was accompanied by an angel of light or an angel of darkness, according to their loyalties (and some were being fought over by both). As I marveled at these things, I turned into my classroom, and there before me was the most hideous creature of all, awful and menacing. I told it immediately that it shouldn't be with me; I knew I belonged to God. That's when it laughed at me and said words I'll never forget: "My name is Anger, and I'm here only because you won't let me go." I awoke with a start, got down on my knees, and told the Lord that even though it was only a dream, I didn't want to have that anger in my life anymore. And finally I forgave her.

Some are skeptical about whether or not God really communicates with us in dreams, or if dreams are just the musings of our own minds sorting out the day's thoughts. But what we do know for sure is that God *did* communicate through dreams in Bible times. Matthew records several instances in which God gave messages to people through dreams. He appeared to Joseph to explain Mary's shocking pregnancy; He warned the Magi in a dream not to report Baby Jesus' whereabouts to Herod; He told Joseph, in a dream, to escape with his family into Egypt; then He sent another dream to Joseph when it was safe to return after Herod's death. A final dream warned Joseph to go to Galilee, and Jesus grew up in Nazareth. All this—through dreams!

I don't know how God plans to communicate with you—whether it be through dreams, other people, His Word, circumstances, or something else. But what I do know is that He will find a way to get through to you, no matter what. Whatever it takes and whatever or whomever He might need to use, He will do His best to reach you. Will you be listening? Would you be open to receiving a message from Him if it were to come to you today?

—MH

What the Crowd Heard That Day

And lo a voice from heaven, saying, This is my beloved Son, in whom I am well pleased.
Matthew 3:17, KJV.

The most memorable thing about my fairly uneventful baptism was the reading of my pet list, which, at that time, numbered about 40 or so. The patient pastor who baptized me went through each of them, one at a time, by name. Toward the end he read "Hershey, Taffy, Salt, Pepper, Cocoa, Cream" and suddenly exclaimed, "That sounds like a cake mix!" Everyone in the audience laughed, and I realized for the first time that I had the habit of naming many of my pets after food products. For a long time everyone talked about my delicious-sounding pets.

The crowd gathered at the baptism of Jesus witnessed something far more memorable and much more amazing than anything anyone had seen at a baptism before or since. First, they saw the Holy Spirit come down out of heaven and rest above Jesus in the form of a dove, and second, they heard the voice of God Himself: "This is my beloved son, in whom I am well pleased." Surely everyone nearby must have been in complete awe at this moment, when all three members of the Trinity were present together—Son, Spirit, and Father. But what God said out of the heavens was far more significant than you may ever have realized.

In the Jewish culture, when a boy became a man and the father wanted to publicly name him as such, they had a certain ceremony. At this ceremony the father would call the boy up in front of all those gathered, and he would announce, "This is my beloved son, in whom I am well pleased." Sound familiar? At this the son was then legally allowed to carry out any type of business transaction in his father's name. He became a legal representative of his father.

Now, imagine Jesus—He didn't have an earthly father. Perhaps He never participated in this ceremony. But everyone in the crowd that day at His baptism knew what those words meant. So when they heard the voice of God, not only did they realize Jesus was His Son, but they also realized immediately that God was presenting Jesus to them as a representation of Himself, and one who was able now to carry out His business on the earth. Amazing! I don't know what your earthly father is like, but if he ever falls short, remember that your Father in heaven is very pleased with you, and He still calls you to carry out His business today.

–MH

What Is the Meaning of Life?*

In the same way, let your light shine before men, that they may see your good deeds and praise your Father in heaven. Matthew 5:16.

Looking out the window toward two graveyards, Alexander Papaderos asked his students for the last time, "Are there any questions?" His institute on the island of Crete, devoted to peace and understanding between Greeks and Germans, was built on the site where a massacre had taken place during World War II. All that remained now were crosses and hatred. And questions, such as the one asked now: "What is the meaning of life?" The class snickered, knowing no real answer to this question existed. To their surprise, Papaderos began one of the most profound answers of all time by pulling a small, rounded mirror from his leather billfold, explaining that as a poor child during the war he'd found it in the wreckage of a German motorcycle.

"By scratching it on a stone, I made it round. I began to play with it as a toy, and became fascinated by the fact that I could reflect light into dark places—into deep holes, crevices, and dark closets. It became a game for me to try to get light into the most inaccessible places I could find. As I became an adult, I realized that this was more than just a game, but a metaphor for what I might do with my life. I came to understand that I am not the light, or the source of the light. But the light—truth, understanding, knowledge—is there, and it will shine in dark places only if I reflect it. I am a fragment of a mirror whose whole design and shape I do not know. Nevertheless, with what I have I can reflect light into the dark places of this world—into the black places in the hearts of men and women—and change some things in some people. Perhaps others may see and do likewise. This is what I am about. This is the meaning of *my* life."

What's the meaning of your life? Do you reflect Jesus Christ, the true light of the world, or do you merely reflect yourself to others? None of us is the source of the light, but as Christian mirrors we reflect only what actually lives inside us. If there's only selfishness, pride, and conceit in your heart, that's what you'll reflect to the world. But if Jesus lives there, your life will become a mirror that reflects Him. Let your light shine to the world so that you will glorify Him! There's no better meaning for any life than to reflect Jesus.

—MH

*Adapted from Robert Fulghum's musical play *All I Need to Know I Learned in Kindergarten.*

Poke Your Eyes Out

And if your right hand causes you to sin, cut if off and throw it away. It is better for you to lose one part of your body than for your whole body to go into hell. Matthew 5:30.

Only once have I ever tried to chop off one of my own body parts. Granted, I was only about 2 years old at the time, but I remember it quite vividly. I was working out in the garage with my dad, doing something really helpful (pushing piles of sawdust around with a stick). Dad was busy sanding something on a belt sander a few feet away in the corner of the garage. I had always been given express orders never to touch, or even get near, the machines when they were turned on, but as I looked at the whirring belt sander I was entranced by the spinning wheels and shapes. They looked so cool and interesting that I found myself slowly meandering in that direction. I could feel a little breeze coming from under the machine, and the smell of freshly cut wood made my head spin a bit. Slowly I reached my hand out to touch the spinning machinery underneath the belt, all those cool gears and shapes, blurring into a mass of metal and wood. My memory of the event goes up until the moment I actually shoved my hand into the gears themselves, and then there was lots of blood and lots of pain. I practically cut off the whole tip of my finger with that little stunt, but luckily it was able to be reattached.

Was Jesus really suggesting we cut off body parts when He made the comment in the verse above? Stated during His famous Sermon on the Mount, He had just finished explaining that lusting in your heart is not much different from adultery. Then He started talking about dismemberment? Well, not exactly. You probably realize that what He's really suggesting isn't as gruesome, but it's still just as difficult. He's saying that if something in your life is causing you to fall into sin again and again, it's better just to get it out of your life as quickly as possible. Whether it is an object of temptation, a person who always leads you into sin, a location in which you repeatedly get into trouble, or anything else that always results in a sin for you—whatever it might be, get rid of it! It's better to lose out on a little down here than to be led astray for good.

What are those certain things, people, places, or situations in your life that always cause you to fall into sin? I bet you know them well by now. Are you ready to be finished with them? Do you feel daring enough to make a rash move today and cut them out of your life forever?

—GH and MH

How to Destroy Your Enemies

But I tell you: Love your enemies and pray for those who persecute you. . . . If you love those who love you, what reward will you get? . . . Do not even pagans do that? Be perfect, therefore, as your heavenly Father is perfect. Matthew 5:44-48.

Technically, teachers aren't supposed to hate their students, but I must confess that one time I came close. Let's call him David. I was a 19-year-old missionary teacher on the little island of Ebeye, and he was one of the worst students you could ever imagine. He completely disregarded everything I said, put his moves on the girls in my class, and blatantly defied and loudly opposed me, even leading others in the class to do the same. He was impossible to control—there was not an ounce of respect in him. One night I fell on my knees, exasperated, and begged the Lord to take him out of my life. The answer I got was a very strong impression that I should just love him. Love him? Impossible!

Well, I tried it. The next morning, when I greeted him cheerfully with a smile, he about fell over in shock. I encouraged him in class. I joked with him and asked him about his life after class, and walked him home and visited with his family. Soon he began paying attention during my lectures. Then he started staying after class to hang out with me. One day he began shutting down any other student who tried to make noise in my class. At the end of the year, at my going-away party, he stood up and said, with tears in his eyes, that I was his one true friend.

I'll never forget "David." He taught me one of the most important lessons of all time: that LOVE is the ONLY thing that ever really changes anyone. Love is the single most powerful weapon you and I have—it turns bad kids into good kids, mean people into nice people, enemies into friends. Love is the defining mark of a Christian—it's the one thing that makes us different from the rest of the world, Jesus said. Everyone loves their friends, but who loves their enemies? When He asked us to be perfect, He didn't mean never to mess up again. He meant to be perfect in love, to intentionally choose to show love to every last person who crosses our path.

Who in your life today do you need to start intentionally showing love to? Think of that person who tries your patience and gets under your skin—that's the one! If you think you can't do it, just start small. Ask Jesus to help by filling you with His perfect, abundant love.

—MH

What We Keep

Do not store up for yourselves treasures on earth, where moth and rust destroy, and where thieves break in and steal. But store up for yourselves treasures in heaven, where moth and rust do not destroy, and where thieves do not break in and steal. For where your treasure is, there your heart will be also. Matthew 6:19-21.

It's hard to describe what it feels like to watch every earthly possession you own burning in flames before your very eyes. The night of our fire, Greg and I came on the scene in time to watch the flames leap from room to room of our home, but not in time to rush in and get anything out. So we were left standing outside in the rain, watching everything we loved and cherished go up in smoke. The fire burned for so many hours that we didn't bother to wonder what was left—except for the clothes on our backs, we knew we'd lost everything. That horrible night as I stood there sobbing, watching my beloved treasures burn—a lifetime of pictures, journals, yearbooks, mementos, even my wedding dress—suddenly out of the night I felt a steady arm around me, holding me tight, and the reassuring voice of my good friend Renee insisting this one bit of comfort into my ear: "This is all only temporary, Melissa! These things—they're just things. All of it is temporary! You can't take it with you anyway."

It's funny how much time and effort and love we put into our things, isn't it? Think of your possessions. What do you treasure, what do you cherish? Anything you would run into a burning building to try to save? I guess Jesus knew how tightly we would cling to our stuff when He uttered the advice above. He knew that our first instinct would be to throw ourselves into collecting treasures and wealth down here, but He also knew that it wouldn't last. Not any of it! As Renee reminded me that fateful night, it's all just temporary stuff that can be taken from us in an instant.

What do you put your time and energy and the best of yourself into? Is it stuff—your things? Or are you investing your life instead into what can't be taken away from you? Are your treasures here on earth, or are your real treasures in heaven? Investing in the lives of other people, and investing in your relationship with Jesus—these are the only treasures that will last beyond this earth. Make sure your treasures are in the right place today, because as Jesus says, you will find that your heart is with them.

—MH

The Prowling Midnight Moose

Do not worry about your life. . . . Who of you by worrying can add a single hour to his life? . . . But seek first his kingdom and his righteousness, and all these things will be given to you as well. Do not worry about tomorrow. . . . Each day has enough trouble of its own. Matthew 6:25-34.

I first heard the thundering footsteps of the giant moose at 3:00 in the morning. Frightened, I curled deeper into my sleeping bag inside our little tent, remembering all the stories I'd heard about moose being mean and aggressive and attacking people. We were on a canoeing trip, camped on a small island in the boundary waters of Minnesota, and we'd been warned not to pester the moose or make them mad. And we hadn't—so why did it continue to stomp angrily around our camp? My heart raced at the heavy footsteps so close by my head. It was almost daybreak when I finally drifted off to sleep. Next morning everyone was asking each other if they'd heard the mad moose. We couldn't figure out why it had come, and what's more, why it had stayed nearby so long! Then just as our fears were subsiding, we heard it again—the thudding footsteps—except there was no moose in sight. Not anywhere! All of a sudden one of us looked up and saw it: two trees growing against each other, knocking together each time the wind blew hard. I'd stayed awake most of the night worrying for nothing!

Sometimes the real worries in our lives seem as big as a moose, only far scarier. So why does Jesus tell us not to worry? Doesn't everybody? Shouldn't we worry, at least about some things? The answer comes in verse 33. Jesus says that instead of worrying, we should put that energy into seeking after Him and His kingdom. At first this doesn't seem to make a whole lot of sense, but think about it. Last year at this time, what problem or fear was worrying you to death? I bet it resolved itself, didn't it? Jesus knows not only that our worries are temporary, but also that He can handle them. When we put our energy into seeking Him instead of worry, He can simultaneously give us peace and work those problems out.

Does worry hang heavy on your mind today? It's hard, but trust Jesus when He tells you not to worry. Throw yourself into chasing Him instead. Have faith that He can work out your problem, and leave those worries in His very capable hands.

—MH

The Unwanted Sunglasses

Why do you look at the speck of sawdust in your brother's eye and pay no attention to the plank in your own eye? . . . You hypocrite, first take the plank out of your own eye, and then you will see clearly to remove the speck from your brother's eye. Matthew 7:3-5.

Tucked away on a high dusty shelf in my room is a pair of sunglasses that I wish I didn't have. My heart sinks each time I see them, so I try to hide them from myself. But I can't. I still know they're mine. I can still see the look on the girl's face when she came asking to borrow them. I was her teacher, and in her culture the word "borrow" is just another (nice) way of saying they want to take it and keep it forever. Because they were nice sunglasses I gave her an firm "no way." But she hung around, kept asking, and acted pretty upset about my repeated refusals. I was angry with her when she left, because I knew she was just being devious and trying to play the pity card so that I would give them to her. How dare she manipulate me! I'm not stupid!

The next day in church I was still angry at her for attempting to weasel me out of my best pair of glasses when in came her older sister, a ball cap pulled down low over her eyes, her head bowed in shame. She sat silently in the back corner, and only once did she lift her head at all, but in that instant I saw it—a large, swollen, puffy black eye. Turns out she'd been beaten up the day before, and her sister had come to me, her trusted teacher, asking for the sunglasses so her sister wouldn't have to be ashamed in church the next day. How completely wrong I'd been!

Ever notice how easy it is to judge someone? Ever find yourself feeling justified when you point out the annoying habits of other people? If so, better check yourself. That's what Jesus says in today's verse. When was the last time you stopped to think how annoying your own habits are? Or what about the faults you have that everyone else so graciously puts up with day after day? It's easy to forget about ourselves when other people around us are so maddening, but we can't do that. Besides, as in my student's situation, we never really know the true pain lurking in the lives of others. We might be judging them harshly when really they're just hurting.

Try to take a good honest look at whatever "planks" may be in your own life today, or ask the Lord to reveal them to you. Then next time you're tempted to criticize or judge someone else, remember that you've got enough problems of your own to worry about first!

—MH

Choose Your Bus Wisely

But everyone who hears these words of mine and does not put them into practice is like a foolish man who built his house on sand. The rain came down, the streams rose, and the winds blew and beat against that house, and it fell with a great crash. Matthew 7:26, 27.

I still say we got so terribly lost in Rome that night because Greg made us take the wrong bus. Well, OK—I stepped onto it too, but it was really his idea. We had wandered the city until well past midnight, visiting the Trevi Fountain, milling around the plazas, meandering past the Pantheon, finally making our way to the Spanish steps. By then we were tired and exhausted, so we waited on a street corner where other young people seemed to be gathering, and hoped a bus would come by shortly. We waited 45 minutes. No bus came. Some concluded the buses stopped running after 1:00 a.m. Others decided just to walk home, but we were miles from our hotel, and the sun would rise before we made it there. So we waited on.

Finally a lone bus came crawling out of the night, and without thinking where it might take us, we hopped on board. Thus began our tour of the entire city of Rome—except the part where we were staying. We rode through suburbs and neighborhoods. We got on a freeway and headed out of town. One by one people got off the bus, until finally we were the last two riding. Then the bus pulled into a lot filled with other buses. The driver turned off the engine, got out, and walked away. We were left sitting there stunned—where were we? And how on earth could we find our way home? It's a long story, but the ending is that we made it to our hotel around 6:00 a.m., just as the sun rose. It would have been better if we'd walked to it in the first place, but the best idea would've been to make solid plans at the start.

Many times we make quick choices without thinking about the end result. What we might forget, though, is that the choices we make today have drastic effects on our tomorrows. Our future life is built on the foundation of today's choices. That's why Jesus encourages us to build our lives on His words, not our own ideas, which are as stable as shifting sands.

What are you building your life on today? Will it hold up when the winds of life start blowing, or do you need to start looking for something sturdier? Try building your life on Jesus, the most solid choice of all.

—MH

He Never Saw It Coming

When Jesus had finished saying these things, the crowds were amazed at his teaching, because he taught as one who had authority, and not as their teachers of the law. Matthew 7:28, 29.

I believe it was the bikini that did it. Let me explain. If there was one thing in my brother's young life that you couldn't take away from him, it was his bike. He'd ride up and down our road and all over the neighborhood, pedaling and jumping and spinning all over the place. The best story about my bro and his bike involves some new apartments that had sprung up not far from our house. He was riding along the edge of the road, casually taking in the scenery, when he saw a girl on a lawn, tanning in a bikini. He stopped pedaling and coasted on by, craning his neck to get a better look. Suddenly he felt the front tire smack into something. In an instant he was thrown into the air and landed with a splat on the windshield of a parked car like some gigantic bug. At the sound of the crash the girl shot upright to see what was going on. My brother moaned and rolled off the car. Grabbing his bike, he fled as fast as he could pedal. He told me that he never saw the parked car—he wasn't expecting it on that side of the road.

Sometimes we can miss out on things because we just aren't expecting them to be there. The people in Jesus' day weren't expecting to hear some of the things He said in the Sermon on the Mount The Bible says that He spoke with authority, like one who was telling you what the law meant, rather than just giving an opinion. "Blessed are the poor in spirit, for theirs is the kingdom of heaven"; "Blessed are you when people insult you, persecute you . . . because of me" (Matthew 5:3, 11).

You just don't expect to hear this kind of thing from a leader. The people expected a declaration of revolt, something to raise up the masses to take on the Roman abuses in their society. Instead they heard, "Blessed are the peacemakers, for they will be called sons of God" (verse 9). Those listening had just as hard a time with some of these things as we do today. But the Sermon on the Mount is probably the best outline of what Jesus taught and lived recorded anywhere in the New Testament. It points us toward an ideal for us to model in our own lives, and shows us the things that are really important to God and His way of life. Jesus isn't always the kind of person we expect Him to be, but that's part of what makes Him so great. So check out the rest of the sermon today, and see what other unexpected things you find in there.

—GH

You Almost Had Me, Philip

Do not worry about what to say or how to say it. At that time you will be given what to say, for it will not be you speaking, but the Spirit of your Father speaking through you. Matthew 10:19, 20.

Why should we even care about Jesus, anyway?" Philip yelled angrily from the back of my classroom. "He's no better than any other god we could serve—Buddha or Muhammad or anyone else! There's no good reason to be a Christian!" All eyes turned to me, and a stunned silence fell over the class as they wondered how I'd respond to this direct attack on both Jesus and Christianity. Philip was known for these scathing outbursts from time to time, and some days when he raised his hand I cringed and waited for the worst. This was the most terrible comment he'd ever made. Was I supposed to defend everything my entire life stood for in one simple explanation? I pasted a smile on my face that let my class know I was calm and prepared with an answer, but inside I was pleading desperately with God: "Please, Lord; I have no idea what to say! It's Your name on trial here, anyway—not mine. I need an answer!"

An uncomfortable 10 seconds passed, and finally I knew I had to say something, so I opened my mouth to speak, still not having a single clue what I'd say. But when I opened my mouth, a strange thought that I'd never even considered before was right there on the tip of my tongue. "Can you please give me the date, Philip—or anyone—can you give me the exact date in history that Muhammad died to save his people? Someone tell me when Buddha was crucified so that we can be free from our sins and not have to work our way into heaven."

The real miracle took place after my question. Philip fell silent. And he later told me why. It was because I had distilled the core reason we do need Jesus, the one thing that makes Him a better God to serve than all the rest: He died to save us. No one else has ever done that. God had given me words to say that I couldn't have fashioned better with a month's warning.

In Matthew 10 Jesus promised that He'd do that for His disciples when He sent them out to preach, but His promise still stands for us today. Do you worry about standing up for God, or being put on trial to speak for Jesus? Don't. He promises that when the time comes, the Spirit will give you the words you need. So be bold and speak out for Him whenever you get the chance. He'll be behind you every step of the way, giving you the words to say.

—MH

The Creepiest Parable Jesus Ever Told

Then [the evil spirit] says, "I will return to the house I left." When it arrives, it finds the house unoccupied, swept clean and put in order. Matthew 12:44.

You would think that putting poison in your house would keep the ants out, not in, but not so, my friends Sean and Helen discovered during their recent ant invasion. Something in the poison smells like food to attract them to it, so it brings ants in instead of keeping them out. Here Sean thought he was ridding his house of pesky ants by the thousands forever, and lo and behold, he accidentally invited them in by the millions!

The ant invasion—which they fought for weeks—reminds me of Jesus' parable about the evil spirits. This isn't one of those warm fuzzy parables. In fact, in my book it ranks as one of the more disturbing ones He ever told. He starts by saying that when an evil spirit comes out of a person, it goes around looking for somewhere to rest and doesn't find a place. So the spirit decides it will go back to the "house" (person) it left. When it gets there, it finds the house empty, swept clean, and put in order. But it doesn't just move back in on its own. No. It brings seven other spirits, and they all move in! The end result is far more terrible than it was in the beginning! So what's this scary-sounding parable about, anyway?

First of all, let's think about the empty "house." Is it bad to be clean or put in order? Of course not. The problem was the emptiness. The evil spirit was cast out, but nobody came to live there in its place. Now, what does this have to do with those of us who don't believe we're possessed in the first place? Simple.

Ever wondered why it's so hard to fight against your sins? Ever get frustrated with how difficult it is to clean up your life, or to keep bad habits out of your "house"? The point that Jesus is making is that we can try all we want to clean up our lives and purge ourselves of sin. But without Someone to occupy our heart—namely, without Him—we are still empty and therefore still open to sin. We struggle to keep sin out of our lives because we haven't let Jesus fill us. The goal isn't to sweep the floors, to clean up our own lives, but to have a Savior at home in the house.

What's the state of your house/heart today? Is it messy, clean, empty, or full? Who's in residence there? Is it time to invite Jesus back in to stay?

—MH

"These men who were hired last worked only one hour," they said, "and you have made them equal to us who have borne the burden of the work and the heat of the day." But he answered one of them, "Friend, I am not being unfair to you." Matthew 20:12, 13.

On a plane headed for Greece the distinguished gentleman graciously approached TV star Telly Savalas in first class and asked for his autograph, claiming his daughter was a great fan. Savalas, annoyed by the hype of his fame and wanting to fly in peace, ignored the man. The gentleman sat down, but about an hour later asked again. Savalas didn't even look at him this time. Just as the flight was preparing to descend into Greece, the man asked for the autograph one more time, stressing how his daughter would simply treasure it. Again Savalas didn't give him the time of day. When the plane finally landed, as he told the story to Johnny Carson on *The Late Show*, Savalas looked out his window and saw an interesting sight: a red carpet rolled out to the plane's steps, big, fancy cars, and crowds of people waving flags. A very important-looking man got onto the plane, went to the distinguished gentleman who had asked Savalas for his autograph, and said, "This way, Your Highness." Savalas said his heart just sank—he had been flying with the king of Greece! The king! He could have enjoyed him all this time, gotten to know him, but he was too stuck on himself even to give him the time of day. What precious time he wasted!

Jesus once told a story that has to do with wasted time, but you might not ever have heard it that way before. The story of the vineyard workers features a man who hires people at all hours of the day—some very early, others at the last hour—but pays them all the exact same wages. The ones who'd worked all day long are mad! This parable is about salvation. Some walk with Jesus all their lives, and some sneak in at the last hour, but the end reward is the same. And sometimes those of us who sacrificed and lived good lives feel mad—we could have been out playing all that time too, and then repent on our deathbeds! Why not live wild and repent last?

Because we could be flying with the King! Let those who convert on their deathbeds tell you about ruined lives, torn-apart families, wasted years. The end reward may be the same, but your life isn't. Don't waste the opportunity you have—choose to "fly with the King" now. Save yourself years of pain and misery and regret, and enjoy the ride of a lifetime with Jesus.

—MH

Does It Make You a Better Lover?

One of them, an expert in the law, tested him with this question: "Teacher, which is the greatest commandment in the Law?" Jesus replied: "'Love the Lord your God with all your heart and with all your soul and with all your mind.' This is the first and greatest commandment. And the second is like it: 'Love your neighbor as yourself.'" Matthew 22:35-39.

It still makes me angry when I think about that potluck day at the church. We'd smelled good things during the church service. It was almost painful to watch Claire and Donald, an ailing elderly couple, creep across the foyer toward the kitchen carrying a big casserole dish. Donald had severe diabetes, and Claire had recently been diagnosed with cancer. They were very poor, so for them to be showing up with food was really a big deal. Claire finally made it to the kitchen counter and proudly slid across the big casserole, liberally covered with thick melted cheese. Now, you gotta understand that cheese was something of a novelty in this church. The majority of them were vegan, so nobody ever brought anything with dairy products to potluck. The woman behind the counter took Claire's dish without a word. During lunch I looked for it on the serving table, but it was nowhere in sight. Later I saw Claire make her way back to the kitchen and sadly ask for her pan, which had never made it to the table. The woman came back with the pan, washed and dried, and handed it to the crestfallen Claire. The entire casserole with its evil cheese had been scraped into the trash to keep us from being tempted by it.

Now, the first thing that comes to mind is a sense of injustice and anger at such a coldhearted response. The Pharisees who asked Jesus about the greatest commandment felt passionate about such things, arguing about clean and unclean foods, weighing mint and cumin, and measuring the steps they took on Sabbath. It was a discussion of right or wrong, good or bad, sinner or saint. But Jesus boiled the commandments down to something surprising: love. He said that all the commandments need to be kept in perspective: Does what I'm doing right now make me a more loving person toward God and people? That makes the commandments both a matter of what *and* why. Instead of seeing them as stiff rules, learn to think about the commandments as the best way to show love to God and the people around you.

—MH

Therefore keep watch, because you do not know the day or the hour. Matthew 25:13

The day of my sixteenth birthday dawned perfect with a rare and unexpected surprise: rain. Because we lived in Phoenix, we got a good rainstorm only a couple times a year. I hoped all day I'd get to enjoy the rain properly, but it was a busy day, and I didn't get an opportunity until my best friend Brooke and I were standing under the eaves in the parking lot, waiting for my parents take us to my birthday dinner. There in the parking lot dozens and dozens of shimmering rain puddles just begged to be jumped in. We took one look at each other, and the puddle-jumping began with a shout. In the gray rainy evening we splashed happily through puddle after puddle as if we were 5 years old again. It was the most fun either of us had enjoyed in months. We were tired with laughter by the time my parents drove up, honking hurriedly. "Come on!" they shouted. "We're going to be late. Jump in quick!" But that was before they got a good look at us, sloppy, soaking wet, and covered in mud, not suitable for any birthday dinner anywhere! We ran back to the dorm to change our wet clothes, but there was no help for it. We were late.

It would be a real shame to get caught playing in the mud when Jesus finally does come again, wouldn't it? But that could happen. Some of you are jumping through the dirtiest habits as if nobody is coming for you, as if there's nowhere better that you're supposed to be.

Jesus told a parable about 10 girls waiting up late at night for a bridegroom to arrive so they could go to the party. Five of them brought extra oil for their lamps, and five did not. When he finally did come, the latter were unprepared and had to go back to town to buy more oil. The doors to the party were closed, and they did not make it into the wedding banquet.

The thing is, if they had known when he was coming they would have been ready, right? Maybe that's why Jesus doesn't tell us when He'll return. Maybe He wants us to be ready every day of our lives. The truth is that none of us knows when our last day on earth might be.

How are you living today? Are you prepared for His coming, or are you messing around in places you shouldn't be? If He came tonight, would He find you ready, or unprepared?

—MH

Water Balloon Ambush

The King will reply, "I tell you the truth, whatever you did for one of the least of these brothers of mine, you did for me." Matthew 25:40.

First, it's only in a place like Phoenix in the summer, when the temps are above 110 degrees, that anyone could possibly think what we did was funny—riding in the back of Jake's truck, throwing water balloons at people out for an evening stroll. We'd crouch low in the truck bed, and Jake would drive up alongside the next victim. Just as he'd almost reach a dead stop, we'd spring up and pelt them with water balloons until they were completely soaked; then Jake would floor it, and we'd speed away. Our first hit was a group of girls dressed up for the evening. We left them soaked, laughing our fool heads off. When we drove up beside a guy on a bike I accidentally hit him square in the head. Boy, was he mad—he actually tried to chase us. I laughed so hard my sides hurt. It was the most fun I'd had the whole burning, boring summer—until we drove up beside that man on his way home from work.

He was riding his bike slowly, shoulders slumped in defeat, head bowed in discouragement. But I was so intent on mischief that I didn't take it all in. I released the balloon from my hand, and it was headed straight for his chest when he raised his head and looked me straight in the eye. His face held so much pain it broke my heart. It was as if his whole world had fallen apart that very night. As the balloon drenched him, suddenly the game wasn't funny anymore. I'd give anything if I'd had the courage to go back and find him, beg his forgiveness, and make sure he was OK. But I didn't. I will always regret it.

We don't know the pain that exists in other people's lives. We're so quick to judge them or make them the butt of our merciless jokes. We have no idea of the suffering that goes on behind closed doors or in other hearts. We Christians have a greater responsibility than the rest of the world, because of what Jesus says in today's verse: Whatever we do to even the very least people (though, of course, class doesn't matter at all), we've done it to *Him*! Remember this the next time you go after someone you think is weird or snotty or you just plain don't like. Choose love and kindness every chance you get. Every kindness shown is as to Jesus Himself.

— MH

Twice Betrayed

Peter replied, "Even if all fall away on account of you, I never will." . . . After a little while, those standing there went up to Peter and said, "Surely you are one of them, for your accent gives you away." Then he began to call down curses on himself and he swore to them, "I don't know the man!" Immediately a rooster crowed. Matthew 26:33-75.

Tara was the last person I would ever have guessed would turn on me, for she was my closest friend and also my roommate that year. Who would have guessed she had a tape recorder under her blankets that night we sat up late talking? I should have been suspicious when she started asking all those strange questions about my boyfriend. I shouldn't have answered them, but he and I were struggling, and it suddenly felt nice to tell someone how frustrated I was with him. She seemed so understanding! I told her everything I felt, and she patted me supportively, all the while wickedly recording our conversation. And what did she do with that tape? Next morning she took it straight to my boyfriend. I was shocked when he suddenly broke up with me, until I found out about the tape. I had never felt so betrayed in my life.

We talk a lot about how Jesus was betrayed by Judas for 30 pieces of silver, but if you think about it, two people betrayed Him that night—Judas and Peter. A few short hours before His arrest, Peter had publicly sworn, "Even if all the rest of these desert you, I certainly never will!" He had professed loyalty before everyone. But at his first chance to show his loyalty, he denied he knew Jesus, just as Jesus predicted he would—right when Jesus needed him most. Two men. Two acts of betrayal. They made the same mistake.

But think of how differently their stories ended. When Peter realized his mistake, he ran off into the night and wept bitterly, but he went on. Three days later, at the first sight of Jesus, he swam to shore like a crazy person to make it right. Peter went on to become the speaker at Pentecost and a leader in the early Christian church, converting thousands of Jews. Judas? Well, he went out that night and hung himself. You see, there are two possible reactions when you find you've betrayed the Lord: give up, or pick up and start over. Think of the thousands who might have been lost if Peter had given up as Judas did. We all let God down sometimes, but it's what we do afterward that matters most. Don't give up. God forgives and sends us out again.

—MH

Two Gardens*

Going a little farther, he fell with his face to the ground and prayed, "My Father, if it is possible, may this cup be taken from me. Yet not as I will, but as you will." Matthew 26:39.

On his knees in the mud he scooped handful after handful of clay and excitedly formed arms, legs, hands, feet, a man's face. His love swelled at the sight of his newest, finest creation of all. "This one will be like us!" He announced to the angels gathered around. "This one will be able to choose." As He bent over to breathe that breath of life into the dusty nostrils, he felt a hand on His shoulder. He turned around to face an angel with brows furrowed, a look of concern in her kind, faithful eyes. "Are you sure?" she asked. "Is it safe to give him that gift—choice? What will happen?"

Leaving the man of clay for just a moment, Jesus took the angel's hand. "You want to know what will happen? Come with Me." Unbound by time, they walked into tomorrow—to a sight of utter joy: Adam's children and their children, singing and laughing, praising and worshipping the Lord together out of true love and devotion. The angel had never seen anything so beautiful. "This kind of love can happen only with choice," He explained. "But walk further with Me." Then they came upon a dark scene—wickedness and hate, war and famine. "This, too, is the result of choice," Jesus explained patiently. "If they want, My children *can* choose wrong." He took a deep breath. "But there is more. Come just a step further."

Nighttime—a garden—and a Man on His knees on the ground, sobbing, blood dripping from His sweaty forehead. The angel gasped with recognition— "You!" Then a hill. Three crosses. Nails and thorns, nakedness and shame. Death. The angel stumbled and fell to her knees. "You again!" she shrieked. "No!"

Then they were back in heaven's garden. "You can't do this!" she pleaded with Him. "You will die for it! Are they worth that?" The Creator smiled, a hopeful, knowing, loving smile, as He answered emphatically, "Yes. They are worth it. They will be Mine."

And with that He bent down again and breathed into the nostrils, and the man came to life.

—MH

*Adapted from Max Lucado's "The Choice."

Thorns

They stripped him and put a scarlet robe on him, and then twisted together a crown of thorns and set it on his head. Matthew 27:28, 29.

When I felt the leash go taut, then limp, I knew something was terribly wrong. I turned around immediately and saw the empty end dangling in the grass, and my terrified cat scampering away at high speed. We were moving from Seattle to Michigan, and someone had talked me into a cat leash for the long trip, which had barely worked for 30 seconds there at the rest stop before Charlie scrambled out of it. I chased him to the edge of a blackberry thicket, but it was too late—he was already yards away, deep inside the thorns.

Knowing I had lost my precious cat, I sat down to cry as Greg ran over to me. I thought he would comfort me, but instead he did something else. Parting the largest thorn branches, he bent down and began crawling through the tangles after my cat. Anyone who knows Greg knows that he's not particularly fond of the cat. But he knew that I was, and Greg is particularly fond of me. I could hear the thorns tearing at his clothes and ripping his skin, but he pressed on. When he reached Charlie, he had to reach around both sides of a giant thorny branch to pull him out. Then he returned through the thorns to me. He was torn and bleeding from head to toe; thorns were stuck in his shirt, arms, shoes, and hair; but he had Charlie. He held my cat out to me with a loving smile, and I knew that he had done this just for me.

Greg is not the only one who willingly chose the thorns for me. Jesus did too—for me, you, and for all of us. They didn't come as a surprise to Him. He knew they would be part of the deal. He knew about the punches and the trials, the whip with shards of glass on its tip ripping through the flesh on His back. He knew His beard would be torn off His face, and His wrists would have nails pounded straight into the largest nerve in His arm. He knew about the anguish of separation from His Father. And He still came anyway, purely out of love for us.

"When He was on the tree, all His thoughts were of you and me. You're worth so much to this Man that He died to make you free."*

—MH

*From Jeff Carlson's "Priceless." Used by permission.

What Can One Person Do?

Go ye therefore, and teach all nations, baptizing them in the name of the Father, and of the Son, and of the Holy Ghost: teaching them to observe all things whatsoever I have commanded you. Matthew 28:19, KJV.

What can one person do?" he asked cynically from the microphone, pouring one single cup of juice into the giant empty fish tank that sat on the stage in front of us. The red juice made a small splash. A few pitiful little drops splattered onto the glass, and that was all. The fish tank remained basically untouched and definitely not full. Then the next person came up. "What can one person do?" She laughed doubtfully, pouring her glass of red juice into the tank. Another splash; and the puddle on the tank floor widened about an inch. "What can one person do?" the third speaker asked hopefully, adding his cup of juice. I watched from my chair as cup after cup was poured in. Soon we could see the juice just barely begin to rise off the bottom. But nobody else came to the microphone. The room was silent as hundreds of us pondered the point.

I'll never know who that first brave soul was, but somebody must have noticed that there were hundreds of full juice cups just waiting on the table. Someone stood to their feet and walked to the front. Another person followed. Each one reached for a cup of juice, poured it in, walked back to their seat, and sat down. Another courageous student stood up then, and another—then five others. As they made their way toward the front, 10 stood up behind me, and a dozen more stood on my right. Then I was on my feet, and in seconds the entire Union College auditorium turned into a dashing crowd headed for the table with the juice. Countless hands reached out of the chaos and picked up a cup and poured, and do you know what? When we left the auditorium that day the tank was full to the brim.

What can one person do? Maybe not much on their own, so many never even try. But if every "one person" does something, we can do anything. When Jesus gave His legendary Great Commission written above, He knew that it would take all of us. Every single Christian man and woman, boy and girl, is included in that call to go into the world and tell His story. And that means you are, too. Are you willing to go for Him today? You are only one person, and you have only one life. But what could your one life do?

—MH

Off the Wall: Jesus the Action Figure

The beginning of the gospel about Jesus Christ, the Son of God. Mark 1:1.

The old painting hung on his wall in a splintered, wooden frame. There was Jesus, solemn and serene, and worlds away. My college friend Jeremy wrote a song about the picture that his parents had hung in his room as if he were talking to the Man: "Is that all You are—a picture on my wall? Can You talk? Can You even understand the problems in my life?"

I've felt like this, haven't you? Sometimes it seems as if Jesus is just a pretty picture, a painting of a man who doesn't quite fit in the real world and who doesn't really get our day-to-day situations. Instead, He seems distant, removed, uninvolved. But this isn't good enough for Jeremy. "Off the wall!" he begs the Jesus in the picture, "and into my life—come and be my God! When religion is confusing and I just don't know, leave the frame and lead me!"

Maybe that's what we all want, for Jesus to come "off the wall." We need for Him to come down from the high places people put Him and out of the distant worlds He's been painted in, and to enter into our real lives. We want a living and active God, not just some pretty-picture God. We want someone who truly understands our problems and our pains, someone who makes an actual, noticeable difference in our daily struggles. We need a God that matters!

Is that the kind of God you've been looking for? If so, the Gospel of Mark is the place for you. In Mark we see Jesus as we've never seen Him before—a God of action! The Man is on the move! He's constantly healing, teaching, preaching, traveling, and performing miracles. In fact, Mark tells of more miracles than any of the other Gospel writers. Another cool characteristic of Mark is that the word "immediately" is used in practically every other story. Jesus immediately does this or that—He's full of power that never ends! Why do Mark's writings have all this energy and movement?

Well, the early Church Fathers agreed that Mark closely resembled the preaching style of Peter. They believed that Mark was Peter's interpreter, and he carefully wrote down all of Peter's memories of Jesus. Some claim that Peter's personality can be found on every page. No wonder this is a book of action! Who better than Peter to capture the real Jesus—to take Him "off the wall," and bring Him to life for those of us who need a lot more than just a picture.   —MH

Near-Death Experience Via Amphibious Electrocution

Very early in the morning, while it was still dark, Jesus got up, left the house and went off to a solitary place, where he prayed. Mark 1:35.

What do a storm drain, a power strip, and a tiny green frog have in common? I found out one day when I went down into our basement after a thunderstorm and saw dozens of puddles from an overflowing storm drain. I thought I had disconnected all the electric plugs down there, so I wasn't worried about electricity as I stomped through the water. What surprised me was that in one of these puddles sat a little green frog. In one wild leap the little guy landed on a power strip that was connected to a computer. Thinking that I could finally capture him, I got down on my knees and dove wildly at the power strip, my hands cupped together. Before I knew what was happening, I felt a stunning jolt and my body convulsed with electric shock. The frog, caught inside my cupped hands, peed (probably from fright), screamed like a banshee (did you know frogs scream like little girls when shocked?), and shared in my wild convulsions as 110 volts of electricity zipped through our bodies. Within seconds I shot back from the power strip, and the frog and I stared at each other until he finally bounded away to hide for his life under a pile of boxes in the corner. Only then did I realize that the power strip had been plugged into the outlet the whole time, creating a great little circuit between the wet, traumatized frog and me.

We all know that if an electric cord isn't plugged into a source of electricity there's no power running through it. Likewise, if we aren't plugged into a source of power there isn't any power running through our lives, either. Jesus knew this, which is why He went out before dawn to find a quiet place to pray. His days required tons of power—for miracles, healing the sick, raising the dead, and teaching salvation to the masses. Jesus couldn't afford to be unplugged. He needed to connect with His Father for power to be running through His life to other people.

Have you been going through life unplugged, wondering why there's no energy or strength or power in you? It might be that you haven't connected to the ultimate Source of power in quite a while. If this is the case, set aside a special time to reconnect with Him today.

—GH and MH

Don't Waste the Chocolate Cake

Then he said to them, "The Sabbath was made for man, not man for the Sabbath."
Mark 2:27.

There it sat on the stage for all to see—a scrumptious, thick, chocolaty frosted cake. It was right before lunch, and we were already hungry as it was, and our mouths watered and our stomachs growled at the sight of that delicious-looking cake. Whom was it for? We couldn't take our eyes off it, so by the time song service was over, some of us were already salivating and drooling for just a bite. Finally, when the pastor asked for volunteers to come up, every single student was on their feet waving their hand in the air. That's why I still can't believe that he even saw me, much less chose me. I couldn't wait! I hurried up front, sat down at the beautifully prepared table, and waited to be served. The pastor appeared beside us in an apron, and I knew that the blessed time had come. But to my utter horror, he took his two giant hands and smashed them directly into that beautiful cake, pulling out a messy sticky glob of cake and rolling it around in his hands, wiping it on his arms, smearing it across the bottom of his shoes, before slopping it down on the plate in front of me. I gasped. I couldn't eat this! Not after it had been served to me this way! He asked for other volunteers, but nobody wanted it now. Nobody would even touch it. That entire beautiful cake went completely to waste.

Sometimes there's absolutely nothing wrong with a belief, doctrine, or teaching, but because of how it's served to us we don't want anything to do with it. Take the Sabbath. Jesus taught that the day is meant to be a blessing, a delight—made for us, created so that we can stop, relax, and reconnect with Jesus and others. We can look forward to it, anticipate a rest stop on a long road trip. But often we dread it. We've lost the joy in Sabbath, because somebody has served it to us wrong. It's been made a list of do's and don'ts, a chore, a burden. And while some still wrestle with what to do or not do on that day to keep it holy, we completely miss the point— what Sabbath truly is. God gave it to us as a gift, a chance to escape the rat race for a day, and it should be as satisfying as vacations, holidays, and your favorite cake.

If Sabbath has been served badly to you, remember that it doesn't mean there was ever something wrong with the Sabbath. The truth is, there was something wrong with the server. Don't let anyone cheat you out of this great way to enjoy life better. Sabbath is for you!

—MH

The Only Time to Trust a Demon

Whenever the evil spirits saw him, they fell down before him and cried out, "You are the Son of God." But he gave them strict orders not to tell who he was. Mark 3:11, 12.

I still say it was because Eddie was "pregnant" that he got twice as much candy as all the rest of us. The costume was his idea, and it worked like a charm. Instead of "Trick or treat," he'd shout, "Eating for two!" and they'd throw in an extra handful. People must have felt sorry for him, walking around with that great big belly. Wasn't his beard and mustache a clue he was a big fat fake? Or maybe the costume idea was super-funny, and they rewarded him with extra candy.

Doesn't it bother you when people pretend to be something they're not? A lot of people hated Jesus because they thought He was pretending to be something He was not: God. They just couldn't swallow the idea that this man could be divine, and that's understandable. Even today some still have a hard time understanding and believing. But there were a certain select few back then that never, ever questioned Jesus' true identity: the demons. In the book of Mark Jesus casts demons out of a whole lot of people. And without fail, they instantly recognize Him for who He is—the Son of God. They fall down and scream it out. But unlike people who try to toot their own horn or become something they're not, Jesus plays it down, tells them to be quiet about it. When you're the real thing, I guess you don't need a lot of publicity.

It's pretty embarrassing to us that even the demons acknowledge Jesus as God, but we humans still struggle with the idea. A lot of people you meet in life will try to tell you that Jesus was just another good man, that the idea of Him being God is completely ridiculous. But if you think about it, there's really only three things He could have been: crazy, a liar, or the actual Son of God. He had no signs of a crazy person. In fact, He seemed very sane and had His wits about Him more so than many. And if He was lying about being God, why would He die for it, and why would His disciples be willing to die for what they too knew was a lie? That doesn't make sense either. All the evidence points to the truth: Jesus was God-come-down-to-earth.

If you've wrestled with this idea, take comfort. You aren't buying into a hoax, or serving a faker. Even the demons testified that Jesus was who He said He was, and they had nothing to gain from it. You're investing your life in the right thing.

—MH

Beware the Birds

Listen! A farmer went out to sow his seed. As he was scattering the seed, some fell along the path, and the birds came and ate it up. Mark 4:3, 4.

There wasn't a single scrap of food left when we returned to our campsite—only wrappers, cartons, bags, and trash scattered across the ground. The robbers lurked above us, mocking with their chatter. Greg and I were enjoying a four-day camping trip in Mount Rainier National Park. Our quaint campsite nestled in a little clearing on the banks of the icy Ohanapecosh River. That summer afternoon when we returned to our campsite after a long hike, starving and ready for dinner, we discovered that those clever crows had robbed us blind. They opened our Rubbermaid bins with the pliers they have for beaks and devoured every single edible thing we had— even the seasoning packet in the ramen noodles had been eaten through! It was already getting dark, but we made the hour-long trip down the mountain to the nearest convenience store and assembled some food items from their understocked shelves for the rest of our trip. We felt so stupid—and so hungry—for the next few days. We'd been outsmarted by birds!

I always think of those pesky thieving crows when I read Jesus' parable of the sower, because I am certain the crows' distant cousins appear in the story! In the parable a farmer scatters seed that meets four different ends, all symbolic of God's Word landing on different types of hearts: The first seeds fall on the path, and the birds snatch them up to eat. Those birds represent Satan, who immediately snatches God's Word (the seed) and leaves the heart empty, and probably starving, too. The seeds that fall on rocky places, that spring up but die immediately, represent people who hear the Word but don't have strong enough faith roots to last when the trials of life come. We can probably all see ourselves in the seed that falls among thorns and gets choked to death, for this is the Word getting crowded out of a person's heart because of worries, the pull of money, and desires for other things. At last some seed falls on good ground and produces a large crop, which is like the heart that accepts the Word and shares it with others.

What is the state of the soil in your heart today? Are there paths wide open to Satan? Are trials making your faith in Jesus wither away? Are worries or other things crowding Jesus right out of your life? Or is His Word growing in you and producing a plentiful harvest?

—MH

Low Expectations

They were terrified and asked each other, "Who is this? Even the wind and the waves obey him!" Mark 4:41.

We weren't even able to be present when the charred building was torn open and our few visible or retrievable items were pulled from the wreckage of our burned home. But my friend Kay was there in our place. I had phoned her from my parents' house and asked her to have the firefighters get one thing, and one thing only, from our ruined home—my silver-plated unity candleholder from my wedding that sat on the top of our entertainment center. I didn't know even if the entertainment center would still be standing, but Kay phoned later and told me that they were able to find the candelabra, and she would hold it for me.

When I got back into town, there were so many things to do that I forgot all about the candelabra. I was too busy buying clothes, trying to find another place to live, replacing driver's licenses and Social Security cards, and all the other details that go with losing all of your earthly belongings. So it was a few weeks later that Kay gave me the candelabra, and I could hardly believe it. I expected something black and charred and twisted, but there it was—beautifully refinished in new silver, looking just as it had looked the day I had bought it. She had far surpassed my expectations! All I had wanted was the charred remains, but she had returned it as good as new.

I know that Jesus often surpassed the expectations of His disciples, too. I know for certain that He did the night the storm came up on the sea when He was asleep in the stern. Mark says the boat was almost swamped when they finally woke Him. "Don't You care if we die?" they asked. What an accusation to wake up to! Jesus promptly told the wind and the waves to be quiet, cut it out—and everything was still in a single instant. The disciples were amazed, speechless. They weren't expecting Him to calm the storm. Maybe they were hoping He would bail water or something. They had no idea He could actually control the weather.

What about us? Do we have low expectations of God? Do we spend weeks praying for Him to help us bail the water out of a situation when He has the power to change the entire thing for us? This God who told the storm when to stop is able still the storms in your life as well.

—MH

A Simple Touch

And a woman was there who had been subject to bleeding for twelve years. She had suffered a great deal under the care of many doctors and had spent all she had, yet instead of getting better she grew worse. When she heard about Jesus, she came up behind him in the crowd and touched his cloak, because she thought, "If I just touch his clothes, I will be healed." Mark 5:25-28.

In my younger years I believed I had an invisible shield against the world. Behind this shield I could roam muddy fields, slide into dusty bases on the ball field, and climb trees without fear. My trusty shield was my jeans. I can remember, though, that my mother was less impressed with the invincibility of my jeans. One day after I had burst out the knees of yet another pair, my mother gave me a brand-new pair of jeans and told me in no uncertain terms that I was not to get these dirty, ripped, or otherwise mangled. For that first day I did well, but our house was surrounded by nice grassy hills that begged to be rolled down. Finally I couldn't take it anymore and rolled myself over the edge of a great-looking hill. I came out of that first roll with such a wildly dizzy feeling that I knew it was going to be one of the best rolls of my life. Afterward my jeans, which moments before had been a lovely shade of blue, were now covered with swaths of green. Afraid for my life, I ran home and changed into a different pair, burying the stained pair at the bottom of the hamper. Not too sharp on my part.

The woman with the 12-year bleeding problem didn't hide her problem, as I did. At that time, when people had a prolonged sickness that seemed incurable, the religious leaders taught that it was a curse from God. When she heard reports of Jesus the healer coming through her town, she dared to hope one last time. She found Him in the crowd and grabbed the hem of His garment—a cultural way of boldly saying, "Help me!" The Bible says that instantly she was healed. Her simple act of faith, Jesus said, was what had made her well. That's when I realize that sometimes I treat Jesus the way I treated my mom with my stained jeans. Instead of coming straight to Him, I shove my mess away and hide it from Him. But this story tells us that no matter how dirty our life gets, Jesus won't turn His back on us but will help us wash out the grime and the stains. But we have to bring it to Him boldly first, in faith, as part of our own free will. Do you have a mess to bring today?

—GH

A Staredown With Death

While Jesus was still speaking, some men came from the house of Jairus, the synagogue ruler. "Your daughter is dead," they said. "Why bother the teacher any more?" Ignoring what they said, Jesus told the synagogue ruler, "Don't be afraid; just believe." Mark 5:35, 36.

I looked down at the still form of my son, Caleb, and thought he was dead. He had fallen 10 feet from a slide and landed flat on his back. He'd let out one earth-shattering scream, then turned blue, passed out, and stopped breathing. His open eyes stared vacantly, and he was completely motionless. Frantic, I began giving him rescue breathing while Greg called 911. On my knees on the cold ground, desperately trying to breathe life into my precious child, I silently pleaded for help. *Don't let him die, Father,* I begged. *Please, oh, please, God, don't let him die! Help me!* An eternity later Caleb began breathing again, opened his eyes, and moved his arms. We rushed him to the hospital, and the plucky little fellow turned out fine.

That terrifying day reminds me of Jairus' frantic push through the crowd to find Jesus and desperately plead with Him to come to his house and heal his dying daughter. He knows that if Jesus doesn't help, she will soon be gone. But instead of coming right away, some crazy woman who's been bleeding for years interrupts Jesus. During the time He "wastes" healing and talking to her, the girl dies. Servants come and tell Jairus to leave Jesus alone for his daughter is dead. At that Jesus gives this memorable command: "Don't be afraid; just believe." A tall order, to be sure, at a hopeless time like that. What did Jairus think? We know that Jesus went with him to his house, and after removing the mourners who laughed at Him, Jesus raised the 12-year-old girl back to life. Once you saw a Man raise the dead, it'd be easy to believe anything else!

We don't often choose belief first. Our first response is usually fear, and that's so very human of us, isn't it? Jesus knows that while we should have complete faith in Him, many times we're just afraid. That's why He tells us to *choose* faith, to decide to believe, even in the presence of terror when all hope is lost. It's an intentional, calculated action that we can opt for over fear and doubt. I don't know what you're afraid of today, but whatever it is, let those words of Jesus echo in your ears: Just believe. Choose faith—even when it seems crazy.

—MH

I Got No Time for Food

Because so many people were coming and going that they did not even have a chance to eat, he said to them, "Come with me by yourselves to a quiet place and get some rest." Mark 6:31.

That smug old Harmony used to make so much fun of me when she'd come into my dean's office around 4:00 or 5:00 in the evening and see my cold, stale lunch still sitting on my desk, untouched. I would try to explain to her that I hadn't even had the time to catch my breath, how I'd been dealing with a never-ending string of back-to-back problems and emergencies, but she would just laugh. "Everyone has time to grab a few bites here and there!" she'd insist.

That was before she became a dean herself! I got a message from her one day, and a very apologetic voice confessed into the phone that though it was now past dinnertime, her sad little lunch sat completely untouched on her own desk. She finally understood that sometimes you get so busy you really truly don't have a moment to eat!

Have you ever had a day like that—when you're too busy even to eat? Perhaps when you're taking finals, or rushing through an airport, or during back-to-back practices and games? After Jesus sent His disciples into the towns to preach, heal, and cast out demons, they returned on an incredible high, excited about all their miracles and successes. I imagine them interrupting one another, giddy like schoolgirls, as they shared story after story. Jesus listens quietly to all the hubbub, not saying much, until finally He makes the suggestion above. He realizes that they have been so busy they haven't even eaten or rested. Though they don't realize it in their excitement, Jesus knows that what they really need is to take care of themselves. Because if they don't, soon enough they won't be able to go on. You can't continue at a frantic pace forever.

Whether we stop to realize it or not, this is what we need as well. We need to come away with Jesus to a quiet place, and get some rest. Life gets really hectic and crazy in your teenage years, and often you rush from one thing to the next without stopping to take care of yourself. We don't eat well, don't sleep enough, and certainly don't find time to spend with Jesus. But unless we stop and take time aside, pretty soon we'll burn out. So avoid the crash. Slow down, take time to care for yourself, and spend some quiet moments each day recharging with Jesus.

—MH

Magnetic Properties

Jesus left that place and went to the vicinity of Tyre. He entered a house and did not want anyone to know it; yet he could not keep his presence secret. Mark 7:24.

Spies were stationed at every corner, in every store, on every boat, behind every building, and along every coast. How else could these people have known every single thing I did from morning until night? The island of Ebeye, where I went as a student missionary, was very small—about a mile long—but more than 12,000 people live together in that mile, making it one of the most densely populated places in the world. So you'd think a person could become anonymous, but not so. "Miss, why did you buy so many potatoes at the store last night?" my students would ask in class, though not a single one of them or their parents had been in the tiny store where I bought my food. "Teacher, why did you walk home along the beach yesterday?" But I'd been alone on that beach! "Why were you reading a book on the boat to get water?" I was clearly the only passenger. Was it because I was a teacher at one of the largest schools on the island? Or that I was one of only six people on the island who had blond hair? How did they know every move I made? It had to be spies. Nothing I did was ever a secret to them.

On a much grander scale, this is what life was like for Jesus. Whenever He entered a town, people were waiting for Him. Even when He tried to keep His presence a secret, He couldn't. Crowds flocked to Him and followed Him, bringing their sick by the hundreds and hanging on every word He said. The day He found out that His own cousin had been beheaded, He went away to mourn, but still the hungry crowds followed and He ended up teaching and feeding 5,000 that day. It seems as though Jesus often wanted rest or solitude, but He always allowed the people to come to Him anyway. People were drawn to Him like a magnet—the more time they spent with Him, the longer they wanted to stay. They couldn't get enough of Him.

This might be hard for us to imagine. We struggle to make time for Jesus, and often we don't feel excited about it or extremely drawn to Him. So what's the secret? The secret is just to start somewhere. Jesus still has those magnetic qualities about Him, so the more time you spend in His presence, the more you will want, and the easier it gets. Keep at it! Soon you'll find you can't get enough. You'll be craving that time with God, and happily looking forward to it.

—MH

The Worst Home Remedy in Palestine

Jesus took the blind man by the hand and led him out of the village. Then, spitting on the man's eyes, he laid his hands on him and asked, "Can you see anything now?" Mark 8:23, NLT.

Tofu was her medical suggestion for every ailment imaginable—just a fatty white slab of tofu. Have a third-degree burn? Smash some tofu onto that charred skin, she would advise, and in less than a day the skin will be good as new! Struggling with acne? Rub some tofu on your face, of course, and it will be cleared up by morning! This poor well-meaning woman truly believed in her tofu home remedies, but I have to say I was a little less than impressed. Home remedies, as a general rule, have not ever been the way to go in my family. Instead of tofu, Aunt Schleria swears colloidal silver is the ticket. Just a spoonful of silver makes any sickness go down! And then there were the days when giant mushrooms the size of dinner plates floated in vats of water in the kitchen, because Aunt Ros insisted that drinking the water would bring us health. Yeah, I'm gonna have to go ahead and vote NO on home remedies.

But it almost seems as if Jesus tried one of them when He spit on the poor blind man's eyes. Using spit was a traditional healing method of Jesus' day—a well-known home remedy, if you will—even though in our day and age it sounds pretty gross. It seems funny that Jesus, who could have healed the man with a word or touch, first employed a popular healing method of the times. It's as though He's trying to say something. He spits on the man's eyes and asks if the man can see anything, and the man can make out only vague shadows of people walking around. So Jesus puts His hands on the man's eyes a second time—just His hands, now—and the man can finally see. Do you think perhaps Jesus was hinting that traditional ways are not always best? God's ways always turn out far better—and more effective—than our ways ever could.

Remember this the next time you catch yourself stubbornly trying to do something your own way instead of God's way. Your own way is kind of like spit—or tofu or giant mushrooms or silver. It's really not the best thing there is. Also, the world will forever try to compete with God, telling you that their way is far better than His old ways, but don't believe it. The world offers only mere shadows of what Jesus can do for you. So give God's ways a try instead, and you'll see that they always bring the truest healing and most satisfaction in the end.

—MH

I Want to Believe You, But . . .

Immediately the boy's father cried out and said, "I do believe; help my unbelief."
Mark 9:24, NASB.

I try my best to believe Greg when he promises not to forget things. Really I do. But it's extremely difficult, and perhaps even a tad bit unwise, to trust him. You see, he has a problem. He's been medically diagnosed with a very large hole in the bottom left corner of his brain— coincidentally the part where memory is stored—and things fall right through that hole into the oblivion that is his neck. At least I think that's what happens. Must be hard having a hole in your head and forgetting every single thing your wife ever tells you, eh? And so it is a joyless exercise in futility to remind this man to do anything, but for some reason I still try. He forgets his keys each and every time we leave the house, and his phone and wallet besides, so I remind him. He gets mad at me and insists that he is not an idiot, that he can remember his own things, and we stand in the rain staring at the locked car because, ah, what a surprise, he did not bring the keys. Every Thursday night I remind him to put out the trash, but the bags and bags of trash collected in our garage bear witness to the success of that. His phone dies and remains dead and useless for days at a time before he remembers to charge it; and forget about leaving him a message—he won't remember to check the 29 he already has without yours added to it! This is why I find it so maddening when he mutters something like "I said I will. Why don't you believe me?"

There is a father in Mark who, I think, would identify with me. He has brought his demon-possessed son to Jesus to heal, for the demon often throws the boy into water or fire to kill him. The father asks Jesus to heal him, if He can. "If I can?" Jesus responds. "All things are possible for him who believes." The father then exclaims, *"I do believe. Help my unbelief."*

I think of this phrase often, and have uttered it myself to God many times. Isn't there a part in all of us that wants to believe, that tries to believe, but still doubts? We doubt because we've been let down before, because we're afraid, or maybe even because we respect God's sovereignty and want to allow Him to say no, as He rightfully can do. He's God, after all. But whatever the reasons, we need a little more faith. I think a little faith is enough when Jesus makes up the rest, because after the father said it, Jesus healed his kid. So next time you need help with unbelief, confess this father's phrase to God. He can make up the difference.

—MH

"What do you want me to do for you?" Jesus asked him. Mark 10:51.

The question He asked both of them that day was exactly the same. Scheming James and John had approached Jesus and demanded, "We want you to do for us whatever we ask" (Mark 10:35). Can you imagine saying that to Jesus? His only response to them is "What do you want me to do for you?" They proceeded to tell Him that they wished to sit on His right and His left in His glory, and I can almost see Jesus shaking His head as He told them that they didn't know what they were asking. His moment of "glory" and victory was the cross, but they had no idea. He counseled them instead that if they truly wanted to become great, they needed to become like a lowly servant.

After this they came to Jericho, and a blind beggar named Bartimaeus began shouting at Jesus like a crazy person. A lot of people told him to shut up, but he shouted all the more, saying, "Son of David! Have mercy on me!" Jesus finally summoned him, and the same people that had rebuked the blind man then said, "Cheer up! On your feet! He's calling you" (verse 39). As the man approached Jesus, He asked, "What do you want me to do for you?" (verse 51). There's that question again! The very same question. But this time, instead of asking for recognition and prominence, this lowly man asked only to be healed. "I want to see," he said (verse 51). And Jesus simply replied, "Go. Your faith has healed you" (see verse 52). I think Mark put these two stories together on purpose.

If you think about it, both of the requests were granted that day. James and John did suffer in the end, as Jesus did. But that very day Bartimaeus walked away seeing, and we are told that he began to follow Jesus down the road after that. We don't know how many people were in the crowd that followed Him, but bright-eyed happy Bartimaeus was one of them.

Jesus can give us what we want. Don't waste your requests on silly, selfish things. Ask for things that lift you up, as James and John did. Ask for something real, such as healing. Bartimaeus cut to the chase and asked for what he needed most in life. He was a living illustration to James and John of how the lowest can become great. What do you want Jesus to do for you today? Do you need healing, guidance, wisdom, strength? a miracle, maybe? Dream big. Ask for what really matters. Our God is capable of anything.

—MH

Camp Pranks and a Difficult Ultimatum

And when you stand praying, if you hold anything against anyone, forgive him, so that your Father in heaven may forgive you your sins. But if you do not forgive, neither will your Father who is in heaven forgive your sins. Mark 11:25, 26, margin.

It truly wasn't nice to freeze my underwear. The other camp lifeguards thought they'd play a funny little trick on me one day, so they had a girl sneak into my room and steal all my underwear out of my drawer Then they stuck it in the freezer while I guarded at the pool. Since they knew my shift, they had my frozen-stiff underwear back in my drawer that afternoon, only minutes before I got back to my cabin. There is nothing so shocking and disheartening after a hot shower at the end of the day than ice-caked underwear, let me tell you.

These particular guys played pranks on all the female staff at camp that year, but I was the only one who stayed mad about it. For the rest of the summer I schemed and planned how I might get back at them. One evening as they left for campfire, I got my opportunity. The director had given me the keys to the kitchen and asked if I'd bring down some supplies. The camp was empty; there was no one around. I rushed into the kitchen and grabbed as many large vats of salsa as I could carry. I quietly sneaked into the guys' room and doused their shower with jug after jug of salsa: salsa splashed across the glass, running down the walls, and clogging the drain. I was so pleased! There were so many pranks going on that summer that I knew they'd never suspect me, but I was wrong. They knew immediately. When I asked how they knew it was me, they said, "Melissa, it was easy. You're the only one who's still angry."

It's easy to hang on to anger, isn't it? Especially when someone damages you or hurts you seriously. You have a right to be angry, but Jesus says that when you withhold forgiveness from someone you're endangering only yourself. When we refuse to forgive someone, God actually will not forgive us! Wow, that's serious! But how can we forgive after significant wrongs? My grandpa Bill practices something amazing called "instant forgiveness." He makes the choice to forgive people immediately, no matter what. It sounds impossible at first, but really, it's just a choice you learn to make, and it's for *you*! So if you're holding anger against anyone today, this might be a good time to begin practicing "instant forgiveness."

—MH

Watch and pray so that you will not fall into temptation. The spirit is willing, but the body is weak. Mark 14:38.

I have a confession to make. Almost every car I've driven during my lifetime has run out of gas at the worst possible time. I've hiked down the interstate looking for the nearest gas station. I've hitchhiked, and even clung to the tailgate of a truck doing 50 miles per hour, just to get to a gas station. I was even reduced to begging for money door to door the one time I forgot my wallet and had no way of buying a gas can or gasoline once I got to the pumps. I especially hate when this happens with other people in the car. They get either angry or hysterical, or openly mock my stupidity. The worst situation was running out of gas on a date with Melissa in the middle of a blizzard. We were coming back from a banquet, so we weren't dressed in the best clothes for hiking through foot-deep snow. I had to walk an hour round-trip in a gale of snow and ice, wearing a suit coat (no overcoat or jacket) and thin pants. She shivered in her banquet dress in the cold truck stuck on the side of the road. I didn't win any points with her on that date, to be certain. The fact is that I never mean to run out of gas; I just forget to look at the gauges at those crucial low times. As Jesus says above—my spirit is willing! But my flesh is just, well, weak.

The disciples didn't mean to fall asleep on Jesus either when they were spending His final night in Gethsemane. They had good intentions, but weren't able to follow through with the support that Jesus needed. Even Jesus Himself said that His own spirit was willing to go through with the trial, but His humanness shrank from the impending disconnection from God that He knew He'd face. The Bible points out that He fell to the ground in agony, experiencing an intense separation from His Father that He had never felt before. He was tempted to give it all up and just go back to heaven. He wanted to throw it all out, but clung to the knowledge that God had not truly abandoned Him. He knew that the world—that's you and me—was worth this price. We all go through times of intense temptation during which it seems we can't make the right decision. We are willing but weak. But Jesus knows. His advice for those times is to watch and pray, and cling to the knowledge that God is not abandoning you to bad habits, broken promises, or glaring mistakes. He's always there to offer help and strength in the face of our weakness.

—GH

The Most Ironic Insult in the Bible

Then some began to spit at him; they blindfolded him, struck him with their fists, and said, "Prophesy!" And the guards took him and beat him. Mark 14:65.

Perhaps you could say that we have Jeff to thank for our marriage. Jeff has been my husband's best friend for almost 10 years now, and never did he do Greg a bigger favor than during the October night he visited my apartment. On tour with his band, Jeff came by to see me after a concert, and we began talking about my current boyfriend. Things had not been going well, and the more I revealed to Jeff, the more determined he became to convince me to leave the guy. But the tactic Jeff used was so clever: he simply compared the guy to Greg. When I described how he'd spent the weekend in bars, Jeff stated that I would rather have a guy like Greg, who didn't drink. As I talked about my boyfriend dancing in clubs with other girls, Jeff insisted I needed someone loyal like Greg—who can't even dance. Not Greg specifically, mind you. Just someone "like" Greg. But the suggestion was enough to sway me, because all along Jeff knew something I didn't: that who I really wanted was Greg. That night Jeff knew me better than I knew myself.

An interesting thing takes place the night of Jesus' trial. The guards have taken Him outside, and they're spitting, punching, beating, and taunting Him. Their demand that He "prophesy" is a joke because they don't believe in Him. But what they don't know is that down below in the courtyard, at that very moment, a prophecy of Jesus' is coming true. Peter is betraying Him, as Jesus predicted he would. Their demand for a prophecy was being fulfilled as they spoke. But Jesus knew it all along. As Peter spewed out curses and denials below, Jesus looked down from above and caught his eye. In this moment Peter's heart was crushed. He had sworn undying loyalty, but he realized that Jesus had been right about him all along.

Jesus knows us better than we know ourselves! He knows what we truly want, even when we think we want something else. He knows what we are going to do, even when we insist we'd never do it. He knows our thoughts, what we're capable of, and how shamefully we'll behave. And . . . He loves us anyway. Take comfort in being known this way, and loved in spite of it. Next time you are trying to get to know yourself, go to Jesus. Listen to His guidance and take His advice, because in the end He is the one who knows you best of all.

—MH

No More Lies

Therefore, since I myself have carefully investigated everything from the beginning, it seemed good also to me to write an orderly account for you . . . so that you may know the certainty of the things you have been taught. Luke 1:3, 4.

I waited for her in the dark that night, forcing myself to stay awake. I just had to see her this time. After what seemed like hours, the door creaked ever so slightly. I squinted my eyes to make out the shadows—was she beautiful? Did she have a gown, wings, a sparkly wand? (My mom worked in a dentist's office, and she had raised all four of us to believe in the tooth fairy because she claimed to be personal friends with her.) I could tell that she was short, and as she crept closer I noticed she had my mother's hairdo. Then I noticed she wore my mother's pajamas and slippers—it was kind of odd for a tooth fairy to borrow Mom's clothing, wasn't it? There was also something about her walk that reminded me of my mother, and her face was so similar. Wait! It was my mother! All this time, all these years of believing in the tooth fairy (who graciously left money under my pillow), I had been fooled. But I had been so certain she existed.

At the time the Gospel of Luke was written, many were already starting to wonder if half the stories about Jesus were true or fairy tales. People wanted evidence, proof, certainty that they could bank their lives on the fact that the stories about Jesus were true. This is the reason Luke gives for writing—so that you may know the certainty of the things you have been taught. Luke, a highly educated Greek, wrote the fullest and most orderly story of Jesus' life. He includes details and stories that all the other Gospels leave out. Like a good reporter, Luke has done his homework, checked eyewitness sources, and tried to come up with the best account possible.

Many of us have been taught from a very young age about Jesus, Christianity, and even Adventism. Some of us don't even remember that first time in beginners when we spoke the name of Jesus or received our very first memory verse sticker. But there comes a time in the life of every one of us raised in religion that we must decide to own it for ourselves. Will we believe the stories, buy into the doctrines, and walk in the ways of the church? Or will we choose a different path? If you have reached this point in your life, the book of Luke offers you a unique opportunity: to build certainty in the things you have been taught. Jump in and see!

—MH

The Hopes and Fears of All the Years

Today in the town of David a Savior has been born to you; he is Christ the Lord.
Luke 2:11.

You remember the waiting and wishing, don't you? How they hoped, how they prayed, how they looked for Him in the face of every baby boy born? Down through the ages He had been promised—first to Adam and Eve, and they thought Cain would be the one. After the Flood Noah and his family still waited. Abraham, Isaac, and Jacob waited. The children of Israel knew good and well that they needed Him when they broke their covenant with God—first at the foot of Mount Sinai, and then time and time again through the years. During the time of the judges things became so terrible that they felt sure He would come. The prophets predicted Him—but He didn't come. Then when the people went into exile they realized anew just how much they needed Him. Seventy years later, returning home to rebuild their broken lives and cities, they wondered if now He would finally come. Years went by. Living under Roman rule, they longed for Him to come and set them free. They knew their covenant with God had been broken beyond repair. They knew they needed more than a second chance—they needed someone to come and make right what they had made so wrong.

As one author put it, He truly was the Desire of Ages. People throughout all the ages were looking and yearning for His coming, which makes it so surprising that they all missed it completely. Well . . . except for some shepherds. As they sat warming their hands by their fires that night, angels appeared in the sky and directed them to something unexpected. Their Messiah, their King, would be found in a stable with stinky barn animals, sleeping in a hay-filled feeding trough, mothered by a young unwed woman. The shepherds went immediately to find and worship Him—a helpless newborn who couldn't even control His bowels or hold His own head up. God, the Savior of the entire world, the one hoped for during thousands of years, came just as we all do. Maybe that's why so many missed Him.

Are we still missing Him today? He may not show up to you in the exact ways you expect Him to, but hey, He's done that before. You may need to search for Him instead in lowly places, unexpected places, places others might miss Him. But keep looking and keep waiting for Him, for one day soon He's coming again—but this time as a King in glory, to take us home.   —MH

When Your Parents Are Clueless

Why were you searching for me? . . . Didn't you know I had to be in my Father's house?
Luke 2:49.

Click! And just like that, the call was dead. As I hung up on them, my parents, on the other end of the line, were furious. It was my freshman year in college, and we were vehemently arguing about several of our favorite fight topics: money, who said what, and why I didn't call them often enough. The way I saw it, they were just plain lucky to hear from me at all—there were lots of people I could call on a Sunday night, but I chose to call them, so they should just be happy about it instead of making me feel bad for not calling earlier! Who wants to call someone when they just make you feel bad for calling! After hearing too much of this, I hung up on them midsentence with a that'll-show-them certainty. I waited for them to call me back yelling, but they didn't call the rest of the night. It was only early the next morning that I heard from my dad, in an e-mail entitled "hung up on." What he said was something I hadn't considered before: the way they saw it. He explained sweetly that they thought of me every hour of every day, wondered where I was, what I was doing, and if I was happy and well. He shared how hard it was to think about someone so much and have no way to talk to them because they don't call you. I had never seen it that way.

It's strange to think about Jesus having a misunderstanding with His parents, but it happened. When He was 12, they left Him in Jerusalem and traveled all day before realizing He was missing. They went back and searched the whole city, and when they finally found Him in the Temple, He told them they should have known where He was all along! If even Jesus had a misunderstanding with His parents, it's no surprise that we sometimes do too. This also means that not all misunderstandings are sin. Sometimes there's no right or wrong person—rather, just two people seeing something differently. Jesus wasn't sinning by being in the Temple, and His parents weren't sinning when they didn't know He'd be there—they just saw things differently.

You may love your parents the way you do best friends, or they may not be some of your favorite people at all; I don't know how you feel. But just remember that when you have a misunderstanding with them, you can talk about it to Jesus, because He's actually been there too.

—MH

He Lost the Look-alike Contest—for Himself

All spoke well of him and were amazed at the gracious words that came from his lips.
"Isn't this Joseph's son?" they asked. . . . "I tell you the truth," he continued, "no prophet
is accepted in his hometown." Luke 4:22-24.

Chaplinitis, as it was called, swept the United States in 1915. The popular co-median and actor Charlie Chaplin had become a household name in just a few short years, and look-alike contests started springing up everywhere. Much like the Elvis or Marilyn Monroe impersonators you might see today, these contests were all about imitation. The goal was to see who could best imitate Chaplin's signature character, the tramp, with his classic bowler hat, cane, and crazy shuffling walk. One such competition was held in a San Francisco theater in the midst of Chaplin's soaring popularity. For the fun of it, Charlie Chaplin himself entered the contest. Obviously, the man who'd created the look was a shoo-in for first prize, and he flawlessly performed his classic shuffle and crazy antics just like people saw in the silent movies that were playing across the country. You can imagine his shock when even before the final round he was booted out by the judges as not being quite realistic enough. In a quote given to a reporter after the contest Chaplin said that he was "tempted to give lessons in the Chaplin walk [to the contestants], out of pity as well as in the desire to see the thing done correctly."

Jesus had a similar experience when He returned to His hometown of Nazareth after touring through the surrounding towns and villages for almost a year. He had been preaching, teaching, and healing the sick everywhere He went, but when He came home to do the same, people said, "Isn't this just the son of Joseph, the carpenter? Who does He think He is?" The people were blinded to who He really was because they'd seen Him grow up. He had repaired their furniture in the carpentry shop. They demanded that He do miracles as proof, and ultimately Jesus was forced to leave when they tried to throw Him off a cliff. Believing Jesus is who He says He is is a matter of faith, but sometimes we mistake Him for something else. Sometimes we make Him out to be a harsh critic or a spineless wimp who wouldn't defend Himself. But He is what He says He is: our Creator and Savior. If you have negative misconceptions about Jesus, I encourage you to get to know Him better. He's a lot more than what people sometimes think.

—GH

For whoever wants to save his life will lose it, but whoever loses his life for me will save it. What good is it for a man to gain the whole world, and yet lose or forfeit his very self? Luke 9:24, 25.

It was like watching those old cartoons of Wile E. Coyote as he's just spun off a cliff, his legs pinwheeling in midair. We'd been playing capture the flag in the dead of night. My friend Nevin and I had been creeping through briars, inching our way up to the hill in the middle of the forest. At the top of the hill was the other team's base, with their flag lying in the center of the empty fire pit. We used all of our stealthy ninja skills to advance noiselessly on the base, looking for any sign of anyone from the other team guarding the flag. Finally, we were less than 10 feet away from the flag, with no sign of a guard anywhere. Nevin crept up to the fire pit, quietly stuffed the flag into a pocket, and slipped off down the hill. Suddenly from out of the inky shadow a deep voice bellowed, "STOP RIGHT THERE!"

We blasted off across the hilltop, Nevin leading the charge. One moment I was staring at Nevin's sweatshirt and fleeing sneakers, and the next he simply disappeared. My hand shot forward to grab onto a tree, and suddenly my feet swung out over empty space. It was then that I saw Nevin running in midair as he literally shot off the side of a 15-foot drop-off. Luckily his momentum carried him out far enough to miss the boulders and rocks directly below, and he landed instead in the soft carpet of leaves that blanketed the surrounding area.

Sometimes what we think is worth pursuing in this life is only leading us off a high cliff. Jesus says, paradoxically, that whoever wants to save his life will lose it and whoever loses his life for Jesus' sake will save it. He's talking about your goals and aspirations—your dreams, even. Life, in His definition, is not confined to the time we spend on earth—it refers to the eternal life we will experience when we get to heaven. Jesus says that focusing on yourself and looking to better your own life in the here and now, though understandable, are the wrong places to look for real salvation. Even if you became emperor of the entire world and had everything you wanted, it would not be worth losing heaven for. What are *you* chasing today? It's not worth it unless it's putting you closer to Jesus and that eternal home that He's promised to all of us.

—GH

The Nerd Finally Gets the Girl

About eight days after Jesus said this, he took Peter, John and James with him and went up onto a mountain to pray. As he was praying, the appearance of his face changed, and his clothes became as bright as a flash of lightning. Luke 9:28, 29.

A college student will do pretty much anything for $20, so when the Student Association declared an official Nerd Day with the voted-for winner receiving $50, I knew my financial worries were about to get a little smaller. I assembled my best nerd attire: plaid polyester high-waist pants, mismatched argyle socks (one pink, one teal), bright-red suspenders over an oversized sleeveless button-up sweater, a huge pocket protector filled with a graphing calculator and every pen I owned, a bulging leather briefcase filled with papers and more pens, slip-on penny loafers, big ugly glasses with a missing lens, greased hair on one side and a comb stuck in the other side (to look cool), and a large "Kick Me" sign taped to my back. Finally, with a computer keyboard tucked under my arm, I made my way from class to class with squinty eyes. As I shuffled into class, Melissa, my not-yet wife, looked up in shock at my transformation and decided instantly there was no way she would be caught dead with me that day. In fact, she refused even to look in my direction until I had gone back to "normal" after the final round of voting. The sick irony is that when I won the $50 prize I took her out on a date. Looking back, it seems that I should've ignored her in return. She claims, "I hardly knew it was you!"

The disciples felt the same kind of shock when they went up on a mountain with Jesus. They thought they were going there to pray, but instead Luke says that Jesus transformed—His face suddenly changed, and His clothes glowed with splendor. What they had thought was Jesus' "normal" appearance was actually a disguise masking His heavenly image. Peter, John, and James were so overcome that they collapsed in fear, and when a voice from a cloud said, "This is my Son . . . ; listen to him" (Luke 9:35), they covered their heads and trembled. Sometimes we forget that Jesus isn't only the smiling picture we see on the wall at church—He's also the God who created the earth from nothing and shook the mountain of Sinai with fire and lightning. He's awe-inspiring and human, all in the same package, and that gives Him a unique connection with each of us. This God-man is both strong enough and gentle enough for whatever it is you need today.

—GH

The Man Who Walked on the Moon

As they were walking along the road, a man said to him, "I will follow you wherever you go." Jesus replied, "Foxes have holes and birds of the air have nests, but the Son of Man has no place to lay his head." Luke 9:57, 58.

I can remember impatiently standing in line with my treasured National Geographic book called *The Moon and Beyond* tucked under my arm. It was the closest I was ever going to get to being next to a real astronaut—James Irwin, a man who had actually walked on the moon during the *Apollo 15* mission! I had already been wowed by the speech and slide show of personal photos and memories that he'd given for the past hour, and finally the school's principal announced that Mr. Irwin would sign autographs after the lecture. I stood there watching everyone else rustling around for something for him to write on, but I was ready. I had a book with a photo of the lunar lander and even a picture of Irvin ready and waiting. When I finally got up to him, he smiled as I handed him the book. After he signed it, he motioned for me to step around the table, and I handed a camera to someone to snap a photo of us. And there I was, immortalized forever next to a man who had been somewhere I could never go; as close to a celebrity as I was ever going to get!

This kind of celebrity view of Jesus was very much the same in His own day. People flocked to Him, simply because of the stories they'd heard about Him. The verse above shows one of those instances as some groupie frantically cries out, "I will follow you wherever you go!" Jesus doesn't get caught up in the celebrity craze that followed Him. At first it just seems as though He's playfully using images from nature to say that He doesn't have a place to stay. But in that day the phrase "birds of the air" was symbolic of the Gentiles and Romans who had taken over the land. And "fox" is a term that many applied to King Herod, who was placed as king of the land by the Roman authorities. So in a sideways manner, Jesus is actually saying to the man who called out that if he wants to follow Him, then he has to be prepared to stand against the Romans and the elected officials, because He's destined to be not a powerful political figure but a rejected one. You might ask yourself why *you* are following Jesus. Are you doing it just because you were born in it, or because it's expected of you? Regardless of your reasons, realize that following Jesus isn't always safe, but it's definitely an adventure worth living.

—GH

Wanna Be Mugged? Take the Jericho Road

"Which of these three do you think was a neighbor to the man who fell into the hands of robbers?" The expert in the law replied, "The one who had mercy on him." Jesus told him, "Go and do likewise." Luke 10:36, 37.

If you didn't want to get mugged, you tried to avoid traveling down the 17-mile stretch of rough, rocky road between Jerusalem and Jericho. Everyone who heard Jesus' story of the good Samaritan would've instantly thought, *Ooh, shouldn't have been on that road alone!* But this story isn't just a random cautionary tale for the daily commuter; it's a response to a lawyer's question: Who is my neighbor? He'd just asked Jesus how he could gain eternal life for himself through his own actions. Jesus affirmed that loving God and neighbor is the highest action one can do, but he wanted specifics to make sure he had a list of do's and don'ts to follow.

Jesus then relates the story of the man robbed on the road who is passed by a priest and a Levite, who fear defilement by a corpse or a person who might not be a Jew. The last person who came by was shocking to the listeners. They expected it would be another religious figure, since the first two were. Instead Jesus spoke of one of the most hated people in Jewish society—a Samaritan man. The history of hatred between the Samaritans and the Jews was centuries old, and, according to historians, they were publicly cursed during Jewish worship services. On a daily basis the priests prayed that Samaritans not be given eternal life when they died. So the fact that Jesus said the third man, the one who compassionately helped the robbed man, was a Samaritan shows both His courage and His sense of irony. When the Samaritan goes above and beyond anything expected of him by rescuing the man, treating his wounds, then taking him to an inn and paying for all his expenses, the answer to Jesus' final question is obvious. First, Jesus makes it clear that our "neighbor" isn't only our friend or relative—he/she is also our enemy. But beyond that, Jesus is saying that we can't just expect to inherit eternal life because we did all the right things! Eternal life is about letting God influence your life and change your heart so that you reach out to *whoever* needs you, even if it's your hated enemy. What we must do to be saved—love our enemies—is larger than what we can do on our own. And so Jesus' point is made: you can't save yourselves. You need grace. You need a changed heart. You need Me.

—GH

The Lord's Prayer for Teenagers

One day Jesus was praying in a certain place. When he finished, one of his disciples said to him, "Lord, teach us to pray, just as John taught his disciples." Luke 11:1.

Our Father. God, sometimes You seem too far away to feel like a father. When I'm disappointed with my own father, I don't want to think of You that way. But it sounds nice to think that You are my parent; my earthly parents make a lot of mistakes. **Which art in heaven.** I can't wrap my mind around heaven. This earth is so different—so much pain and misery, suffering and horror. Heaven seems like an alternate universe. Help me to remember that even though You live in heaven now, You once lived down here in our filth, so You get it. **Hallowed be thy name**. Your name is so often used as a curse, an exclamation, an insult. Teach me to treat Your name with respect. Help me remember I'm talking to the God of the universe.

Thy kingdom come. Well, I'm not exactly ready for that part yet. I mean, I want You to come back and all, but just not yet. There are still some things I want to do, places I want to go, dreams I want to chase! Plus I'm afraid I'm not ready for You to come. I'm scared of the last days, and sometimes I doubt my salvation. I have a lot to learn. Teach me how to look forward to Your coming with certainty and joy. **Thy will be done in earth, as it is in heaven.** That's an even harder one, Lord. I don't always want Your will done; I want my own, my way. I want You to answer my prayers and grant my requests. I hate it when You say no, or when You are silent. But I need to trust You—You do know all. Grow my faith, so that I learn to accept whatever You choose to do.

Give us this day our daily bread. There is so much I need today, God—the list is so long. But I bring it to You. Meet my needs. Fill the empty places in me. Send me help. **Forgive us our debts, as we forgive our debtors.** Another hard one, God. Some people have really hurt me, and I deserve to be angry. Maybe I want to be angry. Change my heart, Lord. Teach me to let go of anger and to forgive as You do. **Lead us not into temptation, but deliver us from evil.** I need this one pretty bad. There's a lot of temptation in my life, and often it looks pretty good. Give me the strength to resist it, and deliver me from all the evil I can't free myself from. **For thine is the kingdom, and the power, and the glory, for ever.** Jesus, You have all the power I need for anything I am going to face this day. Thank You so much. Amen.

—MH

A Nasty Trick

But understand this: If the owner of the house had known at what hour the thief was coming, he would not have let his house be broken into. You also must be ready, because the Son of Man will come at an hour when you do not expect him. Luke 12:39, 40.

I stared lovingly into Melissa's eyes; her coy smile made me feel as if I were the luckiest guy in the world. She reached for my hand and, while squeezing it tightly, whispered "I love you" in my ear. We walked hand in hand down the street, the air crisp and the birds singing—everything was right with the world. Glancing quickly at my watch, I saw that my next class wasn't for another three hours, so we stopped for something to eat, grabbed an ice-cream cone, and browsed the art galleries downtown. Finding a quaint little shop with an outdoor seating area, we ordered a drink and chatted while people strolled by. Again I casually checked my watch and saw that it still indicated I had three hours till class . . . WHAT? I rushed back into the shop and asked the clerk the time. "Why, it's 4:35, dear," she said, and I realized that my class had started about 30 minutes before! I whirled onto the sidewalk in a panic, and there stood my loving girlfriend laughing her head off. "Something wrong with your watch?" she sweetly asked. It was then I realized that while she had been holding my hand and whispering in my ear she had pulled out the little set pin on the watch, which stopped it from running. She still does this all the time--it's her favorite game.

If I had been a little more aware, I would've noticed that my watch wasn't working the way it was supposed to. In this passage in Luke, Jesus calls us to be more aware. He says that we must always be ready for Him because His second coming will be at an hour we do not expect Him. If you're like me, sometimes I get caught up thinking that we have all the time in the world. I plan my life around things that are immediate, and put off until later the things that seem as though they can get done whenever. But the fact is that building a relationship with Jesus isn't something we can just put off for later. He says we must always be ready for Him because He will return at a time we won't expect. The watch of the world will soon stop, and every day that we have is just another day closer. To be ready for the second coming means having a relationship with Jesus right now. So if you haven't started already, why not begin today?

—GH

The Time We Owned a Hot Tub

But don't begin until you count the cost. For who would begin construction of a building without first calculating the cost to see it there is enough money to finish it? Luke 14:28, NLT.

One week my husband and I owned a hot tub. There was this super-great moving sale in town, and the people selling their home claimed that "everything must go," so we went and looked around, and our eyes beheld the treasure of the day: a giant, beautiful, sparkling, eight-person hot tub. It was worth thousands, and the people were getting rid of it for a mere $500. Greg and I were elated! We scraped money together and stole from our savings and purchased it immediately, because our friend Seth was eyeing it as well, and we didn't want to lose it to the likes of him! The people were happy to sell it, their only stipulation being that we had to figure out a way to move it. On the way home we celebrated our good fortune and congratulated each other on finally being the proud owners of a hot tub. We dreamed about the snowy Michigan nights when we'd sit basking in our toasty warm new spa. Wouldn't our friends be jealous!

But then it began to occur to us . . . How were we going to move that thing, anyway? And just exactly where was it going to go? Our landlady would never allow it on the lawn or in the driveway or out back; and when we moved in a year, what would we do with it then? We began to suspect that we had made a terrible mistake. We became sure of it when we looked into how much it would cost just to get it to our house. Frantic now, Greg listed the hot tub online and, thankfully, we sold it a few days later without ever moving it an inch. And that was the only week of our marriage that we owned a hot tub. Every now and then Greg will look at me and say, "Remember the week we owned a hot tub?" And we laugh because of what fools we had been!

If you are smart, you don't buy giant items without first thinking it out. You first consider the cost, as Jesus advises above—can you afford it? What will it take? But He is not talking about hot tubs or other large buys. Jesus is talking about the cost of being a disciple. This is also a life decision that needs to be made thoughtfully, for it will cost you something. It may cost you what the world considers fun and freedom, but think of how much it would cost not to belong to Jesus when He comes in those clouds. Count the cost today, and choose wisely.

—MH

He Just Kept Going Back

Jesus continued: "There was a man who had two sons. The younger one said to his father, 'Father, give me my share of the estate.' So he divided his property between them."
Luke 15:11, 12.

The only thing more pathetic than a couple breaking up because one of them cheated on the other is when the one cheated on takes the cheater back again and again. I remember a guy whose girlfriend kept leaving him for other guys. He'd walk around in a haze of anguish and desperation, leaving flowers on her locker, buying her gifts and cards, or having some big angry fight with her about the new guy she was dating. The big question in all our minds was Why? Why in the world did he keep going back to her just to get his heart stomped on again and again?

The story of the prodigal son feels a lot like watching this guy in high school. What's crazy is that the father here represents God Himself. In Middle Eastern culture the younger son asking his dad for his share of the family estate was exactly the same as saying, "I can't wait till you die to have your money. I want it all right now so I can leave you stranded and have my fun." The father had every right to refuse to give his home and land away; even to cut the son out of the will entirely. What's amazing is that the father gave the son what he asked, taking on the insult and the hatred without saying a word. Money in hand, the son was outta there, squandering it all in a foreign land. When the money ran out, so did his friends. He was so poor and hungry that he wished he could eat with the pigs in a farmer's field. His only option was to return home, hoping that his father could forgive him enough to at least let him be a servant. Again, with the magnitude of the insult everyone would expect the father to reject the boy outright. In fact, a village would have attacked any son who'd done what he did, before he even got back home. So when Jesus said that the father saw the son from afar and ran to meet him, it showed that the father ran ahead to protect his son from the angry mobs. And once he meets his son the father orders a feast to celebrate the boy's return. That's God: taking us back, running down the dusty road to meet us before anyone can point and say, "Look at how you screwed up!" When you come back to God, He doesn't hold on to the past. He runs ahead to meet you with open arms and tears of joy, because really, He just wants us all to come home.

—GH

Throwing Yourself on the Mercy of the Court

Jesus told his disciples: "There was a rich man whose manager was accused of wasting his possessions. So he called him in and asked him, 'What is this I hear about you? Give an account of your management, because you cannot be manager any longer.'"
Luke 16:1, 2.

It worked to throw herself in front of that car. In 1960 the wife of a condemned spy in the Middle Eastern country of Jordan was at her wits' end. In desperation she went to a local official and asked for advice. He told her to wait outside the palace for the king's motorcade to come by. When it was about to pass, this man told her to throw herself in front of the king's limousine and plead for mercy. The woman did as she was advised, and since the king of Jordan knew how the people expected a noble monarch to act in these situations, he released her husband that day.

This is the key to the parable of the unjust steward. The story goes that the manager of a rich man's properties was caught cheating the owner out of money. He was fired on the spot, but instead of throwing him in prison as he deserved, the rich man allowed the deceitful manager to go free. The manager knew that when word got out regarding his dishonesty, he wouldn't be able to find work. So he came up with a plan. He gathered together all the rich man's renters and gave each of them a huge discount in what they owed. When the manager returned to his master with the account books, his master found out that he had indeed been cheated *again* by the fired manager. What's crazy is that the rich man then praised the manager for his wisdom! What's going on here? Is Jesus advocating cheating and stealing as a means to get out of trouble?

The beauty of this parable is that the manager is being praised *not* for cheating, but for knowing the one thing about his master that can save him: his master's mercy. By creating a situation in which all the renters feel that the master has been generous, the manager knows the rich man will not want to risk the renters' anger by changing the rent amounts. He has saved his reputation by throwing himself on the mercy of his master, who, he believes, will be merciful to him again. Jesus is saying, "If this dishonest man was wise enough to place his trust in the quality of his master's mercy, how much more should we place our trust in God's mercy?" Our only option is to put our trust in the unfailing mercy of our generous God. We don't deserve it, no excuses will work, but all we have to do is throw ourselves on the mercy of His court.

—GH

Were You There?

Jesus said, "Father, forgive them, for they do not know what they are doing." Luke 23:34.

Torn and bruised, covered in his own blood and barely able to walk, Jesus struggled to make His way through the jeering crowds bearing that heavy crossbeam on His back. He had just endured the worst night of His life, begging God not to make Him do this. Then He was arrested. All His closest friends deserted or betrayed Him. He spent the wee hours of the morning in ridiculous mock trials, enduring lies, insults, and ridicule, and was beaten, bloodied, and tormented. The same people who had cheered for Him days before when He rode into town on a donkey now seethed in anger and shouted for His death. They chose a criminal—a murderer—to release instead of Him. He recognized a former friend, Satan himself, in the crowd, stirring up the mob, his demons shouting wildly, fanning the flames of hatred against Jesus. Now He was about to die. His carpenter's hands, which had created and blessed, soon would be roughly spread out on splintered wood. Nails would be driven directly into the soft flesh of His wrists and ankles. As He endured unbearable pain, soldiers would casually gamble for His clothes. Naked, cold, and seemingly abandoned by God Himself, He could see that His life would end. But He wasn't thinking of Himself that day.

Even as He dragged that cross through the streets and women followed crying, He reached out to them, trying to tell them not to cry for Him, but rather to cry for themselves because of what would soon happen to Jerusalem. Suspended from nails, pained by every breath, He granted immediate salvation to the thief beside Him simply because he asked. Looking down on the crowd below, He saw His own mother—the woman who had taught Him how to walk, talk, dress Himself—and He made arrangements for John to care for her now. Even as the Roman soldiers were crucifying Him, He prayed that God would forgive their ignorance. He thought of people that day. He thought of you and me. In his last moments, He loved us.

The character of God was never more real than in those hours of Jesus' arrest, trial, and crucifixion. He's not harsh or angry or bitter. He is loving, through and through. Every action, every thought, even during the worst pain imaginable, was love. If you're having a hard time feeling the love of God, go back to the closing scenes of Jesus' life, and realize it was all for you.

—MH

Who Is Lying?

On the first day of the week, very early in the morning, the women took the spices they had prepared and went to the tomb. Luke 24:1.

He burst through the doors of my classroom dressed like a crazy person, threw the stack of copies right in my face, and began to yell at me. My students watched in silent horror as my usually sane husband turned into a raging lunatic. He was a sight to behold. He wore one solitary glove; mismatched shoes and socks; a vest, sweater, and two hats; and carried backpacks and water bottles suspended from carabiners on his belt loops. Shouting that he'd never again make my copies, he stomped out of the room. Every face in the class registered disbelief.

"Take out a piece of paper," I ordered them calmly, "and write down everything you just saw—every word, every action. Leave out no details. Go." Later we collected all their accounts of the incident and had a pretty good laugh. Some students were horrified; others were scared. A few thought it was funny, and several figured out it was staged. But every single account was different—they remembered our words differently, and since nobody was completely accurate on what he was wearing, we brought him back in to compare! Only one out of 74 saw his Band-Aid.

Have you ever wondered why the four Gospels give different details about the same event? I mean, are there mistakes in the Bible? They can't all be right! Take the resurrection of Jesus. How many women were at the tomb? Matthew says the two Marys were there, but Mark lists three women. John says only Mary Magdalene. Did they go at dawn, or while it was still dark? And who met them? Matthew says one angel, Mark says a young man in a white robe, Luke says two men in white, and John says Jesus Himself. Which is right? And why would the Bible contain any variations if it is truly inspired? Is this reason to doubt? Did Jesus really even rise? As my students found out the day that Greg burst in, the fact that people notice different details is normal. As in a court case, if all the stories match exactly, it very likely shows that people got together and made everything up. But the fact that people remember the scene differently means it was recorded by real people who were really there, and were impacted by different things. Its variety is actually proof of its validity. If you ever question the Bible—be encouraged. God let men write it, but He was still behind it. And as for the tomb, they all agree: It was empty! Jesus is alive.

—MH

Why We Don't See Him

As they talked and discussed these things with each other, Jesus himself came up and walked along with them; but they were kept from recognizing him. Luke 24:15, 16.

The night that my husband asked me to marry him I mistook him for a drunk in the bushes. It's embarrassing now, but I tried to run from him. I was home for spring break, and my younger brother, Russell, invited me to hike with him on one of our favorite trails that crested a hill and overlooked the lights of downtown Phoenix. I had mentioned to Greg once or twice that I thought it was an incredibly romantic place, but how could I have known he would plan to propose there? Besides, it was spring break. He was home in Ohio, and I was home in Arizona. I didn't expect to see him for 10 whole days. So naturally it took me by complete surprise when a man emerged from the bushes and called out to me, "Hey, babe!" First of all, in my defense, I'm not really sure why he used that opening line—seems as if he could have thought of some smoother first words—and I thought he was some drunk guy trying to hit on me. I mean, who just comes out of bushes into a path and yells, "Hey, babe"? I was afraid. I turned to run away, scared he might come after me, when Russell said, "Melissa, wait! Turn around!" I looked back over my shoulder and recognized Greg, my beloved, standing there in the path. My brother disappeared somewhere, Greg got down on one knee, and there, overlooking the glittering lights of the entire city of Phoenix, he asked me to be his wife. A magic moment—eventually!

When I tell people the story now, they always make fun of me for not recognizing my own boyfriend, or even his voice. I try to explain that he was completely out of context. It was the last thing I would have ever guessed. I think the two walking on the road to Emmaus would back me up on this. We give them a lot of grief for not even recognizing Jesus as they walked and talked with Him for hours, but maybe it's not such a surprise. They believed He was dead. Gone. Forever. His showing up was the last thing they could have predicted.

I wonder if we still don't do the same thing to Jesus. Are we missing the times He shows up in our daily lives because we just don't expect to see Him? Keep your eyes open today. Look for Him to show up in unexpected places and in unexpected ways. Sometimes the best moments are ones you would never guess on your own.

—MH

The Kidnapping of Bobecia: Looking Back

In the beginning was the Word, and the Word was with God, and the Word was God.
John 1:1.

It's possibly the absolutely worst movie anyone has ever made in the history of all time. *The Kidnapping of Bobecia* (Bow-bee-shah) is a short home movie, filmed at night on the train tracks in downtown Lincoln, Nebraska's old Haymarket district. The plot is awful, the characters are weak, the ending is pointless. But I have to confess something to you: I made the movie. Not alone—with a group of my best girlfriends in college. We called ourselves "the Boyz" back then, for reasons we've long since forgotten. And back in the day, that movie was our pride and joy.

The pitiful excuse for a film features my best friend Alicia as Bobecia the rock star, whom two wayward criminals—Jen and I—abduct and tie to the train tracks. April and Katie are on the scene as confused reporters and detectives, while Amanda, the nervous eyewitness, shares the horrible account of the bicycle abduction of Bobecia. And for effect, Patty, Eunice, and April randomly walk by and stare into the camera, stunned. I told you—it's terrible. Now I have another confession to make: I love that movie. I've watched it literally more times than I can count, and I still laugh till I cry every time. But it's more than just a movie to me—it's a memory, a captured crazy evening from my college days, frozen in time by a cheap old video camera. I treasure that old movie the Boyz and I made because I treasure those friends. I go back and watch it sometimes when I miss being around those girls.

I wonder if that's how John felt when he sat down to document his memories of the life of Jesus. Did he miss his Friend? Did some stories leave him laughing, smiling, or shaking his head? John, who was one of Jesus' three closest friends, wrote a Gospel that is very different from the others. It opens, not with a genealogy or the story of Jesus' birth, but by saying right up front that Jesus was God Himself. This is a powerful way to start, especially from a man who lived with Him. If John, who slept in the same houses with Jesus, walked countless miles and ate countless meals with Him, was actually convinced that He was God, we should pay attention.

When you read this book, read it first as the Word of God and the story of God. But equally important, read it as the story of a man missing and remembering his close Friend. Are you looking for a God today or just for a friend? Either way, John is the place to find both.　　　　　　　　　　　　　　　　　—MH

A Time to Sneak

For God so loved the world, that he gave his only begotten Son, that whosoever believeth in him should not perish, but have everlasting life. John 3:16, KJV.

The dark bruises lining our entire legs top to bottom always gave us away the next day as the girls who had sneaked out of the dorm. The only openings in our academy dorm rooms were these tiny minuscule windows right at the ceiling, about the size and length of a small shoe box, designed by somebody who must have been certain no human being could ever escape through them. Well, whoever they were, they didn't know us! It usually took us the better part of a half hour to get out, and it was actually quite the team effort to do it. Holly would hold my legs, and Sarah would help pull the skin on my legs taut as I would desperately inch my way through. It was painful, I have to admit. Several of us even got stuck halfway out, suspended there seven feet off the ground, straight as a board. And because of the way we had coaxed and poured our bodies through that microscopic metal frame, we were black and blue for days afterwards.

I can't remember why we thought it was worth it to sneak out—except maybe for a few grand-scale campus toilet-papering masterpieces. Mostly it was the excitement of sneaking around campus in the night, I guess. In the end, though, it was just plain painful, and you could hardly enjoy it because every minute you felt as if you were going to get caught.

It was that same fear of being caught that had Nicodemus stealthily sneaking through the night to meet with Jesus, who was not a real popular figure in the crowd he hung around with. Nicodemus had his pride and his reputation to think of, but something in him just had to find a way to see this man. So he snuck out and came to Him at night. And it was during this meeting that Jesus gave us the most famous Bible verse of all time. In one line He perfectly distills the entire gospel message: God loved our broken, bitter, angry world so much that He gave us His most valuable treasure—Jesus. And if we just so little as believe in Him, we automatically inherit the riches of eternal life. It just doesn't seem right. It has that "too good to be true" ring to it, doesn't it? But that's why it's the good news—it *is* true. We don't have to go sneaking around with our heads down, living in fear, ashamed of our sins any longer. When we have chosen Jesus, we can hold our heads high in confidence, knowing that we are saved.

—MH

Caught in the Act

"Then neither do I condemn you," Jesus declared. "Go now and leave your life of sin."
John 8:11.

Headlights shining directly into my eyes were my first clue that we'd been discovered. My boyfriend and I had deserted the basketball game in the gym to go have some kissy time in the bushes, and we thought we were pretty clever. How could they ever keep track of all of us on a crowded game night? But the dean was a lot smarter than we gave her credit for, because within minutes she was driving around campus, searching specifically for us. She spotted our silhouettes in the bushes and drove up within feet of where we stood kissing, so there was no way to lie and nowhere to hide. We would have chosen a much better hiding place if we'd known she'd be on our tail so quickly, but instead we spent the entire next week on "social"—forbidden to make contact with each other in any way.

When the church leaders walked in on the woman in today's text, she was doing a whole lot more than kissing. They caught her in the act of adultery! I'm not sure what they did with the man—oh, yes: *nothing!* He'd set the trap; her they dragged to Jesus, throwing her on the ground to be stoned. Instead of stooping down to pick up a rock, Jesus began writing in the dust. When He stood up and said that the one without sin should cast the first stone, the men were trapped. They had to stare down at their sins written on the ground even to locate a rock, and they couldn't do it. One by one they silently left, until only the woman and Jesus remained. But Jesus was not like those other men. He had no sin in His life—He was the only man eligible to stone her. Even more amazing, He *didn't* condemn her but gave her grace, undeserved, then challenged her: change your ways, clean up your life, leave your sins behind. Today it's still popular to pass judgment on another life and to think that grace gives us the license to do whatever we want. The funny thing about grace? It changes you. When you truly realize that you're a mess and don't deserve this gift, it does something in your heart, creating a desire to be a better person. If grace just left you as you were, you'd live stuck in your sins forever. When God saves you, He wants you to enjoy your new life. And the only way to do that is to leave those sins behind. Does realizing you have undeserved grace change things in your heart today?

—MH

Egging a Car and Outrunning a Cop

Jesus replied, "I tell you the truth, everyone who sins is a slave to sin." John 8:34.

I'm not the one who bought the eggs. Nor was I the driver. But I was still guilty. What were we thinking the day that Penny, Kari, and I decided to get back at Kari's heartless ex-boyfriend? We stalked him to his house, found his extremely nice car sitting in the driveway, and proceeded to bomb it with dozens of eggs. Speeding away victoriously, Penny suddenly thought there might be someone following us. That's when we started to freak out. Had he been home? Had someone been watching out the window? Had a neighbor turned us in? We drove wildly back to campus and hid in the music building all afternoon, praying the cops wouldn't come searching the school for us, terrified of ending up in a jail cell next to someone named Big Bertha. The next time we drove through town we were still looking over our shoulders, afraid of being hunted.

You'd think I would have remembered, the day a cop ushered me over in downtown Seattle, that fear-feeling of being caught that comes hand in hand with a stupid decision. But I didn't. He climbed lazily out of his car and stretched his arms, and at that moment I looked right into the public market. I don't know what came over me. It was like another set of hands took the wheel and turned the car into the market, speeding crazily past the fruit stands, the Starbucks, and the sidewalk musicians. By the time that cop got back into his car and followed, I was long gone, huddled terrified in my car at the bottom of a parking garage. Instead of being triumphant, I was seized with fear. I had committed a misdemeanor! I spent the whole rest of that day in Seattle being afraid, looking over my shoulder, certain that the cop would drive by and recognize me. While my son splashed happily in the fountains on the Harbor Steps, I cowered in fear behind a nearby planter. It ruined my entire day.

That's how sin rules us, doesn't it? It traps us in fear, keeps us looking over our shoulder in shame, even if we didn't get caught. It steals our freedom and sense of security, and robs us of the carefree ability just to enjoy life. The Pharisees thought they were free, but Jesus pointed out that anyone who sins is a slave. You become a slave to fear, guilt, and the sin itself. In a sentence: it's not worth it. Living in fear, looking over your shoulder, is not the life Jesus wants for you. He wants you to be free. And only the truth—Jesus Himself—can set you free.

—MH

Are You Dumber Than a Sheep?

His sheep follow him because they know his voice. But they will never follow a stranger; in fact, they will run away from him because they do not recognize a stranger's voice. John 10:4, 5.

There was that feeling again—that sickening, sinking, foreboding feeling—in the pit of my stomach like a churning knot. I felt it every single time we drove by the house—the one we'd just bought. The process took 30 days, and then the house would officially be ours, but until then we excitedly drove by it each day. Recently, though, every time we did I felt worse and worse about our decision. It became clear to me that something was terribly wrong. What worried me most was that I recognized the feeling. It was the same feeling I'd had in the past when God was trying to tell me that something wasn't right. It's almost like a still small voice whispering in my ear. God has often spoken to me like this when I've asked Him to warn me if I'm making a bad decision, and here it was again. One night I told Greg how I'd been feeling, even though we were so jazzed about owning our first home. To my shock, Greg said that he'd been feeling the exact same thing. So we stopped the deal, got out of the house, and were left to wonder: why did He warn us? Only two years later the housing market virtually crashed and burned, and we had to move at the same time. We would have owned a house that we would never have been able to sell. It would have ruined us financially for the next 10 years. God was right again!

When Jesus compares Himself to a shepherd and us to sheep (one of the dumbest animals alive, by the way), He points out that sheep are familiar with their shepherd's voice. One of my seminary professors visited a shepherd one day and bet the shepherd that if he dressed up in the shepherd's cloak, used his shoes and staff, and went out to get the sheep, they would come to him—certainly they followed only the outfit! Sure enough, when the sheep saw the impostor coming, they eagerly ran to him. He was so pleased that he yelled out, "Come here, my sheep!" Instantly they turned and walked away. They knew it wasn't their shepherd's voice.

The more we get to know Jesus, the more we will become familiar with His voice and the ways in which He leads us. Spending time with Him will help us to really learn that voice. You can also ask yourself, "How has He led me in the past?" Chances are He'll speak to you in the same ways that He has spoken to you before. So take time today to get to know His voice.   —MH

Looking for More Out of Life?

I have come that they may have life, and have it to the full. John 10:10.

Our Bible teacher balanced casually on a stool at the front of the classroom and crunched loudly on a mouthful of giant pretzels. The room was silent except for the rustle of the pretzel bag and his chewing. Instead of taking notes or engaging in some amazing life-changing lecture, for the third day in a row we were . . . coloring! Coloring pictures of Jesus, to be exact, a drawing of Him walking under beautiful flowering vines, His eyes turned heavenward. Our teacher said that this particular picture was to help us realize how much Jesus appreciated the beauty of flowers and nature. *Pointless* was the word ringing in my mind as I angrily did the ridiculous assignment and looked around the room at the various cases of desperation nearby. One of my friends was losing her entire personality to drugs and didn't even care anymore. Another had just begun having sex and wanted to stop, but couldn't find the self-control to do it. The parents of one student were going through an angry, messy divorce. Another was losing his father to AIDS. One had just learned that his brother had committed suicide. All around me people's lives were falling apart, and here we were in Bible class, the very place we should be finding help and answers, and we were coloring! Did God have anything better to offer us, or was He just as pointless as the stupid pictures we were coloring? *If this is really all that religion and God have to offer hurting people in the real world,* I thought, *then it's just not enough. I don't need Him.*

Thankfully, I was wrong that day. Both God and religion have so, so much more to offer us than silly platitudes and meaningless activities. In fact, Jesus offers us something that I think every single one of us is after—the abundant life, life to the fullest! He is talking about being our Shepherd when He makes the above statement, and He says that while other people/things try to kill and destroy His people, He has come so that we might have life to the fullest.

If you've found yourself looking for more out of religion lately, I suggest you take a closer look at Jesus. He's got more to offer you than you may have thought. He's not offering another one of the world's empty promises, He's offering life, *real life*, life to the fullest. So if that's what you're after, choose Him. Living with Jesus is never empty, never meaningless, never pointless or purposeless. It is the fullest and absolute best way to live your life. —MH

The Scent of Christians

Then Mary took about a pint of pure nard, an expensive perfume; she poured it on Jesus' feet and wiped his feet with her hair. And the house was filled with the fragrance. John 12:3.

Oil hung heavy in the air and blanketed the stove top, the walls, the floor, and the ceiling of the tiny camping trailer. We glanced at each other in dread of what we would soon have to eat. My sister Heather and I were camping in Arizona's Superstition Mountains with my best friend Alicia, and we had foolishly consented to letting her cook breakfast for us all. She must have used at least four vats of oil just to fry up some country potatoes. As we sat trapped in that trailer, the oil slowly seeped into our clothes, our hair, even our skin. Late that night my hair still smelled like oil. The next week when I did laundry, that oil scent was still on my jeans.

Funny how some smells can linger, isn't it? As kids, my cousins and I used to sneak into my grandma's closet and hide among her clothes because we loved how the scent of the perfume she wore—tea roses—lingered on each and every shirt. One time when Greg and I had broken up, he said that if a girl wearing my perfume passed him in the mall he'd feel as if I were standing there next to him. Scents carry a tremendous power!

The entire room filled with the sweet fragrance of nard as Mary poured it over Jesus' feet and dried them with her hair. Not only was it completely unacceptable for a woman to show her hair in public, but the perfume, the type that kings such as Solomon used to anoint women in their harem, was worth a year's wages. Its scent lasted for months. Anyone who passed a woman who'd been anointed would know immediately that she'd been with the king. Jesus—and every person in the room that day—would have carried the fragrance for months. As they stood near the cross, the perfume's scent was still on them. Weeks later the scent would identify them as people who had obviously been with Jesus. They couldn't hide it.

When you've been with Jesus, people will know. There's something remarkable and unmistakable about a person who's been with the Lord. You can just tell. You can see it; you know there is something different about them. Though you are far from perfect, when you are spending time with Jesus there will be an obvious quality about your life that other lives won't have. You can't hide it. When you have been with the King, His mark is left on your life.

—MH

The Toilet Thieves

In my Father's house are many mansions: if it were not so, I would have told you. I go to prepare a place for you. John 14:2, KJV.

They actually stole our toilet. Who does that? What kind of people steal a toilet, I ask you! But that was only the beginning of it—the repossessed house we now live in came with holes in each and every window, and giant gaping holes punched in every door and wall. Obviously angry because they could not keep the house, the former owners also stole all the appliances in the kitchen and all the kitchen cabinets. They even ripped out the mantle over the fireplace. There was dried dish soap from wall to wall, disgusting stuff in all the showers, and mysterious red and black stains, as large as a man, on the carpets. You may wonder why we chose such a gem of a place, but to be honest, we've always lived in shabby, less-than-ideal homes. Our first apartment was probably about the size of the closet your clothes are hanging in right now—our friends lovingly referred to it as "the shoe box." When we filled it up with 10 or so of our college friends, they had to sit shoulder to shoulder just to fit inside. In the bathroom you could stand only sideways. If you turned straight, you'd run into the shower door. Our second place wasn't any better; in fact, it burned down. Our third house, a duplex, faced a junkyard, and our fourth place had paper-thin walls and a basement that flooded.

Because it looks as if Greg and I will never own a mansion this side of eternity, I take comfort in knowing that Jesus says He's preparing one for us. This was a promise He made to His disciples during His last days with them. The mansion isn't the best part of the promise, though. What gives me the most comfort is just *knowing* there's a place specifically reserved for me, a spot in heaven where I belong. And where we belong is where we get our identity from, isn't it?

Maybe you don't feel as if you belong anywhere right now. Or perhaps you are searching for your place in life. Where do you fit in? Who are you? Where are you most at home? Remember that no matter how lost or homeless you feel down here, there is a place in heaven where you belong. Jesus has actually made a plan for you, and He's counting on your being there! Next time you struggle with who you are and where you belong, remember your true identity: you are a future mansion owner and a celebrated resident of heaven!   —MH

An Incident With Pickles

After Jesus said this, he looked toward heaven and prayed: "Father, the time has come. Glorify your Son, that your Son may glorify you." John 17:1.

Sometimes it all comes down to timing. I was standing in the aisle while my mother was taking way too long in the bread section. Bored, I looked to my left and suddenly realized that I was standing in front of a towering wall of every kind of pickle imaginable. Glancing sideways, I saw my mother still engrossed in a wheat/white decision, and my hand reached out for a jar. I hardly knew what I was doing, but suddenly I heard the satisfying pop of the lid and had plucked a pickle out of the middle of the jar. On some level I knew this was a bad thing, and as I bit into the pickle I felt too guilty to eat it all. So I put back what was left, closed the jar, and replaced it on the shelf. Then the desire for just one more pickle overwhelmed me, so I took another jar and bit into one from that. Then another. By the time Mom had made up her mind, I was on the seventh jar. She grabbed it from me, yelling, "What in the world are you doing?" As I was hauled down the aisle toward the cash register, I knew that now was not the time to say anything about the other six jars. I did tell her, though—about 20 years later. Better timing!

In light of this incident I've always been profoundly touched when I read in the Gospels where Jesus told people, "Now is not the time." It takes a particular finesse to know when the right time is, and Jesus seems to have known it instinctively. Once He said it to His mother when she suggested He perform a miracle for the wedding feast in Cana (John 2:1-11), and another time He said it to His brothers when they suggested He do some positive PR at the Temple in Jerusalem (John 7). This begs the question When was the right time going to be, anyway?

The only other place we find Jesus calculating the timing of things is in the Garden of Gethsemane when He prays, "Father, the time has come." For Jesus, the timing of His final act of sacrifice was essential for its effectiveness. He knew when the right time had come. His disciples would've disagreed with the timing, especially since they felt that He needed to take over the country's throne rather than give Himself to His enemies. But Jesus' timing has always been better than ours. Trust His timing today in your life. And if you have not yet accepted His sacrifice for you, now is a great time. The timing will never be easier than it is today.

—MH

A Last Request

My prayer is not for them alone. I pray also for those who will believe in me through their message, that all of them may be one, Father, just as you are in me and I am in you. May they also be in us so that the world may believe that you have sent me. John 17:20, 21.

Tonight I called to wish her a happy eighty-sixth birthday. That's a lot of years, my friends—86! Grandma Palmer may be old, but she still runs a marathon each and every night. She prays for us, you see. She prays for every single person in our entire family, by name, with specific requests, each night without fail. There are more than 45 people in our family! But still she does it faithfully. As we spoke tonight, my 3-year-old son lay upstairs struggling terribly with a bad case of pneumonia, but Grandma told me that she had been praying for him since the moment she found out he was sick. She reminded me that she prays for me specifically every night as well, in my struggles and trials in life. Hearing that felt kind of like stepping into a warm bath or wrapping a big fuzzy blanket around me. It was just so comforting! There is no feeling in the world quite like knowing that someone is out there praying for you, is there?

Did you know that Jesus prayed for you? The night of His trial, when He wrestled with God in Gethsemane, John records some of the things He said and prayed for. Just as He was closing His prayer, He prayed for every single person who would come to believe in Him through the message of His disciples. That's *you!* And that's me, and all of us. Isn't it amazing to think about? There in the garden, struggling, during His last night before His death, He was praying for us. But do you know *what* He prayed for, exactly? He wanted us to be united together with each other. What's interesting is that Jesus said it was unity that would let the world know He is real. I guess when we fight and bicker and backbite, it doesn't give a great testimony to the rest of the world, does it? But if we could just be united, that would say something. It would show the world that there is truly something different about us Christians.

Is there anything we can do about all the fighting, gossiping, and finger-pointing that goes on in the church today? There certainly is. The change starts with the person in the mirror, because the church isn't just some big body out there. The church is you! Do your best to honor Jesus' last-night prayer, and strive to be united with the people in your life today.

—MH

Nothing but the Truth

"What is truth?" After he [Pilate] had said this, he went back outside to the Jews and told them, "I find no guilt in him." John 18:38, ESV.

Recently I met a church member at Border's Books to discuss some of the things God has been doing in his life. Having grown up in a legalistic and controlling environment, this grown man is discovering a new freedom to ask questions and explore his faith. And as he has been reading, he has wrestled with the concept of truth—more specifically, absolute truth. It is a struggle for a lot of people.

The idea of "truth" can be especially unappealing if you've been in a Christian environment that often uses such phrases as "we have the truth," comparing itself to other sincere people with different faiths. It can make you feel exclusive and snobbish. And this gentleman was wrestling with this, considering the idea that maybe there is no such thing as "absolute" truth. I have heard many people make this claim—including family. Maybe you have heard it from classmates, parents, or people at work.

It's certainly a much easier way to view things. If there is no absolute truth, then everyone has a piece of it, and we can leave each other alone as we all journey together. It can get us off the hook in uncomfortable situations. When Pilate had Jesus' fate in his hands and was trying to ascertain who He was, Pilate asked rhetorically, "What is truth?" That makes it seem as though truth is relative and wishy-washy. However, to claim we cannot know the truth presents us with a big problem.

To claim you cannot know the truth is, in fact, a statement of truth. In other words, you might phrase it this way to point out the error: It is true that we cannot know what is true. My question, then, is how do you know *that*? How do you know if something is *not* true unless you know what *is* true? My church member was taken aback at this and reconsidered his position.

This is important because we live in a world that prefers to leave truth in the hands of the individual and not get into controversy about what's right and wrong. That's what the devil likes to do. If he can blur the lines between right and wrong, there is no telling how low he can bring us. Our only hope is following the example of Jesus, who is the way, the truth, and the life.

—SP

Famous Last Words

When he had received the drink, Jesus said, "It is finished." With that, he bowed his head and gave up his spirit. John 19:30.

Of all of the words to come out of our mouths throughout life, those that people want to know most often are our last, which are usually written down for posterity. Here are some of my favorites: "Die, my dear doctor? That's the last thing I shall do!"—Lord Palmerston, British prime minister, who died in 1865. "Go on; get out! Last words are for fools who haven't said enough!"—Karl Marx to his housekeeper. "No, life is ugly enough to be looked at frankly one last time."—Babi, the French revolutionary, after being asked if he wanted to be blindfolded at his firing squad. "Don't let it end like this. Tell them I said something."—Pancho Villa. "I've been to the mountaintop. . . . And I've seen the promised land. . . . And I'm happy tonight. I'm not worried about anything. I'm not fearing any man. Mine eyes have seen the glory of the coming of the Lord!"—Martin Luther King, Jr., 1968, the day before his assassination. We all hope that our last words will have some meaning, or at least will let those closest to us know how much we love them. Last words are supposed to convey something of ourselves.

Jesus' last words on the cross—three small words—do exactly that. When He said, "It is finished," the natural question is *What* is finished? To Jesus His death wasn't just the end of life, it was the fulfillment of a promise made by God to Adam and Eve when they left the Garden of Eden. It was the completion of the symbolic sacrifices that God established with Moses and Aaron in the desert tabernacle after leading the Israelites out of slavery. It was the fulfillment of what Isaiah predicted would happen in his prophecies of the Suffering Servant from Isaiah 53. "It" was the plan that had been put together before Planet Earth was created. Knowing they were going to create humans with the freedom to accept or reject them, the Father, Jesus, and the Holy Spirit devised a plan to rescue us if we decided to go our own way. And at the moment of Jesus' death, He saw that this plan had finally been accomplished. It truly was finished. The justice in the law of God was satisfied by One who paid the price that we, the ones who actually broke it, should have paid. Sin, with all its power over us, was finally broken. So these three words, really, are what give you and me the hope that we have in Jesus today. It. Is. Finished.

—GH

A Race, a Name, and a Doubter

Then he said to Thomas, "Put your finger here; see my hands. Reach out your hand and put it into my side. Stop doubting and believe." John 20:27.

There was a myriad of reactions when Jesus rose from the grave early Sunday morning. When Mary found the tomb empty, she hightailed it back to Peter and John, who immediately raced out to see for themselves. John takes time in his Gospel to brag about the fact that he happened to outrun Peter in their race to the grave—evidently this was important to him. But instead of going in, he stopped outside. It was Peter who ran right into the tomb, and it was he who took time to notice that Jesus' linens were neatly folded, a strange detail to include. Do we go racing to Jesus, as Peter did, even after we have denied Him? Or do we sulk in shame?

Mary herself stood by the tomb crying to a nearby "gardener," asking Him to tell her where they had taken Jesus. Mary was a tough girl. She was ready to go and carry off Jesus' heavy body if only she could find Him. At her comment the "gardener" spoke just one word: "Mary." At the sound of her name, she instantly knew who He was. Jesus! Alive! I wonder, would we recognize His familiar voice calling our name if He were to do so today? Is He calling your name now?

When Jesus appeared to the disciples who had gathered in a house, they thought He was a ghost. He actually ate something to prove He was a living, flesh-and-blood person. But one of my favorite responses comes from Thomas, who wasn't there at the time. The other disciples claimed they'd seen Jesus with their own eyes, but he just didn't buy it. In fact, he insisted that unless he actually touched the nail marks on Jesus with his own fingers, he was not going to believe a word they'd said. What I love about Thomas' story is that Jesus humors him, meets him right where he is. He tells Thomas to reach out and feel for himself, then orders, "Stop doubting and believe!"

For this reason he's gone down in history as "doubting Thomas," but would our response be similar? Don't we doubt God all the time? Aren't we constantly searching for evidence and proof that He's even there? Some even refuse to believe in God without proof. Are you one of those? If you struggle with doubt, ask Him to show up in a real way to you, and we know He will. And when He does, it's time to stop doubting, and believe.

—MH

Jesus Had X-Files

Jesus did many other things as well. If every one of them were written down, I suppose that even the whole world would not have room for the books that would be written. John 21:25.

There are four things in life I avoid like the plague: cleaning toilets, writing thank-you cards, making a commitment anytime before the last minute, and signing yearbooks. The last one still makes my academy friends mad at me. They wrote pages and pages in my yearbook, but though I kept theirs for five or six days I didn't write a word. I can't explain why, except maybe to say that the pressure was too much. It was easy to write to casual friends, but how could I sum up my best friendships in just a page or two? It would take weeks and chapters to completely describe all of our memories and capture everything they meant to me. So because I couldn't decide how to narrow it down to the highlights, I didn't write anything at all.

When he got to the end of his book, John also realized that though he actually had written a lot, it was still impossible to capture everything that Jesus had done. So he ends instead with the verse above, the closing verse of all the Gospels, where we end our journey with them as well. So as I'm writing this last Gospel reading tonight, I'm really feeling what John said. If I wrote a story about every amazing thing that Jesus did, this book would never, ever end. We have missed so much as it is: He fed 5,000 people from one snack, raised Lazarus to life, threw furniture in anger in the Temple, and one scorching day at a well told a woman her life's story. He washed His disciples' dirty feet, welcomed grubby little kids . . . there's so much more to say; I could write forever! But even then I would be writing only about the stories *I* know. John says there are many, many more stories that we will never know. Doesn't that make you wonder? Which ones did he leave out, ones that we must wait till heaven to hear? What else did Jesus do and say?

But that's the great thing about Jesus. There is always more to learn. You will never completely know Him. Even if you spend every day with Him and read every single verse in the Bible, you will still have more to learn about this Man. You'll never come to the end of His riches. So if you're starting to feel as if you've already heard everything there is to hear about Jesus, remember that you don't even know the half. Keep seeking Him, and you'll keep learning.

—MH

The One Behind It All

Do not leave Jerusalem, but wait for the gift my Father promised. . . . For John baptized with water, but in a few days you will be baptized with the Holy Spirit. Acts 1:4, 5.

Unless you fight it with all your might, you are going to turn out almost exactly like your parents. This is what my senior Bible textbook claimed, anyway, and as a high school student I guarantee you that the thought struck fear into my heart, as it might do to yours as well. Who wants to have all the annoying habits and tendencies we've already put up with in them for most of our lives? Who wants to make the same bad decisions and mistakes we're hurting from today? Not me! But as I get older I'm starting to realize that the textbook is alarmingly correct—when I'm angry I react the same as they did. In a pinch, my first instinct is to say things they used to say or rely on methods they once used. Thankfully, some of the time this has been great, because as it turns out they weren't the idiots I assumed they were. Either way, because we've spent such inordinate amounts of time with these people, they'll somehow silently be behind much of who we become in the future, like an invisible force we don't even notice.

The book of Acts has an invisible moving force behind it, as well: the Holy Spirit. Many of us don't know much about the Spirit; He's kind of mysterious. What does He *do,* anyway? Acts gives us one of the clearest pictures of just how much this invisible force is responsible for. He is behind almost every good thing anyone can say or do. He's the one who provided all the power for every miracle performed. Peter's escape from prison, Philip's disappearing act, Pentecost, all the healings—everything! He's also the one who first convicts the heart of each person who chooses Jesus. He's the reason for the talents and gifts given to every believer at their baptism. He convicts us of sin, fills people with power, teaches them to witness, and sends them out into the world for God. He's the one who draws us to Jesus, and is the reason we want to repent. In every move we make for or toward God, there is the power of the Spirit. Without Him we couldn't even want Jesus—He grows that in us too!

Perhaps you never realized before how much you need the Holy Spirit in your life. But that's OK, because He is available anytime you ask for Him. Chances are He's already with you, because you know what? If you are reading this, He drew you here in the first place.

—MH

Watch Your Language

And at this sound the multitude came together, and they were bewildered, because each one was hearing them speak in his own language. Acts 2:6, ESV.

When I was at Union College, one of my jobs was to work the desk at Prescott Hall in the boys' dorm. It was an easy job. I'd usually get four short calls in a four-hour shift and have the rest of the time to do homework or chat with friends who stopped by. But one night I answered the call of someone in crisis. The phone rang, and I answered it: "Prescott Hall. How can I help you?" The answer was very quiet and timid.

"José?"

"I'm sorry," I said, "I didn't catch his last name—is he a student here?"

"José?"

It was obvious this woman didn't speak English. No problem. There were only a handful of Josés and I knew most of them, so by process of elimination I found him and attempted to transfer the call. It would have been fine had José not been on his phone giving me a busy signal. I was forced to try to explain to the woman I presumed to be his mother that José was busy and that she should call back. She answered with a shriek: "JOSÉ!"

I was left with only one option. I transferred her to the girls' dorm to let them deal with it. It didn't take long for the call to bounce back with this poor woman wailing for José. Mercifully my Hispanic friend Gil walked in just then, and I frantically handed him the phone. He explained the situation to me, and the problem was resolved. What just happened? Was I telling this woman anything wrong? No, but I wasn't speaking her language.

One of the most amazing occurrences in the book of Acts is Pentecost. God pours out His Holy Spirit on His people, and they all spoke in tongues so that everybody heard the gospel in their own language. Sometimes we think there's only one way to communicate the gospel. Not true! Hebrews 1:1 and 2 tells us that God speaks to His people in many ways. Adults sometimes forget this when they try to connect with youth in church, and sometimes it's easy to forget this when youth try to worship in ways adults don't understand. It's important to give each other grace and seek to find ways to communicate God's love in ways we all understand.

—SP

Let the Party Begin!

While the beggar held on to Peter and John, all the people were astonished and came running to them in the place called Solomon's Colonnade. When Peter saw this, he said to them: "Men of Israel, why does this surprise you?" Acts 3:11, 12.

In college Greg and I became known as the people who would seize any and every opportunity to throw a party. When the first snow blew into town, we threw a hot drinks party, and everyone came with hot chocolate and cider and flavored teas. On hot summer nights we'd throw the windows open and have a jumpin' eighties' music party. We threw a mystery guessing party when we found out we were having a boy, and told friends to bring either pink or blue food, depending on their prediction. Beach bonfire parties, photo scavenger hunt parties, and bring-your-favorite-ice-cream-topping parties are among our favorites, as well as costume parties, soup night parties, couples' board game parties, and international food parties. Someone gets a new job, passes a hard class, or returns from a trip? A party is in order! And why let the dog's birthday go by without throwing a party for her as well! On our list right now is to have an ugly sweater party and a breakfast cook-off party. We don't really need an official occasion to throw a party; we'll jump at any chance to have fun together.

Peter was also the kind of guy who seized every single opportunity that came to him—not for a party, but to speak about Jesus. The book of Acts records that whenever a crowd gathers around, Peter stands up to preach. When he gets attention for healing a man, it's his chance to testify. If he's taken to court, instead of defending himself he shares the good news of Jesus rising from the dead. Peter doesn't need an official invitation or an easy opening. He uses any excuse he can find to tell the world about Jesus.

I'm afraid a lot of us do the opposite today. We shrink back from opportunities to talk about Jesus because we're embarrassed, don't want to feel awkward, or fear people will think we are weird. But wouldn't it be great if we were fearless like Peter? If you have the desire to share Jesus but not yet the courage, ask the Lord today to start sending you small opportunities to share His love and speak up for Him. You don't have to preach to the crowds, as Peter did. All you need to do is find a way and a place that fits your personality and works for who you are.

—MH

People Will Just Know

When they saw the courage of Peter and John and realized that they were unschooled, ordinary men, they were astonished and they took note that these men had been with Jesus. Acts 4:13.

Have you ever eaten something that stayed with you hours and hours later? Here in Seattle we have a joke about people who go to Safeco Field to see a game, and that joke has to do with the garlic fries. It's true that you go to Safeco Field to watch the ball game, but most people admit they have an ulterior motive for visiting the ballpark: the garlic fries! The park is famous for their huge, fat, thick French fries that they cover and smother in freshly grated globs of garlic. If you look down the rows in the bleachers at any given spot in the crowd, you can see hand after hand after hand cupped around a brimming cardboard package of garlic fries. Speak to anyone on the way out, and you'll smell the garlic on their breath. Ask someone the next day about the game, and you will know if they were there in person or if they just saw it on TV. How? You guessed it. The garlic. It's a local Seattle joke that everyone around you for the next week will know that you went to the ball game at Safeco Field, because for that entire week you will reek and stink of garlic. The smell is so strong that people in all directions can get one whiff of you and conclude, "Oh, garlic fries. Musta been to the game."

I've always thought Christianity should be like those garlic fries. Wouldn't it be cool if people could know that you'd been with Jesus just by spending a minute in your presence? Wouldn't it be amazing if the presence of God were so visible in your life that people didn't have to ask—they'd know where you'd been? I want that kind of walk with God, don't you?

Peter and John had that kind of walk with the Lord. In Acts, when they stood up before the Sanhedrin and gave their bold speech, the leaders were amazed. They knew that Peter and John were just ordinary guys, fishermen without any theological training. There was really nothing special or scholarly about them. And yet their lives sported the stamp of a greater power at work. It says then that the leaders took note that these men had been with Jesus.

When you spend time with Jesus, it shows. The effects stay in your life, and they point people to the Lord. People can see that there is something different about you. Ask the Lord today to fill your life so full of His Spirit that people will take note that you've been with Jesus.   —MH

Turning Around

God exalted him at his right hand as Leader and Savior, to give repentance to Israel and forgiveness of sins. Acts 5:31, ESV.

Several years ago I was driving the roads of Arkansas to a speaking appointment at Ozark Academy. And it was at one crucial juncture that my directions evaporated—at least that's the only explanation I can come up with. They were gone—and the highway split into two different directions. I chose the left option.

Soon I found myself cruising along a turnpike with a large concrete blockade separating me from the opposite lanes of traffic. I spent several minutes on the road before my internal compass began flashing warning signs. Something didn't feel right. I fumbled for my cell phone and called "my people" at Ozark, only to have them confirm my worst fear.

I had been traveling in the wrong direction for quite some time.

And traveling in the wrong direction becomes even worse when you can't turn around. On this particular turnpike there were no openings for me to get into the other lane traveling the opposite direction. I just kept driving in my error, completely powerless to turn around and go a different direction. Mercifully, after several miles an exit graciously presented itself and allowed me to turn around and head back in the right direction.

The word *repent* means to "turn around." It has to do with a realization that our life is headed in the wrong direction and we need a change. However, you and I are powerless to make that change. This startles some people who think that it is up to us to repent and gain God's favor—in reality, repentance is just as much God's grace.

In Acts we read that repentance is "given." In other words, we don't repent to get grace. Rather, we sense our need of change and repent as a *response* to God's grace. So when you feel remorse for something you have done, don't let it discourage you and make you think God is a long way away. The fact that you sense your need to change is God already at work in your heart giving you the "exit" you need to turn around.

—SP

Unstoppable

For if their purpose or activity is of human origin, it will fail. But if it is from God, you will not be able to stop these men; you will only find yourselves fighting against God.
Acts 5:38, 39.

He was unstoppable. The movie *Catch Me if You Can* was based on the life of a smart dude named Frank Abagnale, Jr. By 19 he had already impersonated a pilot, a doctor, a lawyer, and a university teaching assistant. He successfully passed off $2.5 million worth of forged checks across 26 different countries during a five-year period starting when he was 17. As he bounced around North America posing as a returning airline pilot in need of a lift to his next station, he began to feel as if he were invincible. Every time the police or the FBI got close, he was able to skip town and start a new life under an assumed name. When he was finally captured in France in 1969, the authorities there sent him to prison for a year. When he was released, they gladly handed him over to Sweden, where he was sentenced to another six months in prison. After his release from Sweden he was sent to Italy, for yet another round of trials, where the FBI finally caught up with him and revoked his U.S. passport. This forced Italy to send him home to Virginia, to a 12-year prison sentence for 12 counts of forgery. But en route to Virginia he escaped from a taxiing airliner, and later from a federal detention center in Atlanta, Georgia. Because the government was so impressed by his skill, they got him out of jail early when he agreed to work for them. They recognized his talent, respected it, and wanted it!

Dealing with truly unstoppable people, the teacher Gamaliel made a similar wise decision about the apostles as told in the book of Acts. They'd been brought before the authorities to be stopped, but Gamaliel urged the others to leave them alone in his "wait and see" ultimatum above. If they truly work for God, he claimed, then they would be absolutely unstoppable, and it would be futile to fight them. But if they were just working for themselves, the movement would eventually fail, as all movements without God finally do. The leaders listened to his counsel, and the apostles walked free. The rest of their lives bore overwhelming evidence that God was behind them.

You may have noticed that a lot of your own goals seem to fail. Be encouraged that when your purpose is in line with God's, nothing on earth can stop you, because all the power of heaven is behind you. To be truly unstoppable today, align your goals with the goals of heaven.

—GH and MH

Gregorio the Magnificent

Now a certain man named Simon had previously practiced magic in the city and amazed the people of Samaria, saying that he was someone great. . . . When Simon saw that the Spirit was given through the laying on of the apostles' hands, he offered them money, saying, "Give me also this power so that anyone on whom I lay my hands may receive the Holy Spirit." Acts 8:9-19, NRSV.

Basically I was the worst magician that ever waved a magic wand. I had read up on everything that I could find on such guys as Harry Houdini and David Copperfield. Countless hours were spent scouring the how-to books until I had acquired a fat list of card tricks, coin manipulations, and scarf disappearances. I put together all the tricks of the trade, such as the shaved decks of cards and false thumb covers. The "stage" was made from an upturned cardboard box painted purple with stars and a big sign that announced "Gregorio the Magnificent" in bright-red letters. With everything ready, I finally assembled my family and friends for my worldwide premier and began my first set. Unfortunately, the card trick didn't come off quite the way I'd hoped, and it took me four tries to pick the volunteer's card from the deck. The rope trick was a total flop, because my younger brother had removed the crucial trick piece of rope. Even my grand finale, a balloon trick that involved running a balloon through with needles, failed miserably when I successfully popped the oversized balloon amid peals of laughter from the crowd.

Simon Magus, a local sorcerer in Samaria, may have felt the same when Philip entered the region and began doing some "real" magic. People were cured of sickness; demons were driven out of the possessed. Simon wanted that power, and he was willing to pay handsomely for it. He begged Peter to sell him these powers, but Peter declared, "May your silver perish with you, because you thought you could obtain God's gift with money!" (Acts 8:20, NRSV).

It's a "tricky" thing, this gift of the Holy Spirit. But the one thing we know is that you don't get connected with God by figuring out the right words or calculating the correct number of hours to attend church. It's not a formula like that; it's a relationship. It's for people who sincerely want to search and find meaning from the Creator of all things. You don't go out and buy the gifts of Jesus—you just humbly accept them.

—GH

The Look That Changed a Lifetime

As he neared Damascus on his journey, suddenly a light from heaven flashed around him. He fell to the ground and heard a voice say to him, "Saul, Saul, why do you persecute me?" Acts 9:3, 4.

Nothing will ruin a date more completely than suddenly realizing you're with the wrong person. It was my freshman year in college, and I had bought a plane ticket for my out-of-state boyfriend so that he could attend the spring banquet with me. All in all, it had been a lovely evening. My dress was beautiful, my date was stunning, the banquet hall was grand, and the food delicious. The night would have been a total success if I hadn't looked up from my dessert. My date turned to talk to someone else and, for some reason, I looked toward the other tables. At that exact moment the crowd parted perfectly, and across the entire room I found myself staring straight at Greg—and he just happened to be staring back at me. We held that gaze for only a few seconds, but in those brief moments something clicked forever in my head. I was chasing the wrong guy. One look into Greg's eyes, and the proverbial scales fell from mine. Suddenly all became clear. I was sitting at the wrong table. I wanted to be at his.

On the road to Damascus, Saul also realized in a heartbeat that he was chasing the wrong person, and that everything he had been putting his life into was completely wrong. He was on a zealous mission to arrest and imprison every single Christian man or woman he could find, when suddenly a light flashed from heaven and a voice let Saul know that he was chasing Jesus Himself. Saul was speechless. He went blind, and his companions had to lead him to a house nearby, where he fasted and prayed for three whole days. Finally, when Ananias went in faith to see this dangerous and feared man, he touched Saul's eyes, and the Bible says that something like scales fell from them. Now he could see again. But this time he could see clearly. The purpose of his life had been changed forever, and he knew what his true mission was.

You wouldn't want to realize suddenly one day, in one sickening instant, that you have been chasing the wrong thing, would you? Have you stopped to think lately about what you are chasing? Is it a person? Are you just chasing yourself? Do you chase goals, dreams, fears, addictions? Or are you chasing Jesus? You don't want to find someday that all your time and energy went to the wrong place. Make a choice today of what you truly want to chase.

—MH

Playing Favorites

I now realize how true it is that God does not show favoritism but accepts men from every nation who fear him and do what is right. Acts 10:34, 35.

One of the worst things you can accuse your teachers of is having favorites. Oh, how mad that used to make me, an almost blatant claim that I am unfair! Teachers actually do have favorites, but we don't ever want you to know that. And we don't choose the favorites the way you think we do. Honestly, some kids are just a breath of fresh air. The ones who actually turn homework in, seem to care about what we say, and at least attempt to listen to the lecture we spent hours preparing—those students just make us happy. We can't help it!

The Jews truly believed that they were God's favorites, the only ones who would receive salvation. That's why Peter was so shocked when God sent him to the Gentiles after his vision of the sheet of wildly unclean animals that God pronounced symbolically clean. It was almost unthinkable to a Jew that God would reach out to Gentiles. All throughout the Old Testament God championed only the Israelites, it seemed, and allowed the destruction of all the other nations around them. God appeared to have a chosen people, a "favorite." But what the Jews didn't understand was that His chosen ones weren't the only people chosen for salvation. Rather, they were chosen to bring salvation to the rest of the world. But they didn't do that, as we saw in the Old Testament. So when His "chosen" instruments didn't reach out to the world, God knew someone else would have to do it: Jesus Himself. Jesus' life was a living testimony that salvation was for everyone—Samaritans, Romans, sinners, centurions, slaves.

God shows no favorites. He wants us all! Unfortunately, we're a little more like Peter than we'd care to admit. We think certain people, races, or social groups are better than others, or maybe even that certain Christians are better than others. Because we have a message that is loyal to the Bible, and because our lifestyle is so beneficial, we Adventists often look down on other denominations. But as Peter found out, this isn't the way God wants us acting. Are there people who you look down on as "unclean" or unimportant? While you may be "hating" these people, God is actively trying to save them. This is a good time for you to ask the Lord to change your heart, as He did Peter's, and teach you to love and appreciate people you've been shunning.

—MH

When Storm Clouds Like Sea Billows Roll

He then brought them out and asked, "Sirs, what must I do to be saved?" Acts 16:30.

It's not the earthquake that surprises me. We've seen that happen before quite a few times. The time doesn't throw me either. Midnight sounds about right. I'm also not fazed by doors flying open, and I'm not shocked about the chains randomly coming loose. All these things are what you would expect when God shows up—it just smacks of Him, it's how He rolls. What surprises me the most is actually the fact that they were singing! Singing hymns, no less, as they sat there with their feet in the stocks. I mean, who does this? Especially from a jail cell, after a long hard day of being attacked by a crowd, stripped naked, beaten up, and severely flogged. But it's how we find Paul and Silas when God shows up—praying and singing to the whole jail.

When I have a bad day, I admit that you won't find me singing. I usually call up lots of people to complain to, or get out my journal and write all my depressing thoughts. Sometimes I put on a movie in order to forget, or beg my husband to take me out on the town to cheer me up. If I'm really mad, I pout or go silent for fear I'll say something I'll regret. And as for Greg, well, he stomps around delivering angry diatribes to imaginary audiences. So we probably aren't the kind of people who'd be singing in jail, though we'd like to be.

Maybe Paul and Silas could have been trying to encourage themselves, or were trying to cheer each other up. Maybe they were putting on a good face for the other prisoners, or hoping they would find comfort in the words of the hymns. But I don't think so. I like to think it was because they knew a secret, a secret Paul wrote about many years later from another prison: "I have learned the secret of being content in any and every situation" (Philippians 4:12).

The secret is both knowing and trusting Jesus. Knowing Him personally gives you that peace beyond understanding, and trusting Him means that you are free to accept absolutely anything that happens to you, even the horrible things, because you believe He has a purpose and a way to bring you through. He's the master of making something good out of a mess. Just look at what happened that night in the jail. When the jailer realized that in spite of the earthquake all the prisoners were still there, he knew that Paul and Silas had something he wanted too. He accepted Jesus, and he with his entire family were baptized right there. We can sing when we trust God with the end.

—MH

Misplacing an Entire Day

Then they took him and brought him to a meeting of the Areopagus, where they said to him, "May we know what this new teaching is that you are presenting? You are bringing some strange ideas to our ears, and we want to know what they mean." Acts 17:19, 20.

The scientific team from NASA stood in front of the computer screens, scratching their heads. After working for months to calculate the paths that satellites will travel, they'd finally been able to predict the positions of the moon and planets to make sure any future satellites launched wouldn't run into any surprises. But the calculations weren't coming up the way they should have. They looked into it further and found that their calculations were off by almost a full day. The moon seemed to be about 24 hours ahead of itself. With no answers coming to them, a Christian man on the team grabbed a Bible and turned to the story of the day Joshua called on the sun to stand still. The scientists were amazed that they had discovered, in the Bible, the reason for their miscalculation. NASA had just confirmed the Bible story!

That would be a great story—*if it were true!* Sadly, some well-intentioned Christian sent it off as an e-mail forward, thinking it would convince nonbelievers. This kind of stuff may be sort of funny, but it's one of the biggest reasons an intelligent society often chooses to throw Christianity out as naive and dishonest. When Paul came to Athens, the capital of the cultural and intellectual world of his time, he didn't lie about his faith to make it sound more spectacular. He just used a simple example from their own culture. Among all the altars to the Greek gods he noticed one that was "to the unknown god." Given the chance to speak, he stood before the philosophers of the city, pointed to that altar, and said, "I come to tell you about the unknown god that that altar was built for." Quoting their own poets and philosophers, he gave a simple view of the Jesus' gospel and sacrifice.

The Bible and its gospel message don't need manufactured evidence to be plausible. They need are people whose lives have been changed because of that message, and can simply tell it in the language of regular people. They need Christians who are living examples of the kind of impact Jesus makes in a life. So don't rely on shady e-mail forwards or someone else's faith to get the message out there. The best evidence for Christianity is your own changed life.

—GH

You Can Just Kind of Fake It

But the evil spirit said to them in reply, "Jesus I know, and Paul I know; but who are you?" Then the man with the evil spirit leaped on them, mastered them all, and so overpowered them that they fled out of the house naked and wounded. Acts 19:15, 16, NRSV.

You can be pretenders!" he claimed. The professor looked over the students. Not from the United States, he'd been a pastor for many years throughout the world. "Here in America you don't really have to have an active relationship with Jesus to be a pastor." The students were a little stunned, but he had their attention. "You can just kind of fake it here, if you're a nice person. If you visit with people in their homes and preach good sermons, everyone will think you're a good pastor. You'll have some problems along the way, but for the most part you can just fake it and no one will know that your spiritual life is dead. But where I come from it's not uncommon for me or another pastor to be up preaching on Sabbath morning, and suddenly some sort of demonic manifestation arises from someone in the audience. If I'm standing there preaching when this happens, I am going to have to deal with it. I have to be involved in a living, vibrant connection with Jesus at that point in my life, or else it is painfully obvious to everyone there, and their trust in me as their pastor is *gone!* If the demon doesn't respond to my commands for it to leave, the lack of my relationship with Jesus becomes apparent to everyone present."

The seven sons of Sceva, from the passage above, tried to fake a connection with Jesus. They were getting paid by people to cast out demons, and since they'd heard about Jesus they decided to use His name when commanding the spirits. But it backfired. The evil spirit said it knew Jesus, but had no idea who they were. Then it literally beat them up!

If you're just faking a relationship with Jesus, sooner or later it's going to become evident. Jesus calls each of us into a lifelong relationship with Him, not so we can become nice people or members of a church. The truth is that we need a relationship with Jesus to protect and direct our lives so that they're the best they can be. It can be easy to fake a spiritual walk. But when things get bad and we need something to hold on to, faking won't cut it. We need something *real* to hold on to. Christianity isn't pointless—it meets our most basic needs. We need a connection, a love without limits. We need a Savior who has been where we are.

—GH

Almost

Then Agrippa said to Paul, "You almost persuade me to become a Christian."
Acts 26:28, NKJV.

What better way to celebrate Thanksgiving Day, the day on which we thank God for all He has given us, by going out and getting more? This year I was primed and ready to go and sit outside all night at a popular electronics store with my sleeping bag just to upgrade my laptop. But to justify this kind of purchase, I had to offload the current laptop and use the money for the new one. So I posted the ad online and waited for the happy consumers to make their offers. I got only two, and one of them was amazing. It was from a fellow who lived outside the United States, and needed the laptop sent to a friend in another country. He was willing to pay more than twice as much as the laptop was listed for, and would send an extra $200 to have it shipped! The dollar figures danced in my head, and I could picture myself getting an even better laptop than I had planned on. I was sold! But then something began to smell fishy. His spelling was off, and his responses came from two different e-mail accounts. He was ready to send me the money that day! Internet transfer, click of the mouse, all mine! Just minutes before I made the deal, I hunted online a little and found a Web site that described a scam eerily similar to what I was experiencing. The buyer would claim that the item never came, so the money transfer site would refund their payment from the seller's account! They'd keep my laptop and get their money back, too! A mean but effective way to be ripped off. I had almost been persuaded, but not quite.

Paul tried his best to convince King Agrippa of the truth of Jesus Christ. Agrippa had asked specifically to hear Paul, and he seemed to listen with interest to his speech—until Paul gave him the chance to make a commitment. Not ready to make such a big decision, he told Paul that he had *almost* persuaded him, but almost isn't good enough when it comes to salvation.

Trust me. You don't want to be a Christian who was *almost* persuaded. So many people today come so close to accepting Jesus, but then decide they need more proof, fewer rules, or something else. A lot of people who go through Christian schools and grow up in Christian homes *almost* commit to following the lifestyle they were taught, but then decide to give it up for worldly goals or desires. In the end, *almost* doesn't bring you into the full richness of the redeemed life. Don't be an *almost* person. Go all the way and commit yourself 100 percent to Jesus.

—GH and MH

Things That Go Boom

I am not ashamed of the gospel, because it is the power of God for the salvation of everyone who believes. Romans 1:16.

I don't know what it is about boys, but I've noticed that they like to watch things blow up. My husband and his friends will watch the same YouTube videos of crazy kids lighting things on fire. It's extremely funny to them if the explosion does not go quite according to plan. I think their favorite video ever has to do with some kids who filled a large pumpkin full of dynamite and firecrackers, and then set it on fire. You'd think the kids would've been content to watch it burn and then explode, but no, they had a better plan. One young witty fellow approached the flaming pumpkin with a baseball bat in hand, reared back, and took full swing at the fiery mass. The pumpkin, of course, detonated, and the Darwin-award-winning kid was immediately encircled by flaming pieces of flying pumpkin. I believe his sandal caught on fire, and he spent the rest of the video dancing around like a madman, frantically trying to kick it off. These examples of quality home entertainment will leave my husband and his friends literally rolling on the floor in crying fits of laughter. What is it about guys and explosions?

As we enter Romans—the most detailed and complete exposition we have on salvation in the entire Bible—we find Paul saying that the gospel is the power of God for the salvation of everyone who believes. This doesn't sound like much, until you realize that the Greek word for "power" is actually *dunamis*—the word we get "dynamite" from. Paul is saying that the gospel is like dynamite. It's supposed to be an explosion, a great fiery inferno of energy radiating out to everything around it. I think back to the videos I've seen of major bomb explosions and the like, and I see the gospel in a whole new light. So often it just seems like "the old, old story"— something we've heard at least a hundred dozen times. But it's not supposed to be mundane like that. It's supposed to have power, like actual dynamite.

If the story of Jesus doesn't feel like that in your heart anymore, maybe it's time you went back and spent some new time with it. Paul claims that the power of salvation should be like dynamite in your life. If it's not that way today, ask the Lord to open the story up for you and make it real, bring it to life. When He does, it'll top any explosion you've ever seen.

—MH

Maybe There Is No God?

For since the creation of the world God's invisible qualities—his eternal power and divine nature —have been clearly seen, being understood from what has been made, so that men are without excuse. Romans 1:20.

So much comic relief comes into a teacher's life simply from having to listen to the wide range of pathetic excuses students come up with. One day Clifton tried to ask me out on a date because he was hoping to distract me from collecting his paper. Joon used to insist that he couldn't do his homework when he was in a fight with his parents, which apparently was all the time. Brandon's excuse was always that he'd been asleep when I gave the assignment. (That was probably true, now that I think about it.) And who could ever forget dear Jeff, whose excuse was his paper-filing method of rolling papers into balls and shoving them into his bag? My favorite excuse of all time came from the girl who hit a squirrel and her grief "paralyzed" her.

If you're listening, you'll hear that people make a lot of excuses when it comes to religion and God, too. Many insist that the Bible is either mythology or a very old record of cultural norms that don't apply to us anymore. Some say Jesus was a farce. Others say truth can't be known this side of eternity, so why bother trying to find it? Perhaps the most devastating excuse of all is that there is no God, and religion is nothing more than a made-up coping strategy.

In the face of all these excuses, the voice of the apostle Paul rings out loud and clear saying that people are absolutely without excuse for their unbelief and evil. Why? Because God deliberately made sure that we have enough evidence to believe in Him. Romans says His power, His character, and His qualities have all been made clear to us through the things He has made, meaning through creation. Isn't that an interesting thought? That in creation there is enough evidence to convict us that God exists, and that His ways are just and right.

Maybe you have toyed with the idea that God doesn't exist—just think, you could do whatever you wanted! Maybe you're frustrated with trying to prove Him or know Him. But even if doubt and unbelief sound tempting some days, don't toy with them. Paul says you'll be without excuse if you do. Decide you will choose faith as many times as it takes, and just trust that the rest of the things we don't see or understand now will be made clear one day soon.

—MH

Missing the Mark

For all have sinned and fall short of the glory of God. Romans 3:23.

During the 2007 season of NFL football the New England Patriots managed to get themselves to the Super Bowl without having lost a game all season long. The stakes were high as they had in their grasp a perfect undefeated season. Their opponents were the Giants, a team with a good—but by no means perfect—record.

I remember watching the game with friends and seeing fans in the stands holding up anti-Patriot signs that read 18-1. The "18" represented games won, and the one represented games lost. In other words, the fans cheering for the Giants wanted them to give the Patriots a less-than-perfect season—making the Super Bowl the Patriots' only loss. The game was fun to watch, and unfortunately for the Patriots, those fans' signs proved prophetic.

They lost.

Their perfection disappeared, swallowed up by a devastating defeat. They had come so far, done so many amazing things, gotten the victory over so many opponents, only to fall short at the end of the championship.

You and I have the same experience. We can go along for a while—living our lives for Jesus, treating others in a loving way, attending and participating in church, and being a perfect example of faith. Then we fall. We give in to temptation, in to sin, and many times in to despair at our lack of perfection. We experience so much victory only to have it all stripped away. Maybe it was losing that spiritual high coming back from a youth rally, or maybe you resolved to be more like Jesus after a previous mess-up— but it all ended the same. Defeat.

That's why I take courage from this famous passage in Romans. Paul is making the case that *everybody*—not just you—messes up. We all need God's grace. This isn't an excuse or a license to sin, but it is a comfort when we feel like we're the only one who can't walk the walk of faith. Next time you fall, remember you are not alone. Even the most spiritual people struggle. The difference is what you do next. Resolve to be the kind of Christian who gets up and tries again.

—SP

Daddy and the Bike

And [all] are justified freely by his grace through the redemption that came by Christ Jesus. Romans 3:24.

We didn't notice the angry dog charging in our direction until it was too late. From my cozy nook in the kiddie seat on the back of the bike, all my 3-year-old eyes could see was my daddy's strong back, swaying as he pedaled, and the white blur of fur up ahead that was our dog, Jake. At the end of our ride Daddy would hook Jake's leash to the bike handles, and he'd eagerly pull us up the last steep stretch of hill. Good old Jake always carried us safely to the top. But when the attacking dog came out of nowhere, naturally Jake lunged at the dog to fight back and protect us. He just forgot one detail: he was still tied to the bike. Instantly we lurched forward, and then were thrown down toward the pavement. Being so small and sitting up so high on my bike chair, I remember the blacktop of the street inching closer and closer, almost in slow motion. Expecting to smash down terribly on the hard ground, I was surprised when I fell instead onto Daddy's much softer body. When we finally untangled ourselves from the mess of bike, leash, and dogs, Daddy was torn up and bleeding, scraped everywhere, and limping as he walked. I didn't understand what had happened until I heard him telling Mom later that he'd thrown himself backward in order to break my fall and save me. For the next few weeks those bloody, healing scabs and scratches seemed to tell me just how much my daddy loved me, because he had thrown himself in harm's way when I couldn't save myself.

As I grew up, this bike story became a metaphor of Jesus for me. Though He could have saved Himself easily, He deliberately threw Himself in sin's way to save us when we were helpless to save ourselves. Romans describes why we are helpless. The law has us strapped up like a seat belt, convicting us of sin but unable to save us, since we can't keep it completely. But a holy God can—and did. We read yesterday that every single one of us has sinned and fallen short. But in spite of our sin, we are still "justified freely by his grace." The fact that we could never earn it makes it so important that it's free. We don't have to buy it, deserve it, or pay for it. Grace is a gift you'd be crazy to refuse. "Free" may sound too simple, but it wasn't simple for Jesus. Recall the blood, see the scars, and know you are loved beyond belief.

—MH

How to Remove a Dead Animal

What shall we say, then? Shall we go on sinning so that grace may increase? By no means! We died to sin; how can we live in it any longer? . . . We were therefore buried with him through baptism into death in order that . . . we too may live a new life. Romans 6:1, 2, 4.

There's nothing that can ruin the joyful discovery of a beautiful shell so much as taking it home and finding something inside that was previously alive—and stinking to high heaven. One day while scuba diving in the islands I found a foot-long conch shell and brought it home. Within hours the foul scent of death testified that the shell and I were not alone. I tried pulling out the long musclelike animal twisted around inside the shell, but only a piece came off. So I put the shell in water. No luck. I consulted with my islander friends, who offered a simple solution: bury the shell, and in a month the animal would be gone. Confused, I asked for clarification about this seemingly magical suggestion. They explained that tiny ants and insects in the ground would eat the dead animal right out of the shell. I had my doubts, but I buried it anyway. Sure enough, when I pulled it up out of the ground and rinsed it off, it was as sparklingly clean as can be.

There's something stinking and rotting wrapped up inside all of us, too— sin. It, too, seems impossible to get out, but God offers a strange-sounding solution through baptism: our sins will be buried with Jesus, and we'll come up a new person. It's not that the waters make us clean, but they symbolize the fact that choosing Jesus' perfect record over our messy one clears sin's hold on our life. We don't belong to it anymore, so we can live in full enjoyment of grace.

Can grace ever be taken too far, though? I want to say no, but Paul says it actually can. He talks above about people using grace as an excuse to keep sinning. We hear this argument from a lot of Christians today—that it doesn't matter what we do because God gives us grace. But Paul strongly disagrees with this idea by saying that once you have died to sin, why would you ever want to go back to living in it? It's not a better, freer way to live. It's bondage! It's stinking, rotting decay in our lives, and it ruins the freedom and peace grace wants to give us.

If you've been thinking about baptism lately, realize that it's the only solution for the rot that is inside you. And once you're free of this nastiness, it's just plain crazy to go back to it!

—MH

When Sin Seems Like a Great Idea

Don't you know that when you offer yourselves to someone to obey him as slaves, you are slaves to the one whom you obey? Romans 6:16.

I haven't really stolen a whole lot of things in my life (besides road cones—see earlier story), so I guess I'm not really in a position to criticize, but one of the stupidest theft stories I've ever heard was about a man who stole a dead dog. This old woman lost her dog and had to take it to the vet to have it cremated. She couldn't just carry him onto the bus in her arms, and she didn't own a car. She decided to pack him into a suitcase and board the bus like a common traveler. Well, the dog turned out to be so heavy that the woman could hardly pull the suitcase on her own. A seemingly kind man offered to help her with the burden, but when he too felt how heavy it was, he asked, "What on earth is in here, lady?" Embarrassed about a dead dog being inside, and too grieved about her loss to explain, the woman simply answered, "Oh, just computer parts." At this the man paused, raised his eyebrows, and then took off with the suitcase. He was never found, but imagine the surprise when the thief opened that suitcase! His computer parts turned out to be a dead dog!

I don't know if that story is even true, but it surely is funny to think about that guy lugging the suitcase all the way home and then opening it. Trying to picture him looking in utter disappointment at a dead dog falling out of his suitcase makes me laugh out loud. Sometimes what we think we're getting away with doesn't always turn out to be that great in the end, does it? You think you're stealing a jackpot. Instead, you unzip a dead dog. Or maybe you think that indulging in a certain sin will bring you a lot of happiness and satisfaction. Instead, you get a really big mess. Ever been there?

We often think that our choice sin is what we really, truly want. We put a lot of effort into that sin, and we drag it around with us, like the man with the suitcase. But in the end, isn't it always disappointing? We thought we were getting freedom and fun, but it's just a big letdown. Then it traps us as well, makes us slaves to it so we can't escape. Don't be fooled by sin. It's not a suitcase of wealth. It's not what it seems to be at all. In the end it usually just ends up stinking even worse than an old dead dog.

—MH

Sand Trap

For I do not do the good I want, but the evil I do not want is what I keep on doing.
Romans 7:19, ESV.

My friend Dennis is an avid golfer—and most of us at church who golf with him are not. Therefore, whenever Dennis has a bad day on the links it makes us all feel a little better. In golf a sand trap is a perpetual menace that's strategically placed around the course. It's a big sand pit that threatens to swallow up your ball and makes it difficult to get back onto the green. If you're good enough with a wedge, you can make it out in one shot and emerge not much worse for wear. When Dennis gets into a sand trap (he rarely does), we expect him to get out in one stroke.

Halfway through our 18-hole outing, we all delighted in Dennis driving his ball straight into the sand trap on the left side of the short grass next to the hole. Dennis works in the auto industry and is a fantastic salesman and one of our best greeters at church. He keeps his cool and is very friendly and personable. There was only a hint of irritation as Dennis went to the trap to get his ball out. But instead of his usual perfect chip shot landing him next to the hole, he botched it up and sent the ball in a gentle arc over the hole and straight into the sand trap on the right. It was a marvelous scene for the rest of us, who were still trying to find our balls in the bulrushes. We clapped and made comments, and Dennis was visibly annoyed and muttered under his breath a few words at himself. Landing in the sand trap is not what Dennis wanted to do, or what he usually did, yet there he was.

Paul tells us in his letter to the Romans that he finds himself in a struggle, doing what he does not want to do. You and I can relate. How many times have you found yourself back in the same habit you told yourself you wouldn't be caught in? Or maybe you have feelings for someone—good or bad—that you said you wouldn't have again and yet— there they are.

We are caught in a war. We have the good thoughts and intentions that come from God that war against the bad habits and tendencies of our bodies. It's a constant struggle. Thankfully, Paul concludes in Romans 7 that even though our minds may want to do the right thing—and our bodies don't—we can trust that Jesus looks at our hearts in times of weakness. Praise God today for the grace He gives you and me when we find ourselves doing what we don't want to do.

—SP

> In the same way, the Spirit helps us in our weakness. We do not know what we ought to pray for, but the Spirit himself intercedes for us with groans that words cannot express. Romans 8:26.

When a good friend is having a hard time talking with the girl he likes, it makes you want to step in and help. So I devised different ways that Ryan could bump into Melanie and strike up a conversation. But he chickened out every time. Finally I got tired of talking about it and demanded that he take some sort of action. I threatened to call her myself and tell her to call *him*. He laughed and said I'd never do such a thing, which for a young man my age was like putting a match to gasoline. "Yeah, you're probably right," I grinned. I gave him about 10 minutes, just long enough to let any lingering suspicions fall out of his mind, and then I looked up the girl's phone number and gave her a call. Luckily she picked right up, and I said, "Hey, my friend Ryan has been trying to get hold of you. You should give him a call. I think he's even home right now." She said thanks and cheerfully hung up to call him back. When I got to school the next day, I waited for my friend to show up. He came right at me like a bolt of lightning. "Melanie called me yesterday and said *you* told her to call me!"

"Uh-huh," I said nonchalantly.

"I didn't have anything to say! I had just gotten a Popsicle out of the freezer and let the whole thing melt in my hand while I fumbled around sounding like an idiot for 15 minutes!"

Sometimes that's exactly how I feel about prayer. I can go to all the trouble to get up early, and wind up praying some weird variation of my lunchtime prayers. So when the Bible says our weakness is that we don't know how to pray as we should, it's not kidding! But the beauty here is found in how the Spirit "helps us in our weakness." I mean, this is God stepping in when *we're* supposed to be the ones talking. The Greek word for "intercedes" means He makes petitions for us. This shows us that even if we don't know how to say something, God is there to fill in the gaps. He's so excited to hear from us that He jumps in to help us communicate when we don't know how. So if you feel as if you don't know what you're asking for, the best thing to do is to just say something anyway. The Bible guarantees us that God will interpret the true feelings of our hearts, even if we don't know them ourselves. Just give prayer a try.

—GH

Stealing Prayers at the Burning Bush

For I am convinced that neither death nor life, neither angels nor demons, neither the present nor the future, nor any powers, neither height nor depth, nor anything else in all creation, will be able to separate us from the love of God that is in Christ Jesus our Lord. Romans 8:38, 39.

Did you know you can visit the actual burning bush of Moses? When I was in Egypt we spent an afternoon at a monastery nestled near the base of Mount Sinai, which claims to house the original burning bush where God dwelt in the fire while Moses stood, barefoot, and received his calling. This giant green, tangled mess of a bush sits at the far end of a stone-paved path in the monastery behind a high wall that has been built around it. I don't know if it's the real burning bush or not (I was skeptical), but what interested me was the large crowd gathered around the bush, praying to it. Many were writing short prayers on scraps of paper, rolling them up, and shoving them into holes and crevices in the wall around the bush, hundreds of them, so many that nobody would ever notice if I read just one. So I did. While the crowds petitioned the bush, I discreetly read its words: "God: Finally, I found a place to talk to You."

That was a curious idea. What else might be in there? I read another. And another.

"I wish I could live here, heavenly Father, close to You in this bush."

"Speak to me here for once, Lord, like You spoke to Moses."

"Do You still love me, Jesus?"

What rang loud and clear in my mind (as I tried not to be caught replacing the prayers) was the thought that people feel so separated from God that they think a big fat regular bush will bring them what they're missing. I wanted to post a big sign up on the wall with the verse above—Paul's guarantee that nothing in all the world can separate us from God's love. We don't need to be in a holy location to hear Him or feel Him. He's with us now.

Are there things in your life that make you feel separated from God's love? Maybe mistakes you hate, habits you love, choices you shouldn't have made? Have you ever had that morning-after feeling when you wake up and wonder why you did what you did yesterday? Take heart and read the list above. It's pretty extensive. Your present, your future, the depths you've fallen to, and the powers that hold you—*nothing* can separate you from God's love. Ever.

—MH

Chili Feet

Do not be misled: "Bad company corrupts good character." 1 Corinthians 15:33.

Walking around for a month with shaving cream residue and garlic salt in your shoes is a great reason not to go to slumber parties. Or at least not to go to any of mine. One of the great joys of my teenage life was Mom's allowing me to invite a houseful of girls to stay overnight. About 15 of us giggled through the wee hours of the morning watching movies, eating junk food, playing truth or dare, and talking about boys. But at some point the scene turned ugly. I had invited several groups of girls who didn't get along, but I thought they would at least try to be civil at my house. I was wrong. About 3:00 a.m. they decided the prank wars would begin. Girls who were dozing off awoke suddenly to a head full of shaving cream. Others came to in a sneezing fit from the pepper that had been sprinkled on their faces. Sleeping bags were doused in soda, makeup was stolen, and shoes were filled with spices.

As my friends silently ambushed each other in the night, I was horrified at their meanness and disappointed that they would ruin my birthday party. I made the mistake of hanging around to watch. More and more pranks were pulled, and pretty soon it became almost funny. Then it was funny. Then it was *really* funny. By morning I was joining in with the rest of them, painting mascara moustaches onto the upper lips of my sleeping friends, sprinkling chili powder in their hair, and filling their shoes with dollops of Elmer's Glue and Pert Plus. I had become one of them.

Paul was pretty clear on the fact that we become like the people we hang around with. The ancient city of Corinth was known for both its wealth and its wickedness, and the new Christian church was struggling to be different. Many of the issues Paul addresses in this letter center on Christian conduct—how to grow and develop our characters. When he writes the above caution, that "bad company corrupts good character," he is advising them not to be influenced by the evil people in the city who might still be their friends.

Most of us think we are strong enough to keep our friends from changing us, but unfortunately the changes can be so subtle and slow that we don't notice them until one morning we wake up a different person. For this reason, make wise choices in friends. Be careful whom you spend large amounts of time with. Soon you just might look like them.

—MH

Doing Your Job

For just as the body is one and has many members, and all the members of the body, though many, are one body, so it is with Christ. . . . If one member suffers, all suffer together; if one member is honored, all rejoice together. 1 Corinthians 12:12, 26, ESV.

During a game on October 5, 2008, the Houston Texans made several bungles that wiped out their massive lead and gave the game away to the Indianapolis Colts. The Texans' quarterback, Sage Rosenfels, had played extremely well, placing his team way out front, so that with only four minutes left in the game the commentators had dismissed the Colts from making a comeback--until the Texans' quarterback made a move that sent the team on a downward spiral to defeat. After the ball had been hiked, Sage looked for an open player. Seeing he had no options, he decided to play like a defensive lineman and run it. Not the best choice, but viable if you run for a few yards then slide, effectively "downing the ball" and ending the play before you get tackled. This is an important move for quarterbacks, since they're not usually built to encounter the opposing team's players head-on. But instead of downing the ball, Sage attempted to leap over three tacklers to get farther down the field. (The result is available at youtube.com if you search "Sage Rosenfels" and "helicopter" together.) Sage made an impressive leap, but was struck by three tacklers in midair.

The result was gorgeous. He was blasted into the air, then spun around a couple times before slamming to the ground and fumbling the ball to the Colts, who scored a touchdown. Fueled by that play, the Colts went on to win the game, scoring one touchdown after another. Sage looked as if he were on another planet. He should have played like a quarterback, not a defensive lineman.

God gives various gifts to various people in the church, and we're all called to work together as one unit, one team. However, some people try to do everything themselves. They don't delegate, they don't share, and they try to do other people's work for them. The result is not only extreme irritation on the part of others, but burnout and exhaustion for the person hogging all the jobs. Today, take a look at what you're doing and ask yourself if it's something someone else should be doing. Are you delegating, sharing the work, or doing everything yourself so that you can be in the spotlight?

—SP

Heads Carolina, Tails California

When I was a child, I talked like a child, I thought like a child, I reasoned like a child. When I became a man, I put childish ways behind me. 1 Corinthians 13:11.

The plan was to tell our mothers we were at the other's house, hop an airplane, and fly away for the weekend to an exotic secret location. My best friend, Brooke, and I made the plan late one night in the dorm when we were feeling especially trapped and locked up. The more we thought about it, the more we loved the idea—nobody in the world would even know where we were! We could fly to New York or Key West or even Honolulu. It didn't matter. We'd flip a coin and decide which direction to go! Our final decision was to earn perfect attendance that semester and make enough cash to fund our escape. For weeks we dreamed about this fairy-tale trip. How we longed for it! Every time we were down or discouraged at school, we'd remind each other of the trip and how we had to wait just another month or so till we were free! It was the greatest dream of our lives at that point in time. I'm sad to say that we never did go.

This past fall, Brooke found herself on bed rest in the hospital for several months with a complicated third pregnancy, unable even to walk. From time to time I'd go online and read her blog, and there she bravely described how difficult it was for her to be away from her kids and her home. If she had just one wish now, instead of longing for an exotic vacation she'd want only a simple day with her family. It's funny how our desires change as we grow up, isn't it?

Right in the middle of "the love chapter," following his list of "love is patient" and "love is kind," Paul makes the above statement about a shift in thinking from childish ways to adult ways. What does this verse have to do with love? Paul is talking about the most excellent way to live—a life full of love for others. He says love matters more than anything else. When we're kids, we think silly things are important. But when we grow up, we realize what really matters most, and what just doesn't. Are you focusing your energy right now on childish things instead of on the greatest thing of all—love? Will what you're giving your time to even matter 10 years from now? Does your life seem to need more patience and kindness and less recordkeeping of wrongs? If so, take a moment to ask God for the things that matter the most in this life we are living. You know, the old staples—faith, hope, and love.

—MH

Jag Alskar Dig—Sej Be Ko Bein

NOVEMBER

11

Unless you speak intelligible words with your tongue, how will anyone know what you are saying? . . . If the whole church comes together and everyone speaks in tongues, and . . . some unbelievers come in, will they not say that you are out of your mind? 1 Corinthians 14:9, 23.

The only time I ever tried to speak in tongues was to an angry security guard at midnight—from a hot tub. Our family had checked into our hotel after the pool and spa had closed for the night. My siblings and I decided to quietly climb the fence and jump into the hot tub anyway. If you knew the four of us, you'd know that we don't do anything quietly, even when we try, so in no time at all we had aroused the interest of a passing hotel security guard. He unlocked the gate and burst into the swimming area, shouting in a thick Spanish accent that we were to get out of the pool immediately. I can't remember now if we planned this or not, but without missing a beat, I looked the man straight in the face and began speaking to him plainly—in perfect Swedish. My brother Russell jumped in and began counting to 10 in German, and I followed up innocently with the entire chorus of a Marshallese praise song, then counted in Japanese. These were the only foreign phrases we knew besides Spanish, and we figured the guard would assume we didn't speak English, couldn't read the "Pool Closed" signs, and forgive us for jumping the fence. And he did! He gestured wildly for us to get out, and in mock confusion we made our way back to the hotel room, where we laughed till our sides hurt.

As you might be thinking, this isn't real speaking in tongues. But what you may not realize is that a lot of what happens in churches today isn't real speaking in tongues either, not according to the biblical description of it, anyway. In 1 Corinthians 14 Paul goes into detail about how speaking in tongues should function and what it should look like. These guidelines say that tongues should be used only if someone who can interpret them is there, and that the main purpose of tongues is to build up the church. So if they aren't interpreted, then they can't build up anyone, and Paul says you'll just be speaking to the air. The idea of a roomful of people mumbling and babbling to themselves doesn't seem to fit Paul's description in this case. Every church practice should always be judged against the Bible, so if something just doesn't seem quite right to you, go back to the Scriptures and check it out!

—MH

A Paper Cut in the Grand Scheme of Eternity

For our light and momentary troubles are achieving for us an eternal glory that far out-weighs them all. So we fix our eyes not on what is seen, but on what is unseen. For what is seen is temporary, but what is unseen is eternal. 2 Corinthians 4:17, 18.

Having already been fighting against a new law that made it illegal to openly "convert" people to their faith, local Christians in the Indonesian town of Meulaboh were trying to come together for a Christmas celebration. They were warned, though, that the public sentiment among the town's Muslim believers was becoming increasingly antagonistic, so they decided it would be safer to move the celebration outside the city to a nearby hilltop. Many of the Christians were upset about this and grumbled their way along to the primitive site over-looking the town. They had pleaded with God that the feelings against them would change, but so far He'd been silent. All through Christmas Day these be-lievers tried to celebrate and enjoy a spirit of festivity, but the knowledge that they had had to leave their homes and church back in Meulaboh gnawed at them. On the morning of December 26, 2004, they made their way down the hillside, only to see that a terrible tsunami had decimated not only their town but a massive portion of coastal Indonesia, as well as the island of Sri Lanka—and their church, where they would have been that morning when the tsunami hit. God hadn't forgotten—He had spared.

How many times in our lives do we feel like God is letting us down, when really He's behind the scenes, somehow using bad circumstances to help us out? I've never been a fan of the idea that God makes bad things happen to test us or to teach us a lesson. That's a sick view of God, in my opinion. I think bad things happen as a result of bad choices that people make, which, unfortunately, can affect those around them; free choice has its consequences. God has a way, though, of making something good come out of a bad thing. Writing during persecution, Paul talks about "our light and momentary troubles," as if the things that happen to us are as trivial as a paper cut in the grand scheme of eternity. These troubles that you and I face can sting like crazy, but God's ability to turn a negative into a positive is a testament to our powerful God. So if you're feeling that sting of "bad things happening to good people," wait on God to show you how He's going to bring good out of it. Odds are that you'll be amazed at what He can do.

—GH

Disoriented at 60 Feet Below

But he said to me, "My grace is sufficient for you, for my power is made perfect in weakness." . . . That is why, for Christ's sake, I delight in weaknesses, in insults, in hardships, in persecutions, in difficulties. For when I am weak, then I am strong. 2 Corinthians 12:9, 10.

When you are diving deep inside the bowels of a sunken ship, the worst thing you can do is to get lost, because once your air runs out you'll die in there. This very thought ran through my head inside the captain's quarters of the grand *Prinz Eugen*, a shipwreck we dove on in the Marshalls. Our guide, whom I was not impressed with, had taken us through a door, down a corridor, and into this room where rusted furniture rested on the ceiling—the ship had sunk upside down. What we didn't realize was that everything around us was covered by a fine layer of sea silt, which, once stirred up, thickly clouded the water like the dead of night. The more we moved around in the little room, the darker the water became, until finally I put my hand in front of my face and couldn't even see it. At that point I was terrified. Not only did I not know the way out—I couldn't even find the door, and the guide had vanished. Panicking, I felt my way blindly around the room, bumping into walls, desks, and rusty chairs. Just when I thought I'd never make it out of that ship, I felt a strong hand grab onto my wrist and pull me through the dark water. I couldn't see the body, but the hand pulled me back down the passageway and into clear water again. The hand belonged to the guide, who was more capable than I had ever realized.

Sometimes our lives become as churned up and as black as the darkest, deepest sea, and it's during those times that we wonder why God has seemingly vanished—where is He in the darkness? Why has He left us here to flail blindly? But Paul says it's during those times that God's power can really shine. In 2 Corinthians Paul is defending himself against harsh accusations and attacks, yet he opens up and shares more of his own feelings here than in any other letter. He mentions a "thorn in his side" (see 2 Corinthians 12:7) that he asked God three times to take away, but God assured Paul that His grace is enough for him and that His power is made perfect in weakness.

It's during the times we are lost and terrified that give God the opportunity to show just how strong He really is. The hardest times of my life have also been the times that I felt God closest to me. If you are going through dark times, expect to see God's power in your weakness.

—MH

They Stick Only if You Let Them

Am I now trying to win the approval of men, or of God? Or am I trying to please men? If I were still trying to please men, I would not be a servant of Christ. Galatians 1:10.

My favorite children's book right now is *You Are Special*, by Max Lucado. If you've never read it, stop by the kids' section next time you're in a bookstore and check it out. (I think it was actually written for teens and adults, too.) The story is profound.

Imagine a world in which prejudices and preferences are expressed through stickers! The book introduces a world of funny wooden dolls called Wemmicks, who go around all day giving each other stickers. If someone is pretty or talented, they get stars; but if they're ugly, clumsy, or uninteresting, they get dots. One Wemmick in particular, Punchinello, has so many dots that it's discouraging for him even to go outside. He begins to believe he's not a good wooden person, for the villagers feel he deserves all those dots.

One day Punchinello meets a Wemmick who has no stickers at all. People try to give them to her, but they don't stick. They fall off. When he asks her for her secret, she tells him to go up the hill and visit the woodworker, Eli. Mustering his courage, Punchinello approaches the giant workshop of this craftsman. He is shocked when the maker knows him, and even more surprised as he picks him up and assures him that he is special—despite all the dots. Finally Punchinello asks Eli how to get rid of the stickers, and Eli gives him the secret: the stickers stick only if you let them. They stick if they matter to you, but if you decide you don't care what others think, they'll fall off. Punchinello is still wrestling with this idea as he leaves the workshop, but when Eli reminds him of how special he is, Punchinello believes it for the very first time. The last picture in the book shows one solitary dot sticker falling to the ground.

I've often read this book to groups of teens to emphasize two things: first, the way we go around criticizing each other and sizing each other up is ridiculous; and second, to remind them that people's opinions should not make or break their confidence. Our true self-worth should be rooted in belonging to Jesus—an idea that sounds nice but is hard to learn to believe, I know. As Paul says above, you have to choose whether to please people or God. You can't really please both. Whom are you trying to please today—God or people? Who matters most?

—MH

Solve It With Ranch

You, my brothers, were called to be free. But do not use your freedom to indulge the sinful nature; rather, serve one another in love. The entire law is summed up in a single command: "Love your neighbor as yourself." If you keep on biting and devouring each other, watch out or you will be destroyed by each other. Galatians 5:13-15.

It's hard to forget the sight of two grown women covered head to toe in ranch dressing. I'm not sure what came over Alicia and Helen that night, but something persuaded them that a ranch dressing fight would be the best way to settle their little spat. In the beginning it looked as if Alicia was winning. She'd put Helen in a headlock and proceeded to smear handfuls of dressing in her hair and across her face. Thinking fast, Helen used the opportunity to spread the white stuff all down the front of Alicia's shirt and pants, as well as across both of her arms. Ranch was flung and splattered while we cheered from a safe distance. At the end of the salad-dressing war there was no clear winner. The two girls were slimy and slippery, and the greasy white residue was equally slathered on both. Oh, how they stank for the rest of that night, and since I had to drive Alicia home, my car reeked for the next week.

There are some things we throw at each other that serve only to make ourselves dirtier in the end—things like insults, gossip, slander, and ridicule. We think we're smearing the other person, but our own hands are stinking too. We mess ourselves up when we try to tear others down. When Paul writes to the Galatians about the freedom we have in Christ, he warns them not to use this freedom to let their emotions run wild. They are supposed to love each other, but instead they are "biting and devouring" one another. Some are insisting that the new Galatian believers still must follow Old Testament Jewish rites, while others, such as Paul, say these legal requirements have been removed. At this Paul is accused of being a false apostle, and so the fighting just goes on and on. Paul warns them that if such vicious behavior continues, everyone will be destroyed in the end. Angry words fly like messy ranch dressing—nobody wins.

We are called to be free from destructive, bitter, petty behavior, yet so many of us still find it a part of our daily lives. It's all too easy, and even satisfying, to tear down other people. If you struggle with this, the only remedy is what Paul suggests. Learn to love and accept them.

—MH

How to Be the Best You

But the fruit of the Spirit is love, joy, peace, patience, kindness, goodness, faithfulness, gentleness and self-control. Galatians 5:22, 23..

Liam and I worked in a telemarketing center making hundreds of phone calls a day. After eight hours of getting cussed out and hung up on, most employees were more than a little overwhelmed. Liam, who worked next to me, noticed that for whatever reason I seemed to respond to the stress differently than did the other workers. He noticed that I didn't rush outside to smoke a cigarette for my nerves, and that I didn't cuss or even get overly upset when yet another irate individual yelled at me. He later told me that sitting there day by day, watching me, told him that something was different about me. In time a door opened up for me to talk with him about my faith. I was doing nothing special, but Liam saw something that pulled him in.

Black holes are nasty things that suck every bit of matter, and even light itself, into their gaping dark maw. The intense gravitational attraction caused by a collapsing star has a way of causing anything within a certain range to begin to fall into the "hole." This area around the black hole where things are drawn in is known as the "event horizon." Once within this field, every type of matter, as well as photons of light, are inescapably caught by the star's overwhelming gravitational pull. All Christians are called to be an "event horizon"—the place where other lives come in contact with Jesus and are magnetically drawn into a relationship with Him. When people spend time with us, they are supposed to notice something different. But what if we don't know how to be different from the world or draw them in? Paul gives a nice list of nine things that set Christians apart from the rest of the world, and he calls them the fruit of the Spirit. At first the list seems simple and easy to produce. I myself used to think that I was just a naturally loving, joyful, kind person. But I began to realize that when I grew distant from the Lord, these qualities weren't in me anymore! I was unhappy, rude, and selfish. That's when I realized that God is the best thing about all of us. He fills us with our best qualities, and then enables us to use these qualities to draw other lives to Him. We can't grow this fruit on our own (though we try) because it is the direct result of the Holy Spirit working in our lives. If you are missing some of these qualities today, ask for God's Spirit to grow them in you.

—GH

The Only Things We Have Left

Let us not become weary in doing good, for at the proper time we will reap a harvest if we do not give up. Galatians 6:9.

At first you didn't see the flames. All I could see was some black smoke starting to swirl around in the living room. At this point I still entertained the idea that the fire would be contained, and must not be very big. I hadn't beaten the fire trucks by more than a minute, but as I jumped out of my car I realized all hope of going inside the dorm, where my wife and I lived while she was an assistant dean, was in vain. I rushed madly around the building searching for Melissa, and found her standing with a group of the girls. "I think everyone is out. I think we're all OK," she told me. "Honey, the fire is in our house." The first flames I saw broke out in our bedroom. From the light they gave off I could see the inside of my closet and thought, *Man, what did I leave in there this morning?* I watched the yellow and orange lights flicker through the windows and dance slowly from the bedroom into the kitchen. My heart sank as I realized that there was nothing stopping it. Suddenly the firefighters broke a window in the living room. A sickeningly black plume of acrid smoke spewed out from the hole, and I slowly realized that I was watching my accumulated life's possessions turning to ash and superheated gas.

In the days that followed we walked around in a daze making constant tallies of everything that burned. After adding yet another batch of items to the ever-growing list, my wife made a profound statement. "You know what? The only things we have left at all in the world are the things we gave away to other people." It was true—photos, artwork, gifts from our travels—all had burned, except the things we'd given away to our friends and family.

This world is going to end in just the same way. With fire, yes, but also with the only remaining things being what we have given to others. The effort we invest into other lives is the only thing that will last. All we can take to heaven with us is one another.

Paul warns the Galatians that you get the fruit of the seeds you've planted—you get what you put into life. He encourages us not to grow tired of doing good works, because someday we will reap a great harvest from them. Shift your perspective today. Challenge yourself to invest in the only things you can keep—the love and time you give away to bring others to Jesus.

—GH

In the Doghouse

For it is by grace you have been saved, through faith—and this not from yourselves, it is the gift of God—not by works, so that no one can boast. For we are God's workmanship, created in Christ Jesus to do good works, which God prepared in advance for us to do. Ephesians 2:8-10.

It was because of a spider that we spent the night in the doghouse. My siblings and I were enjoying a summer family tradition, sleeping outside in a tent in the backyard. The night had grown late and we'd almost drifted off to sleep, when someone spotted the enlarged shadow of a spider crawling somewhere on the tent walls. When we realized we couldn't even find the spider, our imaginations ran wild. It could be anywhere in the darkness—crawling up our backs for all we knew—and how big was it anyway? Its shadow looked pretty menacing! Soon it became clear that none of us would get a wink of sleep if we were sharing a tent with a spider, so we grabbed our pillows and headed on back to the house. But one, two, three pulls on the door revealed a horrible fact: Mom had accidentally locked it. Standing there shivering in the cool night, we didn't know what to do. We couldn't go back to the tent, and we couldn't go into the house. So that's when I suggested the doghouse. It was the only dwelling left! My freezing siblings and I eagerly climbed into the old, dirty wooden box, carpeted with inch-thick layers of scratchy dog hair. Curling up with the dog seemed preferable to curling up with a spider, but it turned out pretty horrible—all of us balled up shivering, smashed into a doghouse. Mom still feels terrible for locking us out that night.

Do you realize that if we had to earn our own salvation, we'd be locked out of heaven forever? If God hadn't sent Jesus, not a single person in history would ever have had salvation. But He did send Jesus, and Jesus became the key to let us into the kingdom. No matter how great a Christian we think we are, there is still no reason for any of us to boast, because not one of us can save ourselves. We have been saved by grace, and we get this grace through faith, as a gift. God created us to accept this gift and then to do good works that spring from the gift.

Maybe you've been feeling locked out in your Christian walk, as if you don't belong in heaven, or you're not quite sure how to get in anyway. But you're not locked out, because entrance is free and nobody else is in any better shape than you are. We all need Jesus to get in.

—MH

Millionaire Sea Captain Goes Broke

Now to him who is able to do immeasurably more than all we ask or imagine, according to his power that is at work within us, to him be glory in the church and in Christ Jesus throughout all generations, for ever and ever. Amen! Ephesians 3:20, 21.

When you have only 24 cents left to your name, what are you willing to spend it on? Joseph Bates, an ex-sea captain and veteran of the War of 1812, decided to spend it on the four pounds of flour his wife needed to finish her baking. When he left the sea to take up the cause of the Seventh-day Adventist movement, he'd used his considerable wealth to pay for publications and speaking engagements around the country. By 1846 the fortune he'd amassed over many years had dwindled down to a single York shilling (about 24 cents in today's currency). When he handed his wife the flour and she asked why he hadn't gotten more, Bates admitted they were completely broke. "What will we do now?" she asked. When he told her the Lord would provide, she stomped off angry and in tears, because this was his typical response during a crisis.

As Bates sat down to work on a tract that covered the biblical understanding of the seventh-day Sabbath, he felt impressed to go down to the post office. There he found a letter that had been sent about a week earlier. "I was impressed to send you $10 this week because it seemed like you would need it," the man wrote. God had been ready for days!

The promise above has always been one of my favorites. I like the idea that God can do way, way more than anything I could ever even imagine, because I can imagine a whole lot! Paul wrote this verse to the Christians in Ephesus, and from what I gather, they also could imagine a lot, because they were loaded. Ephesus was the most important city in Asia minor (now Turkey) because it was an intersection between several trade routes. It had a fancy, large temple and became a commercial center. These people had wealth and money, and they were used to high living. So for Paul to say that God can do more than they could imagine was saying a whole lot. But that's the God we serve—He's really that big. You can't even measure it.

What do you imagine today? What are you asking God for? Do you realize He is capable of doing "immeasurably more" than even your highest, wildest dreams? Maybe you've felt timid in your requests and dreams. Leave all that behind. God wants to outdream even you!

—MH

Whose Ball Is This?

Therefore, having put away falsehood, let each one of you speak the truth with his neighbor, for we are members one of another. Ephesians 4:25, ESV.

For a novice golfer like me, finding a ball is a boon in a sea of stinky shots. It's inevitable that I'll lose a few golf balls on, yes, even a nine-hole course. Golf balls are expensive (even cheap ones), and recovering one helps the accident-prone beginner save a little money. It's also good for morale after messing up several shots to say, "Hey, I found a ball!" One day I was out with some church friends, demonstrating my incompetence, and happened to make one good shot. The ball soared through the air and landed close to the hole. Triumphantly I marched up the hill to where my shot landed—and came across a ball I didn't recognize as any of ours.

"Aha!" I shouted, plucking the ball from its resting spot and holding it aloft. At that moment I saw another golfer making his way down the hill from the green next to ours. *Uh-oh.*

Deftly recognizing what was happening, I flung the ball behind me, pointed straight ahead, and pretended I was yelling to my friend about my ball. Then I ran as fast as I could up the hill before the other golfer saw me. Gasping and wheezing at the top of the hill where my friend waited, he motioned down the hill for me to look. "Close one," he said as we saw the other golfer find what I thought was going to be a new ball for me and hit it back to the course where he was supposed to be playing. If you ask me, a ball shot that bad deserved to be lost to another superior player . . . like myself.

I could have let the guy just puzzle over where his ball went as I stowed it in my pocket—but instead I gave it back. Actually, it would be scandalous if he saw me pick it up and move it at all—but that's not important. The key is that we all encounter times that it would be easy to get away with something at the expense of our neighbor. It doesn't have to be big things. It could be sneaking a look at their text messages on their phone; it could be picking up unidentified money someone left lying around at school; it can even be not owning up to our own mistakes when we inadvertently hurt someone. In all you do today, do your best to be honest and trustworthy with those you come in contact with—especially in areas in which you and God are the only ones who know what's going on.

—SP

Don't Dabble Here

For our struggle is not against flesh and blood, but against the rulers, against the authorities, against the powers of this dark world and against the spiritual forces of evil in the heavenly realms. Therefore put on the full armor of God. Ephesians 6:12, 13.

More Satan stories!" she shrieked, begging her friends to continue the tales of ghosts, goblins, witches, and demons. That night the storyteller seemed unnaturally drawn to the world of evil. Only a young girl at camp at the time, my mom couldn't leave her cabin, so she sat in the circle with the other girls, praying in fear. The girl continued to order more Satan stories, but very suddenly, in the middle of a story, she jumped to her feet, gasping. She couldn't breathe or speak a word, and frantically clawed at her neck, trying desperately to pry something off. Finally she wheezed urgently, "He's choking me!" Terror gripped every girl in the room, but it was my mom who suggested they claim the name of Jesus. At the mention of His name, the unseen hands fell from her neck, and the shaking, exhausted girl could breathe again. Within seconds bright-red handprints appeared on both sides of her neck. She had asked for Satan, and she had gotten him.

This story is true, and I tell it because I want you to know that Satan is real. He's not someone to toy with, dabble in, or mess around near. A lot of kids think they can just try little things such as playing with Ouija boards or reading tarot cards, but nothing is little when you invite the devil into your life. He really exists, and he is *not* a power to play around with. Chances are, you'll get a whole lot more than you bargained for. Paul reminds us in Ephesians that we are not just wrestling against human powers in this life. We are actually fighting a supernatural battle against the powers of darkness at work in the world. That's real, and it's scary, but Jesus can equip us for it. The full armor of God, which protects us against evil, consists of several things: having faith, knowing the truth, possessing righteousness, being ready with the gospel story, being covered by salvation, and knowing the Word of God. These things equip us, each in their own different way, to stand against evil. Next time something goes terribly wrong in your life, remember that you're not fighting just circumstance. You are on a battlefield, and we have an enemy. But we also have a Leader who has already won, and all evil flees at His name.

—MH

The Most Depressing Girl in the School

Being confident of this, that he who began a good work in you will carry it on to completion until the day of Christ Jesus. Philippians 1:6.

I've lost sleep worrying about several different high school friends, but Laurel stands out most in my mind. She regularly talked of killing herself, and I was afraid she'd do it. She made poor choices—terrible choices—and wondered why her life continued to get worse. She seemed so reckless and so depressed that I sometimes dreaded to see her coming toward me. Usually she'd try to talk me into driving her off campus into a nearby neighborhood so she could smoke a cigarette between classes. Or she'd talk about her awful, depressing life. One day she just walked up and pretended to put a gun in her mouth and shoot herself. I was appalled and disturbed. When high school ended, she continued right on this same course of self-destruction—we often remain the same as we were in high school—and I lost track of her. Until our 10-year reunion last April.

There she was—married, pregnant, happy, and beautiful—with her kind, caring husband on her arm for us to meet. She had met him in . . . church—somewhere I never thought she'd go. She chose him because he was a strong Christian. As I talked to her, I was shocked to find out that she, too, had become a strong Christian, trusting in the Lord and joyfully walking with Him each day. Who would have ever guessed that she'd grow into such a beautiful Christian! The way God can change a life! Wow!

I learned something from Laurel about God's long-term persistence. You might see a whole lot of unfinished business in your life. Most of us aren't yet the person we want to be. But that's OK! God promises us that He has started doing a good work in us and He's going to finish it—He'll keep completing it until Jesus comes. You see, the Christian life is not a destination. Rather, it's a journey, and none of us have arrived. As long as we live, God will continue to work on us. So face your mistakes, faults, and unfinished character—not with shame, but with confidence. You don't have to clean up your own mess if you walk with Jesus. God is the one at work here, and He's going to carry you through to completion.

—MH

Glow-in-the-Dark People

Do everything without complaining or arguing, so that you may become blameless and pure, children of God without fault in a crooked and depraved generation, in which you shine like stars in the universe. Philippians 2:14, 15.

You've probably heard that hundreds of years ago sailors navigated their ships by the stars. All their complex calculations were based on a single fixed point in the sky, because without a fixed point of reference everything became jumbled. That fixed point was the North Star. When a sailor could fix sights on the North Star, everything else would fall into place.

As I look back at my life, I realize that lots of people became fixed points that helped me navigate through the various obstacles and times of doubt in my life. One was a college professor named Pastor Case. Not only was his vast knowledge of the Bible something I admired and aspired to, but his incredible understanding of people humbled me every time I sat in his office. We'd discuss all kinds of things—personal and professional—and every time I thought I could stump him, he'd amaze me with some unheard-of insight. To top it all off, even though he had every right to be impressed with himself, he was as humble a man as I've ever met. When I look back and think of the kind of Christian I want to be, I usually find myself thinking about him.

As Christians, our lives are supposed to shine like lights to the people around us in the darkness of this world. Paul tells the Christians in Philippi that if they don't complain or argue, and if they live pure lives, they will stand out as something different. They aren't just nice people. There are lots of nice people in the world. These are people who shine like stars in a world that doesn't understand God. They stand out not just because of their polite manners but because their presence is infused with something from Jesus Himself. They aren't perfect, but their strong relationship with Jesus becomes evident to those around them. It makes them different from other people, even other nice people. Pastor Case is a normal guy, but the Jesus that he walks with on a daily basis is anything but "a normal guy." So Pastor Case stands out in the world and causes people such as me to see Jesus.

Look at your own life today—are you walking with Jesus? Is there something different about the way you live? Are you part of the darkness, or is your life a light shining through it?

—GH

Strive

Not that I have already obtained this or am already perfect, but I press on to make it my own, because Christ Jesus has made me his own. Philippians 3:12, ESV.

My dog, Winston, is a pedigreed Alaskan malamute. At the time of this writing he's about 10 months old and weighs more than 80 pounds. His grandfather won Best of Breed at Westminster, and we were on a waiting list for a year and a half before we welcomed him home. We have high hopes for Winston's learning aptitude. When we first undertook the challenge of housebreaking him we knew it would take a few months. We had to teach him what door to use, where to go outside, and correct him gently when he made a mistake. One day we were playing on the floor with him when suddenly his ears perked up and he stood at attention, looking like a little polar bear. He swiftly turned and began running to the back door. I stood up to cheer—but it was premature. Instead of going to the door to be let out, he ran into it. Headfirst. There was a loud boom, and he toppled backward, head over heels. He shook it off and gave us a goofy look with his tongue hanging out. I'm afraid it'll be a long time before he'll compete at Westminster!

I'm proud to announce that Winston is now housebroken. He can sit, shake, lie down, and speak—all on hand signals. He walks nicely and has decent manners. He also falls down stairs, dribbles after drinking, and makes the occasional smell that will curl your nose hairs. He isn't perfect, but we keep helping him be the best dog he can be.

In today's text Paul says that even he, an apostle, hasn't achieved perfection. His focus is on continually "striving" to be like Jesus. It's hard to continue on when we make mistakes, but we need to "press," as Paul says. It's not a comfortable word—it is akin to "squeeze" and "push," and both require effort. Sometimes we need to put forth real effort to achieve God's plans. Not the plan of salvation, mind you, but working *with* God to do what He asks. Are there areas of your life—school, work, or friendships—that you haven't put much effort into? Is there anyplace in your walk with God you haven't been disciplining yourself in—reading Scripture, prayer, or serving others? While it is true that everything we do is by grace with strength God grants us, God doesn't hijack our bodies and make us do it. If there's an area you feel is sliding, trust God to give you the strength to "press on" as you seek to become more like Jesus.

—SP

My Favorite Verse in the Bible

I can do all things through Him who strengthens me. Philippians 4:13, NASB.

M y hands shook and my heart raced as I sat in the very front row of the church, waiting for the pastor to call on me. You'd shake too if you were only 10 years old and had to do the entire sermon! Well, I wasn't preaching; I was playing my harp—for 30 minutes, a "sermon in music"—and everyone in the whole room would be listening to only me, so I was terrified. A song or two is one thing; a full concert is another. I knew I couldn't do this. I considered faking a trip to the bathroom as an excuse to run out of the church and never come back. I planned to repay my parents later for volunteering me for this misery. I was ready to cry when my mom whispered into my ear: "'I can do all things through Him who gives me strength.'"

I looked at her, confused and slightly annoyed. "It's a Bible verse, a promise you can claim anytime and anywhere," she said. "Whenever you're afraid just say the words to yourself and believe them!"

I repeated the verse to myself until the pastor called me up to play, and then repeated between every single song. It calmed me in a way I had never experienced before. I didn't give a perfect performance that day, but I did learn a perfect strategy for soothing my own nerves: believe you can do difficult things because Jesus will give you strength to face them.

Paul wrote these words from prison. As he explained to the Philippian believers, he had learned the secret for being content even if he was starving or destitute. The secret is knowing that Jesus Christ will give you enough strength to get through anything. Anything! That means the darkest night, the scariest task, the most desperate times, and the most heart-wrenching grief. He can carry you through all of it. We aren't strong enough alone, but with Him we can make it.

I have prayed this verse thousands of times over the years—before countless audiences, during brutal finals, from the depths of depression, and even in the delivery room. It's become my favorite, and I say it when I need to believe that God can get me through. You can use it too—anytime, anywhere, for any situation at all. You can use it today, right now. Whatever you must face today, know that Jesus can give you enough strength to get through it.

—MH

Boardwalk Blunder

So as to walk in a manner worthy of the Lord, fully pleasing to him, bearing fruit in every good work and increasing in the knowledge of God. Colossians 1:10, ESV.

On a student missionary stint in the Canadian province of Newfoundland, the task fell to me to provide chaplaincy services during summer camp. One of the kids in my charge was Tim. He was physically incapable of not talking and would frequently spout off inappropriate (and hilarious) things during meals and worships. It got so bad that even our director wouldn't sit next to him for fear of laughing at an inopportune time. During a field trip to a national park Tim was particularly mouthy, and his counselor, Matt, and I were constantly telling him to "simmer down." He kept running along the boardwalk ahead of our group, prompting us to yell, "TIM! Simmer down!" This went on until Tim began to get irritable. We'd exhort him to "simmer," and he'd mutter, "I *am* simmered." We thought it was good fun, but nothing could have prepared us for what would simmer Tim down for the rest of the day. As we rounded a corner, the wooded path elevated four feet, off the ground, and Tim was dancing on the very edge of the boardwalk. In unison Matt and I shouted, "TIM! SIMMER!"

Tim fell, straddling the edge of the boardwalk, then bounced, and then landed on his crotch a second time. From this painful position, with his legs wrapped tightly around the edge, he swung upside down, hanging like a bat for two or three seconds before falling headfirst into a pile of soft, green moss. As Matt and I peered over the edge we saw Tim lying spread-eagled, eyes rolling around his head, with a dumb grin on his face. He was alive and no worse for wear. After finding his way back atop the boardwalk, for reasons unknown to rational humanity, Tim leaped from the boardwalk onto a tree. The tree was skinny and bent away from the boardwalk before snapping back like a switch and slamming Tim back onto the boardwalk in much the same position he'd been in just moments before.

Paul tells us that we should make sure we carry ourselves (or "walk") in a way that brings God glory and produces good "fruit." It's easy to just walk in our own way and not take time to listen to our "counselor," the Holy Spirit. The results usually aren't pretty. Take time today to meditate and ask God to impress your thoughts with how He would like you to go about your day.

—SP

Maturity

Him we proclaim, warning everyone and teaching everyone with all wisdom, that we may present everyone mature in Christ. Colossians 1:28, ESV.

If you ever have the chance to watch little kids play T-ball, please do it. Especially if you're having a bad day or need a good laugh. This sport is designed to teach the rudiments of baseball and coordination to youngsters who are still unfamiliar with how to operate their appendages. The result is spectacular chaos and calamity.

First, for their protection, the kids are forced to wear helmets that are half their body weight. This means that should they start to run they are so top-heavy their helmet sags forward, causing an involuntary slide into first base or the nearby crowd, depending on how directionally challenged they are. Which brings up my next point.

Should they make contact with the ball, these kids have no idea where to go. They will run to third base, then first base, then home, and finally to second in order to score. Kids wander mindlessly in the outfield. They'll leave the field midplay in order to get a drink, go to the restroom, or blow their nose. I don't know how the coaches manage not to get flustered.

Some kids will throw the ball into the stands, hold it while they run around the bases, or simply cry because they are tired and confused. The parents are a riot because they all cheer instructions to the little ones who can't understand what they're saying because they're all yelling at the same time. Some kids run over to the stands while the game is going on and ask someone what to do—which is too late by that time. It is an amazing experience, and hopefully one that will eventually teach them how to play the real game someday.

A lot of Christians are stuck playing T-ball in their faith because they don't take time to grow. In Colossians we see a desire expressed that we each develop a mature faith. This means that we all go through periods of confusion, mistake-making, and unfamiliarity as to what to do—but it's all directed toward growing and learning. Christianity is a process and a journey. The difference between those who mature and those who don't is a willingness to put forth the effort to listen and learn.

—SP

The Most Misused Verse in the Bible

Having canceled the written code, with its regulations, that was against us and that stood opposed to us; he took it away, nailing it to the cross. Colossians 2:14.

Tears streamed down their faces as they returned to the apartment that night, confused and distraught, questioning everything they once believed. My two friends had visited with a preacher from another church who had smashed their faith foundation apart in one stroke by claiming that the Bible clearly teaches that the Sabbath has been done away with forever.

Today's verse has got to be the most misused verse in the entire Bible, and I'll explain why. People use this verse specifically to target Sabbathkeepers, saying that the law was nailed to the cross, so we don't need to keep the seventh-day Sabbath any longer. But was it really the Ten Commandments that were "nailed to the cross," or something else? This matters! If the law was taken away, we don't have to keep it anymore, including stealing and murder. But what the text says is that the "written code" was nailed. Other versions call it "the record of charges," or the "certificate of debt." The original Greek calls it the "against-us code," a handwritten, legal document of debt. It's similar to the slave document referred to in Philemon. This isn't the Ten Commandments, because they were handwritten by God Himself, not by human beings. Jesus said that He came not to abolish the law but to fulfill it (Matthew 5:17). Christians who believe the law was done away with still keep nine of the Ten Commandments, so what was canceled?

There's a story in the Old Testament about Moses reading the covenant to Israel one last time. That day the entire nation made a commitment before God to keep all of the ceremonial laws and decrees. If they didn't, they'd be cursed, indebted to God. And we all know how that ended—they certainly did not keep the covenant, and for centuries it had been against them, reminding them that they'd broken their promise. No wonder the Pharisees tried so hard to keep every last detail of their ceremonial laws—they were indebted! Then Jesus came and died on the cross, canceling forever our debt of sin, and canceling Satan's claim on the lives of anyone who chooses Him. We're no longer slaves to evil, because our slave certificates have been taken away and nailed to the cross. Don't let anyone tell you that the law was done away with. God's law stands firm. It's our debt that's canceled and gone, and we are free.

—MH

Buoys, Barnacles, and a Bad Idea

It is God's will that you should be sanctified: that you should avoid sexual immorality; that each of you should learn to control his own body in a way that is holy and honorable, not in passionate lust like the heathen, who do not know God. 1 Thessalonians 4:3-5.

We were honeymooning in Tahiti, and all week we kept looking at some little islands just off the coast that seemed to be close enough for an early-morning swim. So with our flippers and gear we set out. After 45 minutes we still hadn't gotten anywhere, so I plunged my mask into the water. Thirty feet below, the sea floor rushed by sideways—we were caught in a swift-moving current dragging us toward the breakwater. We tried to swim against it, but we were virtually powerless against the strong current. Just when I thought we had no hope, I noticed a single buoy floating up ahead, the only possible refuge between us and waves that crashed against a razor-sharp coral wall. Swimming for all I was worth, I caught hold of the barnacle-encrusted buoy and hung on for dear life. My legs were bleeding as I fearfully clung to the buoy. I saw Melissa, caught in the rushing current, heading to her doom on the breakwater nearby. As she swept past, I caught her, and we both clung to the buoy, realizing how close we'd come to disaster.

Paul was taken away from the Thessalonian church after only three weeks, so when he writes to them he doesn't delve into heavy theology. He's still going over the basics. And one of the things he finds important to warn them about is controlling their own bodies. Let's face it. Sexual immorality is pretty much the strongest temptation you have to face right now, and if you're normal you're going to fight it every day, sometimes every hour. Our culture bombards us with sexuality everywhere. It's in songs, movies, TV shows, on billboards, and in magazines. It's even in the way we dress. If you live on Planet Earth, you can't escape the barrage of sexual messages every single day. You can fight it, but the pull of sexual immorality is strong enough to sweep us all away. We hardly stand a chance of swimming against its current—unless we have Jesus. Jesus is the one thing in this sea of temptation that we can reach out for and hang on to for dear life. So when you feel as if you're fighting an impossible current, cling to Jesus. Only by fixing our eyes on Him do the "things of earth grow strangely dim." Get out your Bible, talk to Him, sing a song, or go talk with a friend. Whatever you do—swim for dear life.

—GH

Meltdown in the Walmart Cheese Aisle

For the Lord himself will come down from heaven, with a loud command, with the voice of the archangel and with the trumpet call of God, and the dead in Christ will rise first. After that, we who are still alive and are left will be caught up together with them in the clouds to meet the Lord in the air. And so we will be with the Lord forever. 1 Thessalonians 4:16, 17.

My son has an addiction. No, it's not alcohol or drugs, or even his blankie. My son is addicted to string cheese. He's only 3 years old, but he can eat nine pieces before noon and go through entire packages in a single day. If the house is silent and we haven't seen him in a while, you can pretty well guess where he'll be—sitting on the kitchen floor, arms deep in the fridge, mouth full of giant globs of string cheese. That's why it was so difficult for us to evacuate Walmart last week. Caleb had his giant package of string cheese clutched in his little hands when the fire alarm went off. Lights flashed, sirens wailed, and the Walmart employees rushed through the store screaming, "This is *not* a drill! Abandon your carts. Evacuate the store immediately!"

I picked up Toby Jacob, our 3-month-old, in one arm, and tried to hoist Caleb up with the other, but he wouldn't budge. I told him that there was a fire, and we had to leave the store *now*. He wouldn't come. "Caleb not leave string cheese!" he screamed. I pulled and pulled, but he wouldn't leave the cart. Other customers rushing for the door stared in sympathy at my screaming child, probably thinking he was scared of the sirens instead of risking his life for a package of string cheese. At last another woman took the baby, and I put Caleb in a two-arm straitjacket. All the way out he wailed, "Caleb's string cheese!"

Kind of sounds like us, doesn't it? It's probably not string cheese, but there are plenty of things you care a lot about, aren't there? If Jesus came today, would you be happy to go home, or are there things here you couldn't bear to leave? We think things down here are pretty great, but we have no idea that what's waiting for us is infinitely better. The verse above describes what the glorious coming of Jesus will be like. The excitement! The reunion! Don't get so caught up in this life that you aren't ready for the next.

—MH

"It's a Small World After All"

Pray without ceasing. 1 Thessalonians 5:17, KJV.

When "the sex guy" came to our school with his slides and presentations and all, he tried to tell us that we can't control our own thinking. I didn't buy it until he played three choruses in a row of "It's a Small World" and then told us not to sing the song or even think about it for the rest of the day. Naturally, it was impossible! It was permanently stuck in my head for a week, and there was nothing I could do about it. The whole school sang it for days. (Go ahead. Try it. Sing the song to yourself three times and see if you don't sing it all day long!)

It just goes to show that whatever you put into your head is going to stay there awhile. He was making a point about sexual images in movies or on the Internet, but really, anything you allow into your mind for an extended period will show up later, and later, and later. Take an argument, for example—the more you re-hash it in your mind, the longer your anger will stay. Or what about the one you have a crush on? Once you start thinking about that person, it's impossible to stop, isn't it? The guy was right—what you put into your mind stays there.

Lucky for us, that goes for good things as well as bad things. When it comes to our relationship with God, time we spend with Him equals time we'll spend thinking about Him later. I used to read today's verse, "Pray without ceasing," and conclude that such a thing was impossible. How could anybody pray all day long? We have to talk, and eat, and think about other things—it's just not reasonable! But over the years as I continued to consider this ideal of Paul's, I realized that he is talking about a state of mind. It is possible to have our minds set on God throughout the entire day. Even though we'll take time to do other things, our minds can keep drifting back to God, as it would go back to a song that's stuck in our head. The only way to make this happen, though, is to put Him into our minds in the first place. In the morning, afternoon, or evening—whenever you will be certain to make the time—if you spend time with God, your mind will stay on Him. Then it actually is possible to have a constant running commentary in your head with Him, kind of like an ongoing conversation that you pick up on right where you left off 10 minutes ago. Be purposeful about spending time with God, and you will soon discover yourself in regular talks with Him—praying without ceasing.

—MH

The Last Ferry Leaves at 8:00

We hear that some among you are idle. . . . Such people we command and urge in the Lord Jesus Christ to settle down and earn the bread they eat.
2 Thessalonians 3:11, 12.

Somehow we get stuck on an island every single time our friends Seth and Angela come to visit us. I blame my husband for this. The first time they came to the Pacific Northwest, we decided they'd love a trip up to the San Juan Islands. So we packed the car and headed to the ferry docks, where the ticket attendant assured us that we could stop for a quick visit on Orcas Island before continuing on to Friday Harbor where our cabin was. Greg decided to just take his word for it, instead of consulting the official ferry schedule. We ended up stuck on Orcas in a thunderstorm with every room in the three solitary hotels booked solid. For a while there it looked like we'd all have to sleep in the car, but we ended up on someone's floor.

The second time Seth and Angela should have been wary, but they boarded another ferry with us, headed this time for Victoria, British Columbia. That morning Greg had looked up the sailing times on the Internet, so when I encouraged him to pick up a ferry schedule, he swore he could remember the times without one (see the earlier reading on Greg's rare memory disease). Well, you guessed it. We went to line up for the ferry that night, and lo and behold, it had already sailed, leaving us stranded on another island, checking into another hotel at midnight.

This year our friends invited us to visit them instead. I'm thinking they were tired of getting stranded in strange places because of our inability to be prepared.

There were a few church members in Thessalonica who did not want to be caught unprepared when Jesus came, so they just stopped everything altogether and waited. They didn't go to work. They didn't farm. They didn't buy anything. They just waited—all day, every day. They expected Jesus anytime. When Paul realized they had misunderstood his meaning of the word "soon," he quickly wrote them a second letter to encourage them to keep living their lives.

Learning to look forward to the coming of Jesus, but also continuing to live life as normal, is a difficult balance. Maybe Jesus didn't give us a return date because He knew that we wouldn't seek Him or get ready till the last minute. None of us is guaranteed tomorrow—He wants us to be ready each moment. Don't go quit your job today—but do set your heart in order.

—MH

How Studying Geography Can Save Your Life

Don't let anyone look down on you because you are young, but set an example for the believers in speech, in life, in love, in faith and in purity. 1 Timothy 4:12.

The next time a teacher tells anyone in Tilly Smith's elementary school class that what they're learning about could save their life, they'll take it seriously. In December 2004 Tilly Smith and her family vacationed on the beaches of Thailand. Shortly before the trip, Tilly had learned about tsunamis and the warning signs that happen just before a tsunami hits a beach. One day as she walked along the beach with her parents and younger sister, she noticed the frothing foam on the edge of the tide and a sudden receding of the ocean. She stopped walking and told her parents, "A tsunami is coming." They chuckled and kept on walking, but she became insistent and said that she was going back to the hotel. After a few more minutes they finally agreed, and Tilly told a passing hotel manager what she believed was happening. The manager rushed everyone off the beach, and more than 100 people came hurrying back in towels and flip-flops. Within minutes of the last persons scurrying for safety the tsunami hit with full force in what ultimately turned out to be one of the most destructive tsunamis in recorded history. More than 295,000 people lost their lives that day, but 100 or more on the beach with Tilly Smith were saved because of the well-learned lessons of a 12-year-old girl.

Young people can make a big difference in today's world, in spite of an older generation that seems to think otherwise. Paul encouraged a young man named Timothy, who was working hard to share his faith with the people of Ephesus, to use his youthful energy to do something great. Paul was decades older than Timothy, but he told him not to let anyone look down on him because of his age. He knew Timothy could be an incredible example of faith to the people around him. Notice here that Paul didn't say Timothy should rebel against those who looked down on him, but that he should "set an example" for them. He calls on young people to be examples to older ones! This not only upsets conventional wisdom, but also puts the younger generation in a place of responsibility. God wants us to be faithful to Him in how we live—not just when we're older and responsible, but right now, when we're young. You might even be able to teach the adults a thing or two if you clean up your act before they do!

—GH

Taking a Stand

Fight the good fight of the faith. Take hold of the eternal life to which you were called and about which you made the good confession in the presence of many witnesses. 1 Timothy 6:12, ESV.

The famous boxer Muhammad Ali tells a great story about the neighborhood bully he had to contend with while growing up. His name was Corky Baker, and everybody avoided his street. Corky whupped everybody and "terrorized" the entire neighborhood. He was such a brute that he made money taking bets on how high he could lift the back end of cars. He could also knock out adult men. Corky was the undisputed king of the streets. Ali said that even with all his skills he knew he wouldn't get very far unless he faced this local bully. "If I could whup Corky, I could whup the whole world," said Ali. Since Ali knew he wouldn't win in a no-rules street brawl, he arranged for a boxing match at Columbia Gym for the title "King of the Street." This match wasn't about money. It was about being able to see himself as a champion.

In round one Corky came out swinging, "throwing big hard punches," but Ali kept on moving and began to wear out the big bully. Ali ducked punches, and fought faster and smarter. Before the second round was over, the big bully whined, "This ain't fair," and ran out with a black eye and bloody nose. Ali "won the respect of his peers and knew he could face anything."*

This world can be an intimidating place to be a Christian. A casual stroll down the bookstore aisles reveals books from such authors as Christopher Hitchens (*God Is Not Great*) and Richard Dawkins (*The God Delusion*) that can make you cringe. Yet Paul writes to the young pastor Timothy, telling him to take courage and fight. The early Christians lived in a world with church fights as well as persecutions from the government. It wasn't an easy job.

On occasion you may be tempted to simply put up with bullying because it feels safer. But God has called us to confess Jesus to this world. This means we need to study as well as have experiential knowledge of God in order to prove ourselves. Today, take time to review why you have accepted Christ and how you can take a stand for Him.

—SP

The Soul of a Butterfly (New York: Simon & Schuster, 2004).

He Can't Disown Himself

If we are faithless, he will remain faithful, for he cannot disown himself. 2 Timothy 2:13

For a time during my high school sophomore year, I felt that ending my own life would be a relief. I was depressed, dejected, hopeless, and tired of living. I'd grown tired of God and made deliberate decisions against Him to let Him know I didn't want to live for Him anymore. Life became darker and darker until finally one night my hopelessness reached an all-time low. I was ready for the end. When I got home well after midnight, my early-to-bed mom was waiting up for me. She said she'd been impressed to do so. At that, I broke down and spilled everything. She listened quietly until I was finished. Then she told me about Jake.

Jake, a sweet joy of a yellow Labrador, had been our dog all my life. My parents had bought him as a puppy just before Mom became pregnant with me. They'd often walk in the meadows together, Jake running off to investigate things, returning periodically to check on Mom. One day as they walked, Mom said she suddenly felt two strong hands push down on her shoulders. She stopped dead in her tracks—and looked down at a huge rattlesnake coiled where her next step would have been. As she stared in horror, Jake bounded toward her. She was terrified he would run into the snake, causing it to strike her. But a mysterious thing happened. Instead of coming to her side as usual, Jake stopped short, looking high above Mom's head, wagging his tail at something unseen, and ran off again. She believes Jake saw her guardian angel, whose hands had stopped her in her tracks.

She told me the story that night to assure me that God had a purpose for my life—that He had been directly involved in making sure I was born. I had never heard anything like this before, but it filled me with a brand-new feeling of hope and purpose that has never left me since. What amazes me the most, looking back, is that though I wasn't being faithful to God in the slightest, that night He orchestrated circumstances to save me. He was still faithful to me. The verse above has become one of my favorites because it gives us an idea of just how loyal God is to us. Even if we leave Him completely, He will remain faithful to us—why? Because He can't disown Himself. This means being faithful to us is part of who He is! You can't separate it from Him. It's a guarantee. Whether you feel it or not, God is faithful to you.

—MH

The Bible as Swiss Army Knife

All scripture is inspired by God and is useful for teaching, for reproof, for correction, and for training in righteousness, so that everyone who belongs to God may be proficient, equipped for every good work. 2 Timothy 3:16, 17, NRSV.

There are just some tools that you find yourself using almost all the time. For some guys it's one of those snazzy Leatherman multitools. For others it's the cell phone, or even duct tape. For me, it's a little magic trick with toothpicks. I find this little trick extremely handy, especially in times of great boredom. It's really a simple thing. I just take two toothpicks and hold one horizontal in my right hand. With my other hand I let the second toothpick rest on the first, and suddenly without the slightest motion I cause the second toothpick to hop wildly off of the first. I've used it as a bargaining tool to get people to trade me something. At times I've used it to calm down an unruly mob of young children at a school event. One time I even used it to distract my young son while we were waiting for Melissa to come out of a store at the mall. Depending on my skill that day, I can sometimes even make the second toothpick fly off at the command of the viewer! The beauty of this little trick is that it's compelling enough to get anyone to stop and look at it for at least a few seconds, if not longer. I use it whenever I want to change the subject to something more interesting. One kid even paid me $10 for it!

A good tool is one that can be used in a variety of ways. The Bible is this kind of tool. If you're looking for inspirational characters, it's there. Need encouragement or find meaning in life? It has it. Trying to figure out tough personal questions? There's help for that, too. Even when you don't want to know what it says because you're doing something you know you shouldn't, it has help to bring you back around. Want to know what's going to happen in the future, or why things happened in the past? You'll find answers in its pages. The Bible has stood the test of time simply because it's so versatile. With more than 40 authors, from shepherds to farmers to kings, the Bible is able to reach into the life situations of anyone who picks it up. God made it that way so that everyone would be able to get something out of it, regardless of age, profession, or social standing. It's the ultimate multitool for the human experience. Begin learning how *you* can use it in your own life, today.

—GH

Don't Throw In the Towel

I have fought the good fight, I have finished the race, I have kept the faith. Now there is in store for me the crown of righteousness, which the Lord, the righteous Judge, will award to me on that day—and not only to me, but also to all who have longed for his appearing. 2 Timothy 4:7, 8.

The stinky, overflowing toilet was the last nail in my coffin. After breaking up a fight, being bad-mouthed by all the friends of a girl I had kicked out of the showers after lights-out, and being lied to twice, this was it. From my doorway I dejectedly watched gallons of water and sewage spill out into the carpeted hall, and I knew I couldn't face another day. Without a word I turned around, went back into my office, shut the door, and wrote a very pointed message to my boss in the dean's log. Though it was only my first month working in the dorm, I angrily assured her that I was through—this job wasn't for me, I hated it, I wanted to give up and find something—*anything*—better than this.

The next afternoon she penned a short note in her thin handwriting beside my diatribe: "Don't throw in the towel until you have stayed long enough to reap the rewards." At first I didn't understand what rewards she could possibly be talking about, but I did stay. In no time at all I began to form relationships, and I grew to love the 83 girls in my dorm. Some stayed up late in the night talking and laughing with me in my office; others came to me for spiritual guidance or Bible studies. The girl I threw out of the shower that night not only became a close friend, but I had the privilege of baptizing her the day before she graduated. Working as a dean turned out to be one of the greatest blessings of my entire life, and I still count it as one of my favorite jobs of all time. My boss was right—the rewards did come, and they were worth it!

One of the last recorded bits of Paul's writing is the verse above. He has come to the end of his ministry, and he knows his time on earth will soon end. Looking back at his course, he announces victoriously that he has fought a good fight, and he has finished the race. Now the rewards await him—a crown of righteousness and a resurrected life with Jesus forever.

Sometimes you may be tempted to throw in the towel, to give up your fight in the Christian life when it just seems too difficult. But stay the course and finish the race, because in the end the rewards are so worth it. Ask the Lord to help you fight the fight and keep the faith.

—MH

Run Amok

For an overseer, as God's steward, must be above reproach. He must not be arrogant or quick-tempered or a drunkard or violent or greedy for gain, but hospitable, a lover of good, self-controlled, upright, holy, and disciplined. Titus 1:7, 8, ESV.

On a routine trip to Target one of my church members lost control of her dog, Sophie, who is known to be slightly, well, wild. Sophie's a beautiful black Lab with an enormous amount of energy. She likes to run and jump and bark and jump and run and—you get the idea. So as Lauren was shutting the car door, Sophie decided to jump out. She struck a course straight for Target, miraculously avoiding being hit in the busy parking lot. She managed to enter the store via the automatic doors and continue her wild excursion. Naturally her master ran in after her only to find Sophie in the café area behind the counter. "Get that dog under control and take it out!" people said. But nobody actually offered any help. Eventually Sophie was caught and dragged back to the car, where she remained for the rest of the shopping trip. I personally followed up with this story by going to Target and inquiring into the matter. To this day every employee denies any dog of any kind was ever in the store, much less the café. That's a shame. It would have been great to purchase the security video to show at church.

Paul tells Titus, who is pastoring on the island of Crete, that one qualification for an "overseer" or an "elder"—or a leader—is self-control. Why? When someone can't control themselves, others are forced to chase after them, cleaning up a wake of destruction. While most people wouldn't run amok in Target's café, many do take on too much work, have emotions they can't control, try to please everybody, or give in to personal temptations. The results can be devastating, especially if an influential leader can't learn to keep themselves under control. This doesn't mean we won't have bad days, or that we should lose spontaneity. But we should strive for balance in those areas we tend to run wild in: spending money, spending time online, or listening to our iPods instead of talking to family members. You know what I'm talking about.

If we strive for balance now, God will honor it, and we may find ourselves with increased responsibility and leadership—both in our church and community. Our world is starving for good, balanced leadership, and there is no reason that you can't start becoming that leader today.

—SP

So Happy About a Stolen Car

Perhaps the reason he was separated from you for a little while was that you might have him back for good—no longer as a slave, but better than a slave, as a dear brother. He is very dear to me but even dearer to you, both as a man and as a brother in the Lord. Philemon 15, 16.

I have a love/hate relationship with my car. We've had our issues. There have been days when it dies or runs rough or seems to drink up way too much gas. I've considered getting a different car more than once, but I never do because it's just easier to keep it. Early one Sunday morning I was on a run to the grocery store. As I fumbled for my keys and headed for the car, I was suddenly confronted with an empty driveway and realized that someone had stolen it! My first thought was *Good! I can use the insurance for something better!*

But then I thought about all the stuff in my car and the little knick-knacks that had accumulated over the years. As I called the police and described the car, I even felt a little nostalgic, thinking of all the trips we'd taken in it across the country. I was surprisingly excited when the police called in less than an hour. "We found it in a parking lot five miles from here."

Sometimes you don't realize you want to keep something until it's taken away from you. That's kind of what happened with Philemon, the man Paul wrote a letter to, whose slave had run away after stealing from his master. Paul encouraged Philemon to take Onesimus (his slave) back without any hard feelings. From the letter we get the idea that Philemon was pretty upset with Onesimus, but grew to miss his company and his usefulness around the house. Paul is sticking up for Onesimus here, and he also informs Philemon that his former servant has become a Christian since he's been away. From the tone of Paul's letter we can assume that Philemon is indeed eager for Onesimus to return, but his feelings have changed and more than likely he will welcome him back, no longer as a slave, but as a brother and fellow Christian. But until Onesimus was gone, Philemon didn't know how much he wanted him around.

I often feel like this when I skip devotions, and the value of God in my life is much more acute when I notice that I haven't been meeting with Him. My life is a better ride when I include Him, and sometimes I notice it only once it's been gone for a while. It's a sad state of our fickle human nature, but thankfully God is always ready and willing to jump back in with us.

—GH

Slip 'n' Slime

For we do not have a high priest who is unable to sympathize with our weaknesses, but we have one who has been tempted in every way, just as we are—yet was without sin. Hebrews 4:15.

Skinny-dipping is a bad idea, especially for two young girls at night. It's simply not safe. But Peggy and I weren't thinking about that as we crept across campus that dark desert night. We were thinking about that big empty pool just waiting for us to jump in. It was early spring, and we hadn't been swimming in months, but tonight was the night! When we hopped the gym wall surrounding the pool area, we were surprised to find the pool lights off and the water unusually dark, but we thought nothing of it. In the name of adventure, we tore our pajamas off and jumped in—but was it ever slippery! We couldn't figure out why, but the bottom of the pool was slick as ice. We just could hardly stand up on it. Our feet slipped and slid in every direction. I tried to steady myself against the walls, but they wouldn't hold me up either. Even on the steps I could hardly sit down in one place. It was when we climbed back into the dorm that we noticed our feet, legs, backs, and arms were covered in some sort of slimy, dark-green algae. It was in my hair, under my fingernails, between my toes. And it smelled hideous! The next day when we peeked through the fence into the pool area, we discovered what happens to pool floors during winter. They get blanketed in layers of thick, blackish-green, bubbly algae. There in the slime we saw our footprints, and around campus that day the gym workers were talking about some idiots who went swimming in pond scum last night. Boy did we ever feel stupid—and gross!

Sin is just like that, isn't it? It seems like a great idea at first, but then it doesn't turn out so cool. We end up covered in filth, and our mistakes leave permanent marks on our lives and the lives of others. We can't clean sin's slime off of us because it's part of us. But Jesus didn't have that problem. The slime didn't stick to Him, and He wasn't full of sin like we are. Hebrews says that He was tempted in every way that we're tempted, so when you struggle with temptation, realize that He gets how hard it is for you. He understands. He just never slipped and fell for it Himself. This is why He's the perfect High Priest for us—the high priest stands in place of the people, to represent them before God and make atonement for their sins. Only a sinless High Priest could ever make true atonement for us slime bags down here.

—MH

Six Weddings and a Sabbath School

Now faith is being sure of what we hope for and certain of what we do not see. This is what the ancients were commended for. Hebrews 11:1, 2.

She was afraid she'd never get married. She'd been a bridesmaid in six weddings that summer and had attended almost a dozen more during the year. Just out of college and fresh into the working world, she knew her chances of meeting a Christian man were likely past. The last of all her friends still to be single, she came to the Lord one night in tears. "Find someone for me," she pleaded. "I want a family, Lord. I want to raise my children to know You."

As she was praying, she had a strong impression that the Lord would answer her prayer. She didn't hear a voice or anything; she simply felt a surety. As more of her friends became happily married, that surety stayed with her, and she chose faith instead of discouragement. She didn't know how it would work out, but she was sure that the Lord would bring someone into her life—she just felt it. She hadn't attended church for a while, but one day she decided to go back. In Sabbath school she found a handsome young man teaching the lesson. He noticed her as well—and took her out on a date that week. They dated for two years, then married, and I'm one of the four kids she raised to know the Lord.

Is this faith, this being sure God will work out a problem for you because He fills you with hope? Hebrews 11, the Bible's faith chapter, gives a long list of what faith actually looks like. Here are some examples: Faith is believing in Creation, though we can't prove it. It's believing that God exists and earnestly seeking Him, as Enoch did. Faith is Noah building an ark though he'd never seen rain before. Faith is Abraham following God's call to a strange new land. Faith is Abraham offering his son on the altar. Faith is Moses' parents hiding him, unafraid of Pharaoh's punishment. Faith is the Israelites marching around Jericho like fools—with no weapons. Faith is Rahab's cord in the window, knowing God would save her and her family.

The common thread I see in all of these stories is that though they couldn't fathom the outcome, these people trusted God anyway. Today we act as if we need to understand the end before we put our faith in God, but that's not faith. Having faith like the heroes of old means believing that God has a way to work things out, especially when they seem impossible. —MH

"O God, I Can . . ."

Let us fix our eyes on Jesus, the author and perfecter of our faith, who for the joy set before him endured the cross. Hebrews 12:2.

Some said it was because she was very fat. Others thought perhaps she had a medical complication or was just terribly out of shape. Whatever the case, she was still running the marathon a full three hours after every other runner had crossed the finish line, her progress marked by inches with each step. Still, she plodded on, one foot in front of the other. As she topped the last hill and could see the finish line in the distance, it was as if her eyes became permanently fixed on it. She began repeating something to herself, again and again. When the news cameras covering the story finally zoomed in on her face, every viewer could perfectly make out the words: When she lifted her right foot she gasped, "O God . . ." And when she lifted her left she claimed, ". . . I can!" People in the crowd feared she might die there on the road, but as that woman crossed the finish line she triumphantly shouted, "O God, I can!"

This is a great idea for how we should run the Christian race—depending on God for each and every step that we take, especially when we don't think we can move another inch. That's what "fix our eyes on Jesus" means in the verse above. Like a finish line, zone in on Him and don't turn to the right or to the left. He will get you through, because He is the "author and perfecter" of our faith. Do you know what an author of a book is responsible for? Every single word. Every thought, plot, wrap-up, and ending—everything. This is Jesus, responsible for every single part of our faith. He grows it from a tiny seed and brings it to ultimate perfection in the end. What a great anchor to fix our eyes on!

But do you know what Jesus fixed *His* eyes on when He had to endure the cross? It was you. Hebrews says that "the joy set before him" kept Him going— and that joy is us. We are His joy, the joy of ransoming us back and welcoming us into heaven with Him someday kept Him saying, "O God, I can!" You were His finish line. Are you running full steam today, or is your faith slowing down and losing courage? Does it hurt with every single step? Steal the mantra of the exhausted runner and use it at every corner, at every turn: "O God, I can!" With Jesus, victory is yours.

—MH

Disappointment With God

When he asks, he must believe and not doubt, because he who doubts is like a wave of the sea, blown and tossed by the wind. . . . [He] should not think he will receive anything. James 1:6, 7.

When Greg and I graduated from the seminary and returned to the Washington Conference, the number one thing at the top of my prayer list was a job. Day and night I told the Lord that I desired to work with teenagers again, ideally teaching Bible, or something along that line. When I learned that a teaching position had opened up at a nearby school, I was elated. And when they called to question me about the job, I was simply ecstatic. I knew the Lord was working things out for me and answering my prayer. I had faith He would come through for me.

And they gave the job to someone else! How are we supposed to believe that God will answer our prayers when sometimes He actually doesn't? He has that right—He *is* God. He doesn't have to do things our way, but what do we do about verses like the one above that says when we ask for something we must believe and not doubt? Do we have to believe that we'll get what we want, but God doesn't always have to give it to us? Is this crazy-making?

Since I didn't get a job I became a stay-at-home mom, and spent slow, quiet, carefree days with my son. We explored zoos and forests, made crafts and Play-Doh castles, and read about a thousand books. A few months ago I had my second little boy, and suddenly the slow, quiet days disappeared. I'm running all the time—busy, stressed! The baby needs me constantly. It takes all day just to dress myself and put food on the table. The other night someone reminded me about how hard I'd once prayed for a job, and it was like a blinding light suddenly glared in my face: God *had* actually given me what I wanted! Had I known the end from the beginning, as He does, I would have seen how precious and fleeting those quiet days with my little boy really were and chosen them, hands down, over any job out there. God knew! He didn't answer the prayer that I so strongly believed He would—He gave me what I really wanted.

That story is just a start to answering the questions we asked above—the rest is a journey you'll have to take. For what it's worth, here's what I've learned: to trust that God *can* do something is more important than insisting He *must* do it. To trust that God *will* do what's ultimately best frees you to accept any answer He happens to give.

—MH

Fight!

For where jealousy and selfish ambition exist, there will be disorder and every vile practice.
James 3:16, ESV.

I am beginning to prefer college sports games to the professional ones. The college games I've been to are not only full of hysterical fans but always provide giveaways, contests, hilarious games, and much better seating (not to mention that they're cheaper). One of my first college games was a hockey match between the rival Wichita, Kansas, and Tulsa, Oklahoma, teams. What made the evening memorable was their animosity and rivalry for each other nearly prevented them from playing the game. Hockey tends to be a very physical game, but this game took it to a whole new level. The fans screamed for action, and the teams didn't hesitate to give it to them—and each other. I think there were more fights than goals. Pads flew as fast as fists, and the referees had to constantly break up fights. The best was during a face-off, when the ref dropped the puck and neither of the players even noticed. As soon as the puck hit the ice they threw down their equipment and started whaling on each other, to the delight of the crowd. I was both entertained and a little disturbed.

James's book is full of lots of practical wisdom, including the one mentioned above. Selfish ambition is one of the most fundamental sins—if not the essence of sin—in that it seeks to put oneself first above everything else, including God. And when all that matters is your own personal happiness, you'll easily sacrifice the happiness of others to get it. People who are self-centered are willing to do any "vile practice" to get what they want.

World news is full of examples like Bernie Madoff, who stole from his own people billions and billions of dollars for his own personal gain. At any given moment parents kill unwanted babies for being in the way of what they want, kids kill their parents, people cheat in business and in school to get ahead, and the list could go on and on.

This is why it is so important that we constantly check our motivation for what we're doing; and it's why Scripture constantly tells us to love our neighbor and even place their needs above ours. It's not just for the benefit of others, but also for our protection.

—SP

A Verbal Beating From a High School Dancer

But in your hearts set apart Christ as Lord. Always be prepared to give an answer to everyone who asks you to give the reason for the hope that you have. But do this with gentleness and respect, keeping a clear conscience, so that those who speak maliciously against your good behavior in Christ may be ashamed of their slander. 1 Peter 3:15, 16.

My hands clenched into tight balls. About 80 pairs of eyes watched my sluggish march across the front of the room filled with public high school students who had just spent the last half hour listening to a presentation on Seventh-day Adventist beliefs as part of their world religions class. My part was to wrap up the class with a question-and-answer time. The part about the beliefs was what had made me nervous. My friend, in a moment of spontaneity, had gotten up and rattled off a list of the things that Adventists weren't allowed to do: eat pork, dance, go to movies, wear jewelry, attend church any day but Saturday, etc. It was after she had finished and rushed away from the podium that I started my long march. Silence. Fidgeting. Death by the sheer absence of sound. Then a young girl stood to her feet in the back row.

"I'm a dancer," she said, a slight quiver in her voice. "I dance because it's part of who I am and how I express myself. I *don't* dance for any sexual reasons, or anything like that, and I don't go to the clubs. I dance because I have to be me, and because I feel like there's no other way to show that to the world. *Are you telling me that I'm going to hell because I dance?*" I didn't know what to say and, frankly, the class went downhill from there. That day we had given our peers the impression that what we believed in was a lot of negatives.

Sometimes we Adventists are called to give account for what we believe. Maybe your time won't be as dramatic as mine, but it will come (if it hasn't already). Peter says we're to be ready to give an answer for the *hope* we have. Hope is positive, not negative. We're to focus on the good things, not the things we *don't* do, or *can't* do. Who wants to join a group that lives by a big list of no's? Why not focus on a weekly vacation day, living 11 years longer than the rest of the world, not worrying about ghosts, looking forward to Christ's coming, and so much more? In both our actions and our words let's exhibit the hope that we have and the relationship with Jesus that gives us that hope. Are you ready to share that?

—GH

The Scariest Animal of All

Your enemy the devil prowls around like a roaring lion looking for someone to devour. Resist him, standing firm in the faith. 1 Peter 5:8, 9.

When I first heard the scream we were sleeping in an open, three-sided shed in the middle of the woods. It sounded like a woman or a screaming child, and by that I knew exactly what it truly was: a mountain lion, a man-hunter, somewhere nearby. Was it aware of our presence there in that open shack? Was it circling, watching us? Mountain lions come pretty near to the top of the list of all the things in the world that I'm afraid of because they are such cunning, clever hunters. I once did a study on them to try to face my fears, but it only made me more terrified than I'd been before. I learned that they will stalk and track you for miles before they actually attack. They watch for any sign of weakness and attack you there. For example, if a person is limping, they'll go right for the sore leg. If you have small children with you, they'll go for the smallest one. They're most likely to attack people who are hiking alone. In all the attack stories I read most of the people had no idea a lion was anywhere around until it was upon them. One woman was sitting by a stream when suddenly her head was being forced under the water, held there by giant fangs, in an effort to drown her! So you see, mountain lions are wicked and horrible, and they scare the daylights out of me!

With very good reason, the apostle Peter compares the devil to a lion. Peter says he prowls around and looks for someone to devour. Somehow I can picture this, can't you? I mean, think of how I just described mountain lions. Doesn't the devil act in the exact same ways? Doesn't he study us carefully and attack us right where we're weakest? Doesn't he strike when we least expect him? And isn't he more likely to have power over us when we are alone, without the support of others? Our enemy is just exactly like those evil lions!

Has it occurred to you lately that the devil is hunting you? Do you realize that the enemy would like to have your heart and soul as his own? Don't take it lightly. There is a real battle in the universe, and the battleground is your life. So don't mess around on his territory and don't allow yourself to become his prey. Resist him, cling to Jesus, and make it clear whom you belong to.

—MH

Romantic Musings From the *Encyclopaedia Britannica*

Above all, you must understand that no prophecy of Scripture came about by the prophet's own interpretation. For prophecy never had its origin in the will of man, but men spoke from God as they were carried along by the Holy Spirit. 2 Peter 1:20, 21.

The little love letter oozed with mooshy goosheyness. I don't know which of my friends had found it, but it was definitely one of the most nauseating pieces of romantic fluff that had ever been composed. As we all stood around, reading over each other's shoulders, we came to a poem on the last page. As one of my buddies read it aloud in his best Shakespearian impression, just to give it the proper air, I began to feel as if I had heard all this before. Halfway through the poem I *knew* I'd heard it before, so I grabbed an encyclopedia and turned to a love poem written by Emily Dickinson. This wannabe Romeo had plagiarized a love poem! Suddenly the owner of the letter, a fiery red-haired girl, exploded into the crowd, yelling at all of us, spitting venom in all directions. "But he copied the whole thing out of the encyclopedia!" I shouted, handing her the volume. She turned a deeper shade of pink and stomped off in search of lover boy.

In the world of school papers and reports, if the teacher finds out that you've been copying someone else's work, you can be pretty sure you're not going to fare well on that paper. But when it comes to God's Word the question has always been Did God write the Bible word for word or did the men writing it just kind of make it up? The answer, according to Peter, is a little bit of both. Inspiration for writing the Bible wasn't a word-for-word dictation in which the human suddenly turned into a robot. If that was how it worked, then having a human write would've been an unnecessary step. Peter says the Bible writers were "carried along," or given divine thoughts, but left up to their own experiences and words in writing those thoughts down. For some reason God felt it was important to include humans in the writing of His Word, so He allowed them to participate in its creation. I find that reassuring because we know that nothing got lost in the translation. God made sure that they communicated His idea accurately, without losing that human touch.

Like Jesus Himself, the Bible is a great combination of human and divine. So when you read it, trust that it's come to you exactly the way God wanted it to.

—GH

Crazy

> But false prophets also arose among the people, just as there will be false teachers among you, who will secretly bring in destructive heresies, even denying the Master who bought them, bringing upon themselves swift destruction. 2 Peter 2:1, ESV.

The number of nutty people in this world never ceases to amaze me. I just finished a conversation with a Christian who told me that I need to make sure people are "operating in their manifestations." This means that all the spiritual gifts in 1 Corinthians 12 and 14 belong to everybody; and if we can't heal people or discern their "spirit" at first glance, we're not truly Christians. As we chatted about other topics, this man was very knowledgeable, impressing me with his serious study. Yet the overall conversation exposed serious oversimplifications in his theology and views of God. I'm not sure if I would completely call him a false teacher, or not.

On a lighter note, I received an e-mail several months ago with the headline "TruTh fRoM a CRazY GuY in OmaHa!" It was nice of him to let me know he was a false teacher right off the bat. And as I read the nonsensical e-mail he repeated what I have come to believe was his theme throughout: "I am not on drugs." Sure buddy, and I'm not going to delete this e-mail. Actually I didn't. I get so many weird e-mails that I have a folder labeled "crazy," and I'm getting quite a collection. The important thing to note is that not all false teachers come with labels. What's scary is that some come with credentials. Our job is to make sure we take the time to test their words against God's Word and not be surprised if we discover they are false—even if they have all the titles and degrees in the world.

One of the key identifiers in the above passage is the word "secretly." Peter says they will be sneaky about how they present things to get them into the church. In my experience this doesn't necessarily mean secret conspiracies. What I have found many times is that the false teachers market themselves as having *discovered* secret conspiracies or truths and then sell them to an audience with a dramatic presentation.

Don't be deceived. There is no substitute for doing your own research if someone says something sensational, critical, or overly dramatic. Take time to search God's Word and talk to people you trust if something doesn't sound right. And don't be afraid to ask hard questions.

—SP

Endure

For this is a gracious thing, when, mindful of God, one endures sorrows while suffering unjustly. For what credit is it if, when you sin and are beaten for it, you endure? But if when you do good and suffer for it you endure, this is a gracious thing in the sight of God. For to this you have been called, because Christ also suffered for you, leaving you an example, so that you might follow in his steps. 1 Peter 2:19-21, ESV.

Terry Bradshaw, a famous quarterback in the National Football League, had a shaky start when he first arrived in Pittsburgh in 1970. With nicknames such as the "blond bomber" and "Louisiana rifleman," everyone expected him to do great things. When he didn't have the seasons he wanted, the crowds turned ugly. Rather than supporting the young player, booing him became a favorite sport in Pittsburgh, Bradshaw reported later. He tells what happened when his mom came to visit for several weeks to encourage him. "It can't be that bad, Terry," she said. Then they went to a hockey game together and were both booed. "They booed my mother!" exclaimed Terry. "They were booing her for giving birth to me. How awful is that?"*

In this passage in 1 Peter, the followers of Jesus are told to endure under unjust rulers who persecute them, even though they haven't done anything wrong. Peter tells them that Christ, too, experienced persecution while doing what was right. If we're serious about our faith, doing our best to act as Christ would, we're bound to encounter trouble.

Have you ever been "booed" because of your faith? You're trying to be moral, kind, and a good example, but people don't seem to appreciate your efforts. Or maybe you've stumbled in your walk with God, and people noticed. You're "supposed" to be a Christian, and you fell short, so they rub it in your face. But Peter says to endure, and by enduring we honor God. Who knows what may happen when we continue to be a Christian in the midst of persecution? Terry Bradshaw eventually led his team to four Super Bowl titles and accomplished other amazing feats in his career, silencing his critics. The Christians in Peter's day continued preaching Christ, and it has impacted countless millions of peoples. Imagine what God has in store for you!

—SP

Then Madden Said to Summerall (Chicago: Triumph Books, 2009).

Dear friends, since God so loved us, we also ought to love one another. No one has ever seen God; but if we love one another, God lives in us and his love is made complete in us. 1 John 4:11, 12.

He always sat in the front row. Every week this hunched, decrepit old man, with ghastly burn scars up and down his arms and legs, hobbled slowly to the front, and inched down into his seat. And every week someone would ask him to speak. He was the most interesting man in town. As a young man he'd had a fierce temper. He once spent several years on an island, where he said he had visions and dreams of beasts and angels and dragons, and he survived being boiled in a vat of oil because government leaders were afraid of him. He'd stood at the cross near Jesus' mother and watched his dear Friend die. He had walked inside Christ's empty tomb. Because he had lived through so many amazing experiences, the little church of Ephesus would wait on the edge of their seats each week to see what he would say. Would he describe his experiences on Patmos? Recount the Transfiguration? Surely he would talk about the cross!

But no. Every single week, no matter what, John stood up front in the little church and said the same exact thing: "Brothers, love one another!" That's it. Then he would creep back to his chair and sit down. Week after week, it was all he would ever say. After everything he'd seen and done, the Church Fathers record that this one thought is what he wanted to leave with people. It must have been the idea he believed was most important.

Reading 1 John is like sitting in the second row of the church in Ephesus, because here we have John saying the same thing, over and over again, in many different ways. He wrote this letter during a time when the church was under severe attack from false teachers who claimed that Jesus was not really human at all. John's goal in the letter is to combat this idea, but in the middle of doing this he seems to get carried away again on his favorite topic: that we ought to love one another. It's like he just can't help himself. God's love transformed his own life so much that he just has to pass it on to other people. I know there are people in your life who are hard to love, but God loves you, and loving others makes the experience of His love complete. So ask Him for the grace to love the unlovable today.

—MH

Not Merely Man and His Arguments

Watch out that you do not lose what you have worked for, but that you may be rewarded fully. 2 John 8.

Do not imitate what is evil but what is good. 3 John 11.

During July 1857, in a dusty, crowded tent on the fields of Greenvale, Illinois, a series of tent meetings was held for the local farmers and residents. After many nights of sermons a young man walked down the aisle and accepted the teachings of the church. The man's name was Moses Hull, and he soon became a powerful preacher and evangelist. He was well known for taking on the spiritualists, a group that believed you could communicate with the dead. But in his debates he began to get arrogant, as if the gospel couldn't continue without him. Finally he challenged a local spiritualist named Jamieson to a debate in Paw Paw, Michigan. During the debate Hull found himself confronting a demon named Downing, whom Jamieson was channeling. Ellen White later warned him in a letter: "In discussing with spiritualists you have not merely to meet man and his arguments, but Satan and his angels." Instead of taking her advice, he began to forget his personal devotions and to rely more on himself. Some of the doubts that began to bother him he took to the spiritualists, trying to learn from them. Not long after, he left the Adventist Church altogether and began to preach for the spiritualists.

As if it were written to Moses Hull himself, 2 John warns us that it is possible to lose everything we've been working toward. Third John echoes that we should not even imitate evil, as Hull thought he could do. At the time John wrote, the gospel was being taken from place to place by teachers who visited in homes. Both of these tiny letters were written to help believers know which teachers they should trust, and which ones were teaching error. The biggest mistake Hull made was letting his devotional life slide. That daily connection with God's Word left him open to doubts and questions. When we ignore the Bible, we're neglecting the source where we can find answers for our lives. Hull's faith was killed by separating himself from fellow Christians.

Do you have questions about your faith? *Good!* We need them to keep our spiritual walk from turning into a crawl, but we need to take them first to the Bible, then to trusted Christian mentors who've been where you are. Don't let anything cause you to lose all you've been working toward with Jesus.

—GH

Good Defense

To him who is able to keep you from falling and to present you before his glorious presence without fault. Jude 24.

One of the great tragedies of my life is being a Vikings fan. I am a born and raised Minnesotan, and each year I get to watch our sports teams get to the playoffs and lose. The loss to the Saints in January 2010 is particularly painful. Nevertheless, they did win one playoff game against the Dallas Cowboys on January 17, 2010, that was a particular joy for me to watch.

The Vikings were not favored to win. However, we silenced our critics as we defeated—nay, devastated—our opponents, winning 34-3. One of the keys to our victory was the Vikings' defense breaking through the ranks of the Cowboys' offense and sacking their quarterback (the player who throws the ball). This means we sat him on his rear end before he could throw the football.

The Cowboys' quarterback, Tony Romo, a gifted athlete, hadn't been sacked in nine consecutive games. So you can imagine how demoralizing it was when the Vikings sacked him six times in that one game. Time and time again Romo found himself plastered on the ground or, as one commentator put it, running for his life. It was an unfortunate outing for the Cowboys, as their offensive line couldn't keep their quarterback from falling. By the end of the game he was so delirious that he threw a pass right to one of the Vikings for an interception. It was a long, frustrating game for them to think about as they made their way back to Dallas.

Thankfully, the Christians' defense is much better.

The above verse from James is one of my favorites in the Bible. We are surrounded by much that tries to "sack" us. Each week brings new anxieties, stresses, and fears. We know our own faults all too well, and we can be tempted to think that somehow they are too bad for God to be able to defend. But James tells us that Jesus is able to give us adequate defense against the enemy's opposition. This doesn't mean we won't experience trials and failures—but it does mean that we can feel secure in the midst of them as long as we look to Jesus for help.

—SP

Who Makes the First Move?

The revelation of Jesus Christ, which God gave him to show his servants what must soon take place. Revelation 1:1.

For years my siblings and I have secretly harbored suspicions that our youngest brother, Josh, would never find a woman. It's not that he's ugly or strange, but rather that he's picky and shy—a deadly combination. Plus he doesn't go out and do a whole lot of social things, and he's never had the courage to approach girls in the first place, which is the reason we worried that he'd never meet anyone. That's why we all just about dropped dead of shock when we learned that he would be taking a smart, funny, cute, and caring young woman to the spring banquet. We gasped when we saw the pictures—she was gorgeous—and we gaped when we met her. She was wonderful; a perfect fit for my brother. No wonder they are now engaged! We just couldn't understand it, though. How did this miracle come to be? Just recently we finally learned the secret: she had approached him. Brittny had taken the initiative to ask him out the first time. If she hadn't made the first move, I guarantee you that nothing would've happened between them at all, and I wouldn't be getting a new sister-in-law this summer, or ever!

The book of Revelation is a giant example of God taking the initiative toward us. God initiated the encounter with John, sending the visions for him to write down. Even the name, the Revelation of Jesus Christ, indicates a God who wants to reveal Himself, wants to make the first move, wants us to know Him. People are confused and overwhelmed by Revelation, but actually this book is all about God revealing His character to us. Revelation paints one of the most beautiful pictures of Jesus in the entire Bible. Read it for yourself: see Him as He dies for us, fights beasts and dragons for us, finds ways to protect us, sends us warnings about the future, seals His people from horrid trials, and promises to come again. One writer says that in the book of Revelation all the other books of the Bible meet and end. Jesus is uplifted as the center of all hope.

Maybe you've gotten a picture of a God who expects you to come chasing after Him, or who is waiting for you to clean up your act so He'll be pleased with you, but that's all wrong and backwards. God is the one who chases us, reveals Himself to us, and helps us get to know Him. He takes the initiative every time. Haven't you seen Him reaching into your life recently?

—MH

The Ultimate Report Card

To the angel of the church in Ephesus write: These are the words of him who holds the seven stars in his right hand and walks among the seven golden lampstands. Revelation 2:1.

Having your grades mailed to your parents at the end of a semester is about the worst policy schools can ever adopt. Even if you're a good student you're left sitting around over a break stressing about what the card says. Maybe the teacher wrote some special gems in the margin about your disruptive attitude in class, or something. I used to become super-obsessed about the mailman's schedule, watching for him so that I could intercept any letter coming from school. I wanted a heads-up on things before my parents saw it.

The seven churches listed at the beginning of the book of Revelation were getting a report card of sorts too. In this vision Jesus Himself is both an encouragement to them, but also a little scary, since He points out some of their weaknesses. I used to think, *Man, getting a report card on your spiritual life from Jesus—that must have been kind of harsh!* However, when you take a closer look at these letters the picture of Jesus isn't that of some principal getting the churches in trouble; it's one of a tender guide who knows these people inside and out. For example, in the letter to the church of Pergamum Jesus says He's going to give them a white stone with a name on it that only they will know. Back then, during a trial for someone's life the jury voted guilty or not guilty by placing a black or white stone in a basket. A white stone meant that the juror voted not guilty, and the prisoner was set free. Jesus is voting not guilty for these people; He's saying He's on their side! Even in the harshest letter (to the church of Laodicea) Jesus uses imagery only they would get. He calls them lukewarm, like water that is neither hot nor cold. Instantly the people understood, because their city's water source came through pipes from a hot spring five miles away. It was lukewarm by the time it got there, and everyone had to either chill or heat it to make it useful. Jesus used things they understood, coming to them in just the way they needed. He's that way for us, too. He knows everything about us, good and bad. There's no reason to hide things from Him. He's a safe place to take your shortcomings, because you can be sure you already have the white stone of grace on your side.

—GH

Hold On!

Only hold fast what you have until I come. Revelation 2:25, ESV.

Jeremiah had never held the ball. Ever. He wasn't the type of kid you passed it to or handed it to—and I don't think he wanted it any other way. Not built for athleticism, Jeremiah either stood around chatting with the girls or on the sidelines by the teacher, his arms folded, muttering under his breath. The lack of ability wasn't only because of physical deficits; we were merciless in taunting and mocking every facet of his life. This didn't help his self-confidence. I tell you this so you can appreciate the miracle that occurred during one football game during PE.

The teams were lined up midfield, facing each other, when the signal was given and the ball went into play. I have no idea how it happened, but Jeremiah found himself not only holding the ball, but holding the ball downfield at least 20 yards away from the opposing team. Now, even the simplest mind knows (especially if it is attached to a weak body) that if you have the ball near the opposing team's goal, you run for dear life. For a moment the entire field was in shock, and nobody moved or breathed. Then bedlam erupted.

"RUN! RUN, JEREMIAH!" we screamed. "RUN, OR THEY'LL KILL YOU!" He needed no further encouragement. He bolted. Well, sort of. He ran on dry ground as most people run on wet ice. Even so, he made progress, and the other team couldn't get to him. He was within 10 yards of a touchdown when he panicked. Whether it was confusion over all the shouting or fear of death at the hand of the opposing team, Jeremiah did the unthinkable. Seconds away from achieving praise and adoration from his peers—he threw the ball. Into the end zone. *To nobody!* Then he stopped, turned around, and crossed his arms. He looked puzzled at the immediate outburst of screams, hoots, and boos.

Jesus asks a church in Thyatira to hold on to what they know, and to hold on to Him in the midst of persecution, because He is coming. We don't know when, but Scripture tells us that it will be fast and when we least expect it. We need to hold on to Jesus, despite the discouragements that surround us, because our "goal" might be closer than we think.

—SP

The First War

And there was war in heaven. Michael and his angels fought against the dragon, and the dragon and his angels fought back. But he was not strong enough, and they lost their place in heaven. Revelation 12:7, 8.

Why do bad things happen to good people? Why didn't God just kill Satan before he made a mess of things? Couldn't God have started over with new people after Adam and Eve sinned, rather than letting the world get into the mess it is today? These questions have haunted Christians for years, and they're the kind of questions that can cause lasting doubt in many people's faith. Though I don't claim to have an answer for everything, I do think that there's one Bible teaching that points us in the right direction; and it starts in the verses above.

You've heard of "the great controversy," right? It's not just a great one among many—it's *the* controversy around which all others hinge. In these verses we get a glimpse into the time *before* earth was created. We see heaven, not as the joyous place where angels sit around playing harps, but as the site of a great struggle. The dragon, Satan himself, fought against Michael and the heavenly angels. Isaiah 14:13 and 14 says that Satan grew angry and vengeful toward God, even desiring to overthrow Him and take the heavenly throne for himself. He said, "I will raise my throne above the stars of God. . . . I will ascend above the tops of the clouds; I will make myself like the Most High." With this singular motive the war rages on through the centuries, now here on this earth, through the lives and decisions that generations of people have made. Satan is still challenging God, and we all are given the choice to follow one or the other.

Everything we have been through this year—every single book of the Bible, all the stories of nations, people, and kings, all the prophecies, every promise and warning, the life of Jesus and the grace from Calvary—every single bit of it climaxes and culminates here in Revelation. The Bible has spanned the sweep of the great controversy itself. It is the history of the cosmic battle between Jesus and Satan over the character of God. Here in Revelation we are shown how the great controversy will come to an end once and for all. You and I are engaged in the war too, because God gives each of us a choice. Love can never force someone to love back, so God allows all of us to accept or reject Him. What is your choice in this war going to be?

—MH

The One Thing Everybody Is Looking For

They overcame him by the blood of the Lamb. Revelation 12:11.

W hy do you matter? A crazy energetic young preacher came to our church recently and told how one day he talked to a giant biker dude, with tattoos from head to toe, in the supermarket line, sharing the gospel with him right then and there. I admire this guy because I'm not sure that's something I would do. We are supposed to share the gospel with the people we come in contact with, but isn't it a rather hard thing to do these days? We're afraid. We don't want to sound dumb, and let's be real—people just don't want to hear it.

So what do we say? Unbelievers don't struggle with petty church doctrinal differences. What *do* they struggle with? Value. You see, if the devil, "the accuser," died today, we'd all do a pretty good job of continuing his work in our own heads. We accuse ourselves, never feel good enough. We base our self-worth on trivial, shallow things, and we still haven't learned to love ourselves. Because we feel worthless, we don't value other people, either. To distract ourselves, we do all sorts of things—smoke stuff, buy stuff, eat stuff, watch stuff, say fake, shmoozy stuff—none of which brings real value. There's only one source of infinite value: Jesus. Look at the above verse: "They overcame him by the blood of the Lamb." If you told some street people that they can overcome by the blood of the Lamb, they wouldn't get it. What we can say is that the fact that Jesus died on the cross for us means *we* have infinite value. And value, in a nutshell, is the key to a changed life; it's the key to the Christian life. When we know we have value, we become brave enough to take an honest look in the mirror and not flinch at what we see or try to hide it. We can face the dark sides of ourselves because our value won't be changed by what we see. But until we know we're valuable, we won't face these things. We'll run instead.

Are you struggling with self-worth today, trying to believe that you're valuable? Are you searching for value in distractions, habits, relationships? Is the accuser trying to tell you that your life isn't worth much? Well, consider Jesus. He knows all about you, down to the last detail. He loves you just the way you are. He is committed to being part of your life forever. Overcome that accuser with "the blood of the Lamb"—with the fact that Jesus' death for you makes you valuable beyond measure, and frees you from the battle of self-worth. —MH

Are You a Leftover?

The dragon was wroth with the woman, and went to make war with the remnant of her seed, which keep the commandments of God, and have the testimony of Jesus Christ. Revelation 12:17, KJV.

That sour odor came rushing out every time I opened my fridge today, and filled my whole kitchen with the deathly scent of stench. Because it was just that horrible, I finally had to dig in and find its source. After rifling through containers, cartons, packages, and bags, I came upon a small Tupperware bowl in the very back, filled with wilted, disintegrating cooked broccoli—leftovers from a meal we'd forgotten about long since. I'd take the diaper pail any day over the smell of week-old broccoli. The real dilemma was whether or not to keep the Tupperware, because I could do so only at the expense of taking off the lid and freeing the awful odor to permeate my entire house. In the end I decided the container wasn't worth it.

To be called "leftovers" doesn't sound like a desirable thing, but that's exactly what Revelation calls the faithful people in earth's last days: the leftovers. The word remnant means the ones who are "remaining," or "the rest." These are the last people at the end of time who are still true. They haven't followed the beast, and they haven't compromised their integrity.

You'll hear a lot of talk in the Adventist Church about the remnant. Who are they? The verse above gives clues. The remnant will do two things: (1) keep the commandments of God, and (2) confess that they belong to Jesus Christ. Next, we can jump ahead a few chapters to Revelation 19:10 and see that the last-day people will possess some type of visionary, prophetic gift. This group will also focus on the gospel (Rev. 10; 14), have a special emphasis on Daniel and Revelation (Rev. 10) and the sanctuary (Rev. 11), and have clear teachings on judgment and commandment-keeping (Rev. 14). Eventually they'll be the object of worldwide attention and have a message of worldwide significance. God's remnant will have all these qualities. Does this remind you of a church alive today?

I don't know if you'll be alive at the time of the end, but if you are, you'll have to make some serious decisions about whom you worship and follow. If it is your desire to be among God's remnant people, then begin by making sure that you belong to Jesus completely today.

—MH

How Will We Know?

Fear God and give him glory, because the hour of his judgment has come. Worship him who made the heavens, the earth, the sea and the springs of water. Revelation 14:7.

How did you know Greg was the one?" More teenage girls (and guys) than I can count have asked me this question. And my answer is always the same: sooner or later, it will just become obvious. It'll be clear as day. Even scarier than the how-will-you-know-whom-to-marry question is the how-will-we-know-when-it's-the-"last days" question. Most people are afraid they won't recognize the end times or be prepared for them, but Revelation contains a special clue for how we'll know the last days are approaching. In the very center of the book, the place of highest importance in a Jewish book, we find the verse from the three angels' messages above that's a call for the world to make a decision about whom they're going to worship. The last days begin with a cry for people to worship God, the true Creator of heaven and earth.

But inside this verse is a hidden message that you as a twenty-first-century American might never recognize, though it would have been obvious to the people in John's day. The hidden message is found in the words "worship him who made the heavens, the earth, the sea and the springs of water." Now, this may sound like just another description of God to you, but that's because you don't recognize where it comes from. If I quoted a line from one of today's most popular movies, you might know it right off. Or if I said, "For God so loved the world, that he gave his only begotten Son," you would know right away that I was quoting John 3:16, the best-known verse in the Bible today. And the words that John quotes above actually come from one of the best-known scriptures in *his* day—the Sabbath commandment. A string of exact words is not an accident. It is a deliberate and purposeful quote to draw people back to something. Every reader would recognize it, and know that in this call for the world to make a decision about worship, Sabbathkeeping would be a central issue.

Here's the punch line: the last days begin with a worldwide call to return to worshipping the Creator God on the Sabbath day. The Adventist Church is seen as an end-time movement because we are making *that* call, right now. What does that mean for you? The end times have begun, my friend. Time for you to make a solid choice today: whom will you worship?

—MH

375

Blessed and holy is the one who shares in the first resurrection! Over such the second death has no power, but they will be priests of God and of Christ, and they will reign with him for a thousand years. Revelation 20:6, ESV.

As I was scrolling through the news a few months ago I found a delightful story of a Major League baseball player who had a very frustrating strikeout. If you ignore the fact that many baseball players are "juiced" or on "dietary supplements" of a suspect nature, they can be capable of feats of strength. Like breaking a Louisville Slugger baseball bat over one knee.

I have never tried to break a full-sized hardwood bat over my leg. I have not done this because I place a great deal of value on my leg and depend on it to help me function. But this particular player was going to teach that dumb bat a lesson for its role in his strikeout as he walked back from the batter's box to the dugout. With tens of thousands of people watching, he raised that bat high and brought it crashing down on his leg.

It didn't break. He tried again—still didn't break. After a third time without even putting a hairline fracture in the bat he shook his head and made his way back to the dugout—doing his best to hide any hint of a limp. However, hiding the public shame he just experienced was impossible. I laughed and found the video on youtube.com, and watched it several times.

In this final book of the Bible we are given a tremendous promise that death cannot overpower those who follow Jesus and are resurrected to new life at His second coming. No matter what death may throw at us—cancer, car accidents, crashing planes, or colliding tectonic plates creating catastrophic earthquakes—our life cannot be broken. Death will be shamed in front of the entire universe, when He will wipe away every tear from our eyes, and the old earth will pass away.

When Jesus promises us life, He means it. I hope you will make the decision to embrace the life He has promised and we can stand together and watch as death will be "thrown out of the game" forever.

—SP

The End

Surely I come quickly. Amen. Even so, come, Lord Jesus. Revelation 22:20, KJV.

Just like that it was over. Everything. All the late nights in the dorm spent laughing. All the lunchtime stories. All the Saturday nights. All the classes and tests, all the jokes and pranks, and all the memories. Done. Finished. On graduation day I drove out the gate of my high school campus for the last time, with the very final feeling that a chapter in my life had slammed shut with a bang. I couldn't go back and do anything again—no last day with my friends; no last afternoon in class. For the rest of my life it would be only a memory. My cap, gown, and diploma lay on the seat beside me, and as my car sped down those familiar streets one last time I began to do something strange. I began asking myself, *Did I live it well? Did I seize every chance, capture all the fun, and enjoy every moment?* I thought of all my regrets, all the opportunities I missed, the people I was mean to, the risks I hadn't taken. And then I realized: I wasn't ready for high school to end. Oh, I was ready for the classes and tests to be done, for sure, and I was excited to be going to college, but I wasn't ready to leave my friends or our good days together. I wasn't ready for the end to come so soon.

Today we have come to the end of this book, the end of our trip through the Bible, and the end of one more year of your life. It's been a long journey, but there are more ahead waiting. What chapter of your life are you in at the moment? High school, college, something in between, or something later? This chapter too will end for you as well, and before you know it you'll be looking back on today, thinking, *Those were some good times.* So my advice to you before it's all over? Live it well. Make the most of each day by walking with Jesus along the way, and minimize your regrets by following in His ways and being true to His commands. I'll say it one last time—His way is the absolute best way to live. It's the abundant life.

This chapter in earth's history is quickly coming to a close as well, you know. Jesus is coming soon! We don't know how soon, but I do know one thing: I want to be ready. I don't want to see Him coming in the clouds and be afraid. I want to have the confidence of salvation, and the joy of a life spent with Him. Instead of trembling in fear, I hope we both can stand up at that day and echo the words of John with joy and excitement: "Even so, come, Lord Jesus!"

—MH

Notes

Notes

_____

_____

_____

_____

_____

_____

_____

_____

_____

_____

_____

_____

_____

_____

_____

_____

Notes

Notes

Notes

Notes

Notes